J ust for a change of pace, this time I designed a cover
with a background. I've wanted to do something
like this for a while, but I've been afraid that the
faces would look too small. (I get nervous if the
characters' faces don't pop—especially on title pages
and covers.) I was hesitant to try it but now that it's done,
I'm pleased. It grounds the characters and gives the
sense that Train and his pals really do live in this world.
Next time I think I'll draw Train and crew in the city.

—Kentaro Yabuki, 2003

Kentaro Yabuki made his manga debut with *Yamato Gensoki*,
a short series about a young empress destined to unite the
warring states of ancient Japan and the boy sworn to protect
her. His next series, *Black Cat*, commenced serialization in the
pages of *Weekly Shonen Jump* in 2000 and quickly developed a
loyal fan following. *Black Cat* has also become an animated TV
series, first hitting Japan's airwaves in the fall of 2005.

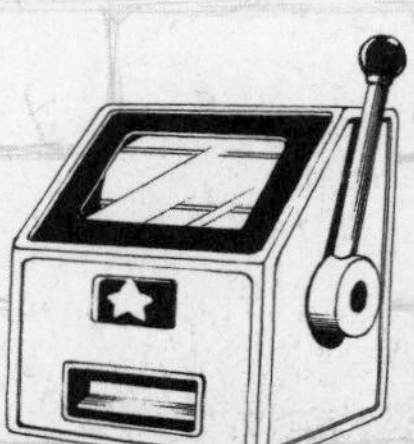

BLACK CAT VOL. 14
The SHONEN JUMP Manga Edition

STORY AND ART BY
KENTARO YABUKI

English Adaptation/Kelly Sue DeConnick
Translation/JN Productions
Touch-up Art & Lettering/Gia Cam Luc
Design/Courtney Utt
Editor/Jonathan Tarbox

Editor in Chief, Books/Alvin Lu
Editor in Chief, Magazines/Marc Weidenbaum
VP of Publishing Licensing/Rika Inouye
VP of Sales/Gonzalo Ferreyra
Sr. VP of Marketing/Liza Coppola
Publisher/Hyoe Narita

BLACK CAT © 2000 by Kentaro Yabuki
All rights reserved. First published in Japan in 2000 by SHUEISHA Inc., Tokyo.
English translation rights arranged by SHUEISHA Inc. The stories, characters
and incidents mentioned in this publication are entirely fictional.

No portion of this book may be reproduced or transmitted in any form or by
any means without written permission from the copyright holders.

The rights of the author(s) of the work(s) in this publication to be so identified have
been asserted in accordance with the Copyright, Designs and Patents Act 1988.
A CIP catalogue record for this book is available from the British Library.

Printed in the U.S.A.

Published by VIZ Media, LLC
P.O. Box 77010
San Francisco, CA 94107

SHONEN JUMP Manga Edition
10 9 8 7 6 5 4 3 2 1
First printing, May 2008

THE WORLD'S
MOST POPULAR MANGA

www.viz.com

www.shonenjump.com

SHONEN JUMP MANGA EDITION

BLACK CAT

ブラック・キャット

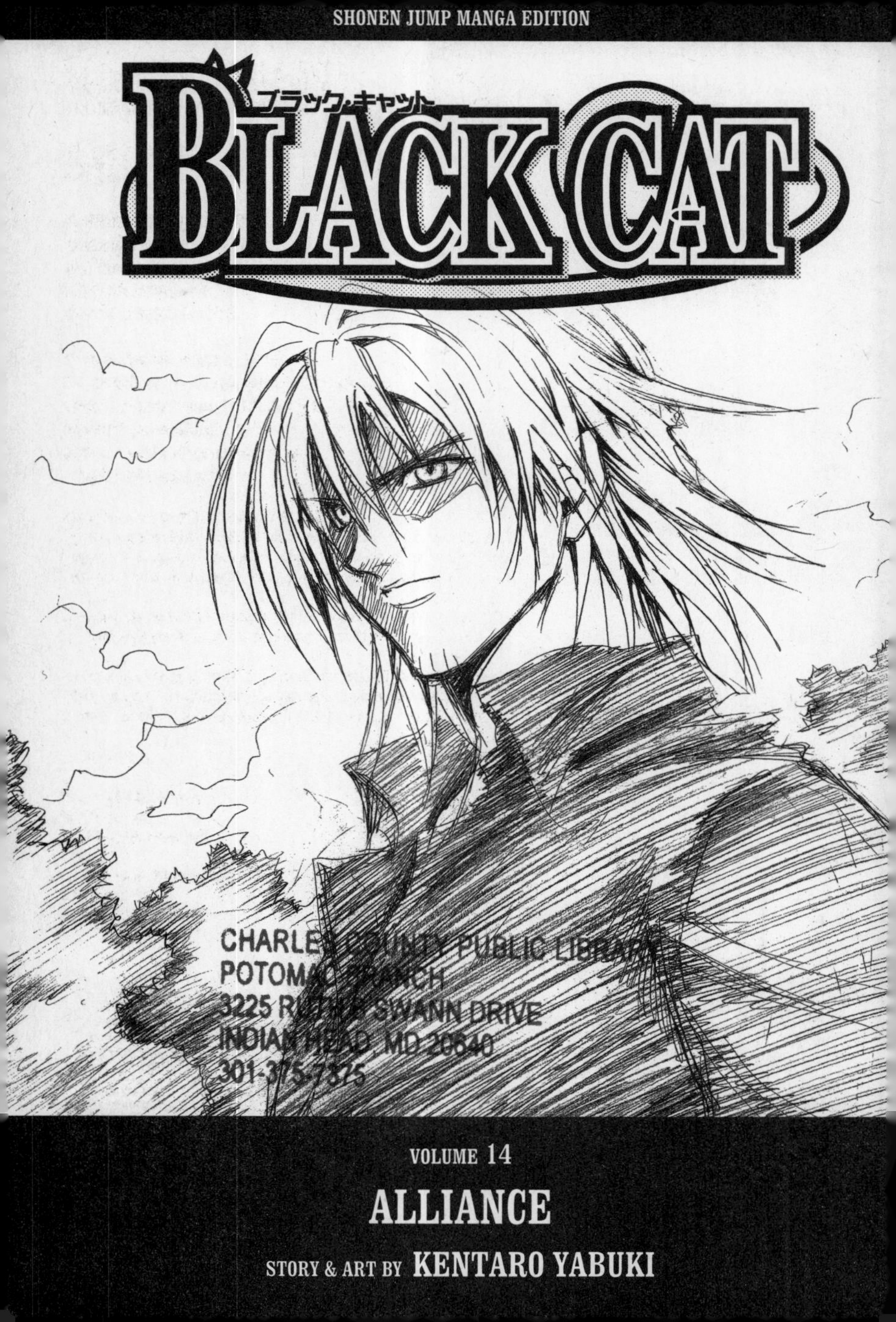

VOLUME 14

ALLIANCE

STORY & ART BY KENTARO YABUKI

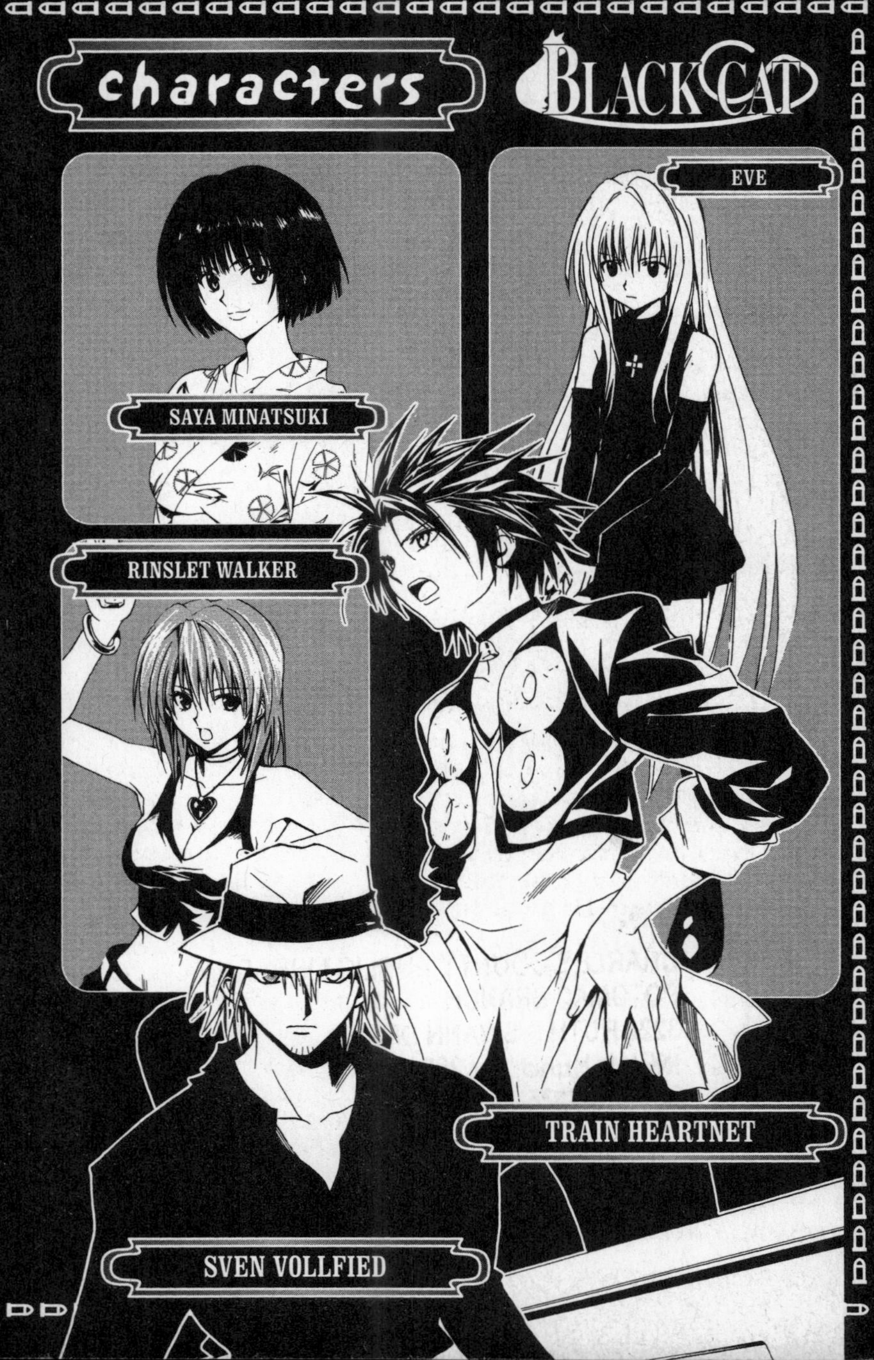
characters
BLACK CAT
EVE
SAYA MINATSUKI
RINSLET WALKER
TRAIN HEARTNET
SVEN VOLLFIED

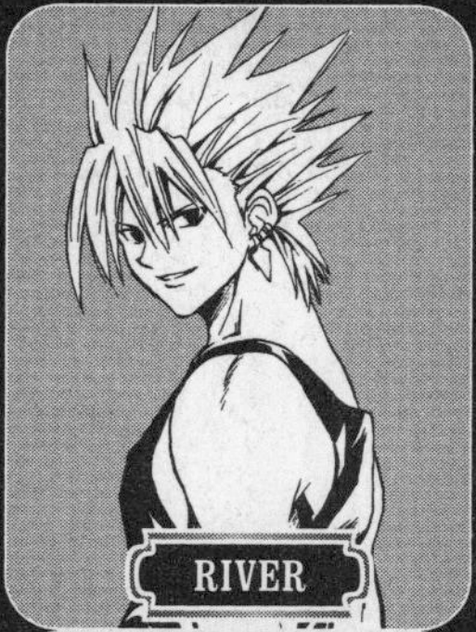
RIVER

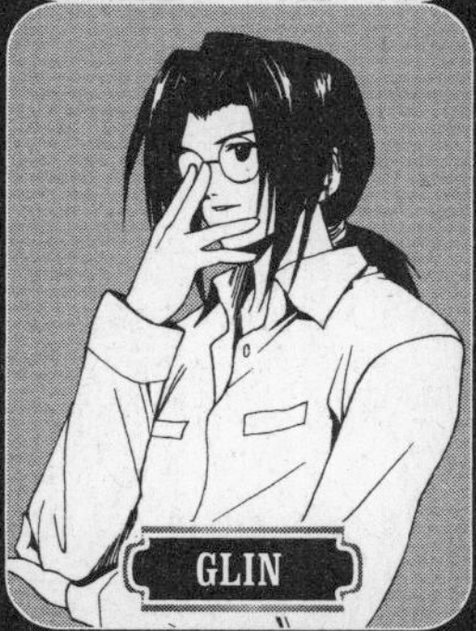
GLIN

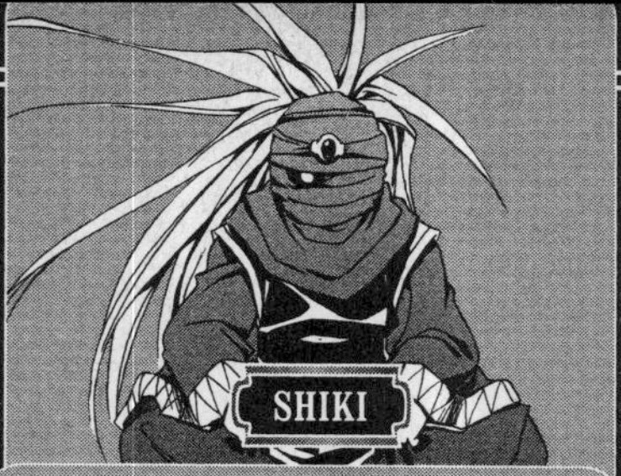
SHIKI

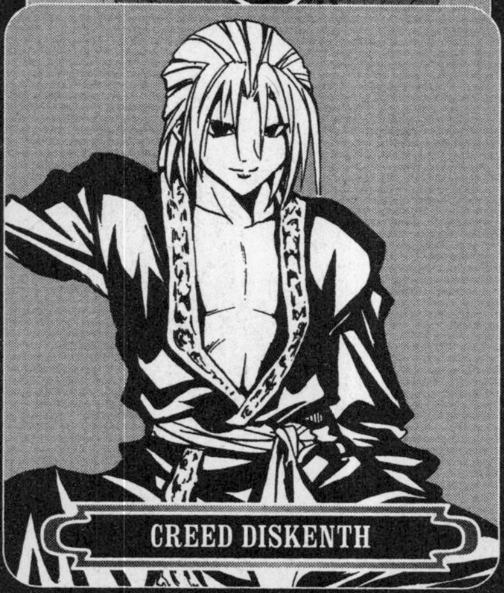
CREED DISKENTH

A fearless "eraser" responsible for the deaths of countless powerful men, Train "Black Cat" Heartnet was formerly an assassin for the crime syndicate Chronos. Train betrayed Chronos and was supposedly executed for it, but two years later he lives a carefree life, working with his partner Sven as a bounty hunter ("sweeper") while pursuing Creed Diskenth, the man who murdered Train's beloved friend Saya. The two sweepers are allied with sexy thief-for-hire Rinslet Walker and Eve, a young girl (and experimental living weapon) whom they rescued from a nanotech lab.

When Creed attempts to kill Sven, Train takes the bullet and winds up infected by a nanotech weapon called LUCIFER. It doesn't kill him, but it causes his body to revert to that of a small child. The team's search for a cure leads them to Dr. Tearju, the nanotech specialist who created Eve.

When Train and friends finally reach Dr. Tearju's home, they again come under attack by the Apostles of the Stars. Train changes back to his normal size and attains a new power, "Rail Gun," which he uses to overcome their foes. The team decides that Creed is too dangerous to walk free, and that he should be their next sweeper target. To gather intel, Train and Eve head for the Sweepers' Café where they meet a man who claims to know where to find Creed—but to get the scoop, Train must first battle a sweeper with supreme confidence in his fists, a man named River!

BLACK CAT

VOLUME 14 ALLIANCE

CONTENTS

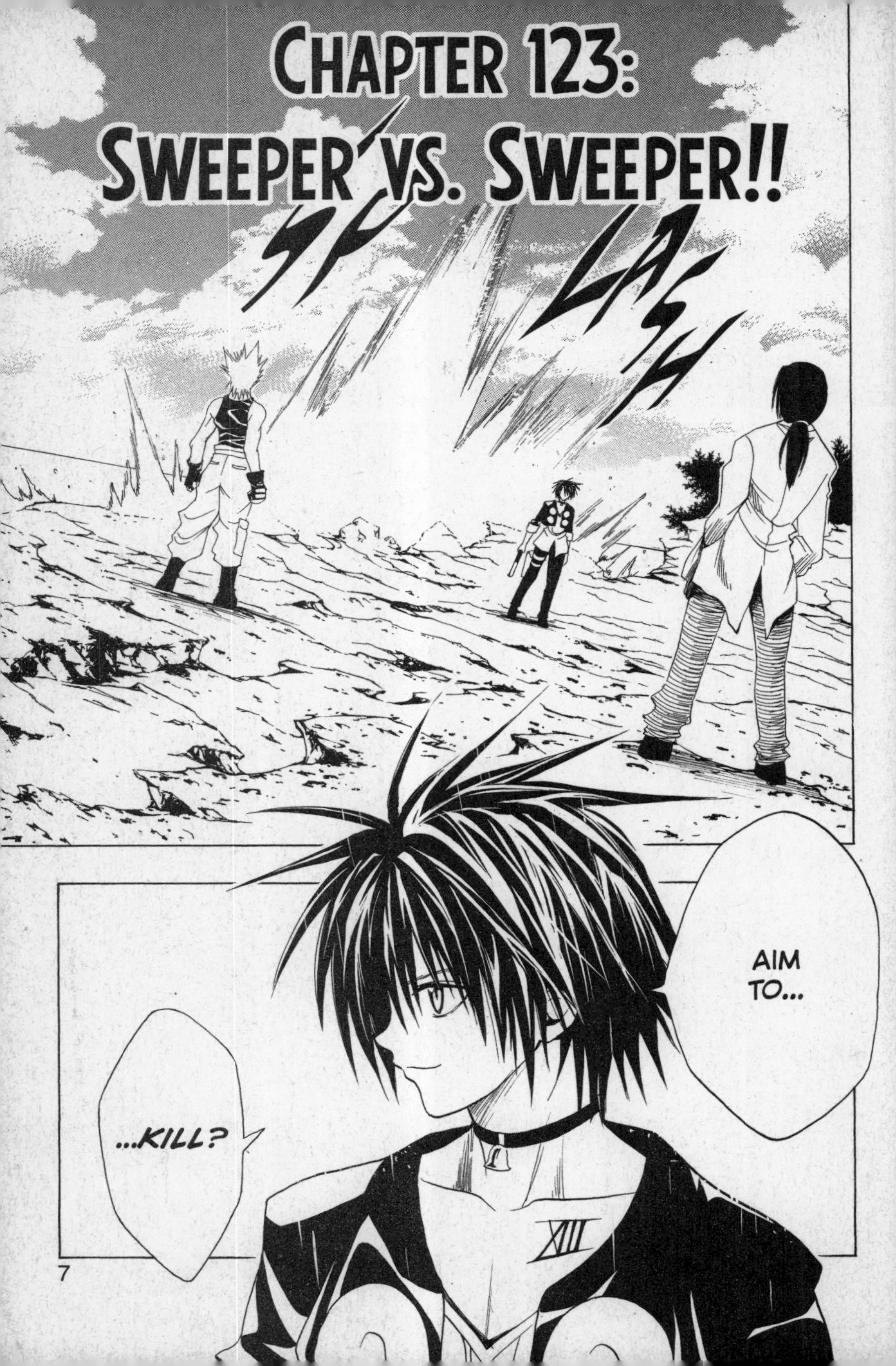
CHAPTER 123:
SWEEPER VS. SWEEPER!!
SPLASH
AIM TO...
...KILL?

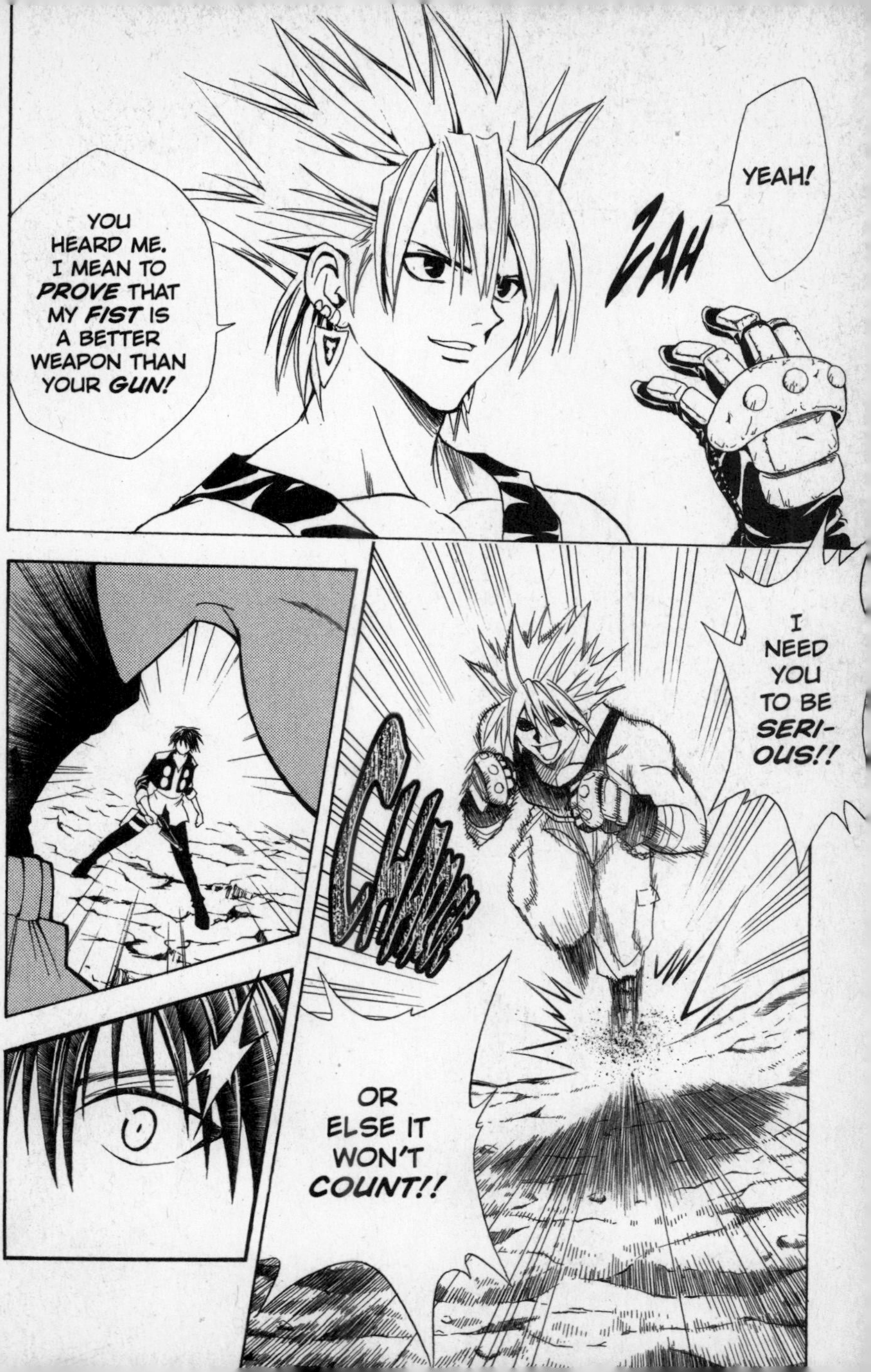
YEAH!
ZAH
YOU HEARD ME. I MEAN TO *PROVE* THAT MY *FIST* IS A BETTER WEAPON THAN YOUR *GUN!*
I NEED YOU TO BE *SERI-OUS!!*
OR ELSE IT WON'T *COUNT!!*

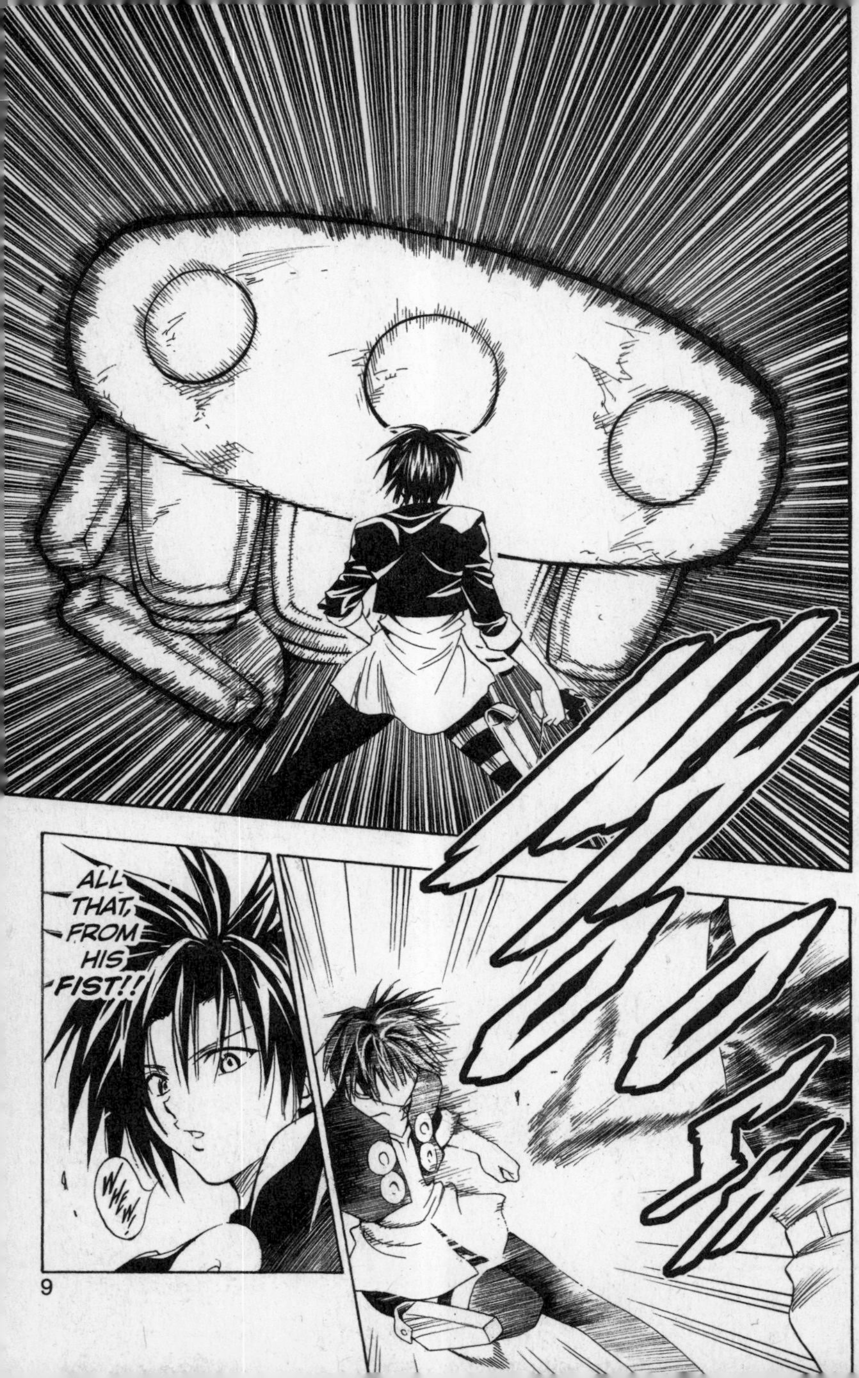
ALL THAT, FROM HIS FIST!!
WHEW!

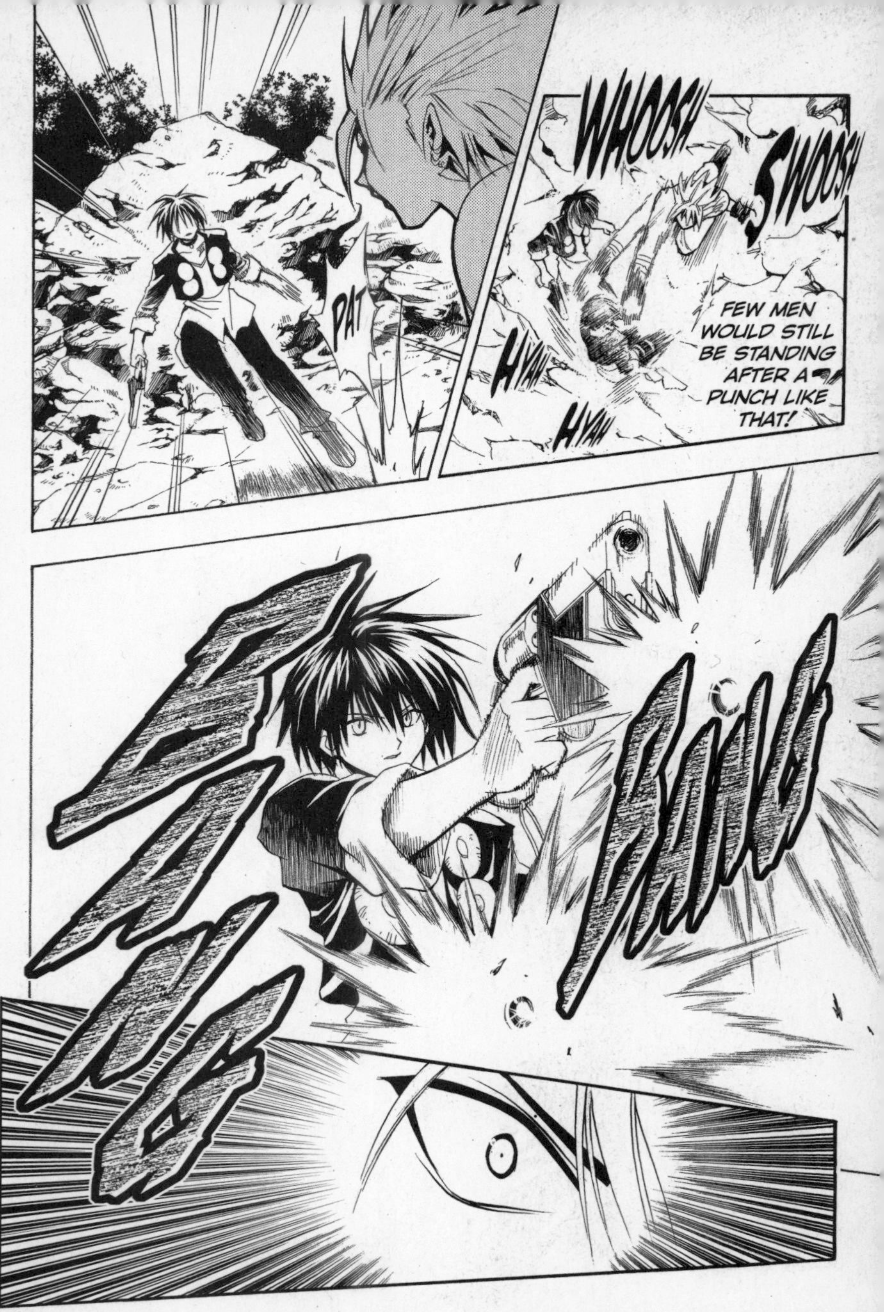
WHOOSH
SWOOSH
FEW MEN WOULD STILL BE STANDING AFTER A PUNCH LIKE THAT!
HYAH
HYAH
PAT

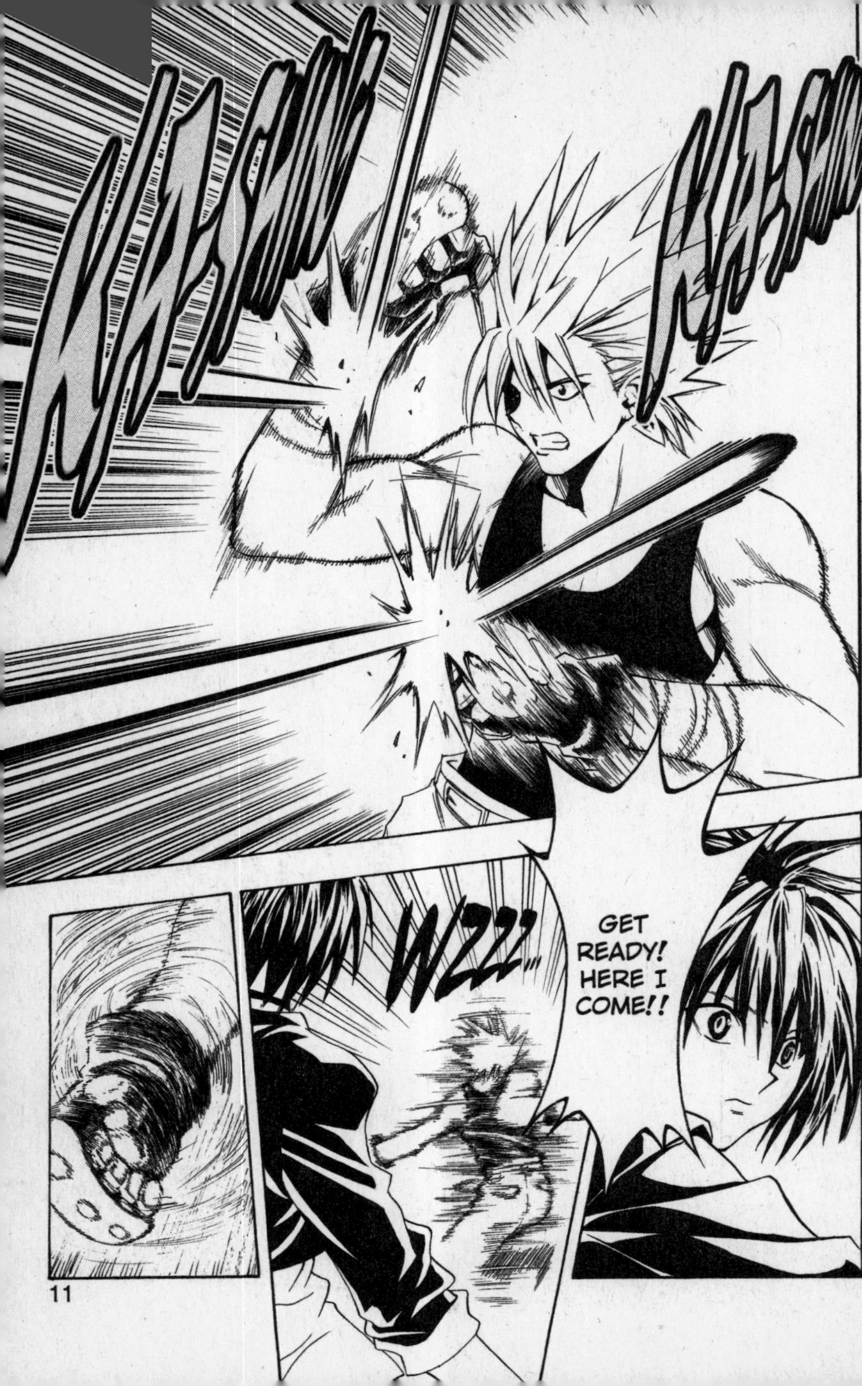
GET READY! HERE I COME!!
WZZ...

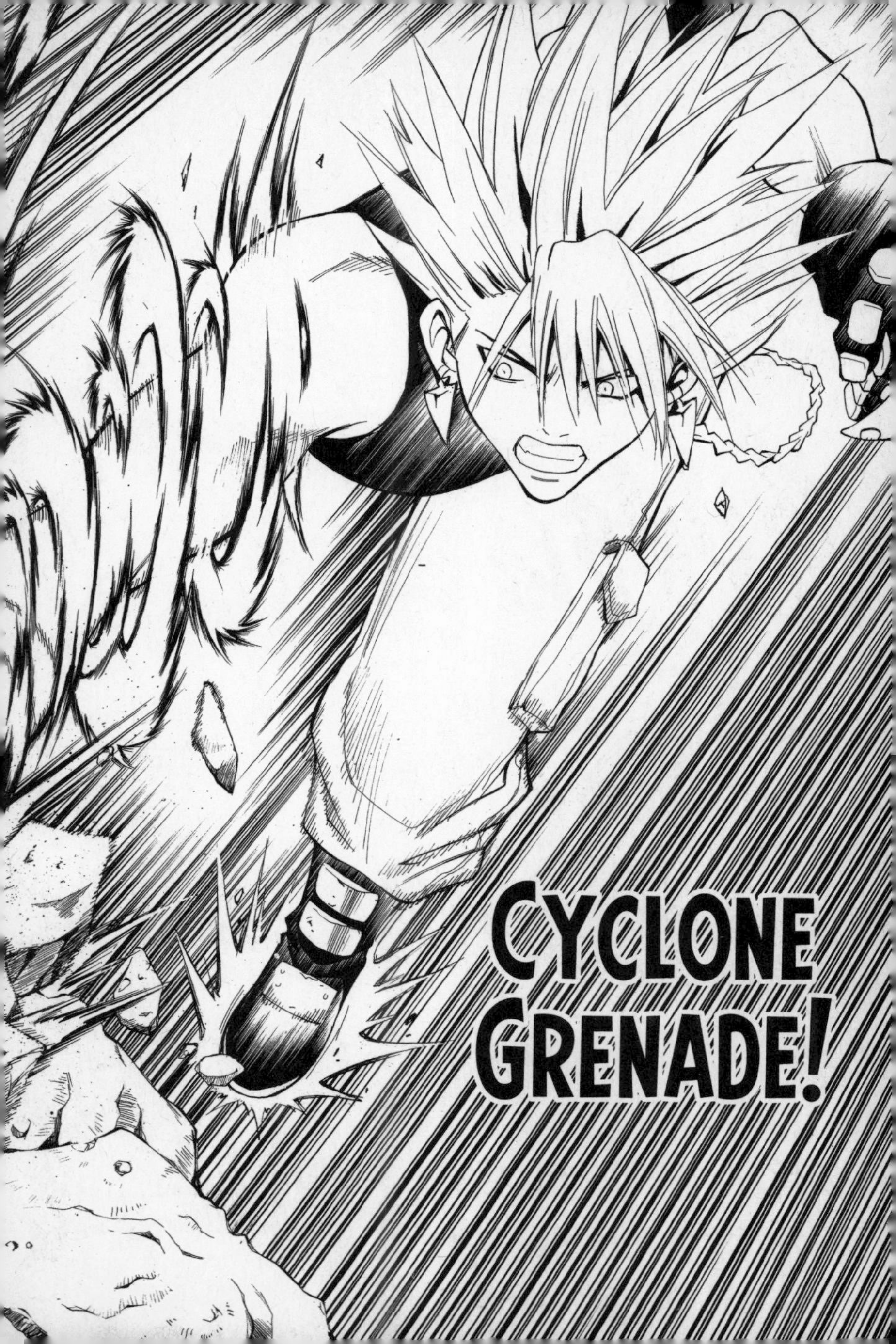
CYCLONE GRENADE!

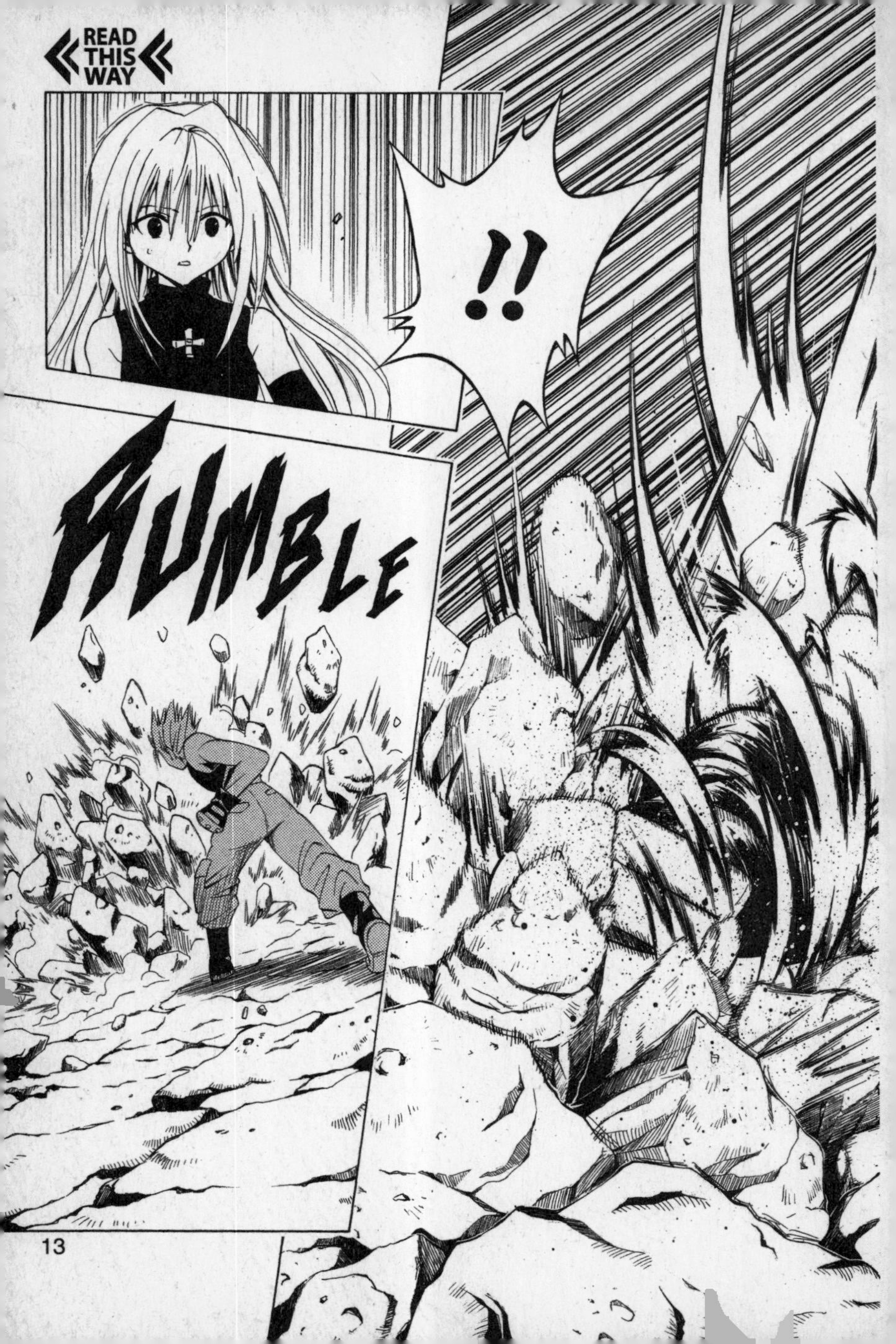
READ THIS WAY
!!
RUMBLE

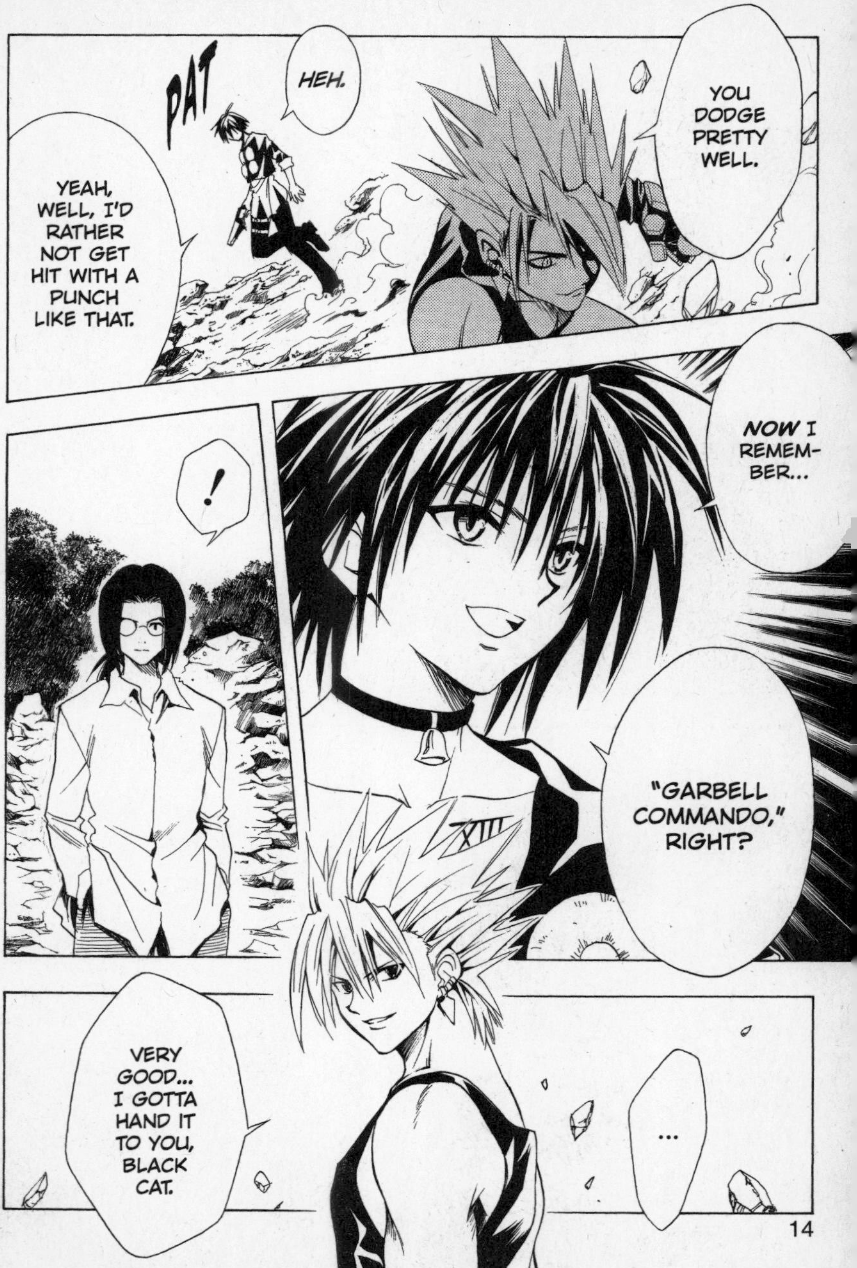

YOU DODGE PRETTY WELL.
HEH.
PAT
YEAH, WELL, I'D RATHER NOT GET HIT WITH A PUNCH LIKE THAT.
NOW I REMEM-BER...
"GARBELL COMMANDO," RIGHT?
!
...
VERY GOOD... I GOTTA HAND IT TO YOU, BLACK CAT.

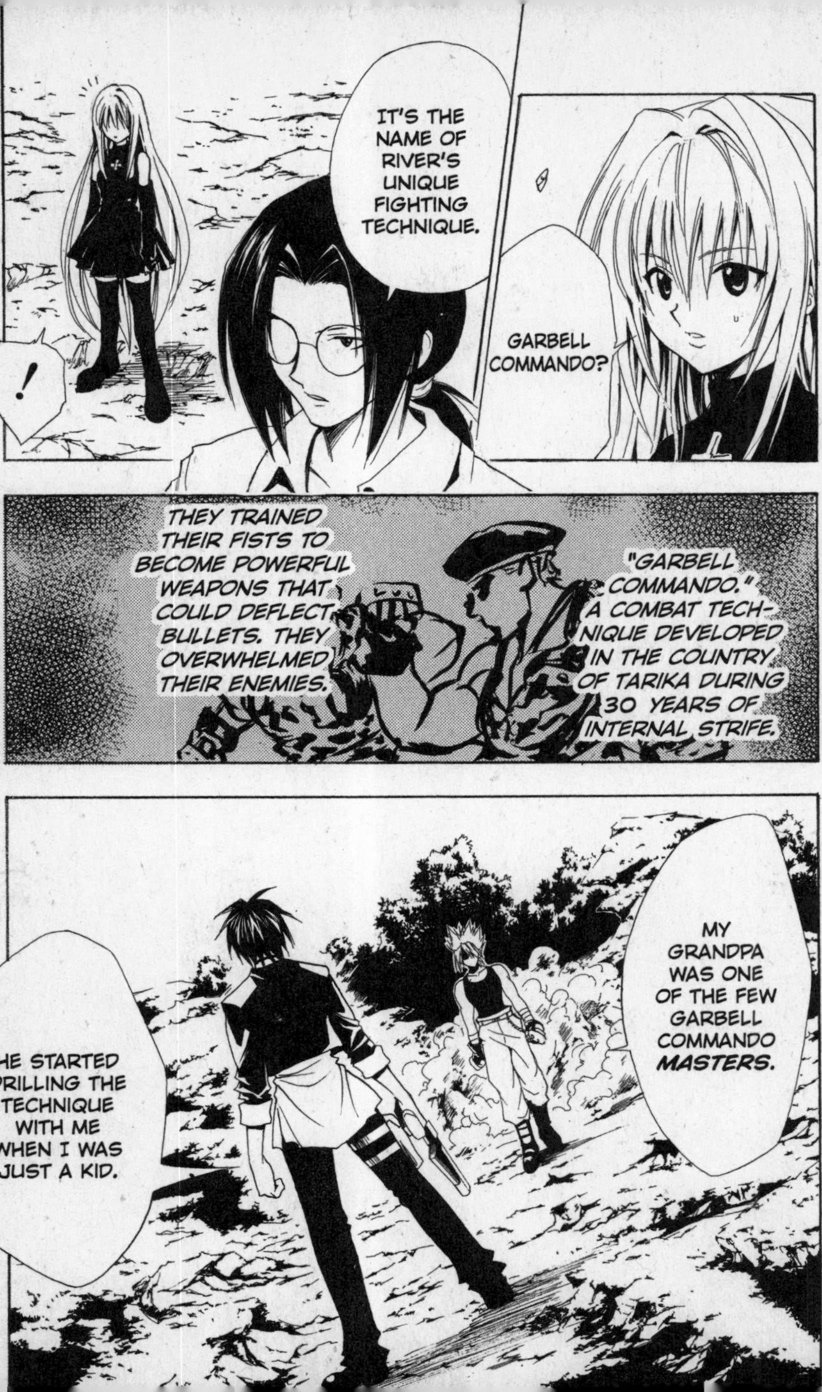
GARBELL COMMANDO?
IT'S THE NAME OF RIVER'S UNIQUE FIGHTING TECHNIQUE.
!
"GARBELL COMMANDO." A COMBAT TECHNIQUE DEVELOPED IN THE COUNTRY OF TARIKA DURING 30 YEARS OF INTERNAL STRIFE.
THEY TRAINED THEIR FISTS TO BECOME POWERFUL WEAPONS THAT COULD DEFLECT BULLETS. THEY OVERWHELMED THEIR ENEMIES.
MY GRANDPA WAS ONE OF THE FEW GARBELL COMMANDO MASTERS.
HE STARTED DRILLING THE TECHNIQUE WITH ME WHEN I WAS JUST A KID.

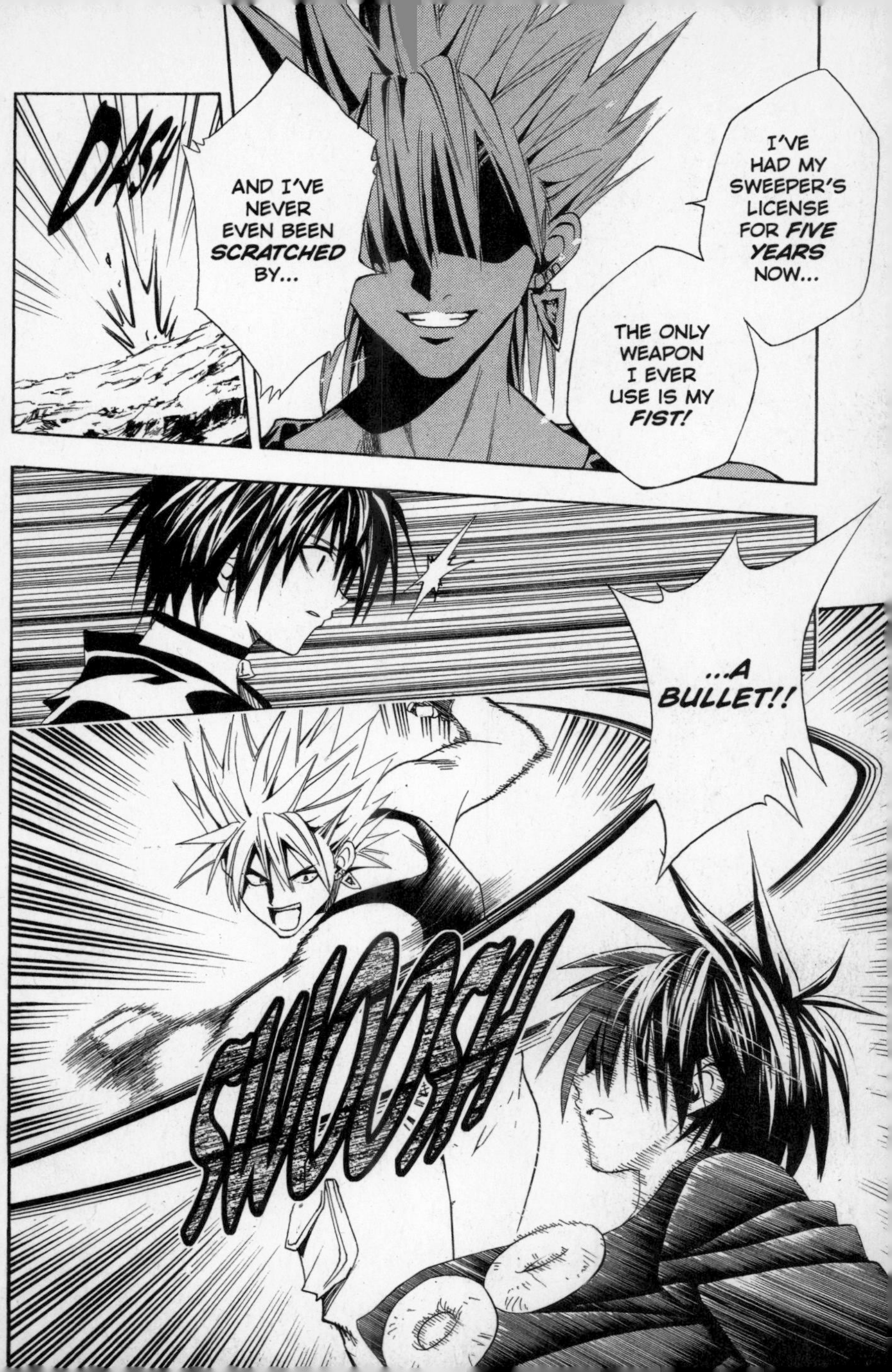
I'VE HAD MY SWEEPER'S LICENSE FOR *FIVE YEARS* NOW...
THE ONLY WEAPON I EVER USE IS MY *FIST!*
AND I'VE NEVER EVEN BEEN *SCRATCHED* BY...
DASH
...A BULLET!!
SWOOSH

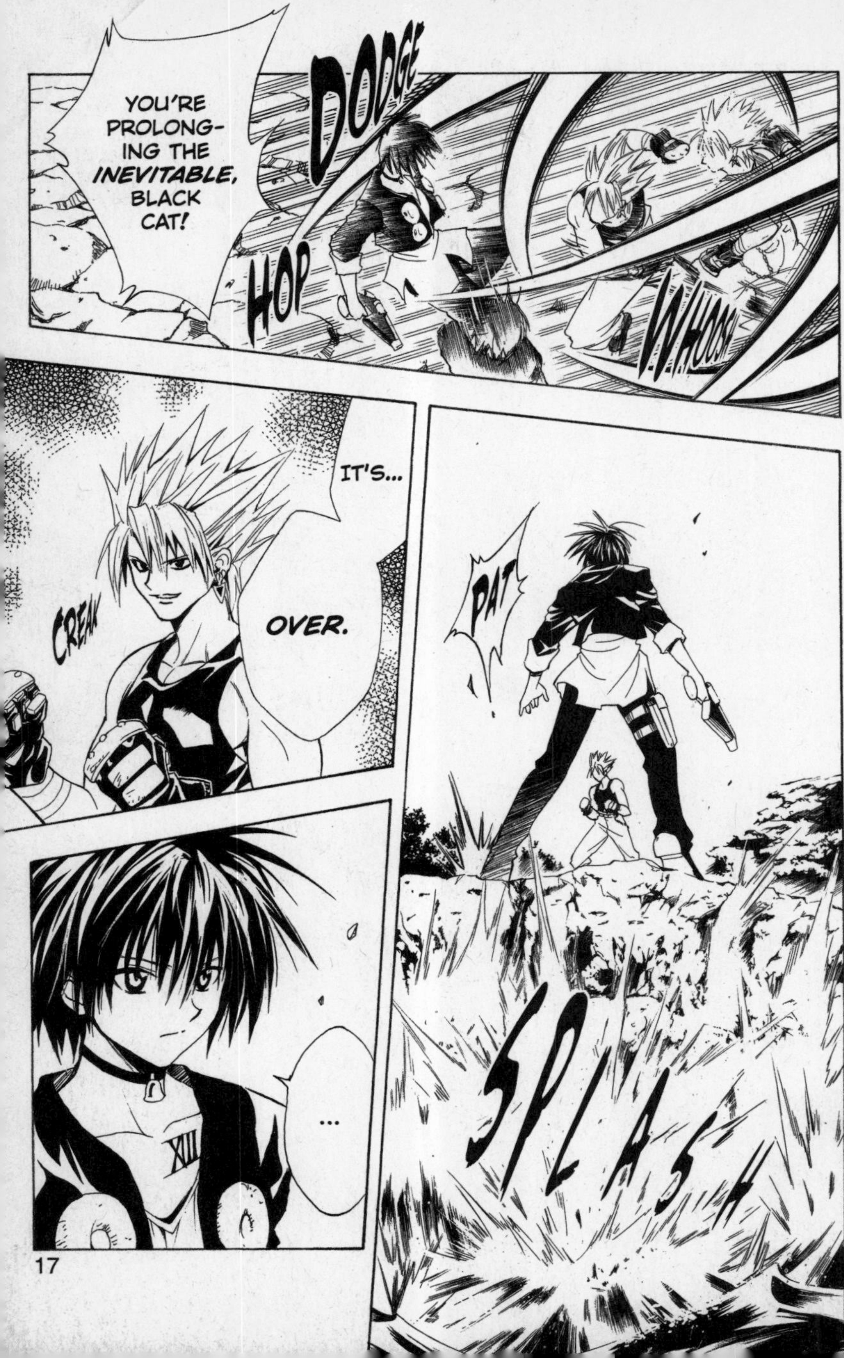
WHOOSH
DODGE
YOU'RE PROLONGING THE *INEVITABLE*, BLACK CAT!
HOP
PAT
SPLASH
IT'S...
OVER.
CREAK
...

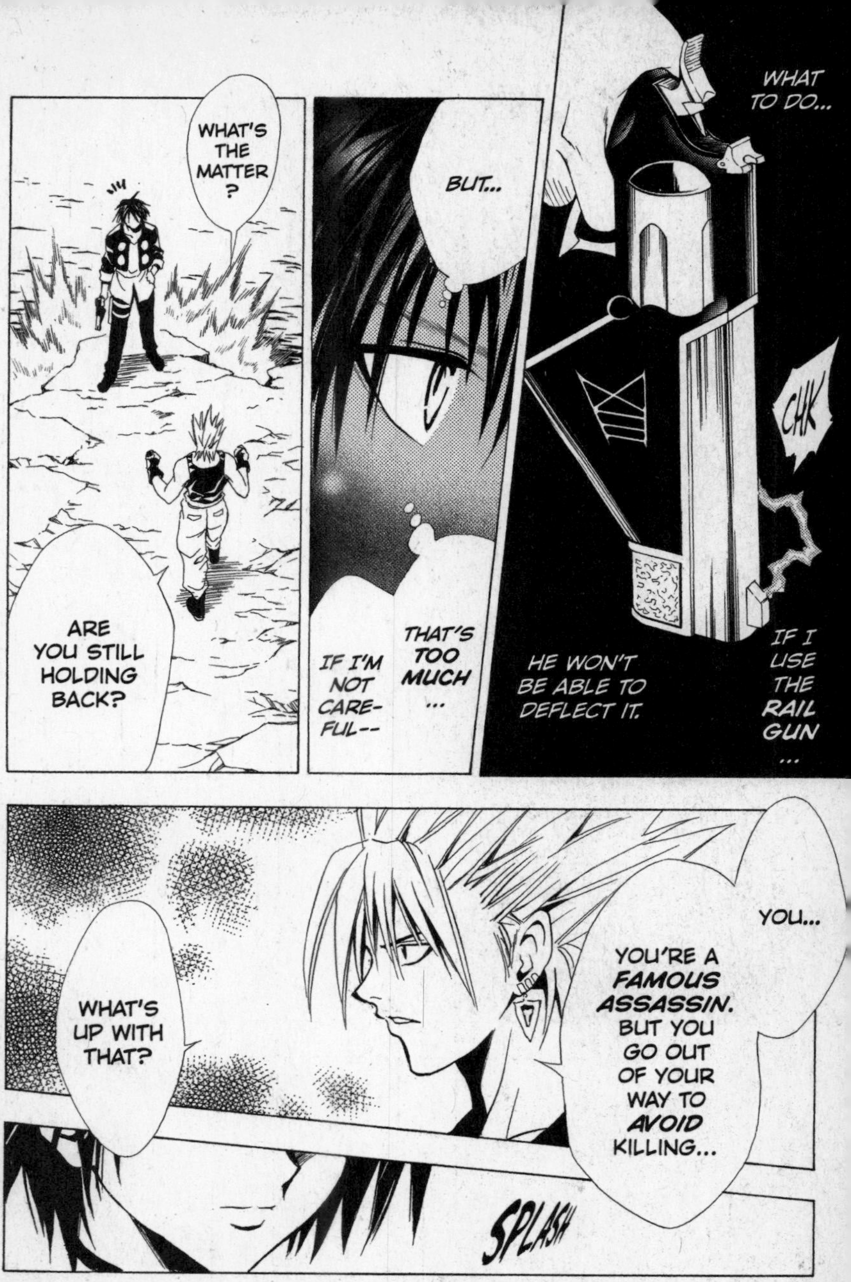
WHAT TO DO...
CHK
IF I USE THE RAIL GUN...
HE WON'T BE ABLE TO DEFLECT IT.
BUT...
THAT'S TOO MUCH...
IF I'M NOT CAREFUL--
WHAT'S THE MATTER?
ARE YOU STILL HOLDING BACK?
YOU...
YOU'RE A FAMOUS ASSASSIN. BUT YOU GO OUT OF YOUR WAY TO AVOID KILLING...
WHAT'S UP WITH THAT?
SPLASH

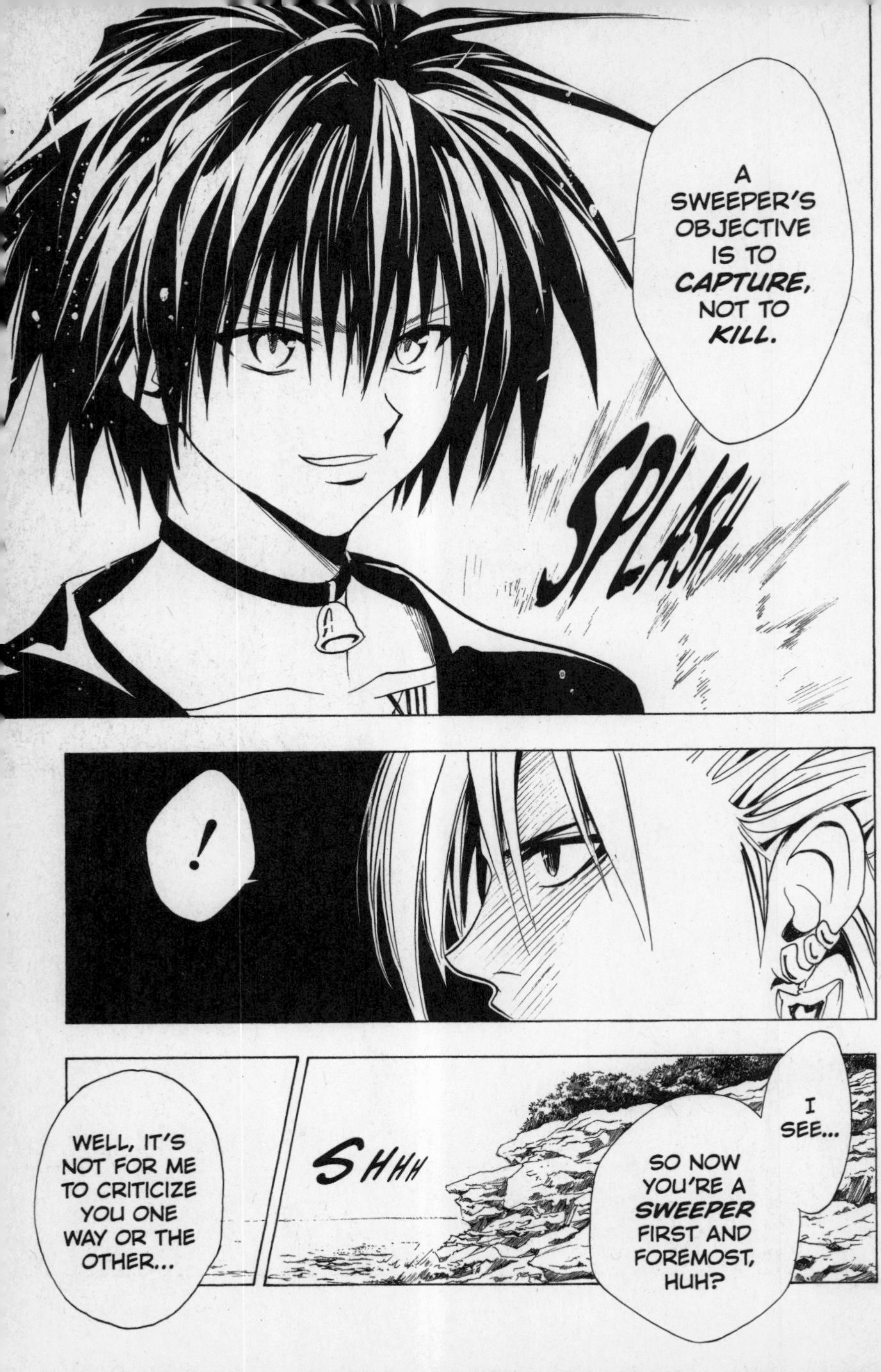
A SWEEPER'S OBJECTIVE IS TO CAPTURE, NOT TO KILL.
SPLASH
!
I SEE...
SO NOW YOU'RE A SWEEPER FIRST AND FOREMOST, HUH?
SHHH
WELL, IT'S NOT FOR ME TO CRITICIZE YOU ONE WAY OR THE OTHER...

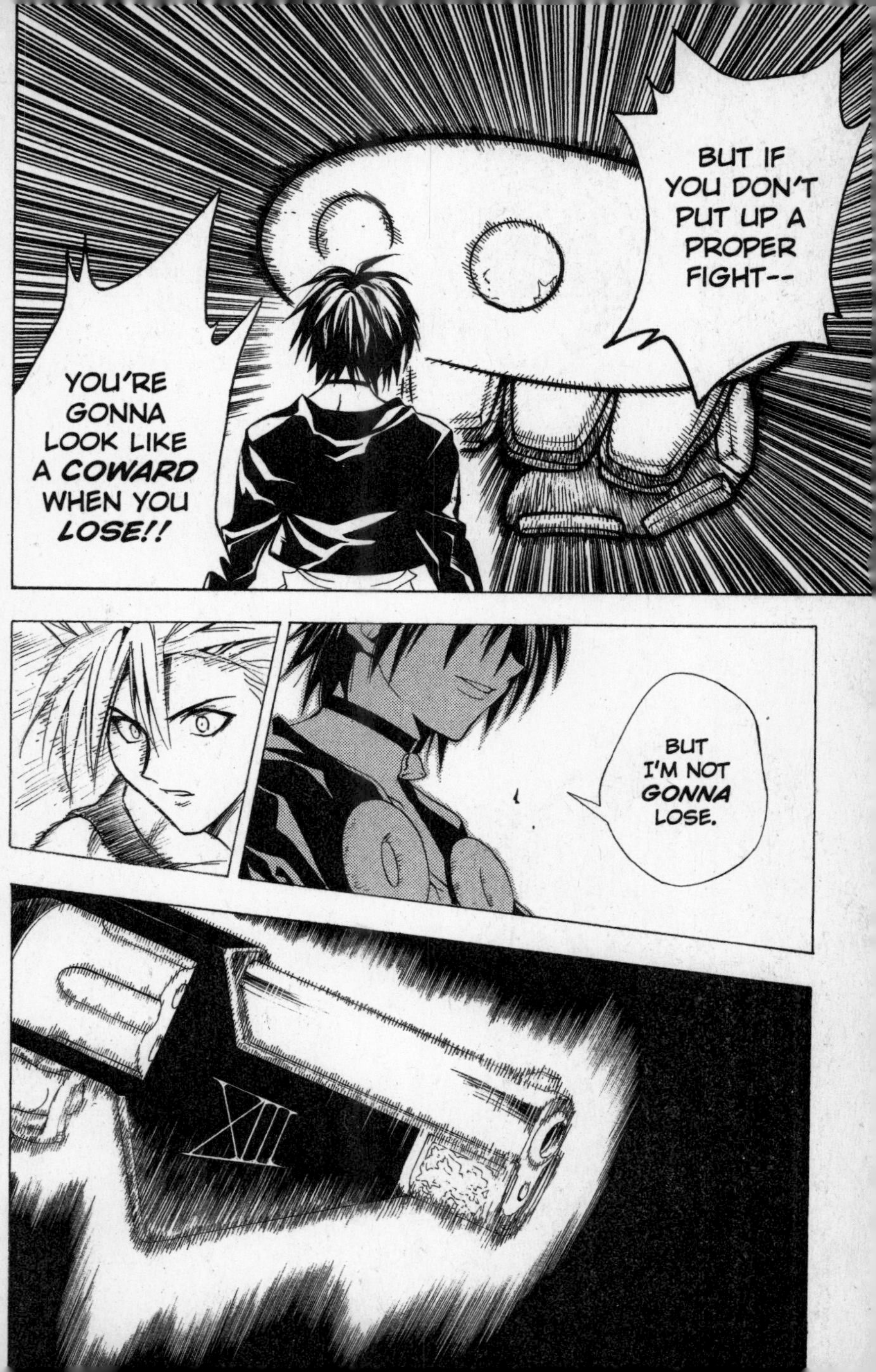
BUT IF YOU DON'T PUT UP A PROPER FIGHT--
YOU'RE GONNA LOOK LIKE A COWARD WHEN YOU LOSE!!
BUT I'M NOT GONNA LOSE.

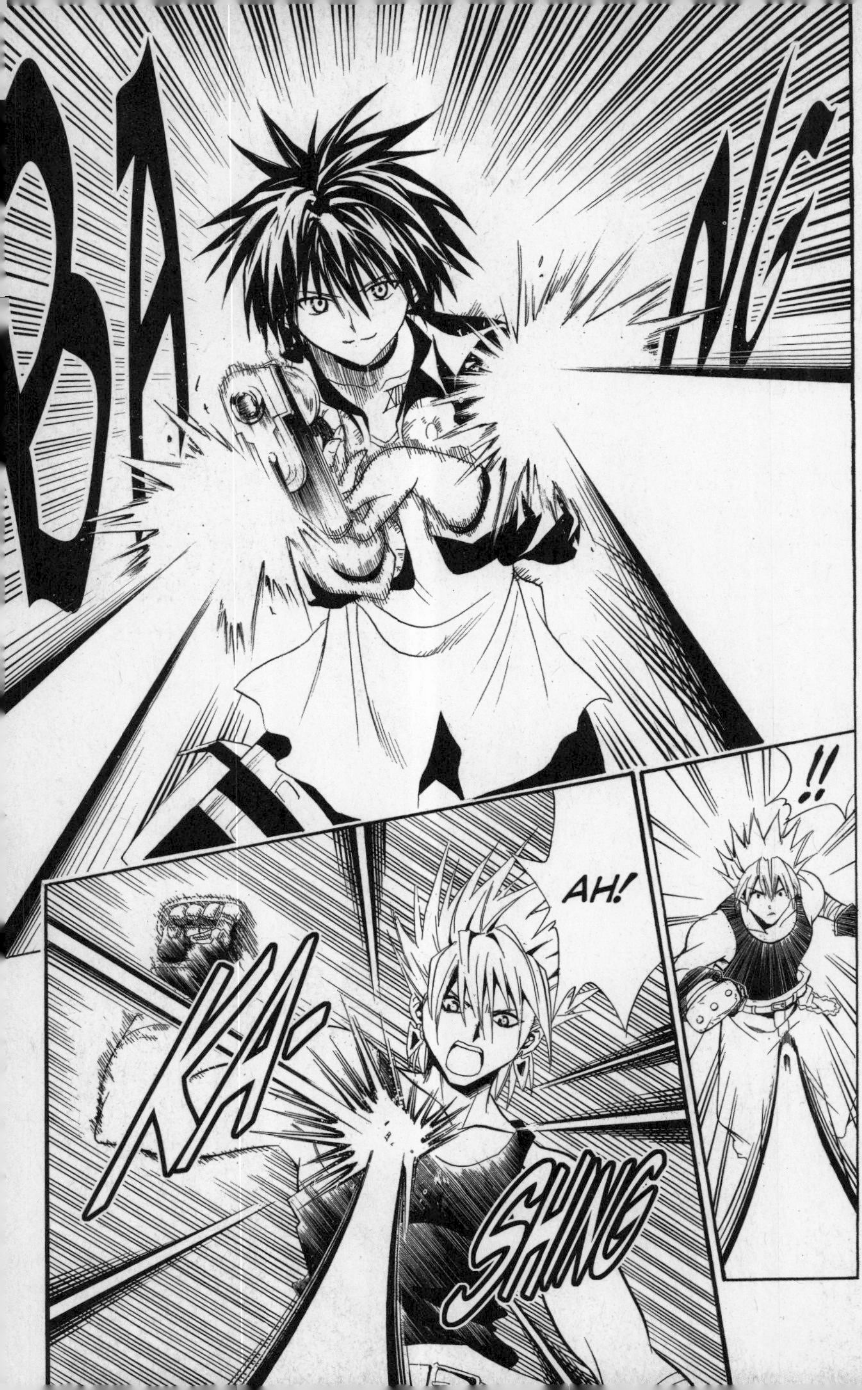
!!
AH!
KA-
SHING

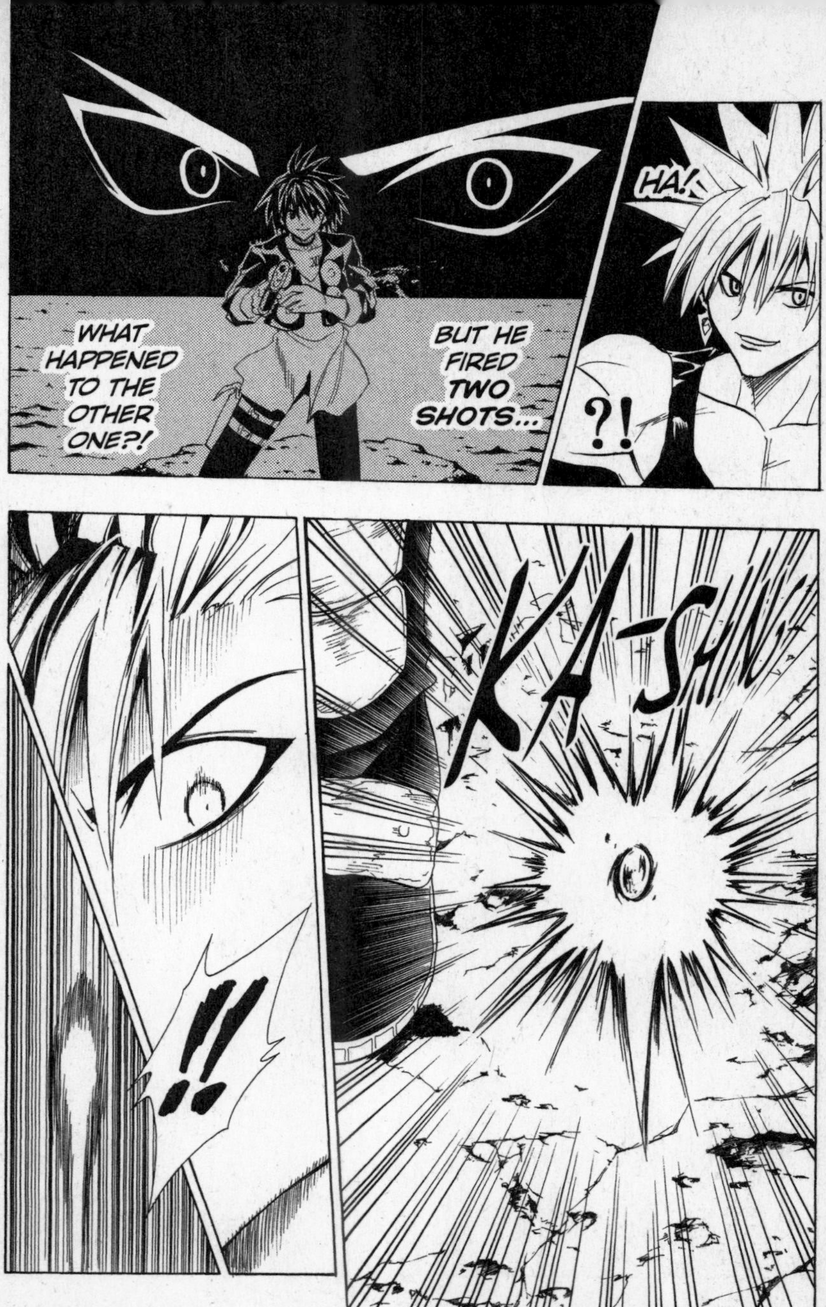
HA!
?!
BUT HE FIRED TWO SHOTS...
WHAT HAPPENED TO THE OTHER ONE?!
KA-SHIN
!!

READ THIS WAY

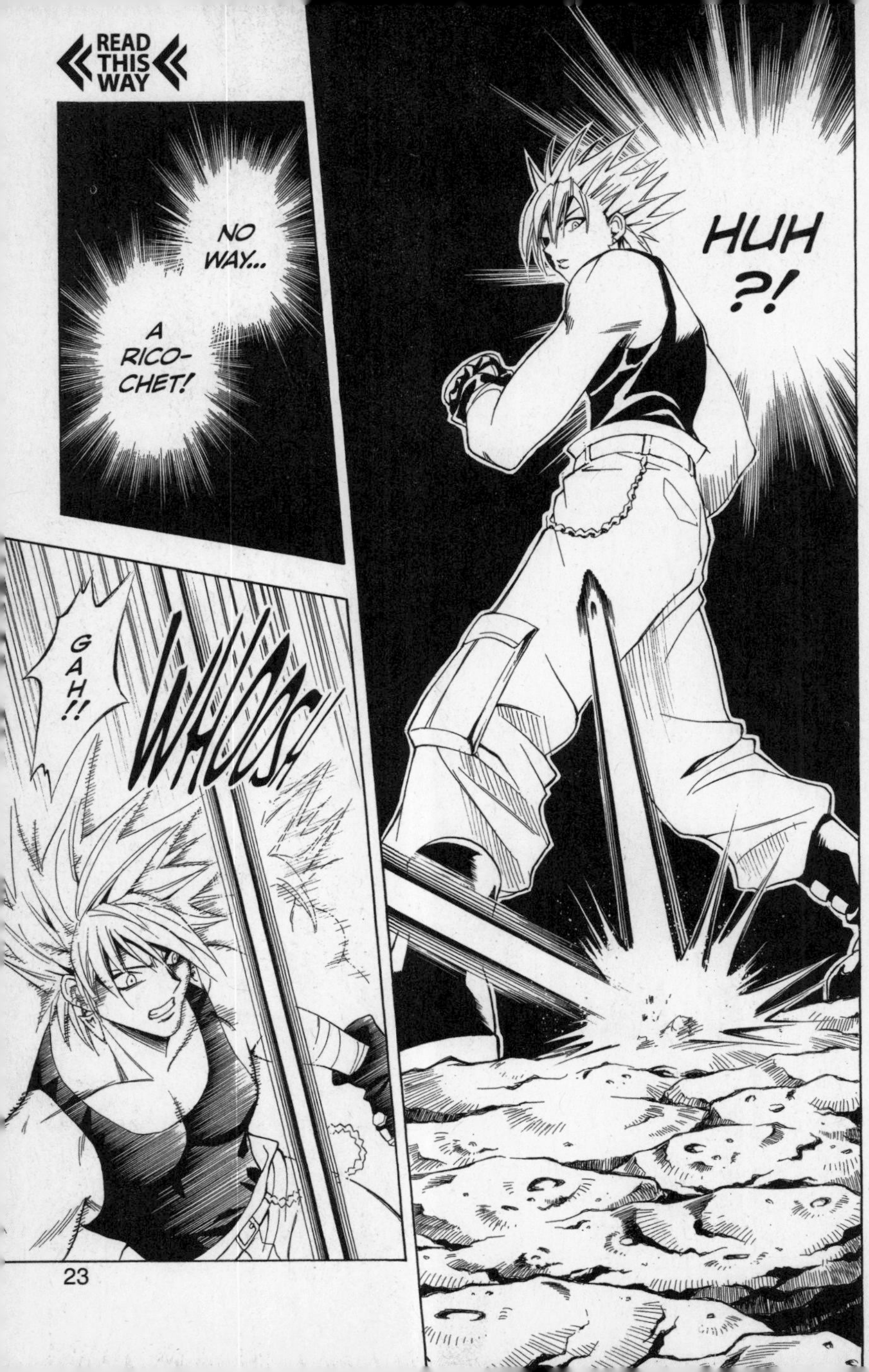

HUH ?!
NO WAY...
A RICOCHET!
GAH!!
WHOOSH

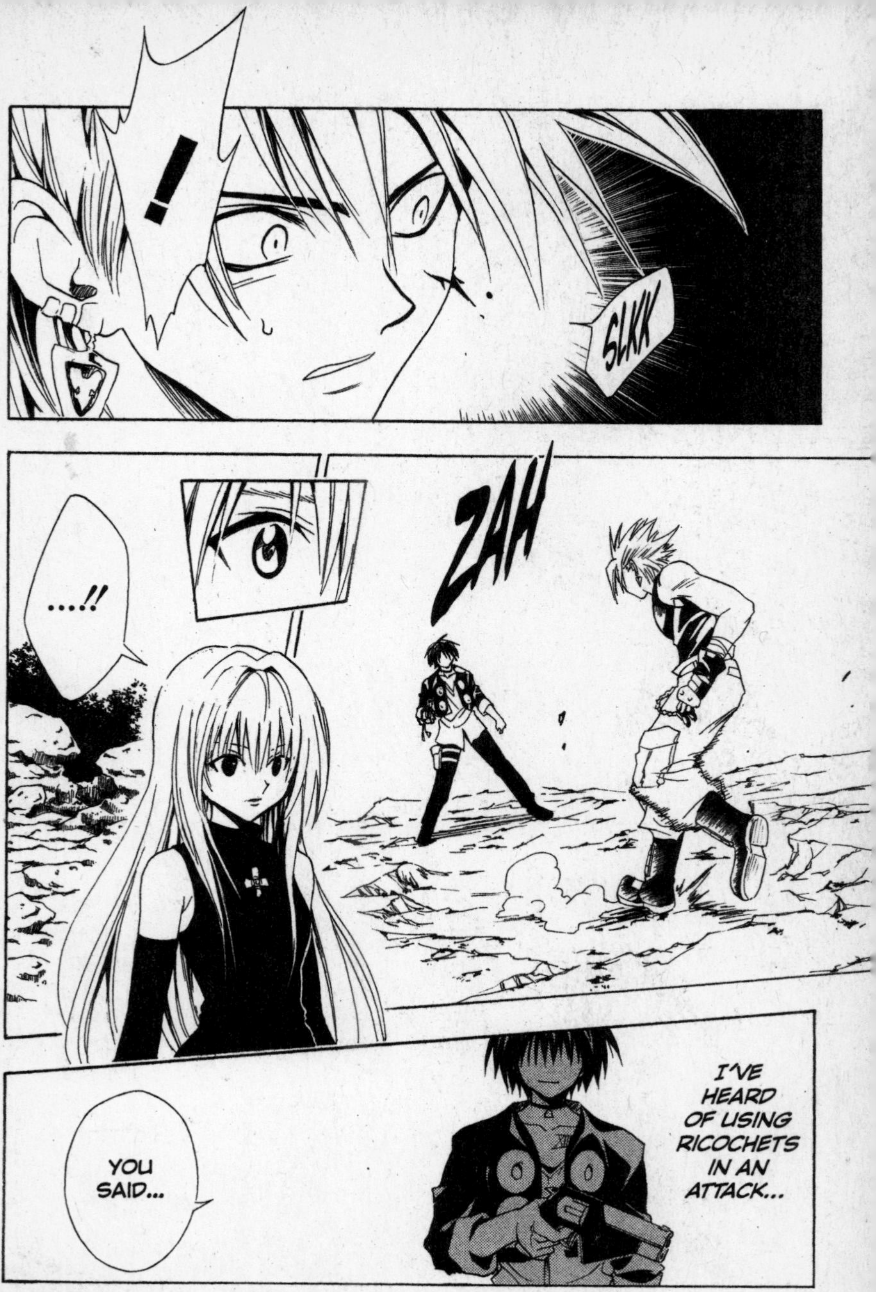
SLKK
!
ZAH
....!!
I'VE HEARD OF USING RICOCHETS IN AN ATTACK...
YOU SAID...

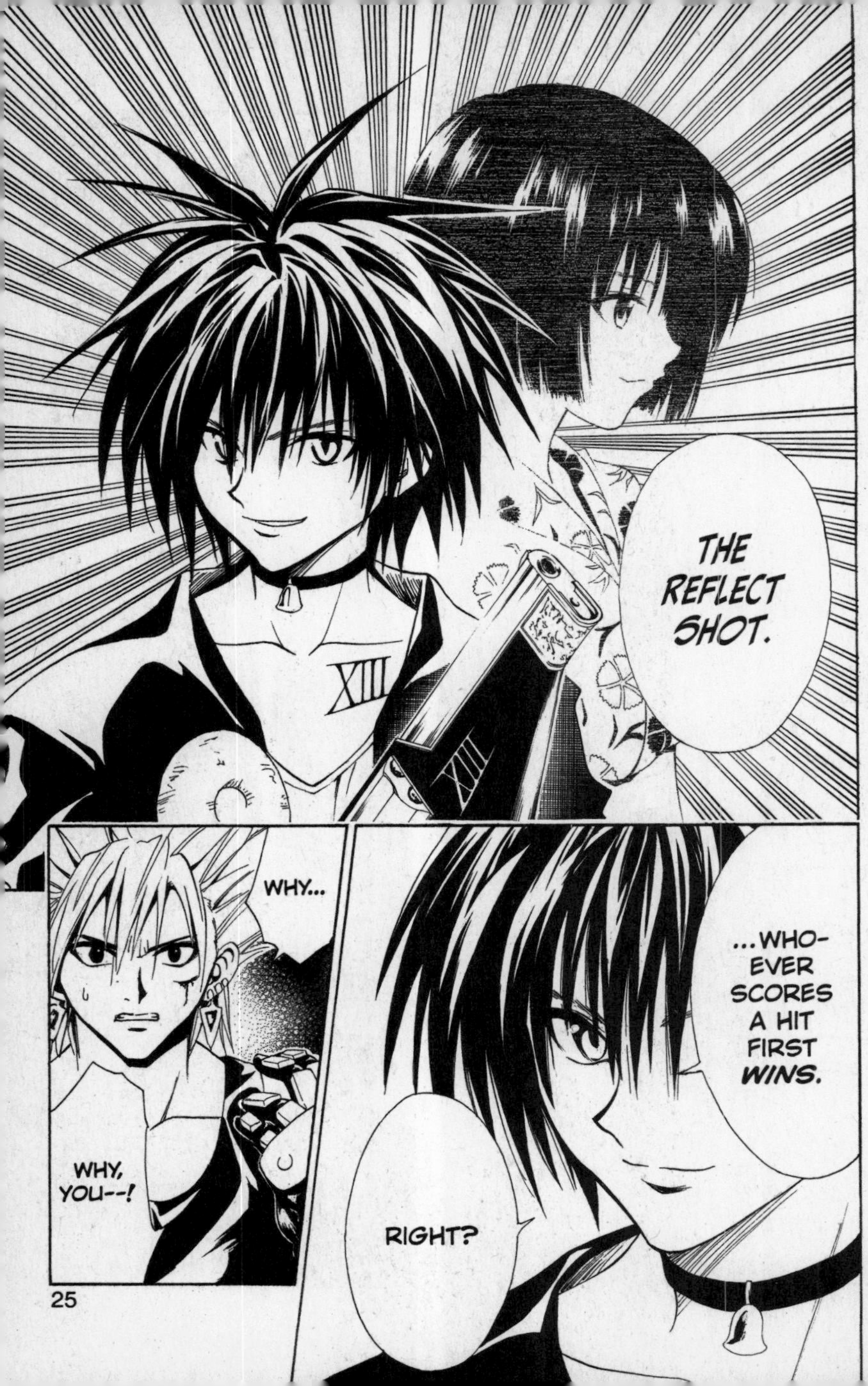
THE REFLECT SHOT.
...WHO-EVER SCORES A HIT FIRST WINS.
RIGHT?
WHY...
WHY, YOU--!

NOSTALGIC SERIES

NUMBER 1—SHION (FROM "YAMATO GENSOUKI")

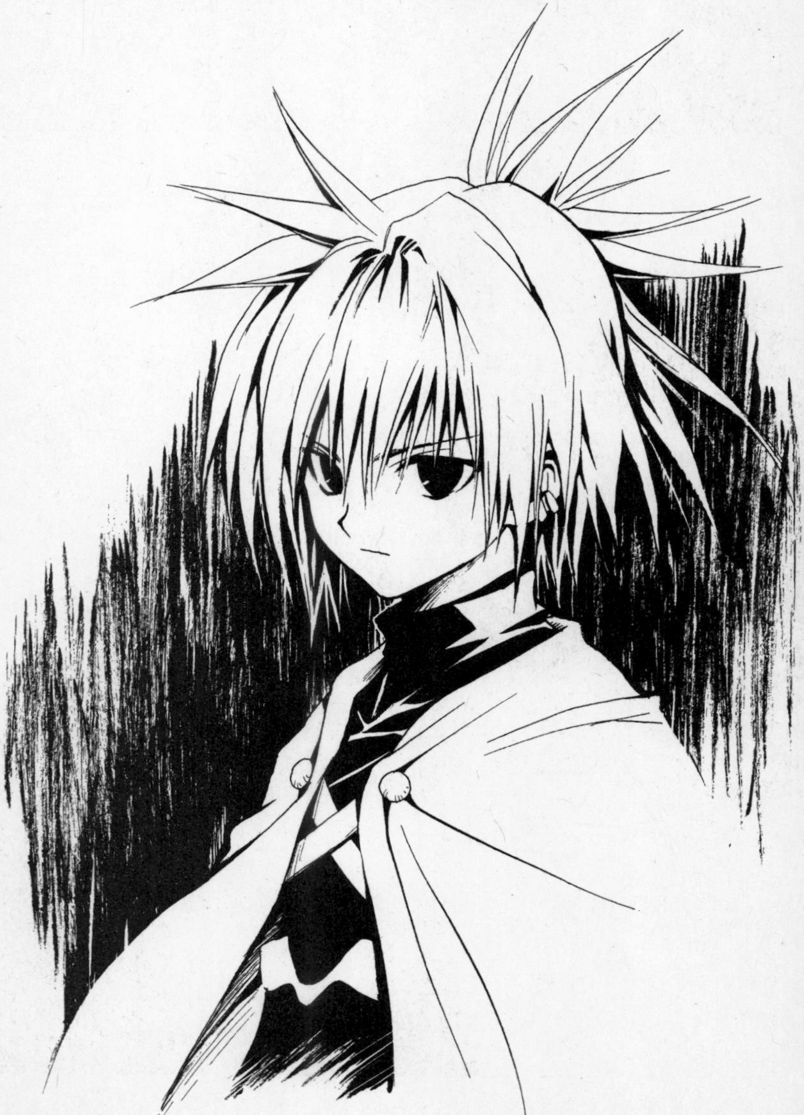

READ THIS WAY

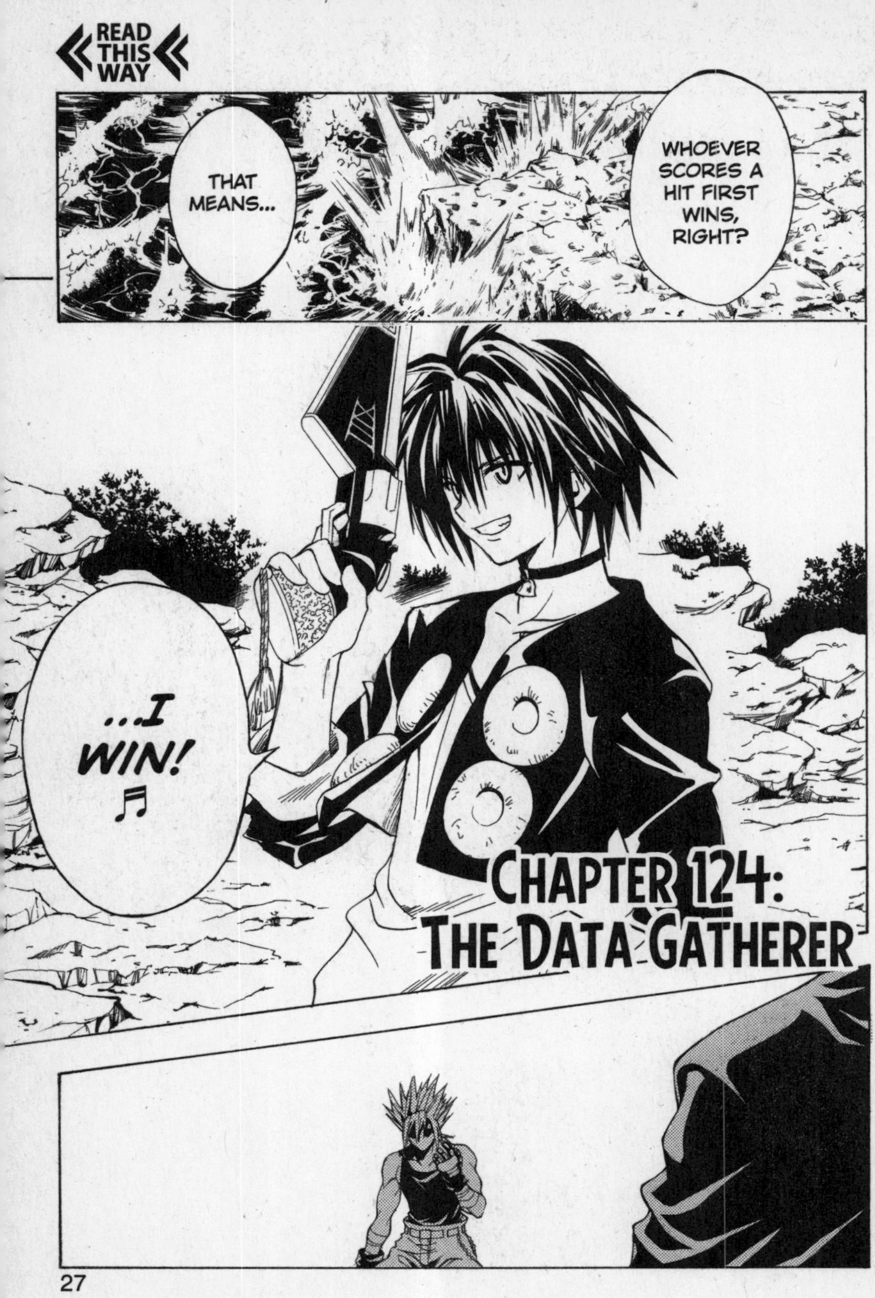
WHOEVER SCORES A HIT FIRST WINS, RIGHT?
THAT MEANS...
...I WIN! ♬
CHAPTER 124: THE DATA GATHERER

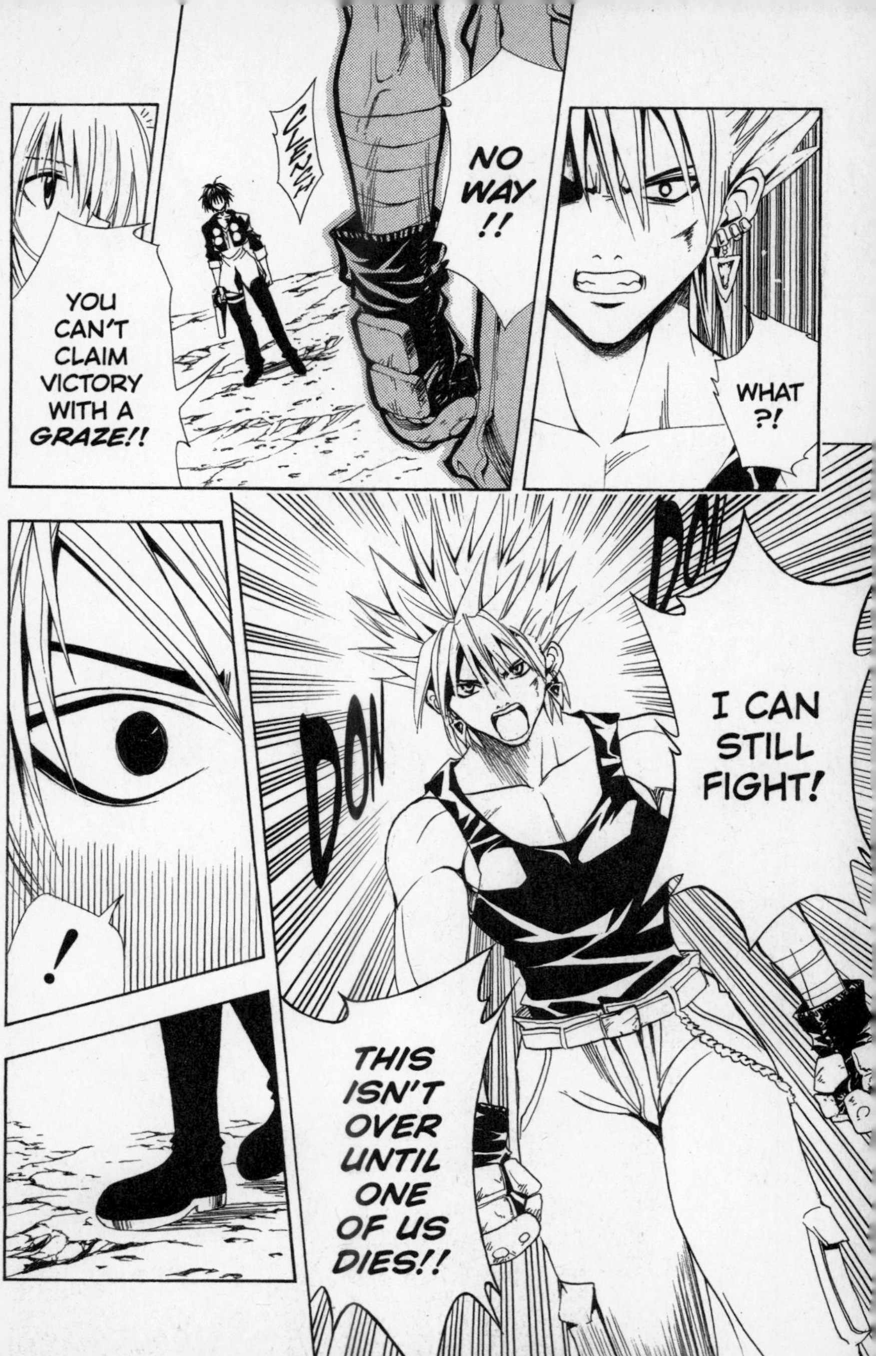
WHAT?!
NO WAY!!
YOU CAN'T CLAIM VICTORY WITH A GRAZE!!
DON
DON
I CAN STILL FIGHT!
THIS ISN'T OVER UNTIL ONE OF US DIES!!
DON
!

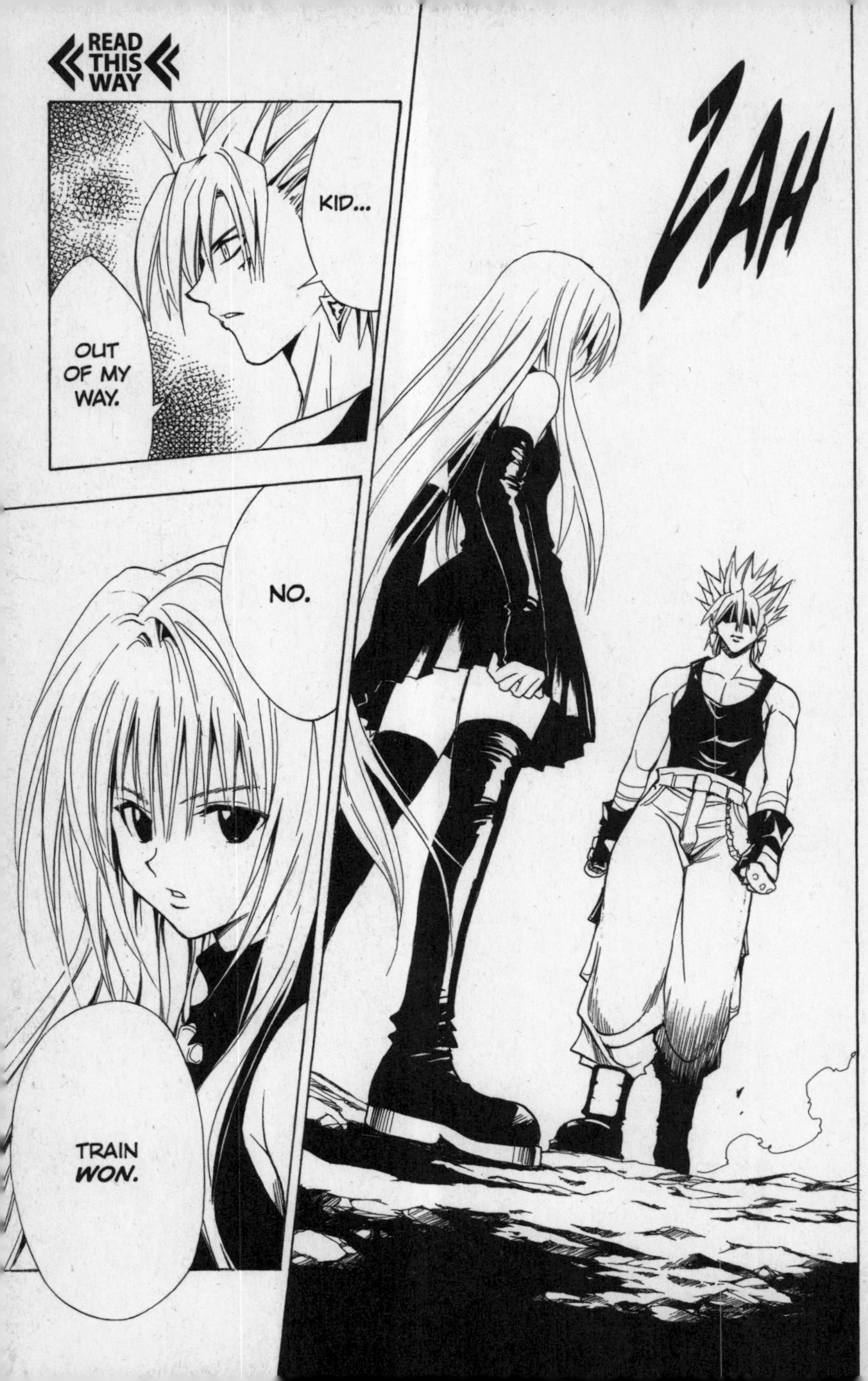
READ THIS WAY
ZAH
KID...
OUT OF MY WAY.
NO.
TRAIN *WON.*

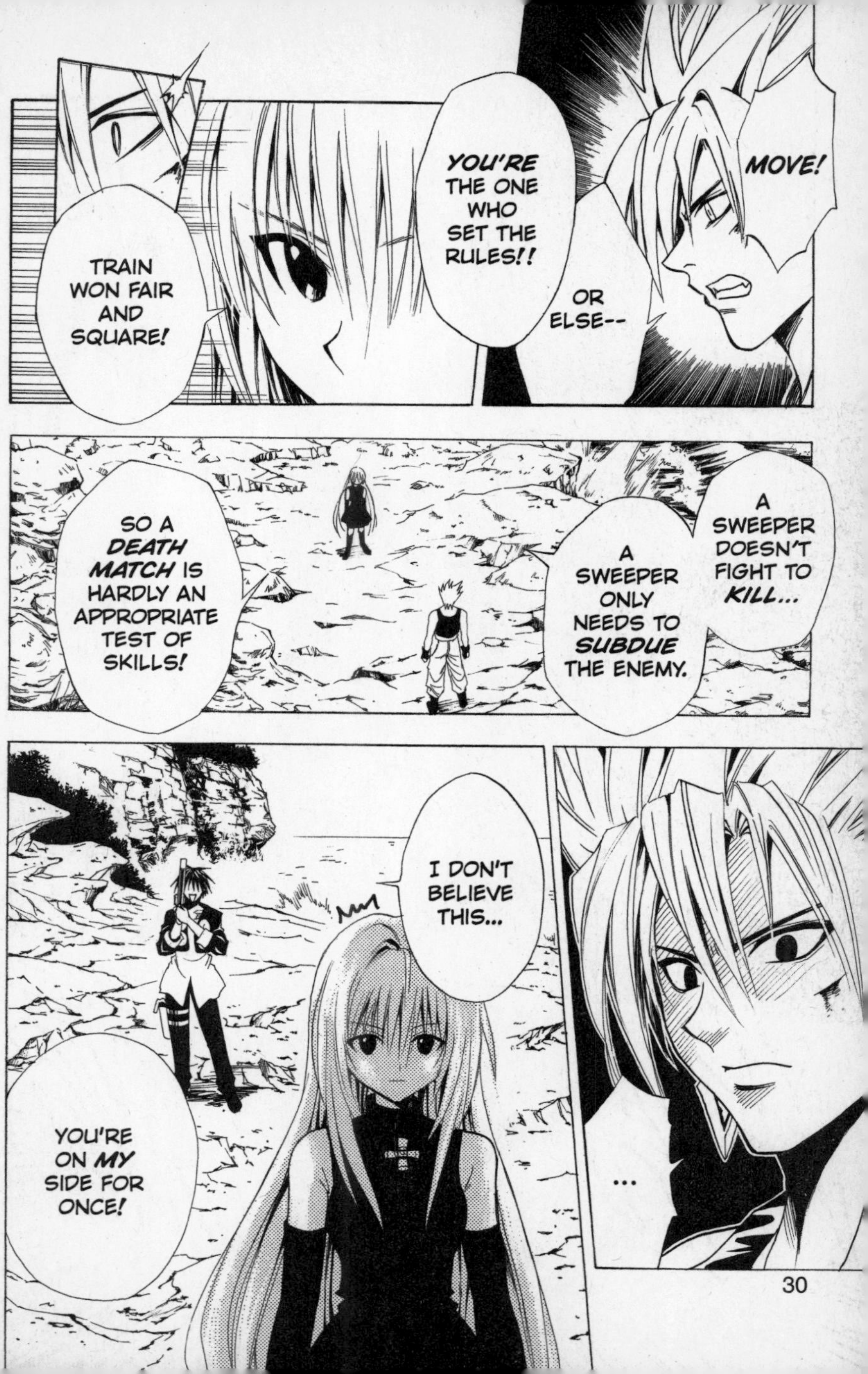
MOVE!
OR ELSE--
YOU'RE THE ONE WHO SET THE RULES!!
TRAIN WON FAIR AND SQUARE!
A SWEEPER DOESN'T FIGHT TO *KILL*...
A SWEEPER ONLY NEEDS TO *SUBDUE* THE ENEMY.
SO A *DEATH MATCH* IS HARDLY AN APPROPRIATE TEST OF SKILLS!
...
I DON'T BELIEVE THIS...
YOU'RE ON *MY* SIDE FOR ONCE!

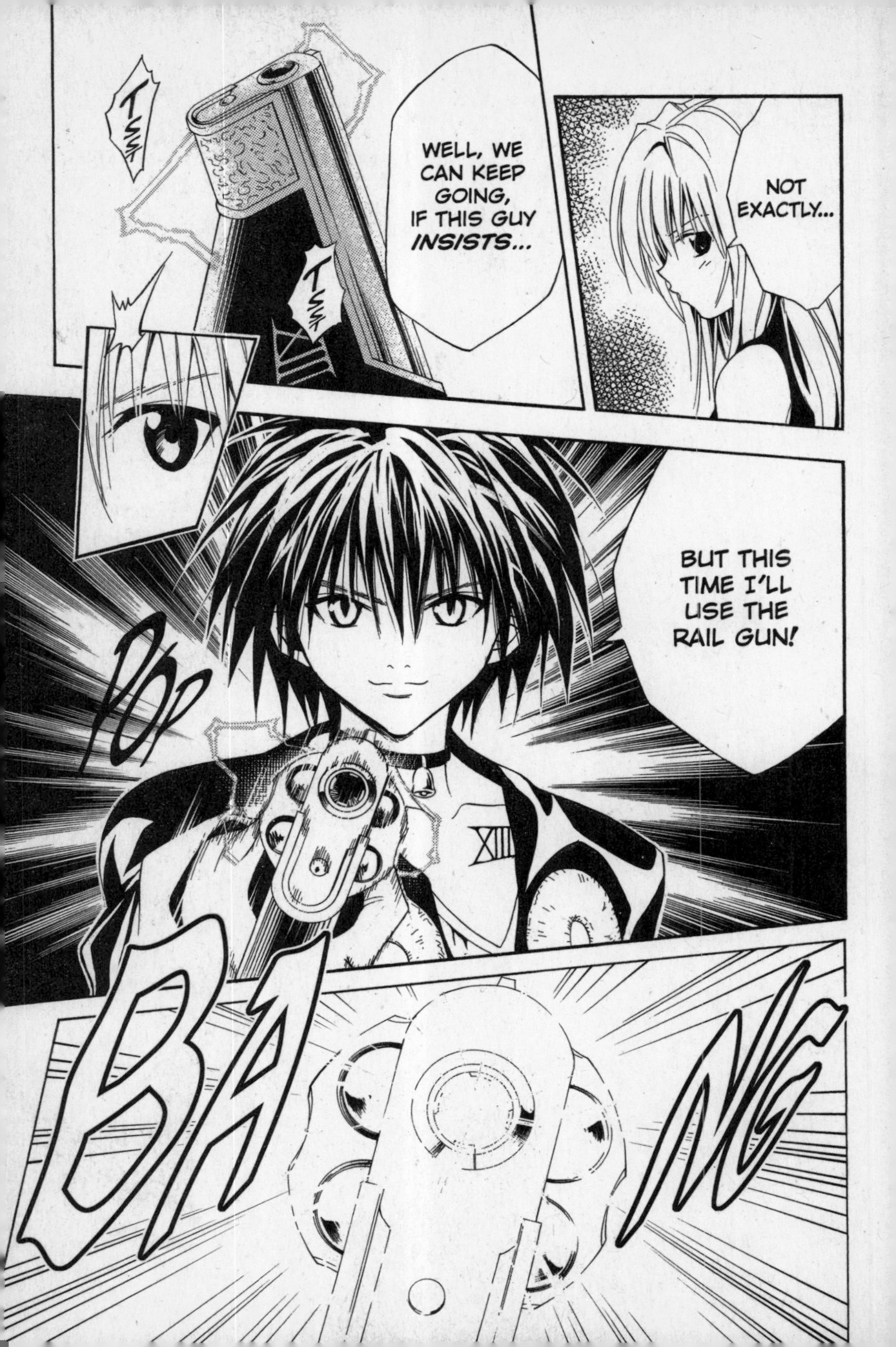
NOT EXACTLY...
WELL, WE CAN KEEP GOING, IF THIS GUY *INSISTS...*
BUT THIS TIME I'LL USE THE RAIL GUN!
POP
BANG

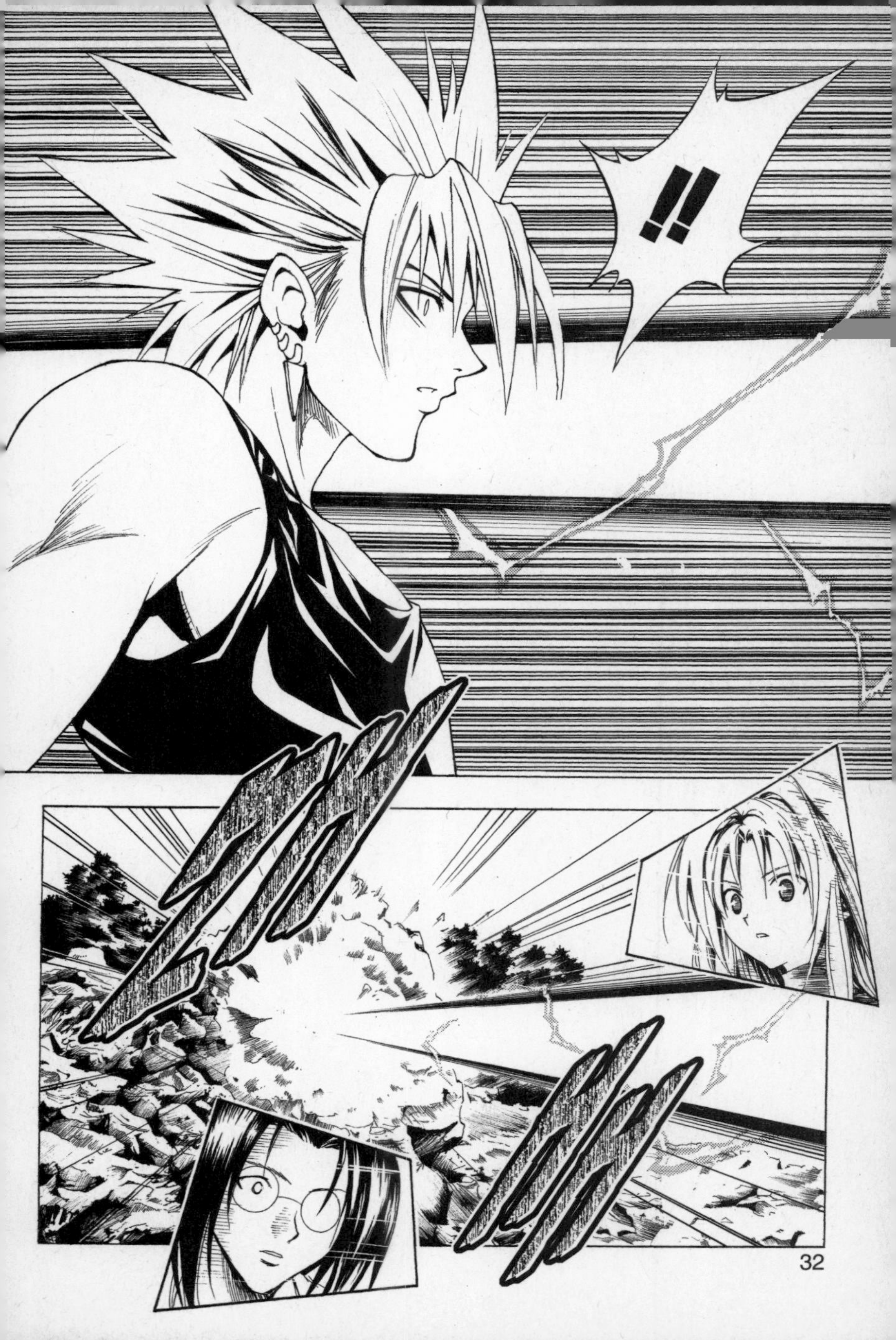
!!

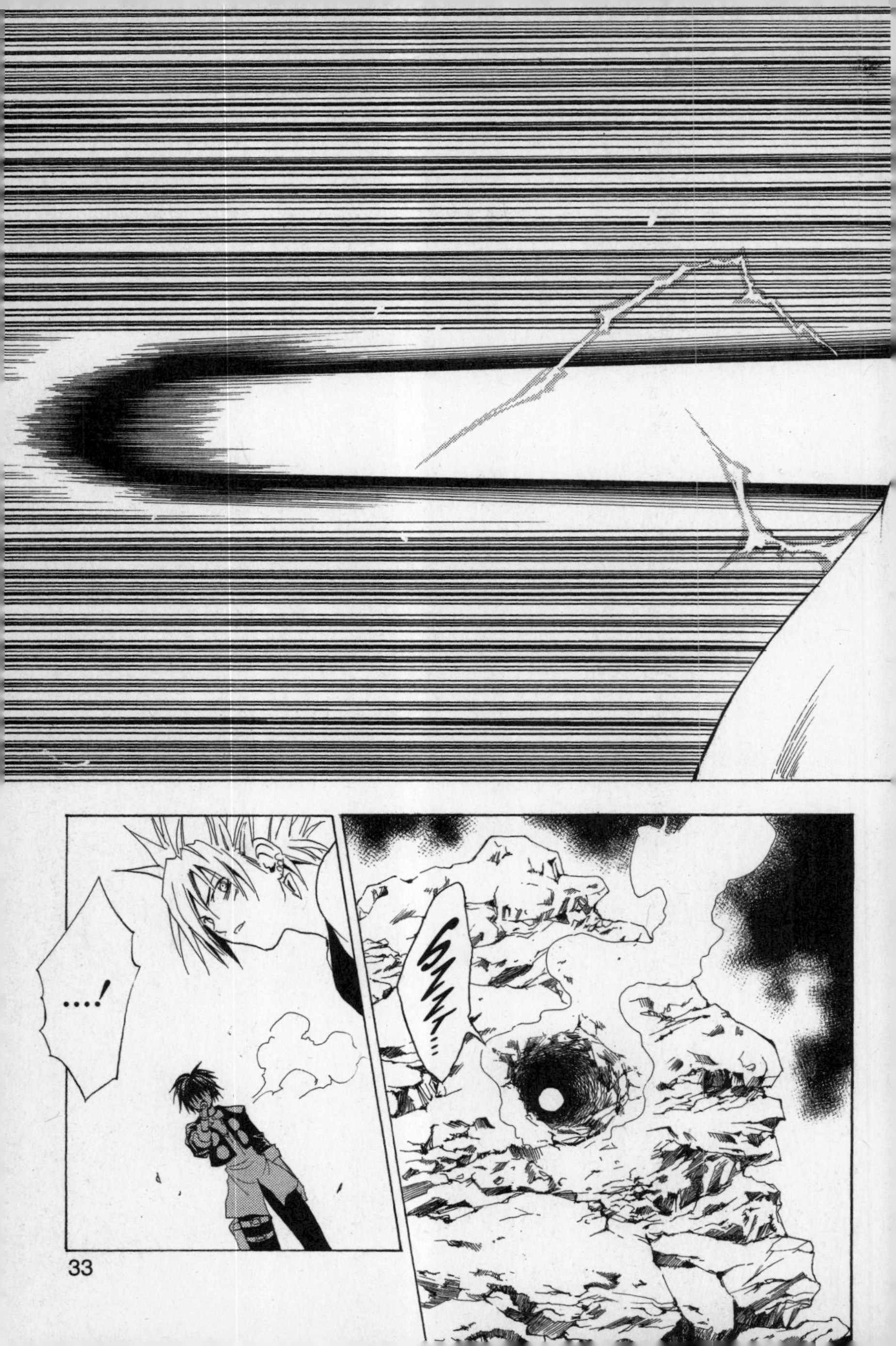
SZZZ...
...!

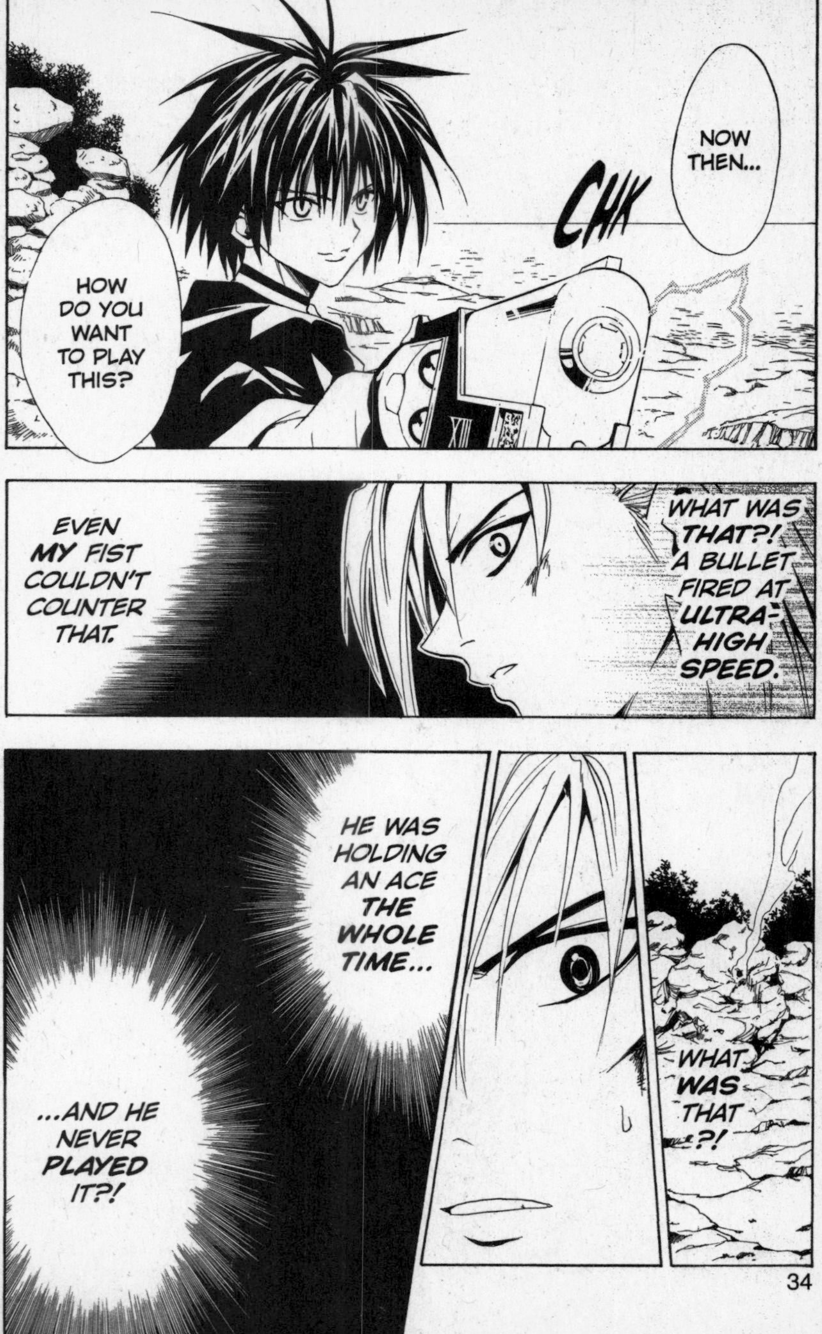
NOW THEN...
CHK
HOW DO YOU WANT TO PLAY THIS?
WHAT WAS THAT?! A BULLET FIRED AT ULTRA-HIGH SPEED.
EVEN MY FIST COULDN'T COUNTER THAT.
WHAT WAS THAT?!
HE WAS HOLDING AN ACE THE WHOLE TIME...
...AND HE NEVER PLAYED IT?!

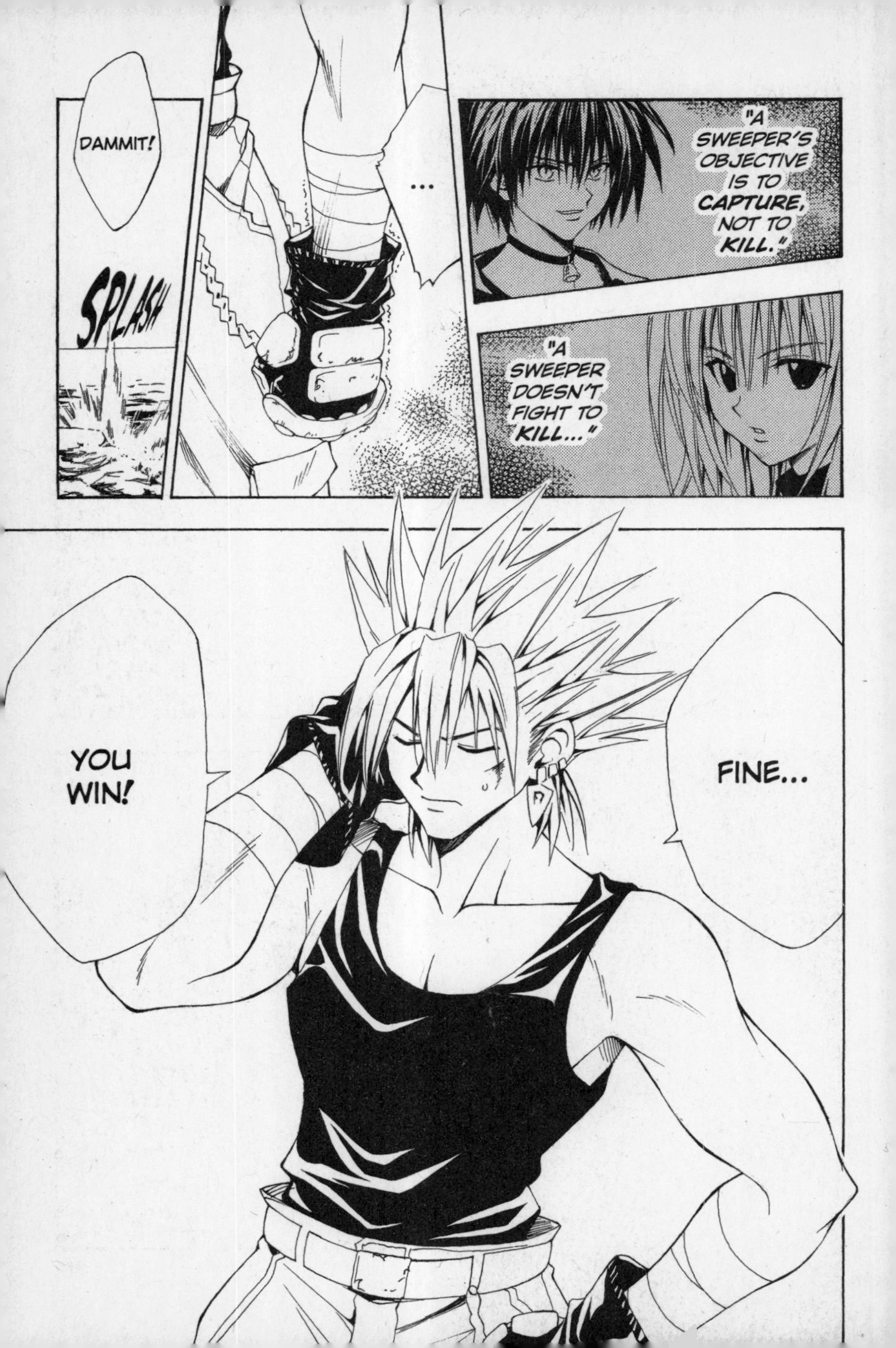
"A SWEEPER'S OBJECTIVE IS TO CAPTURE, NOT TO KILL."
"A SWEEPER DOESN'T FIGHT TO KILL..."
...
DAMMIT!
SPLASH
FINE...
YOU WIN!

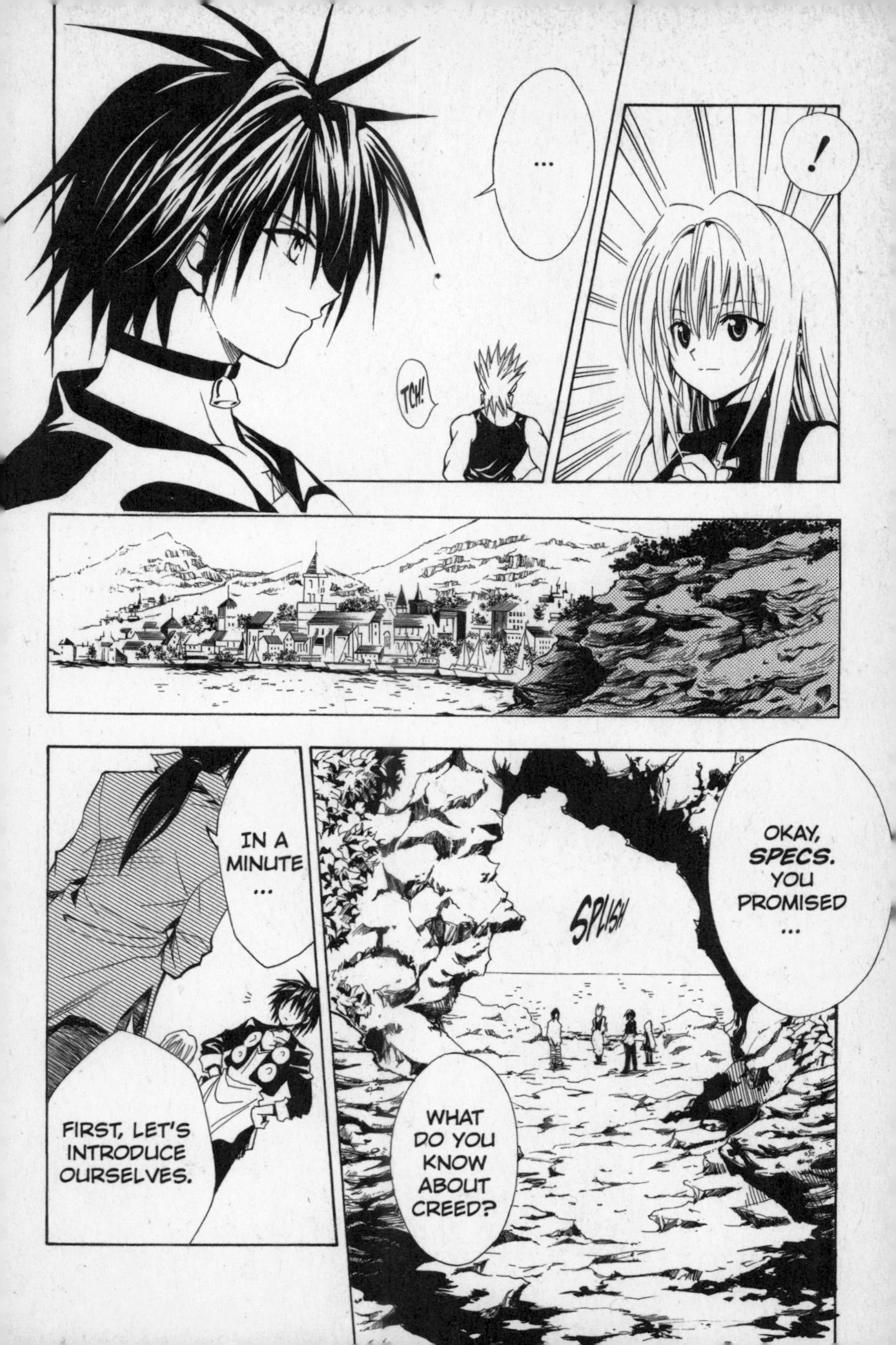
!
...
TCH!
OKAY, SPECS. YOU PROMISED ...
SPLISH
WHAT DO YOU KNOW ABOUT CREED?
IN A MINUTE ...
FIRST, LET'S INTRODUCE OURSELVES.

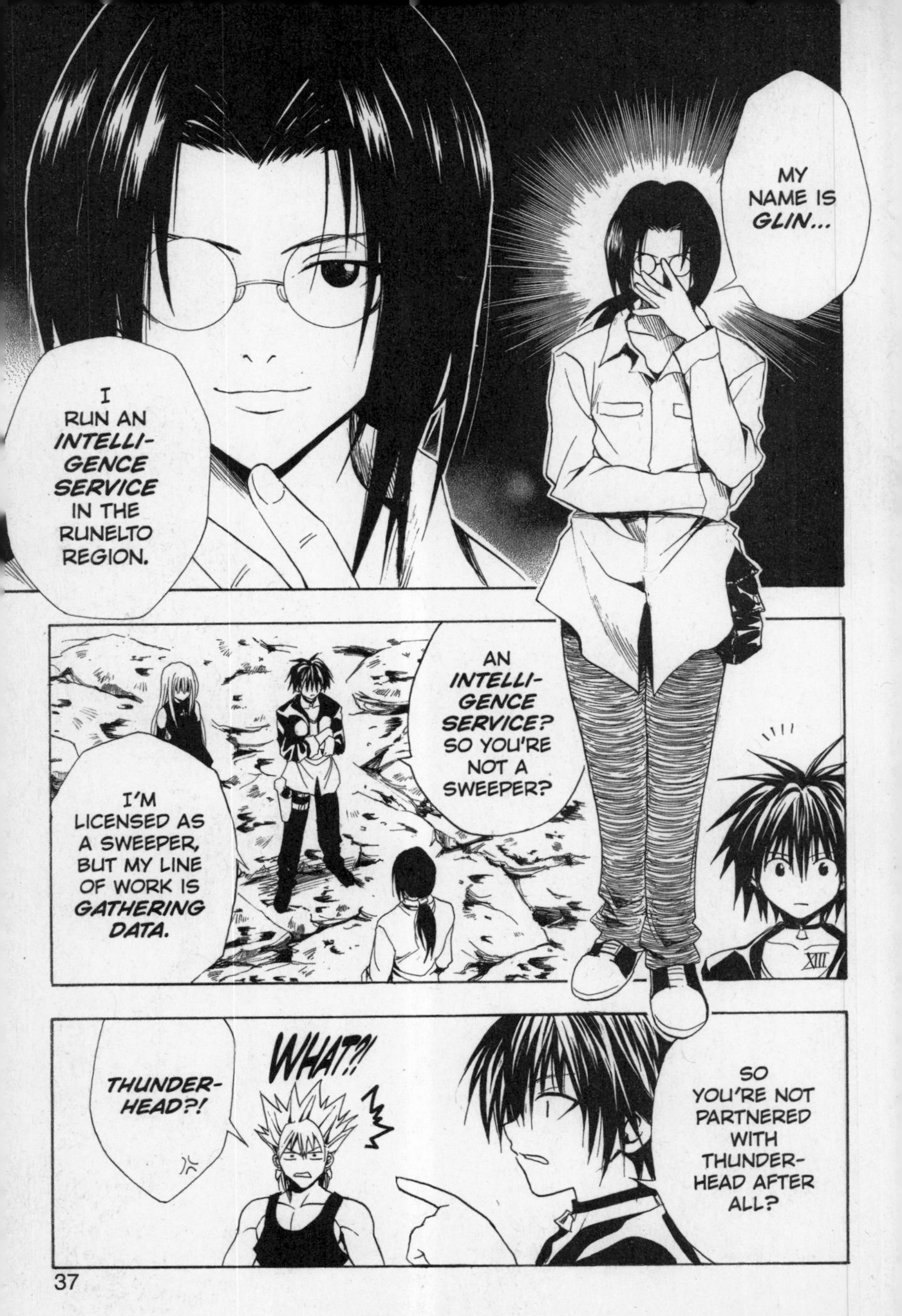
MY NAME IS GLIN...
I RUN AN INTELLIGENCE SERVICE IN THE RUNELTO REGION.
AN INTELLIGENCE SERVICE? SO YOU'RE NOT A SWEEPER?
I'M LICENSED AS A SWEEPER, BUT MY LINE OF WORK IS GATHERING DATA.
SO YOU'RE NOT PARTNERED WITH THUNDERHEAD AFTER ALL?
WHAT?!
THUNDERHEAD?!

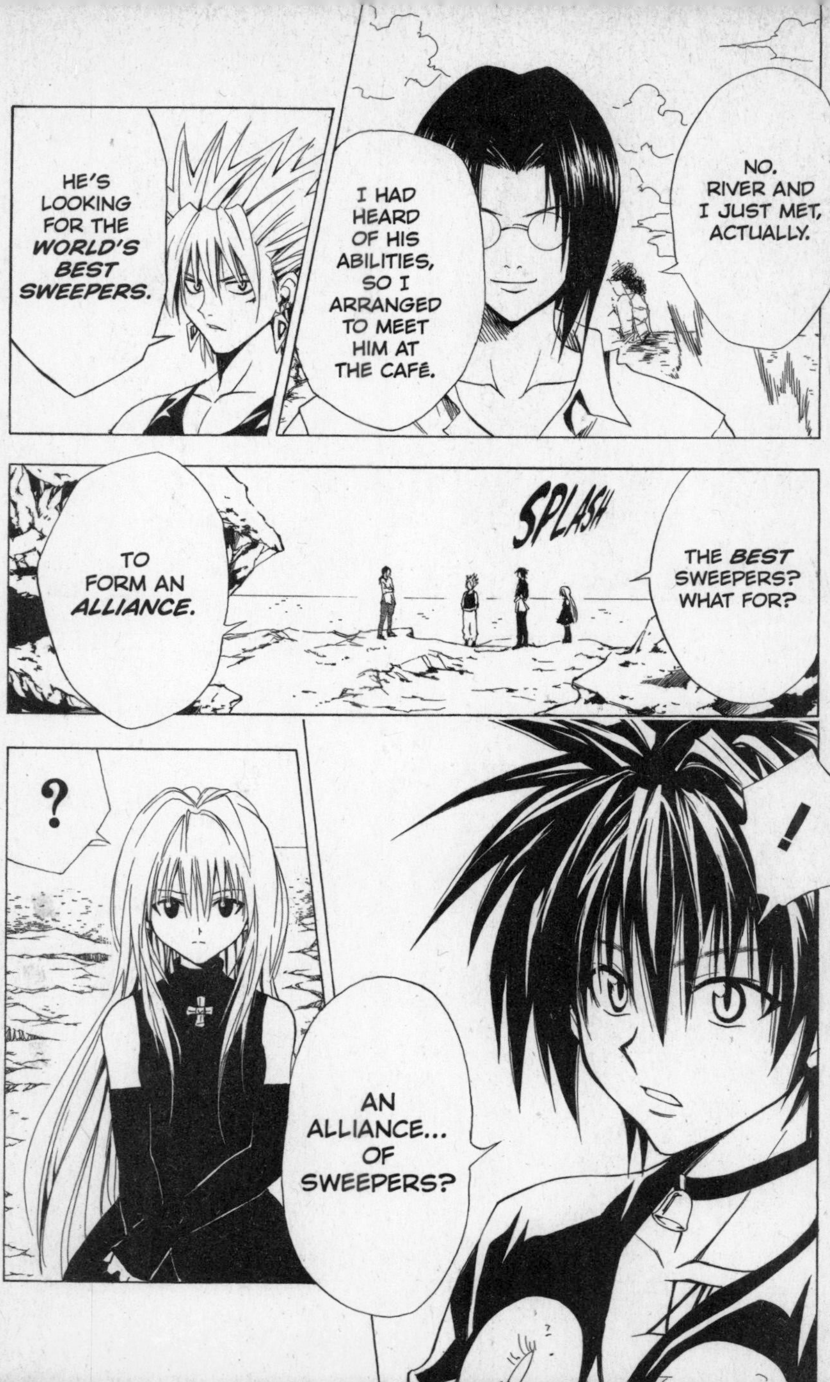
NO. RIVER AND I JUST MET, ACTUALLY.
I HAD HEARD OF HIS ABILITIES, SO I ARRANGED TO MEET HIM AT THE CAFÉ.
HE'S LOOKING FOR THE *WORLD'S BEST SWEEPERS.*
THE *BEST* SWEEPERS? WHAT FOR?
SPLASH
TO FORM AN *ALLIANCE.*
!
AN ALLIANCE... OF SWEEPERS?
?

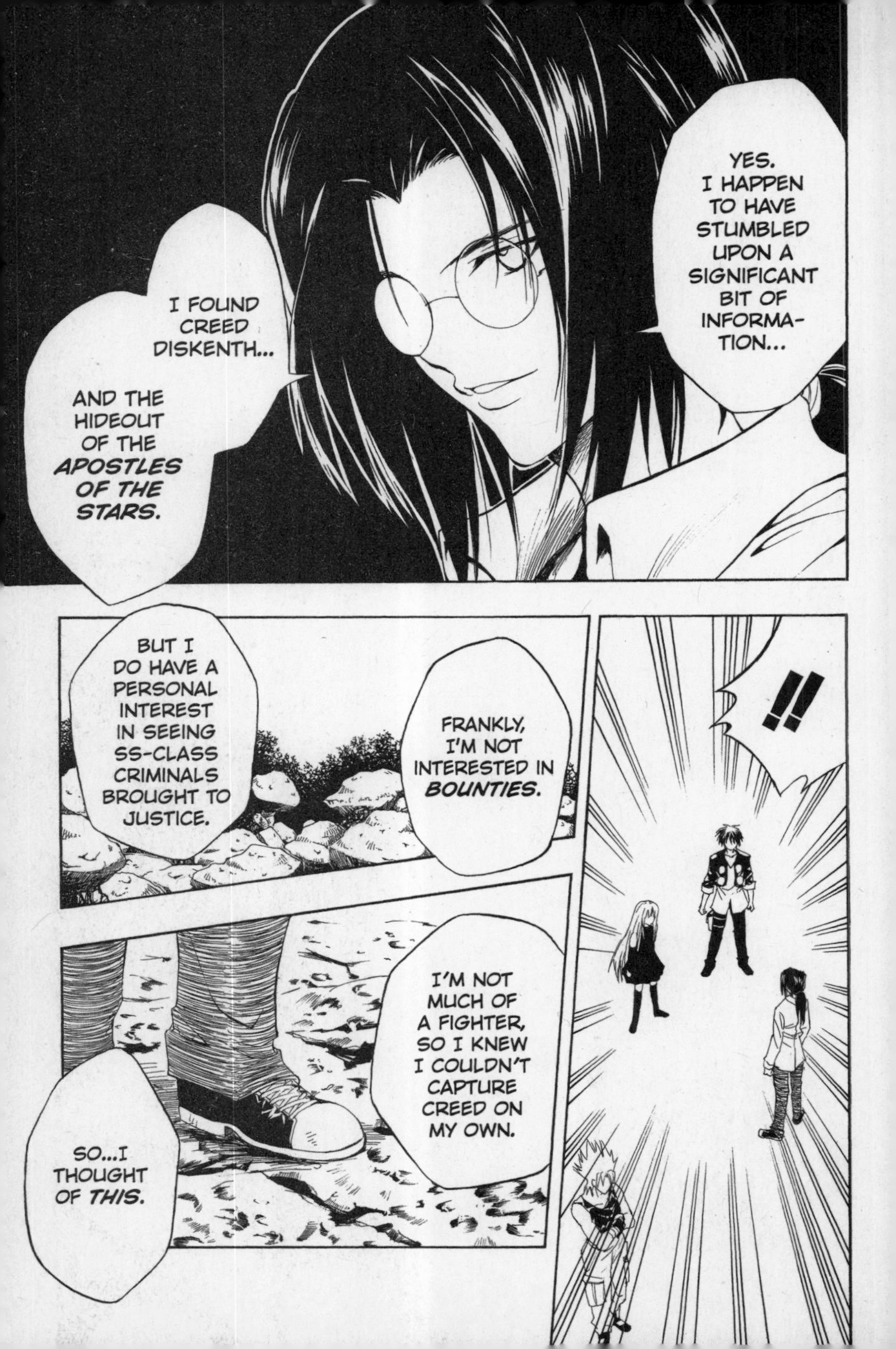
YES. I HAPPEN TO HAVE STUMBLED UPON A SIGNIFICANT BIT OF INFORMATION...
I FOUND CREED DISKENTH...
AND THE HIDEOUT OF THE *APOSTLES OF THE STARS.*
!!
FRANKLY, I'M NOT INTERESTED IN *BOUNTIES.*
BUT I DO HAVE A PERSONAL INTEREST IN SEEING SS-CLASS CRIMINALS BROUGHT TO JUSTICE.
I'M NOT MUCH OF A FIGHTER, SO I KNEW I COULDN'T CAPTURE CREED ON MY OWN.
SO...I THOUGHT OF *THIS.*

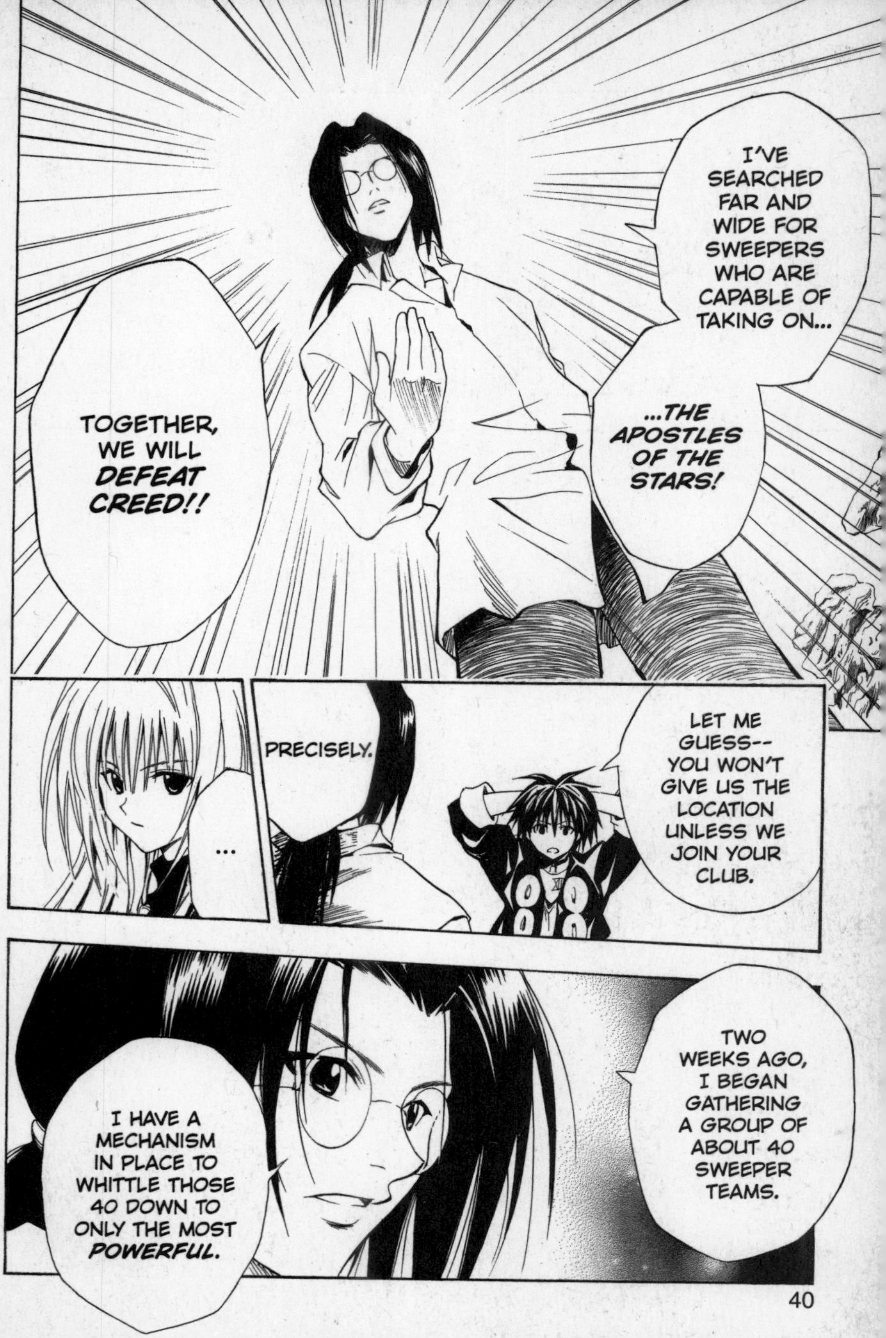
I'VE SEARCHED FAR AND WIDE FOR SWEEPERS WHO ARE CAPABLE OF TAKING ON...
...THE APOSTLES OF THE STARS!
TOGETHER, WE WILL *DEFEAT CREED!!*
LET ME GUESS-- YOU WON'T GIVE US THE LOCATION UNLESS WE JOIN YOUR CLUB.
PRECISELY.
...
TWO WEEKS AGO, I BEGAN GATHERING A GROUP OF ABOUT 40 SWEEPER TEAMS.
I HAVE A MECHANISM IN PLACE TO WHITTLE THOSE 40 DOWN TO ONLY THE MOST *POWERFUL.*

READ THIS WAY

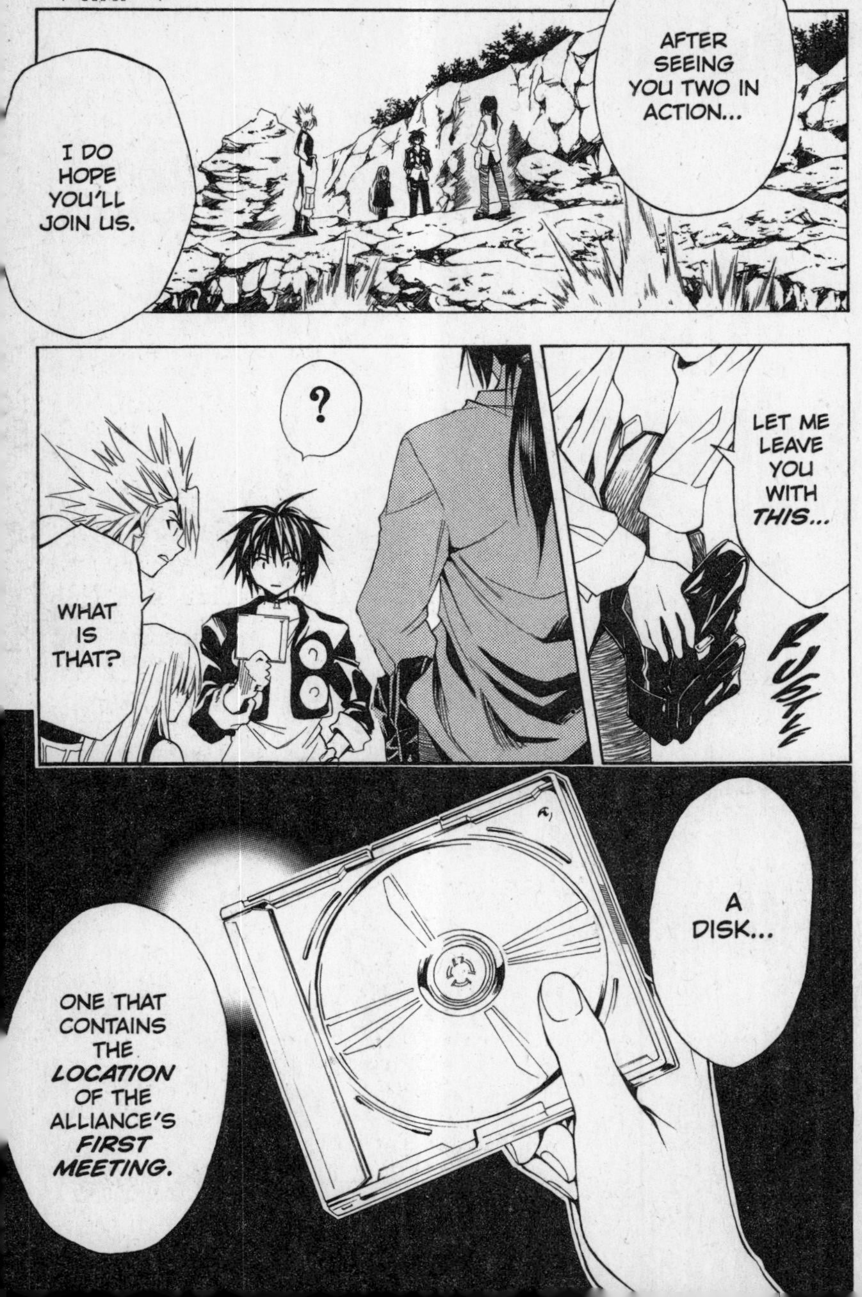

AFTER SEEING YOU TWO IN ACTION...
I DO HOPE YOU'LL JOIN US.
LET ME LEAVE YOU WITH *THIS*...
?
WHAT IS THAT?
A DISK...
ONE THAT CONTAINS THE ***LOCATION*** OF THE ALLIANCE'S ***FIRST MEETING***.

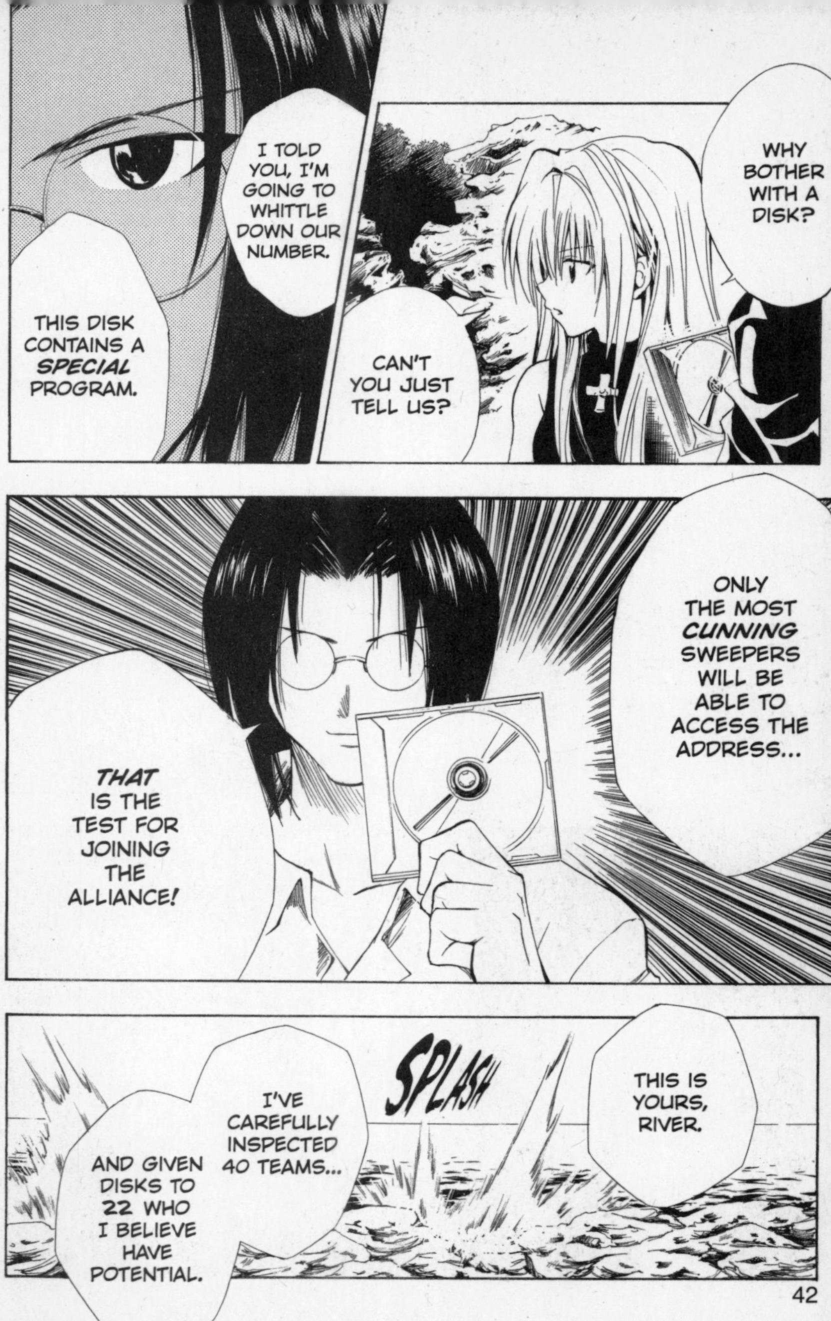
WHY BOTHER WITH A DISK?
CAN'T YOU JUST TELL US?
I TOLD YOU, I'M GOING TO WHITTLE DOWN OUR NUMBER.
THIS DISK CONTAINS A *SPECIAL* PROGRAM.
ONLY THE MOST *CUNNING* SWEEPERS WILL BE ABLE TO ACCESS THE ADDRESS...
THAT IS THE TEST FOR JOINING THE ALLIANCE!
THIS IS YOURS, RIVER.
SPLASH
I'VE CAREFULLY INSPECTED 40 TEAMS...
AND GIVEN DISKS TO 22 WHO I BELIEVE HAVE POTENTIAL.

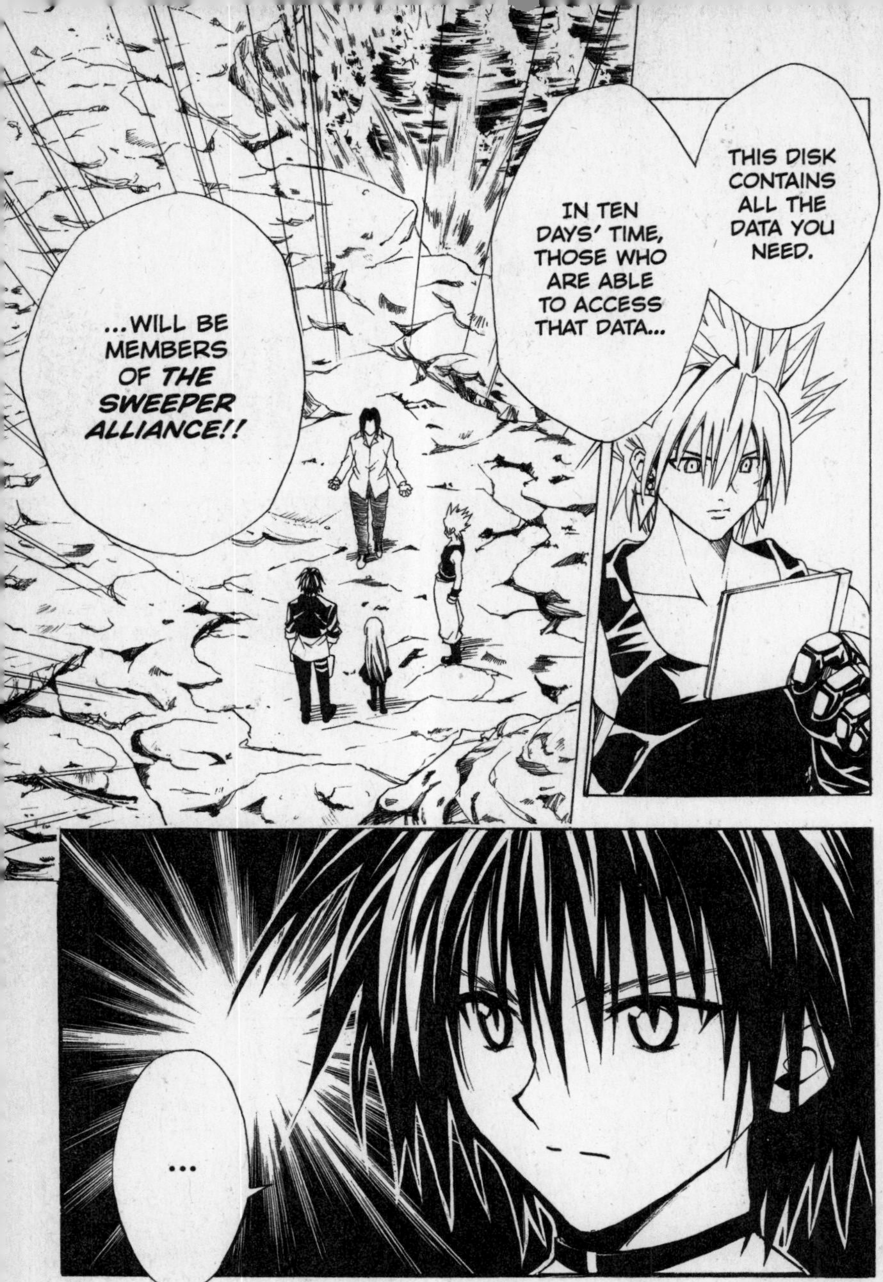
THIS DISK CONTAINS ALL THE DATA YOU NEED.
IN TEN DAYS' TIME, THOSE WHO ARE ABLE TO ACCESS THAT DATA...
...WILL BE MEMBERS OF *THE SWEEPER ALLIANCE!!*
...

UMBER 2—IYO (FROM "YAMATO GENSOUKI")

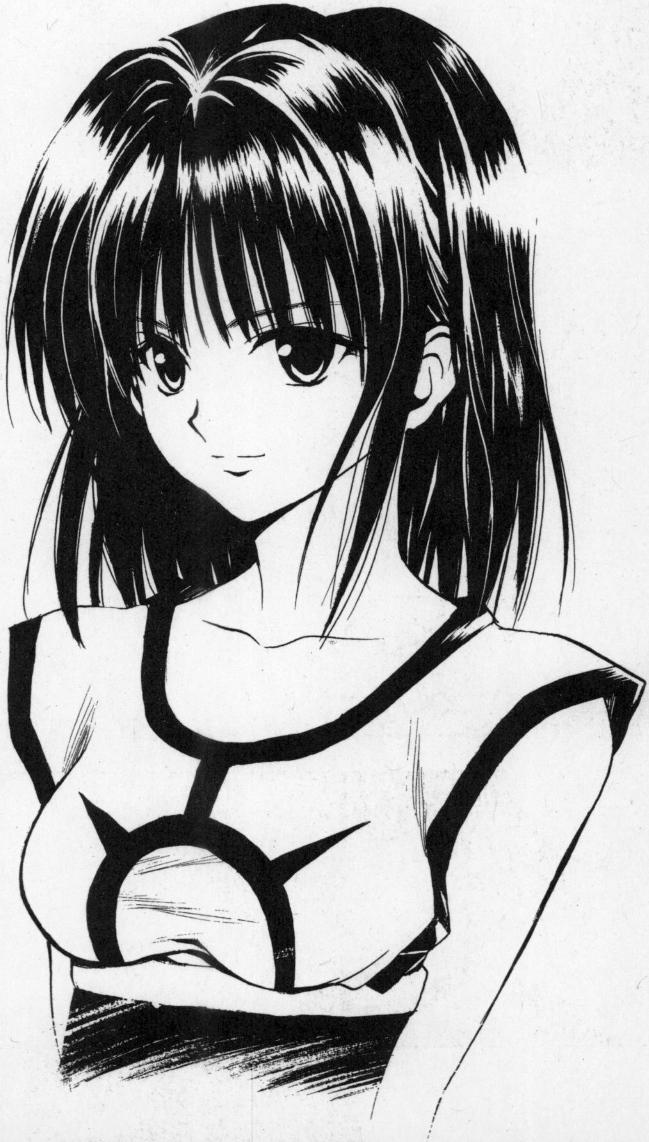

CHAPTER 125: DISK OPERATION

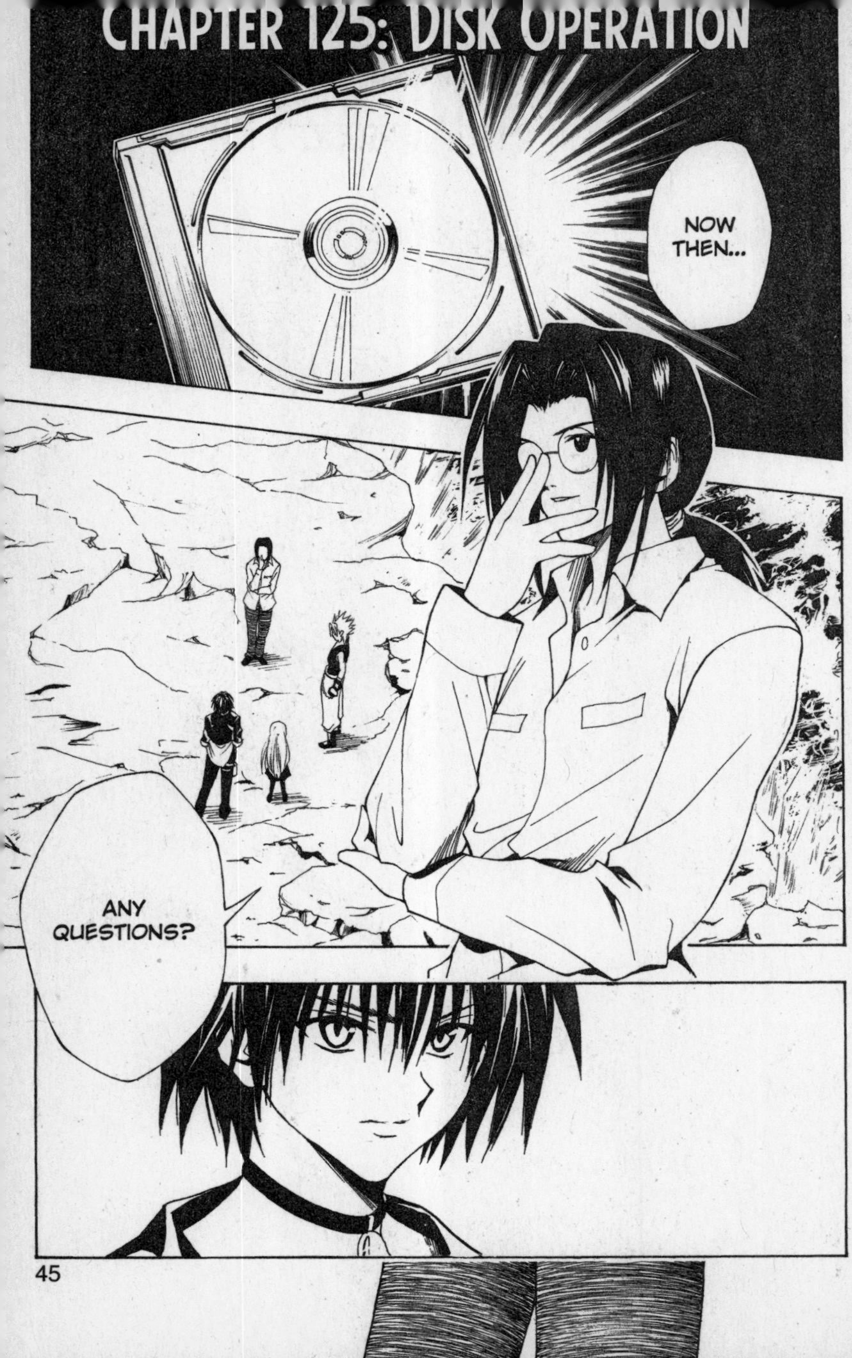
NOW THEN...
ANY QUESTIONS?

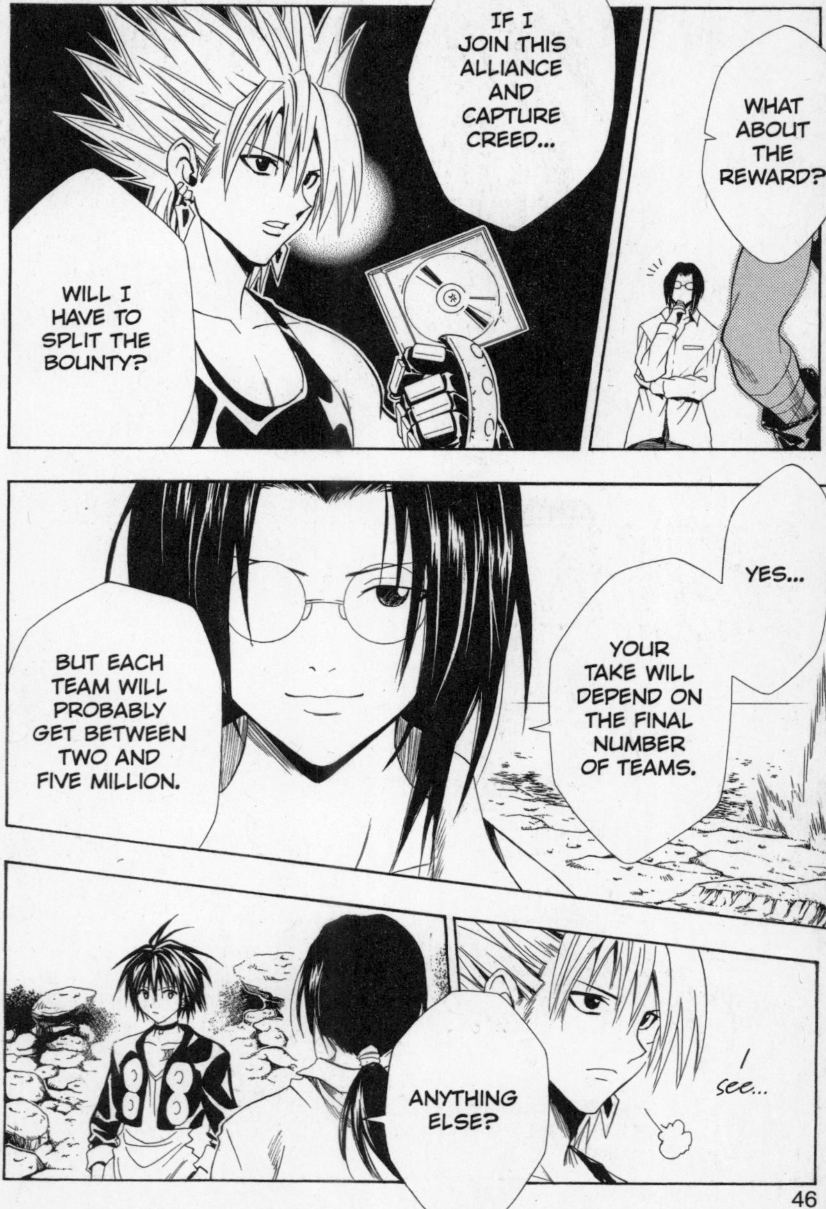
WHAT ABOUT THE REWARD?
IF I JOIN THIS ALLIANCE AND CAPTURE CREED...
WILL I HAVE TO SPLIT THE BOUNTY?
YES...
YOUR TAKE WILL DEPEND ON THE FINAL NUMBER OF TEAMS.
BUT EACH TEAM WILL PROBABLY GET BETWEEN TWO AND FIVE MILLION.
I see...
ANYTHING ELSE?

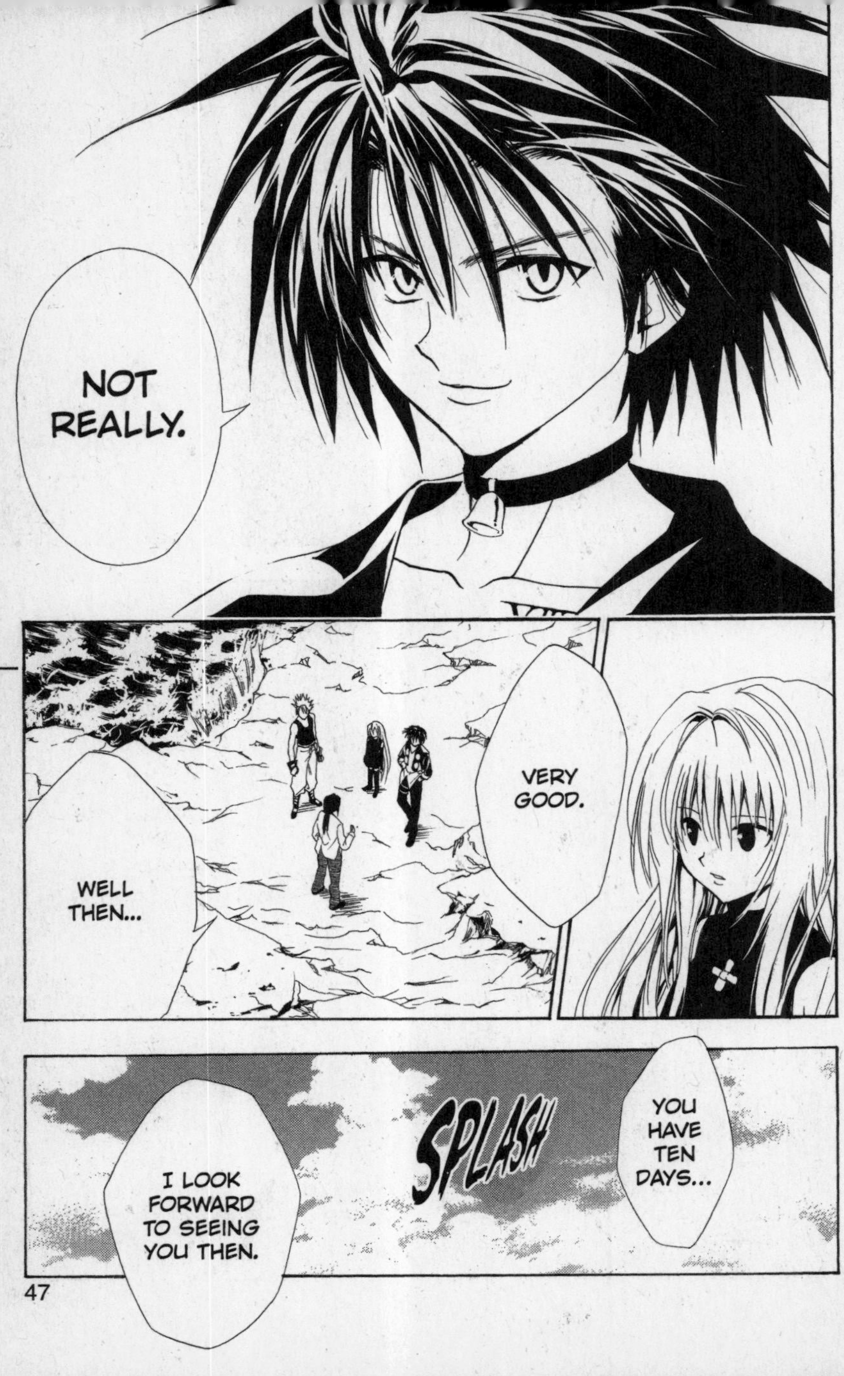
NOT REALLY.
VERY GOOD.
WELL THEN...
YOU HAVE TEN DAYS...
SPLASH
I LOOK FORWARD TO SEEING YOU THEN.

Chapter 125: Disk Operation

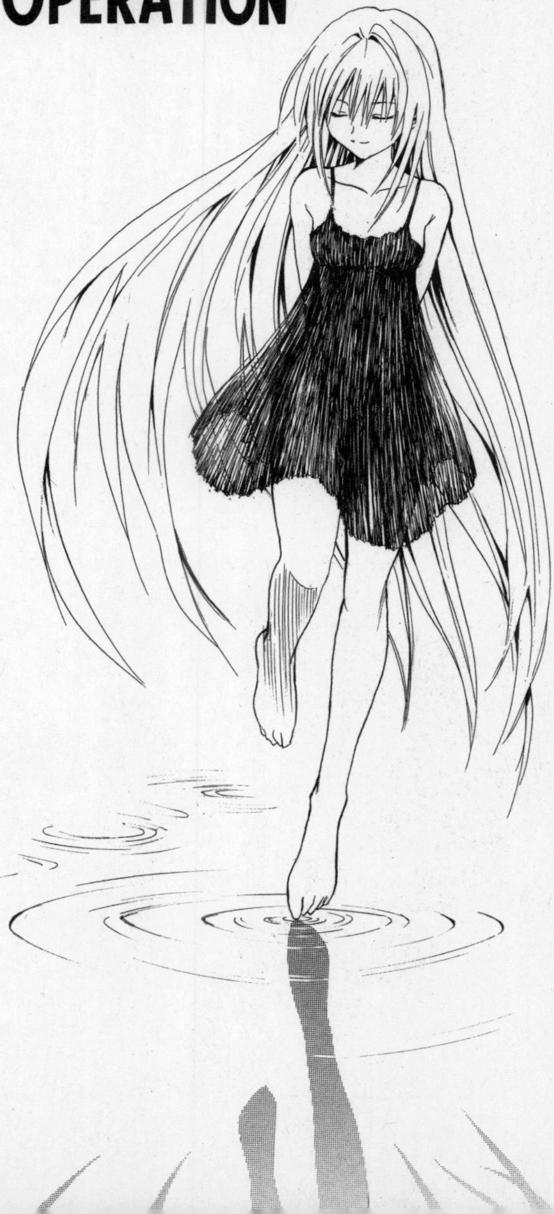

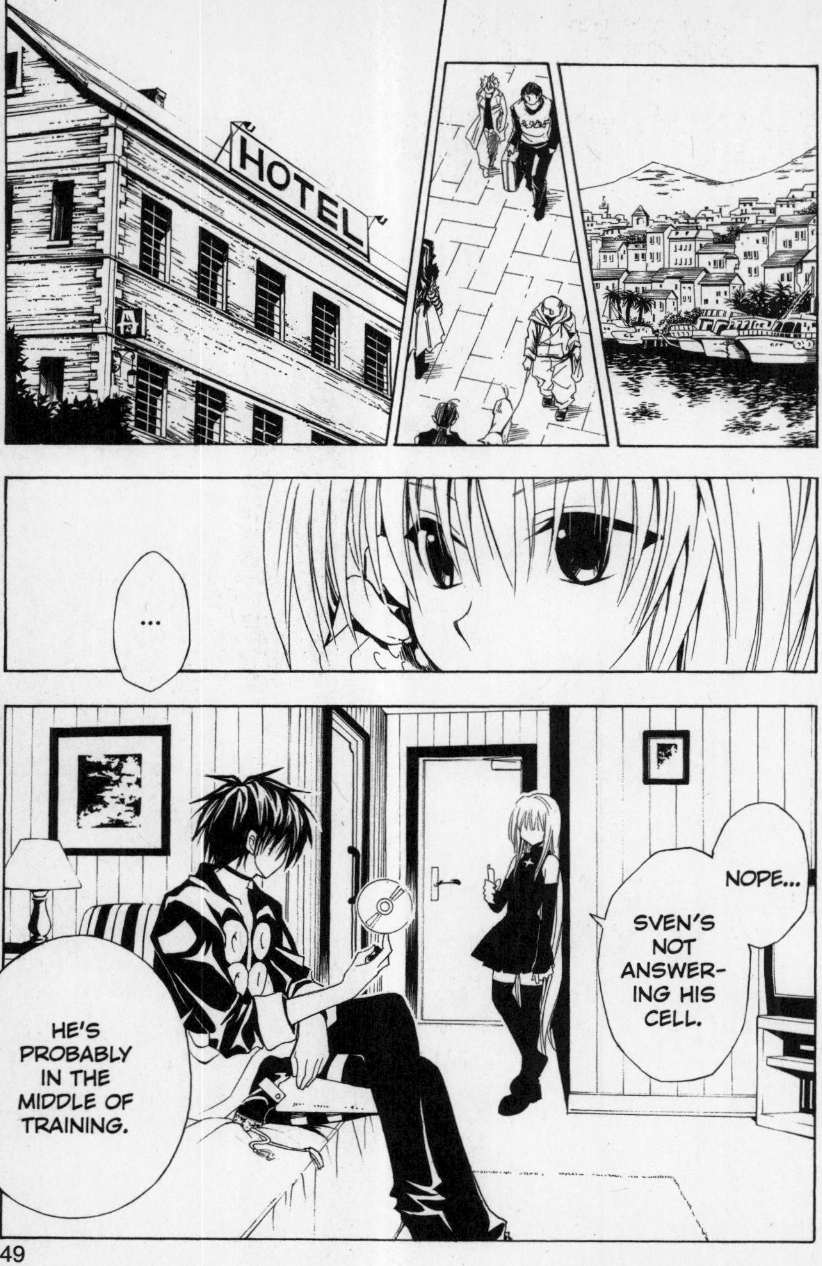
HOTEL
...
NOPE...
SVEN'S NOT ANSWERING HIS CELL.
HE'S PROBABLY IN THE MIDDLE OF TRAINING.

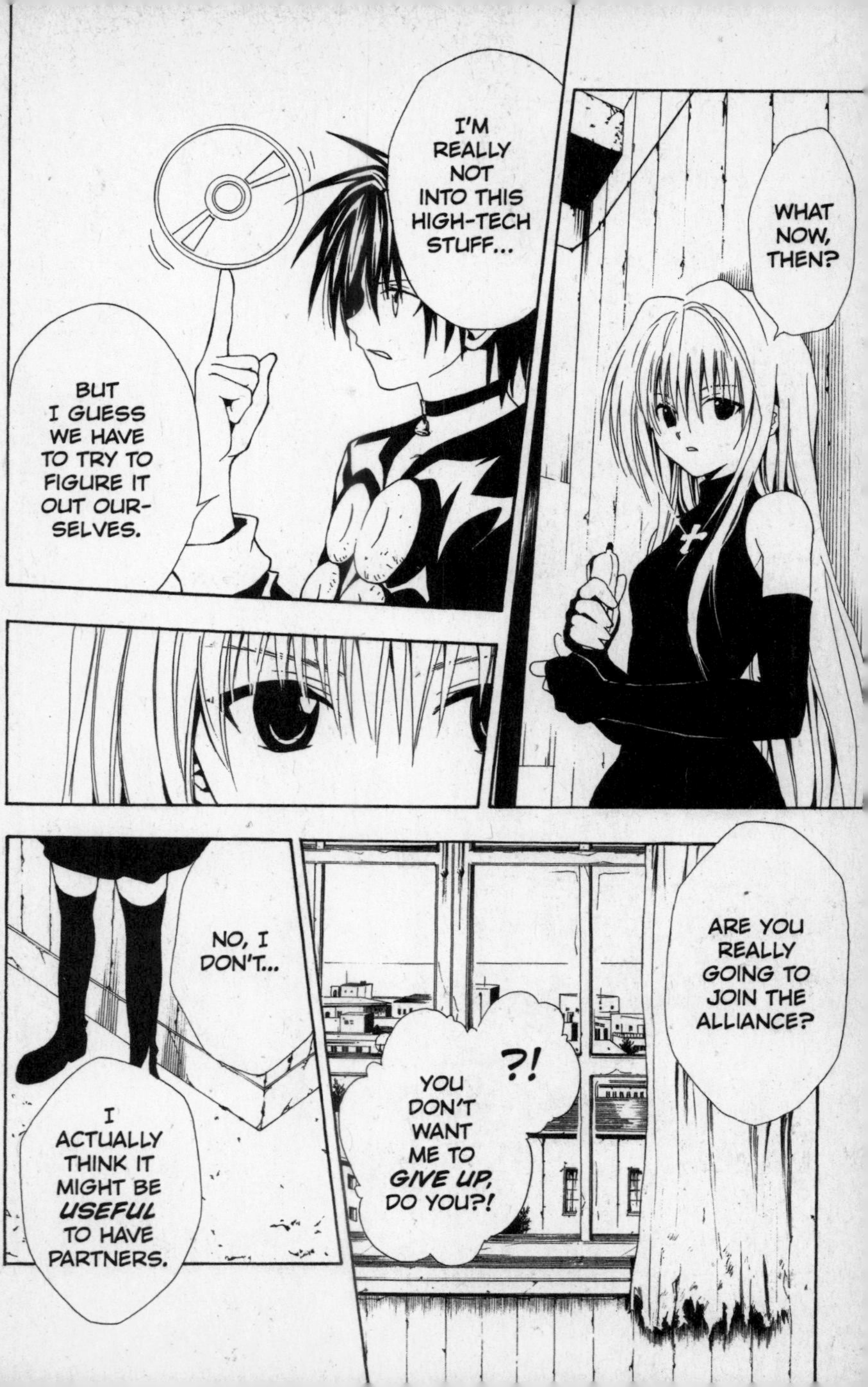
WHAT NOW, THEN?
I'M REALLY NOT INTO THIS HIGH-TECH STUFF...
BUT I GUESS WE HAVE TO TRY TO FIGURE IT OUT OUR-SELVES.
ARE YOU REALLY GOING TO JOIN THE ALLIANCE?
?!
YOU DON'T WANT ME TO *GIVE UP*, DO YOU?!
NO, I DON'T...
I ACTUALLY THINK IT MIGHT BE **USEFUL** TO HAVE PARTNERS.

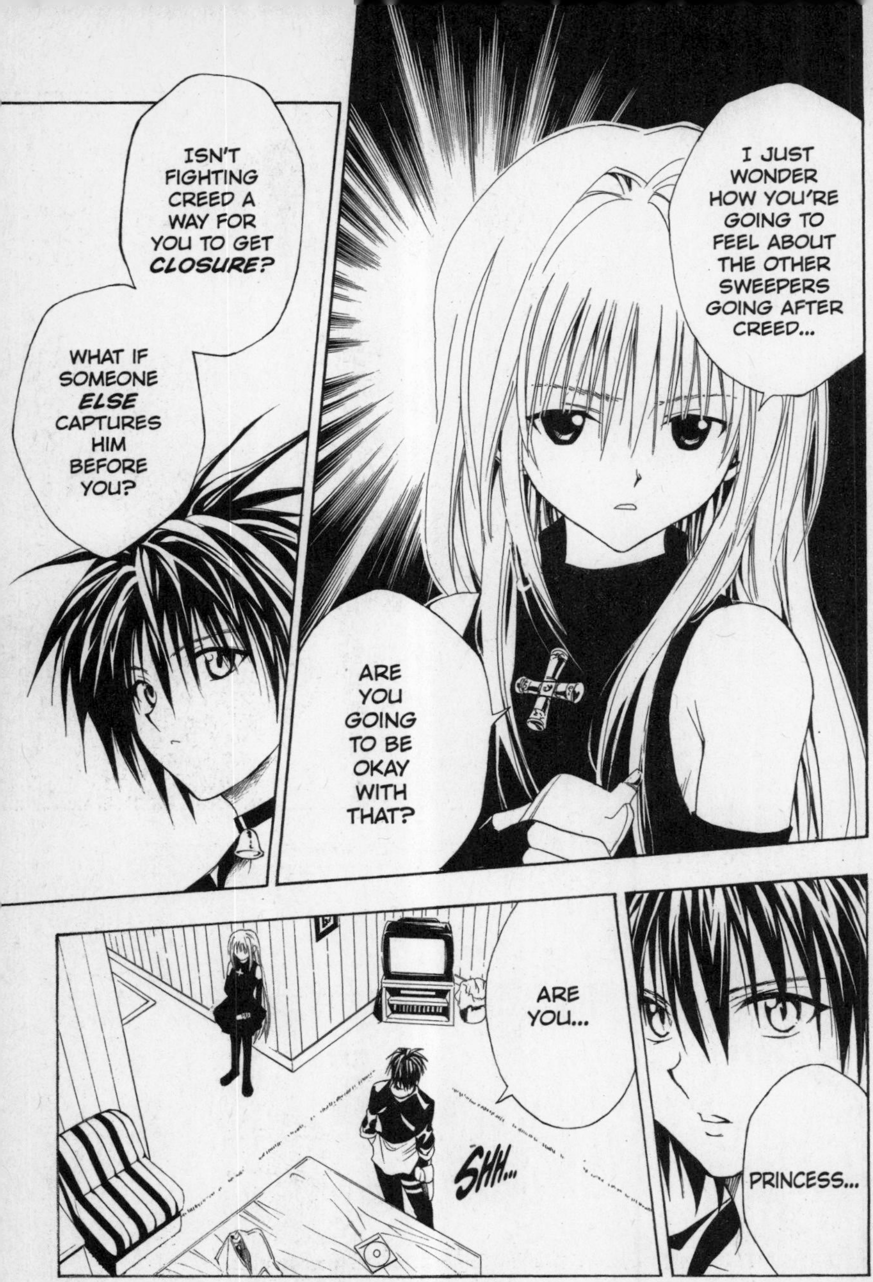
I JUST WONDER HOW YOU'RE GOING TO FEEL ABOUT THE OTHER SWEEPERS GOING AFTER CREED...
ISN'T FIGHTING CREED A WAY FOR YOU TO GET *CLOSURE?*
WHAT IF SOMEONE *ELSE* CAPTURES HIM BEFORE YOU?
ARE YOU GOING TO BE OKAY WITH THAT?
ARE YOU...
PRINCESS...
SHH...

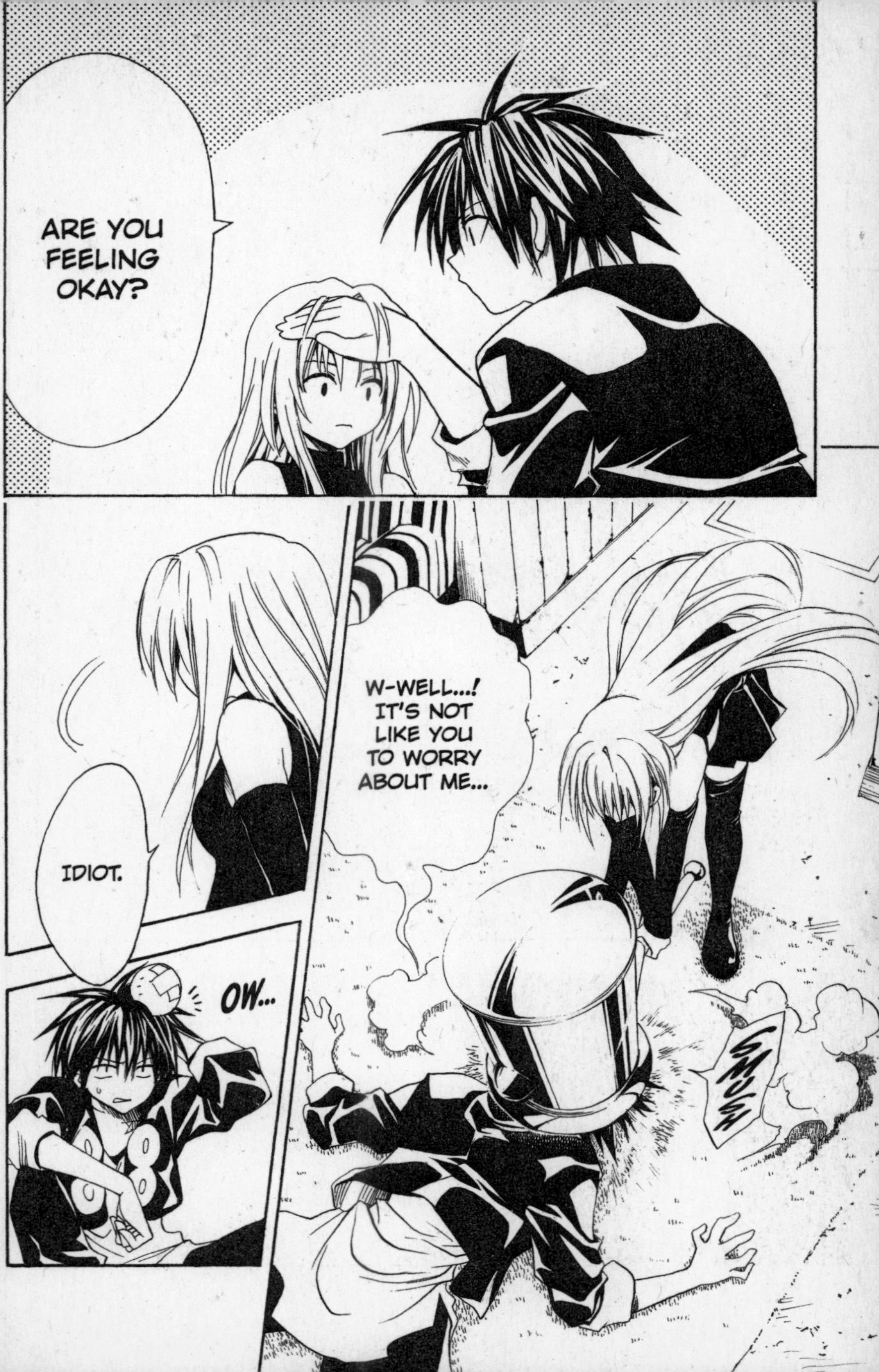
ARE YOU FEELING OKAY?
W-WELL...! IT'S NOT LIKE YOU TO WORRY ABOUT ME...
IDIOT.
OW...

READ THIS WAY

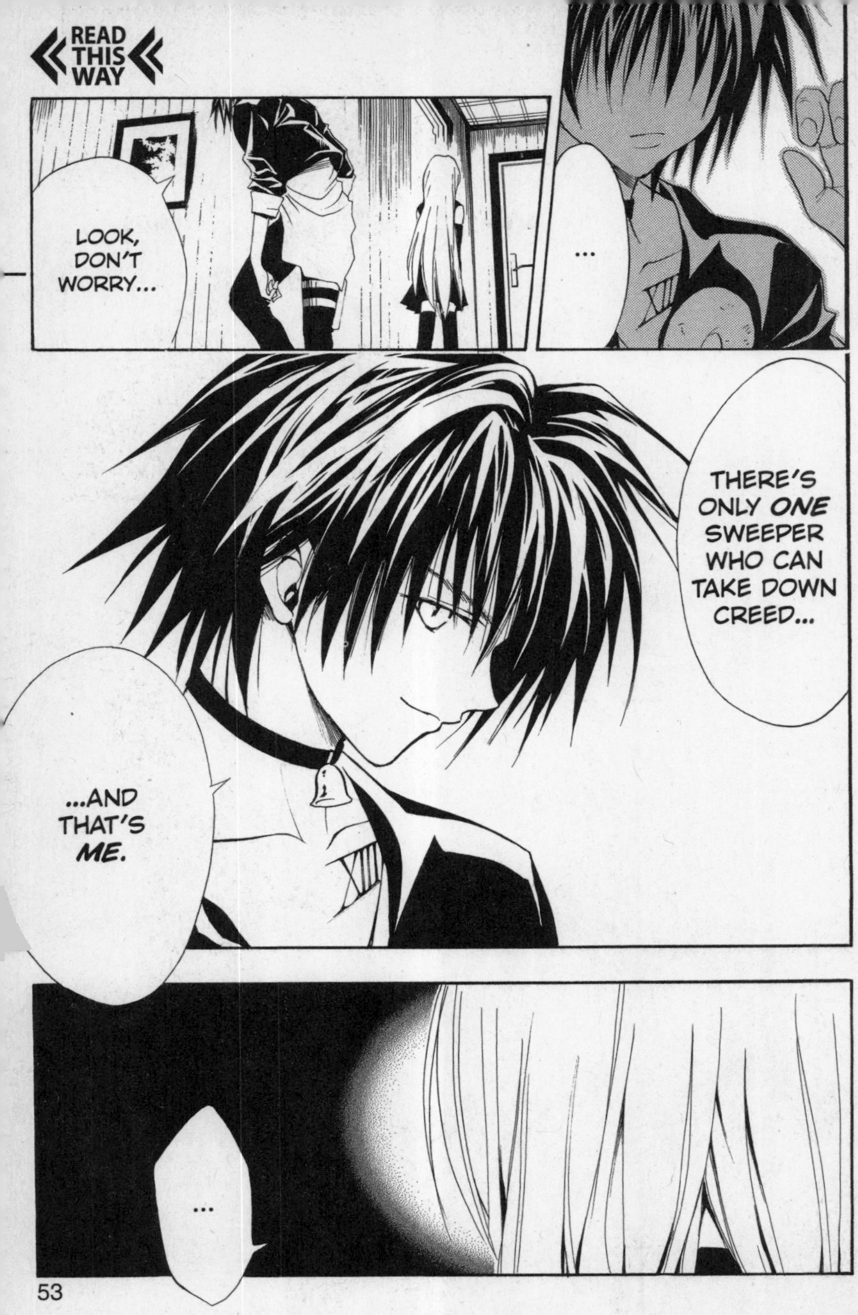
...
LOOK, DON'T WORRY...
THERE'S ONLY *ONE* SWEEPER WHO CAN TAKE DOWN CREED...
...AND THAT'S *ME*.
...

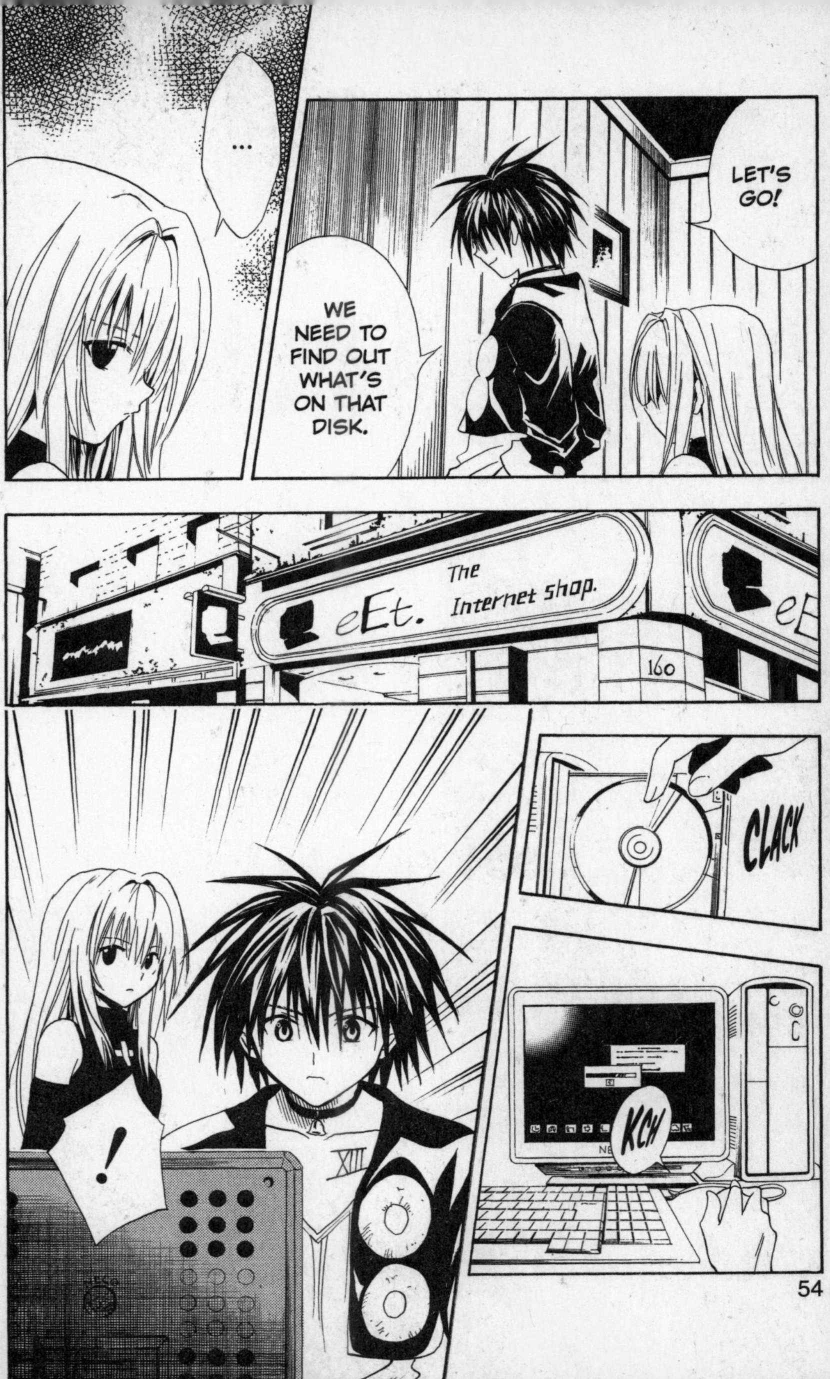
LET'S GO!
WE NEED TO FIND OUT WHAT'S ON THAT DISK.
...
eEt.
The Internet shop.
160
CLACK
KCH
!

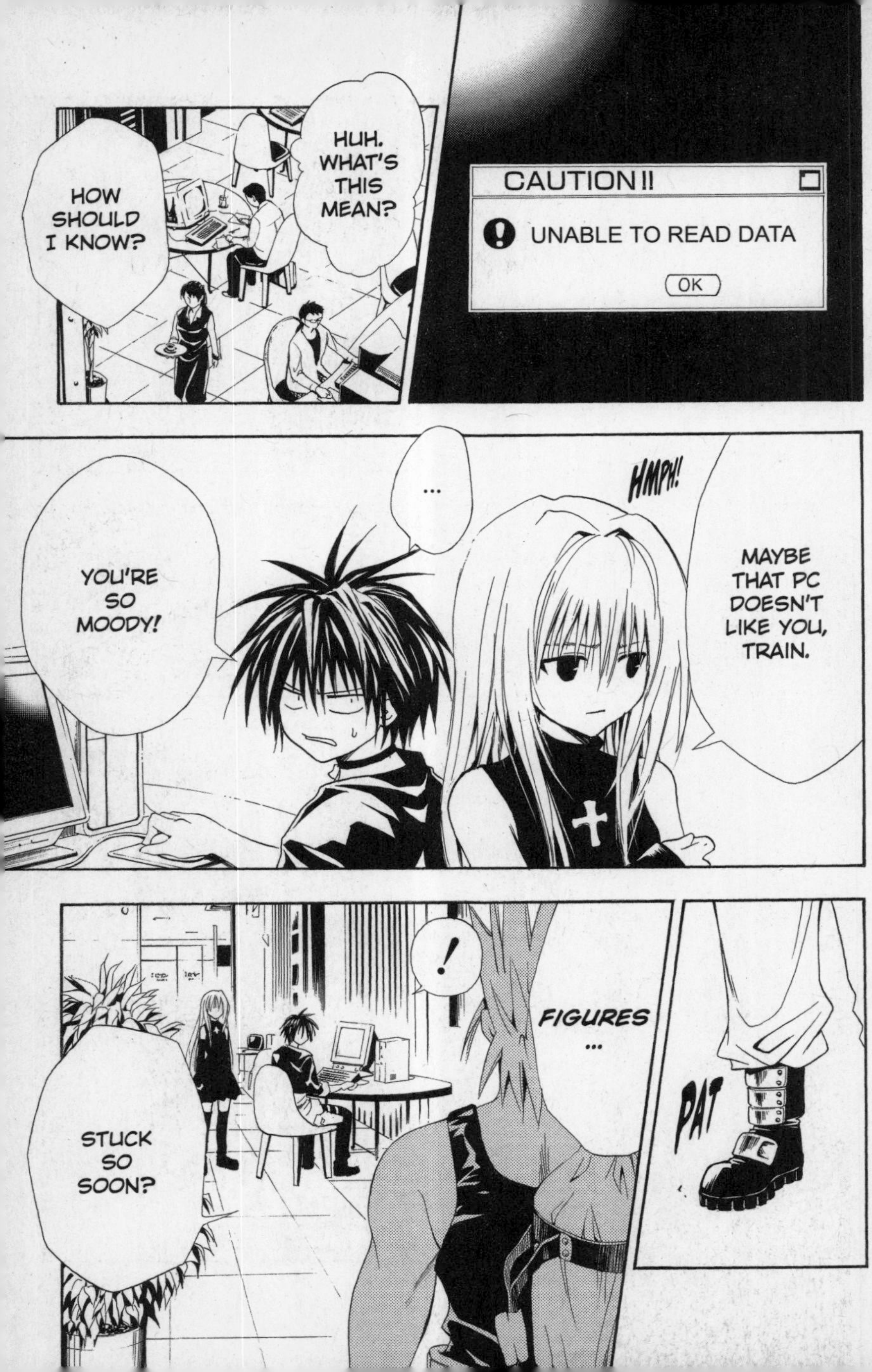

CAUTION!!
UNABLE TO READ DATA
OK
HUH. WHAT'S THIS MEAN?
HOW SHOULD I KNOW?
MAYBE THAT PC DOESN'T LIKE YOU, TRAIN.
HMPH!
...
YOU'RE SO MOODY!
PAT
!
FIGURES...
STUCK SO SOON?

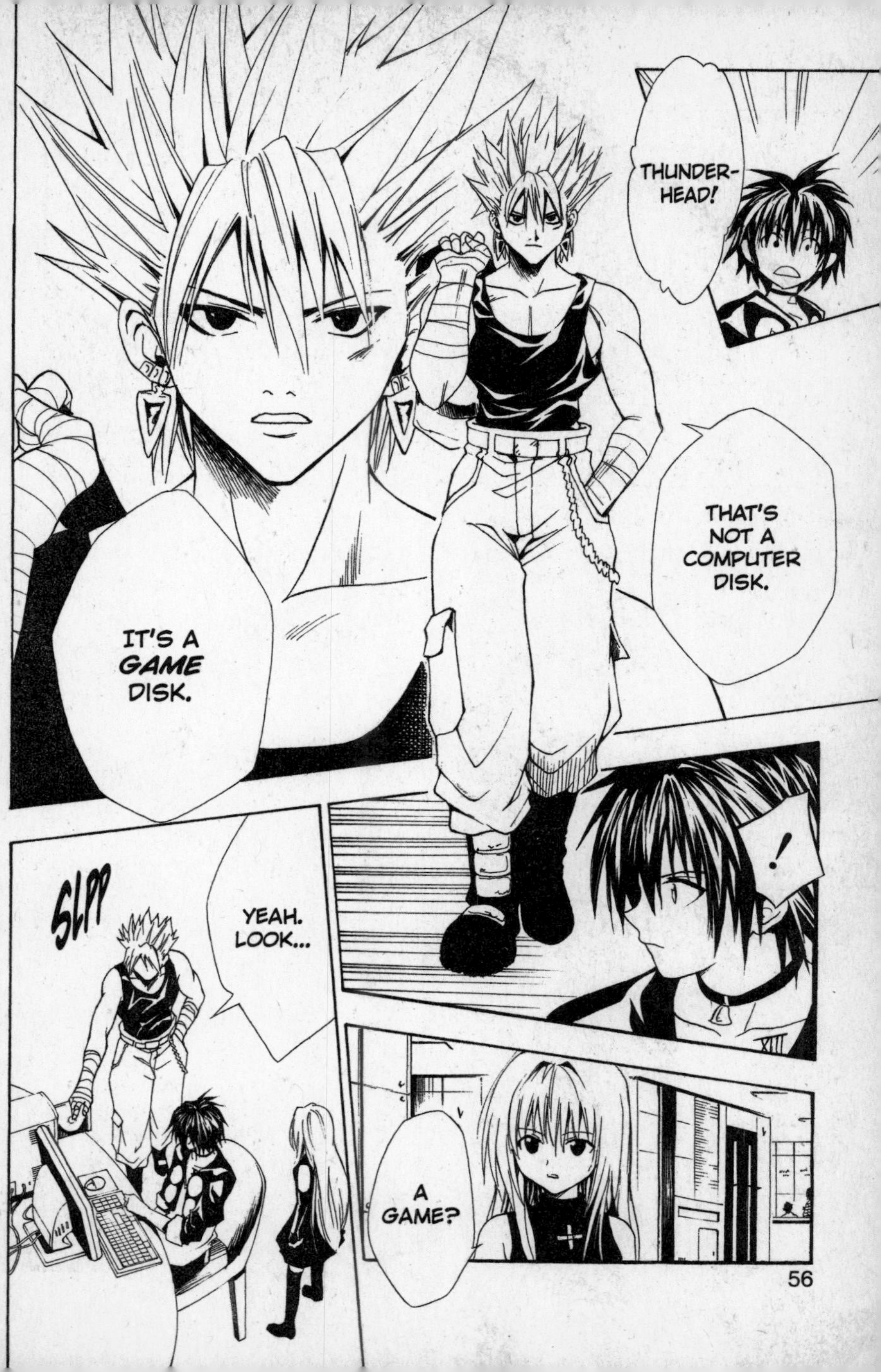
THUNDER-HEAD!
THAT'S NOT A COMPUTER DISK.
IT'S A *GAME* DISK.
!
A GAME?
SLPP
YEAH. LOOK...

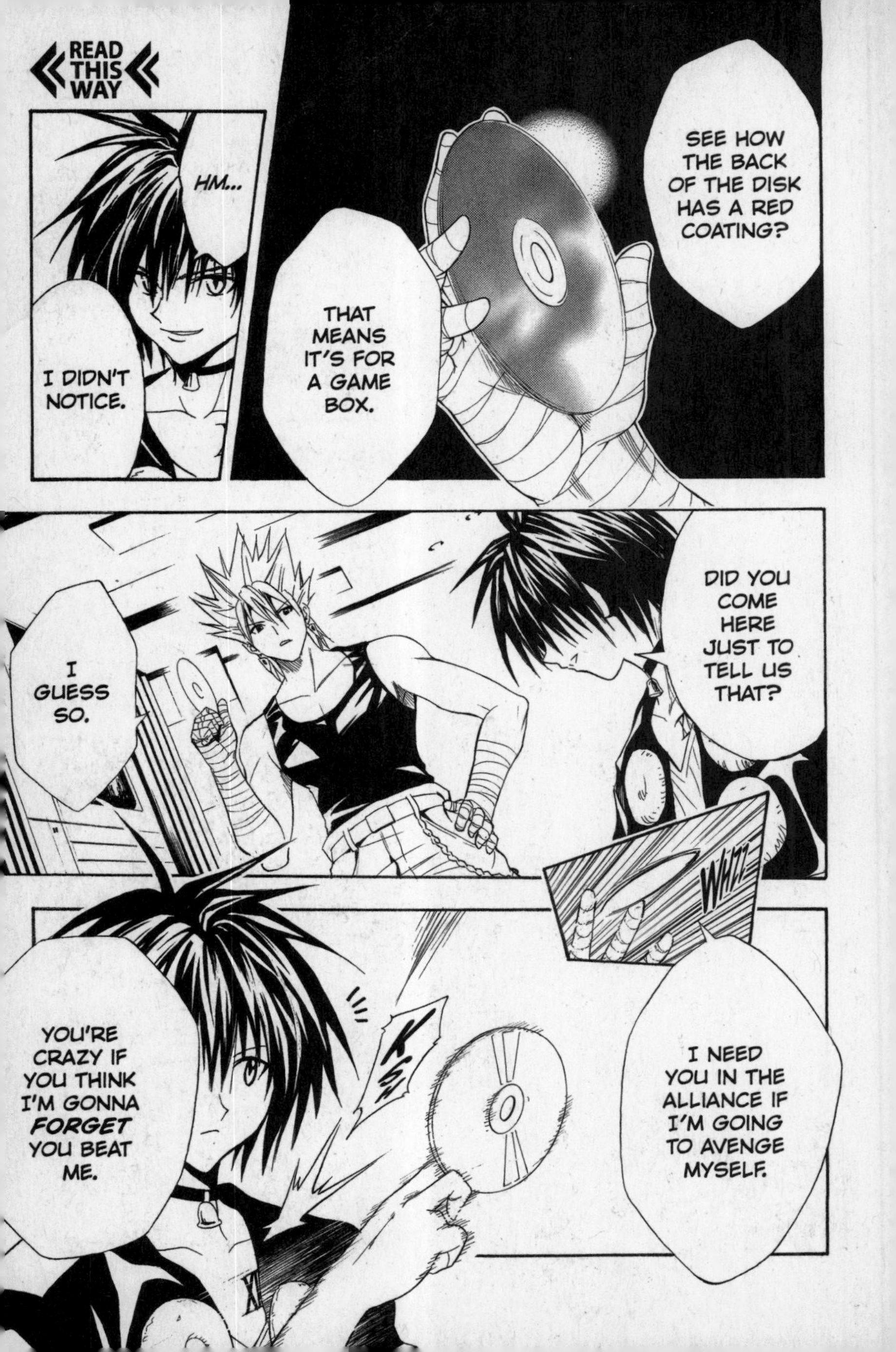
READ THIS WAY
SEE HOW THE BACK OF THE DISK HAS A RED COATING?
THAT MEANS IT'S FOR A GAME BOX.
HM...
I DIDN'T NOTICE.
DID YOU COME HERE JUST TO TELL US THAT?
I GUESS SO.
I NEED YOU IN THE ALLIANCE IF I'M GOING TO AVENGE MYSELF.
YOU'RE CRAZY IF YOU THINK I'M GONNA *FORGET* YOU BEAT ME.

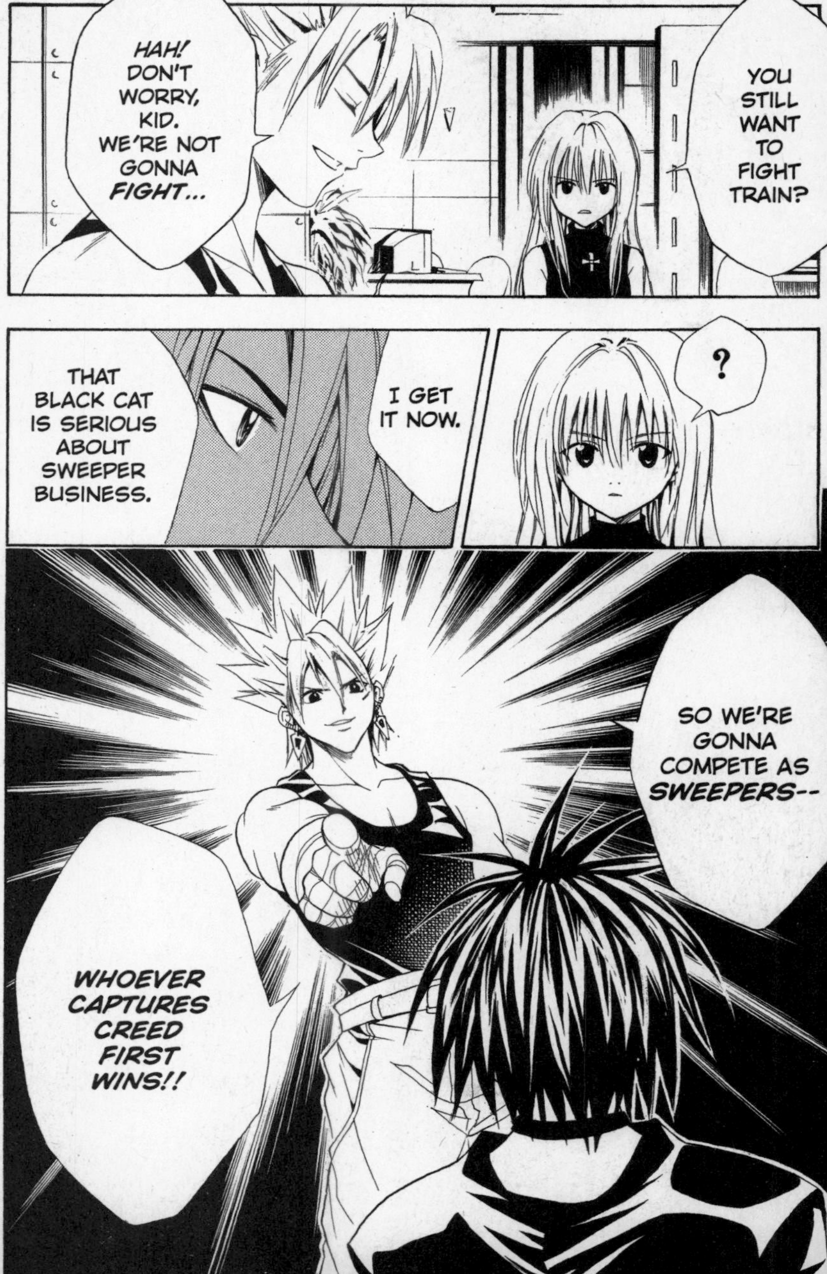
YOU STILL WANT TO FIGHT TRAIN?
HAH! DON'T WORRY, KID. WE'RE NOT GONNA *FIGHT*...
?
I GET IT NOW.
THAT BLACK CAT IS SERIOUS ABOUT SWEEPER BUSINESS.
SO WE'RE GONNA COMPETE AS *SWEEPERS*--
WHOEVER CAPTURES CREED FIRST WINS!!

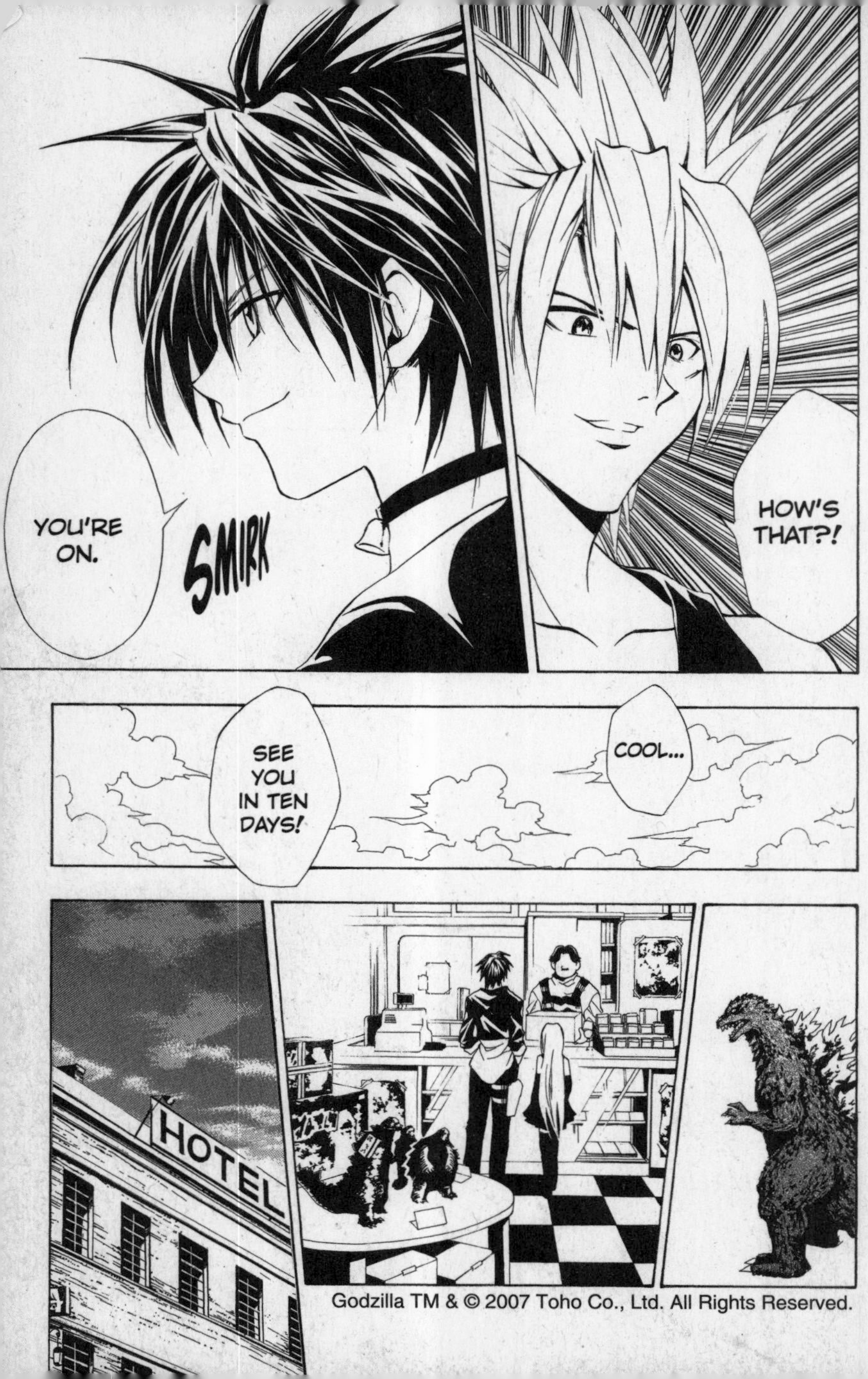
HOW'S THAT?!
YOU'RE ON.
SMIRK
COOL...
SEE YOU IN TEN DAYS!
HOTEL

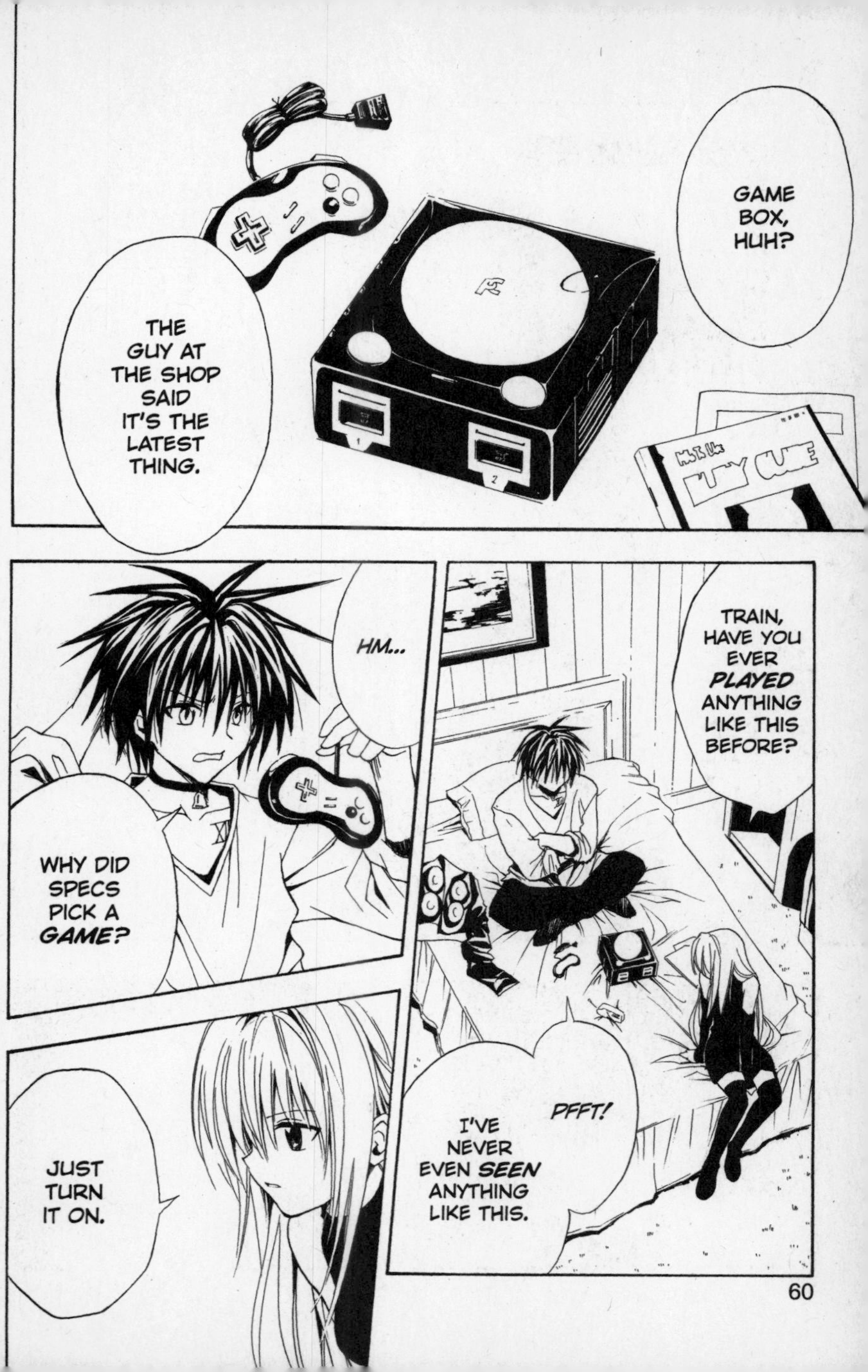
GAME BOX, HUH?
THE GUY AT THE SHOP SAID IT'S THE LATEST THING.
TRAIN, HAVE YOU EVER *PLAYED* ANYTHING LIKE THIS BEFORE?
PFFT!
I'VE NEVER EVEN *SEEN* ANYTHING LIKE THIS.
HM...
WHY DID SPECS PICK A *GAME?*
JUST TURN IT ON.

READ THIS WAY

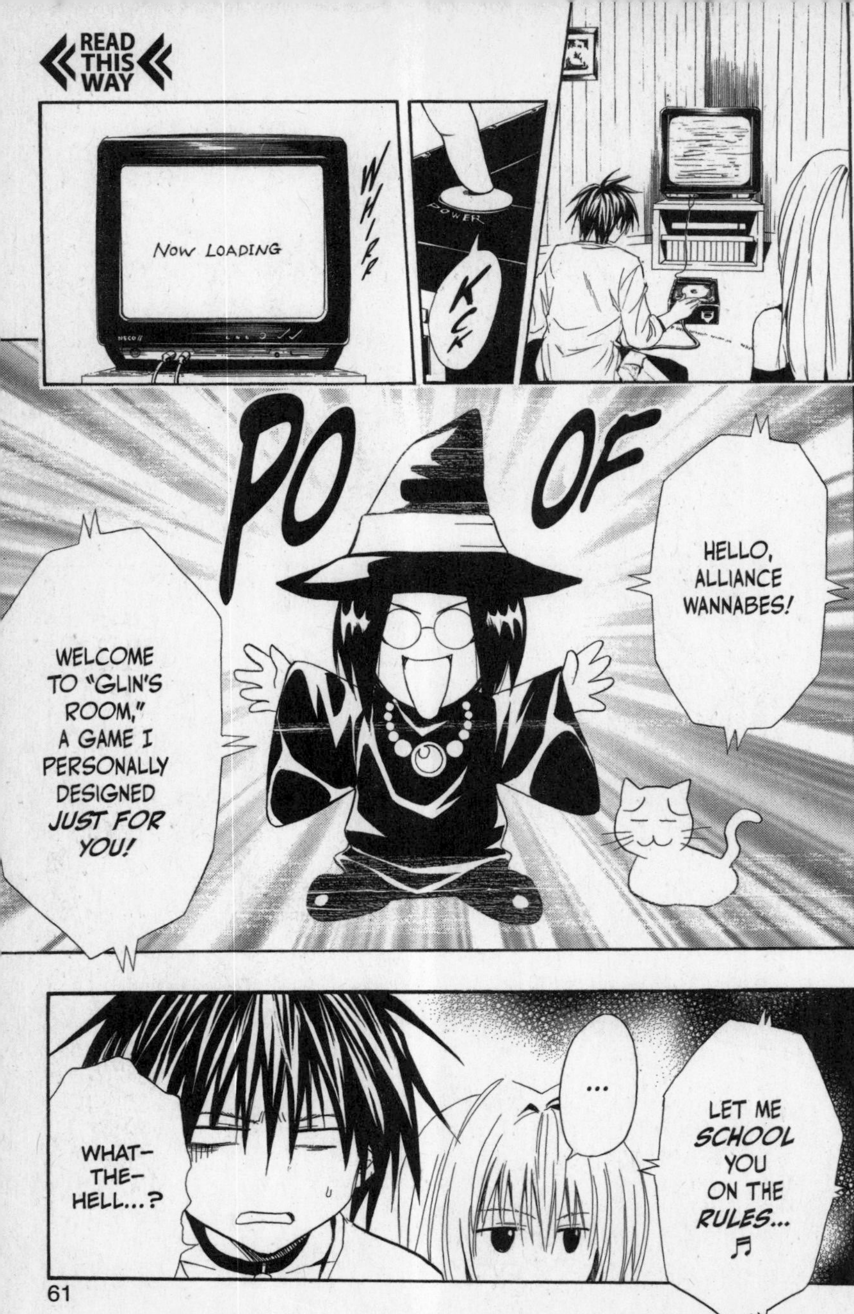

POWER
WHIRR
KCK
NOW LOADING
POOF
HELLO, ALLIANCE WANNABES!
WELCOME TO "GLIN'S ROOM," A GAME I PERSONALLY DESIGNED *JUST FOR YOU!*
LET ME *SCHOOL* YOU ON THE *RULES...* ♬
...
WHAT-THE-HELL...?

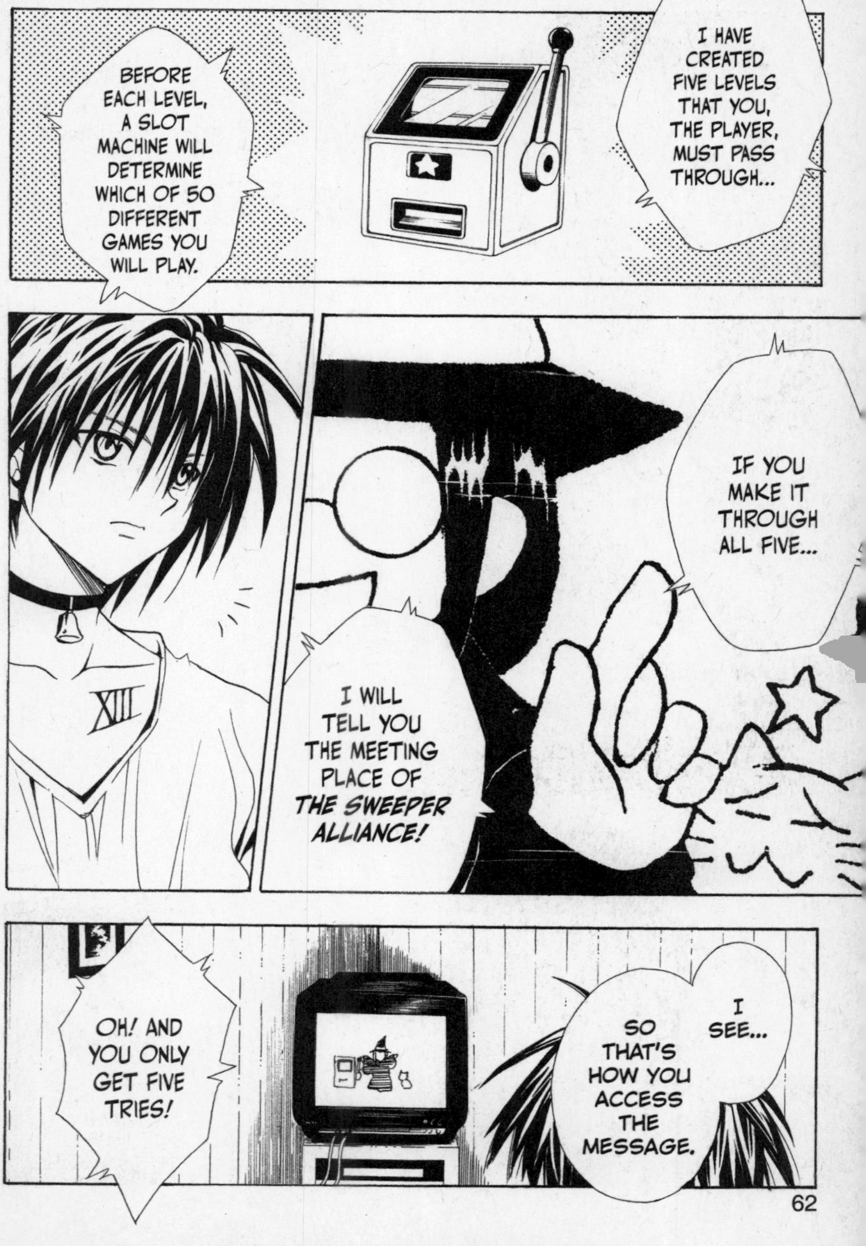
I HAVE CREATED FIVE LEVELS THAT YOU, THE PLAYER, MUST PASS THROUGH...
BEFORE EACH LEVEL, A SLOT MACHINE WILL DETERMINE WHICH OF 50 DIFFERENT GAMES YOU WILL PLAY.
IF YOU MAKE IT THROUGH ALL FIVE...
I WILL TELL YOU THE MEETING PLACE OF *THE SWEEPER ALLIANCE!*
I SEE...
SO THAT'S HOW YOU ACCESS THE MESSAGE.
OH! AND YOU ONLY GET FIVE TRIES!

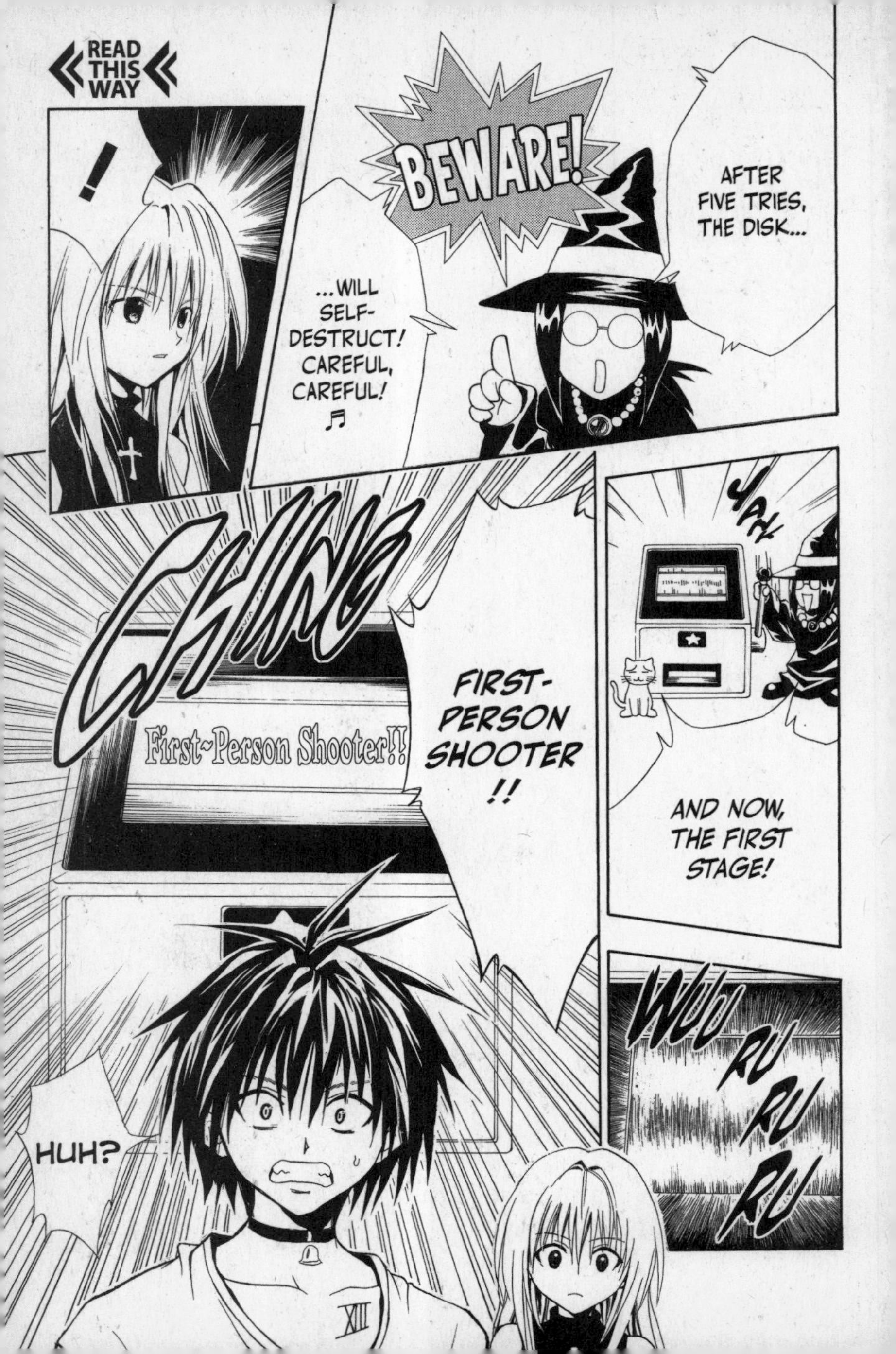
READ THIS WAY
AFTER FIVE TRIES, THE DISK...
BEWARE!
...WILL SELF-DESTRUCT! CAREFUL, CAREFUL! ♬
!
YAH
AND NOW, THE FIRST STAGE!
WUURURURURU
CHING
First~Person Shooter!!
FIRST-PERSON SHOOTER !!
HUH?

NOSTALGIC SERIES

NUMBER 3—GYANZA

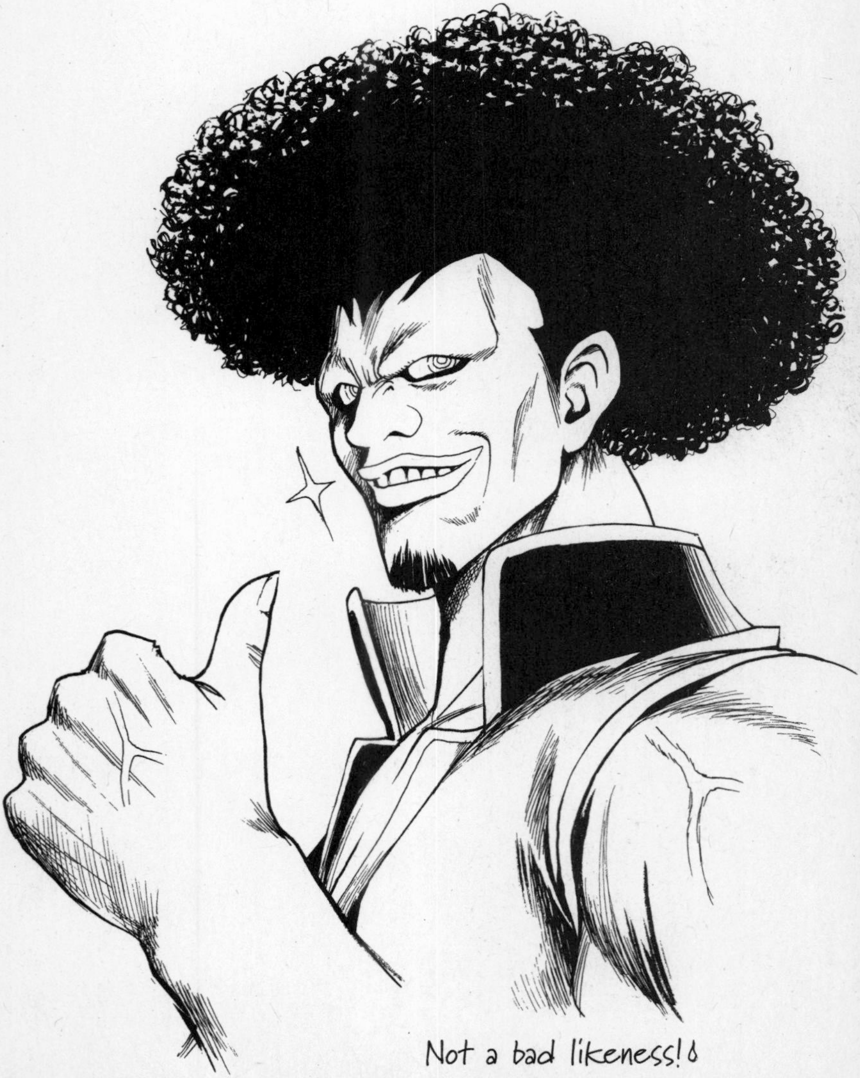
Not a bad likeness!

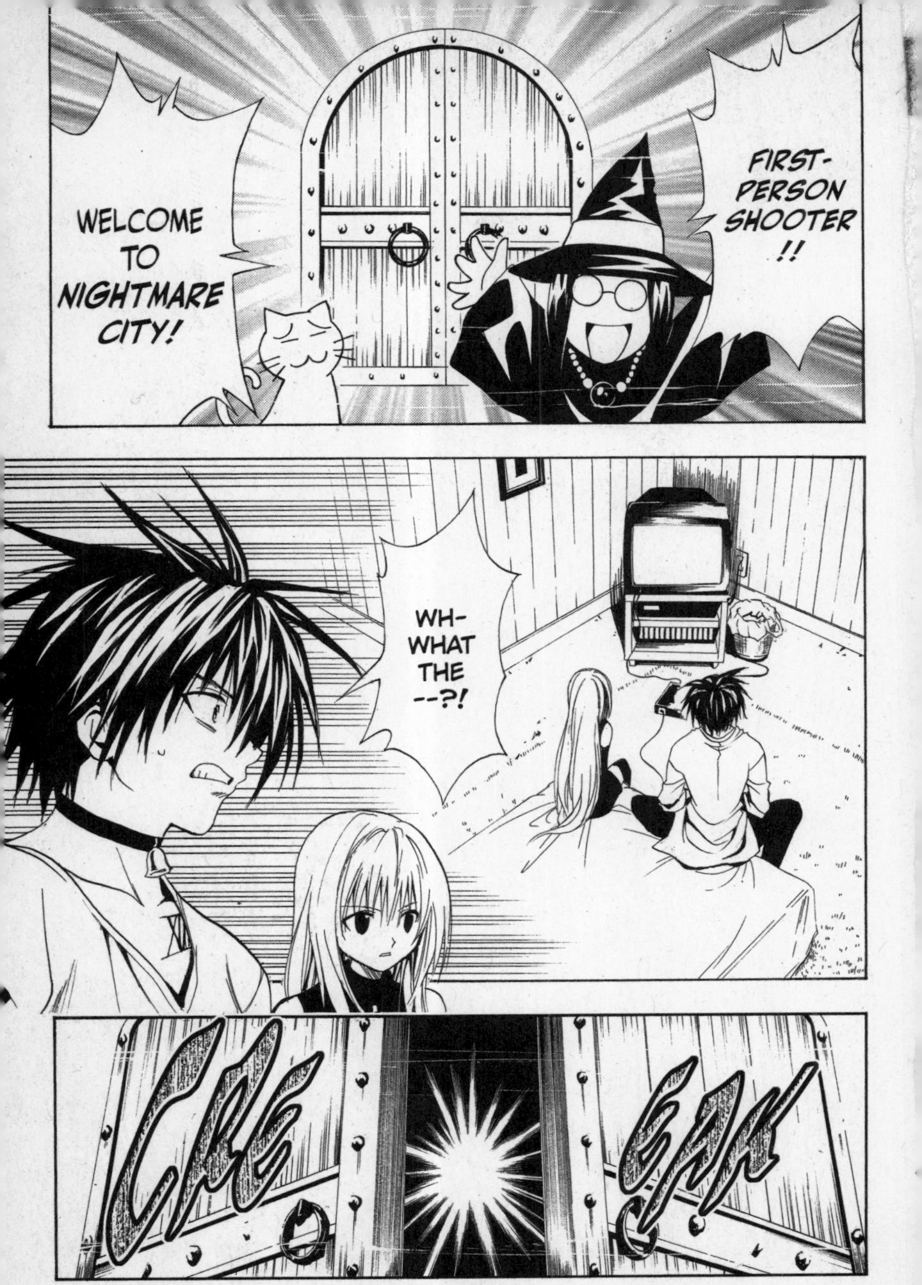
FIRST-PERSON SHOOTER!!
WELCOME TO NIGHTMARE CITY!
WH-WHAT THE--?!
CREEAK

Chapter 126: Nightmare City

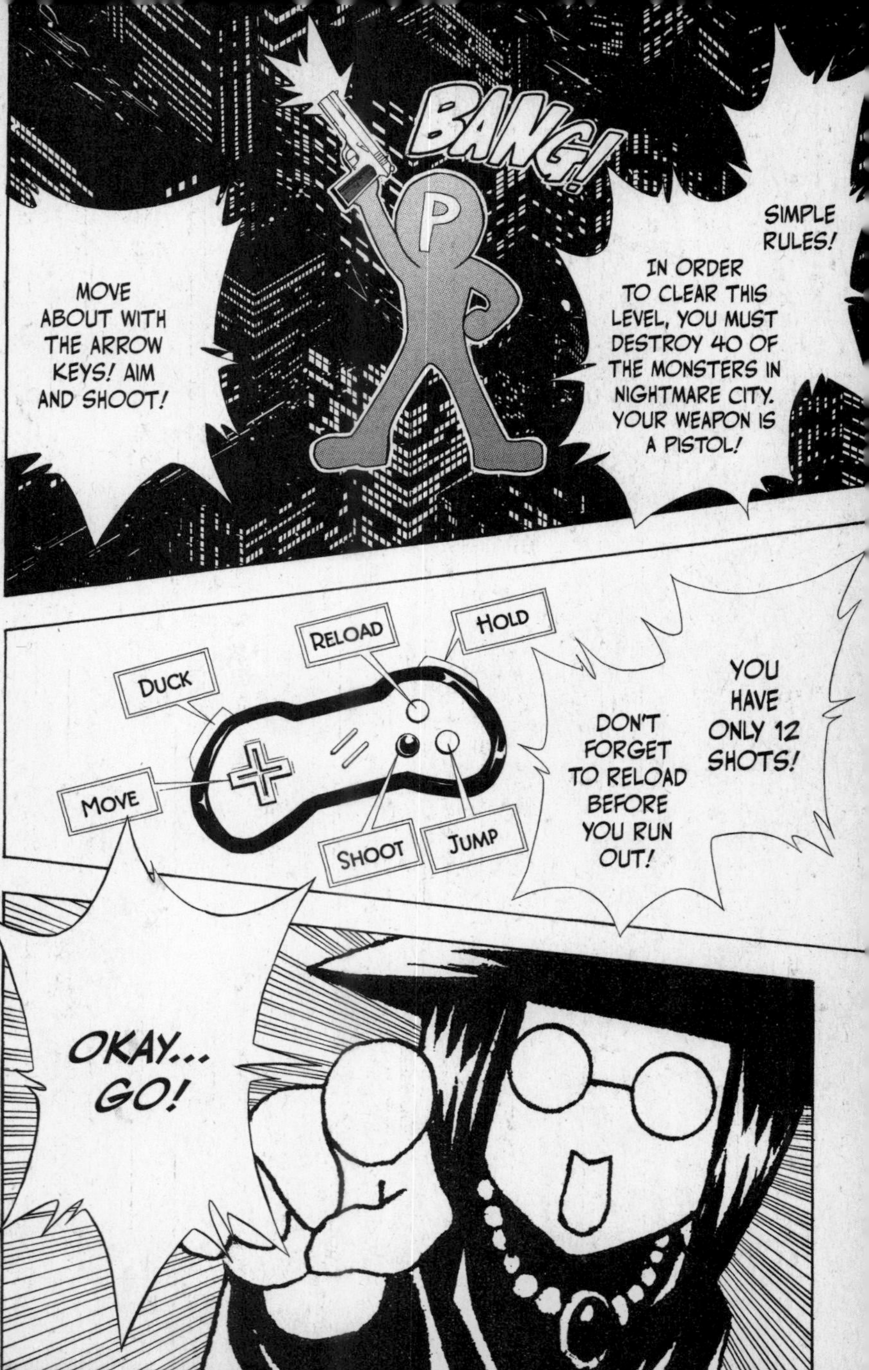
BANG!
SIMPLE RULES!
IN ORDER TO CLEAR THIS LEVEL, YOU MUST DESTROY 40 OF THE MONSTERS IN NIGHTMARE CITY. YOUR WEAPON IS A PISTOL!
MOVE ABOUT WITH THE ARROW KEYS! AIM AND SHOOT!
YOU HAVE ONLY 12 SHOTS!
DON'T FORGET TO RELOAD BEFORE YOU RUN OUT!
HOLD
RELOAD
DUCK
MOVE
JUMP
SHOOT
OKAY... GO!

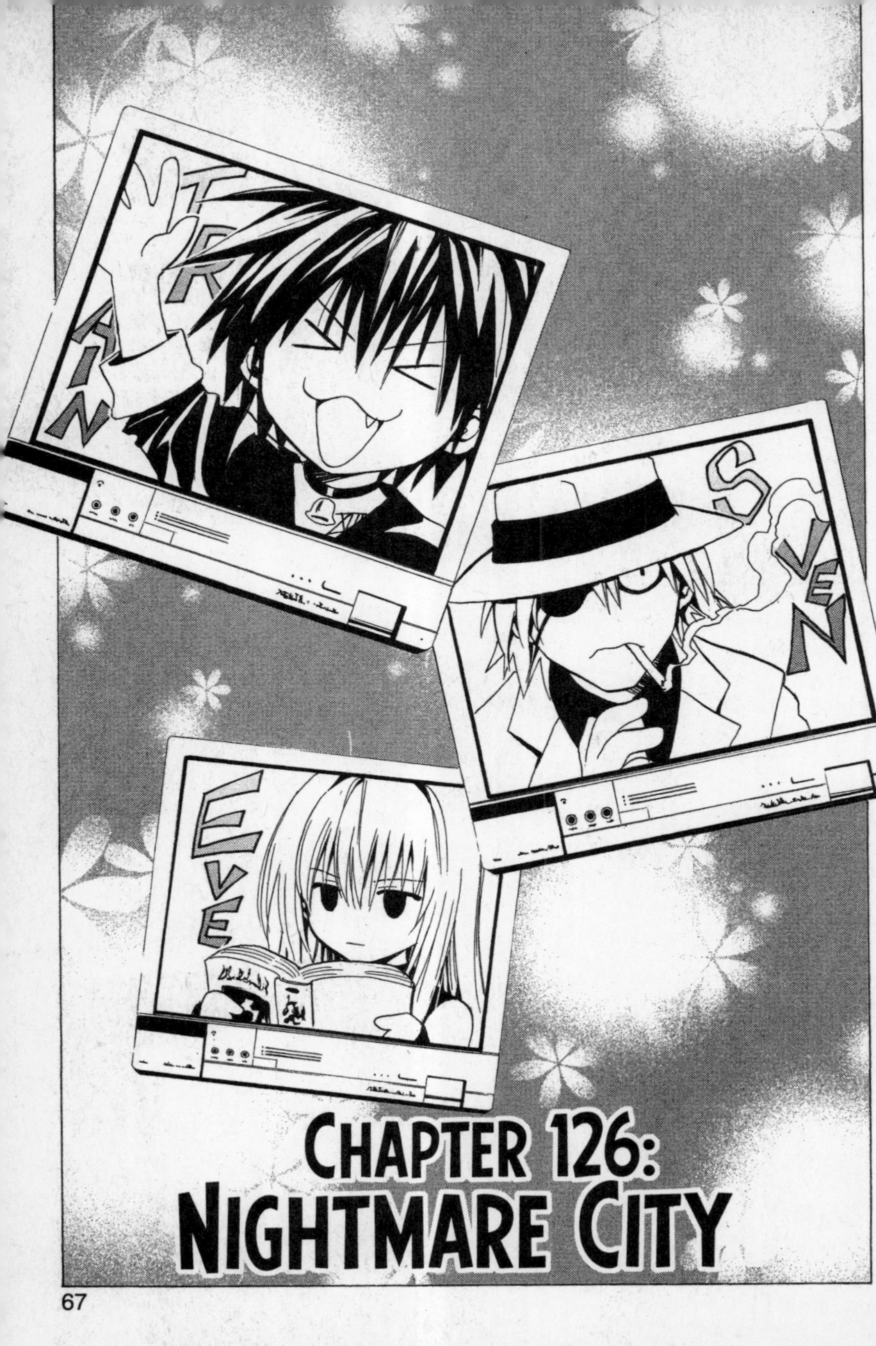
TRAIN
SEVEN
EVE

Chapter 126: Nightmare City

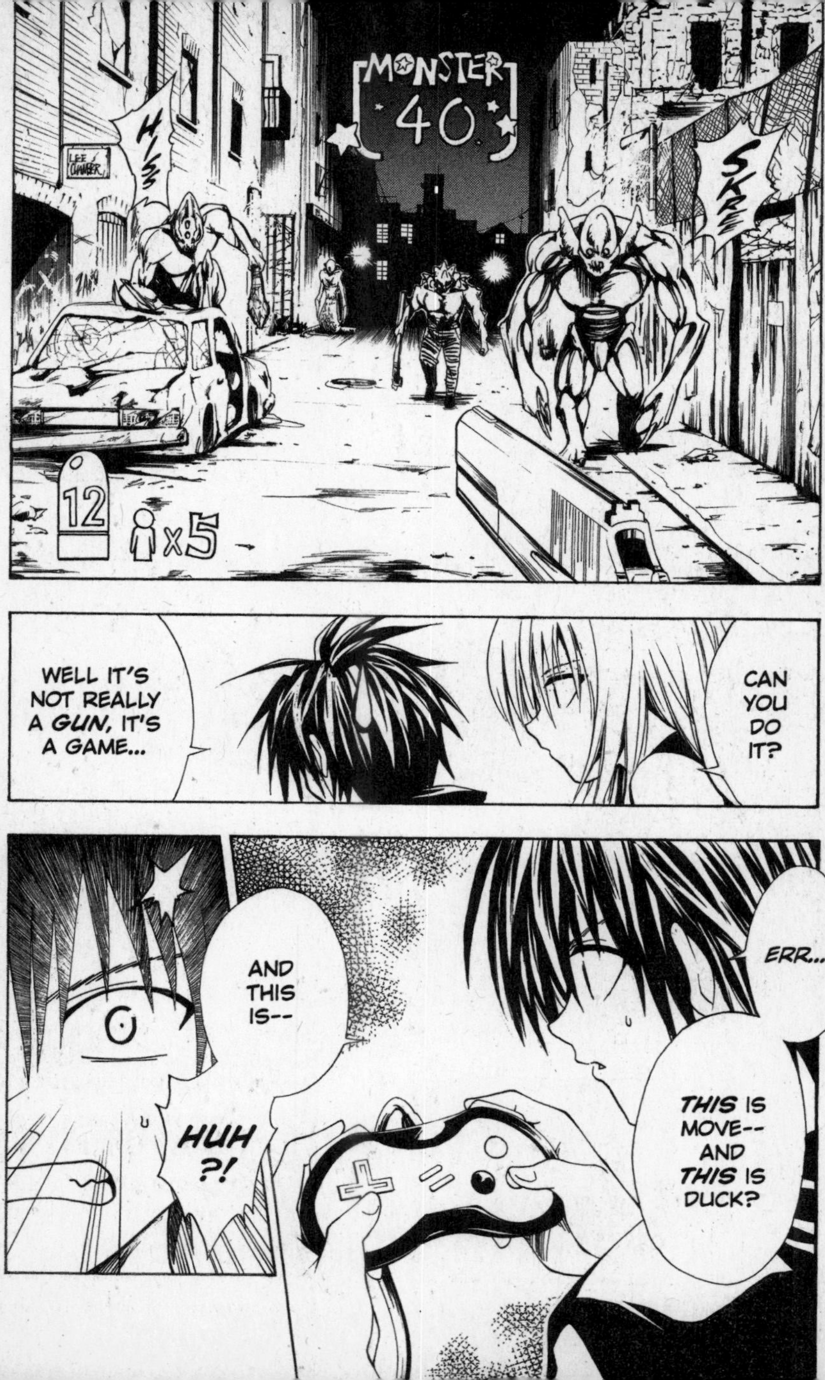
MONSTER 40
SKRE
HISS
LEE CHAMBER
12
x5
CAN YOU DO IT?
WELL IT'S NOT REALLY A *GUN*, IT'S A GAME...
ERR...
THIS IS MOVE-- AND *THIS* IS DUCK?
AND THIS IS--
HUH?!

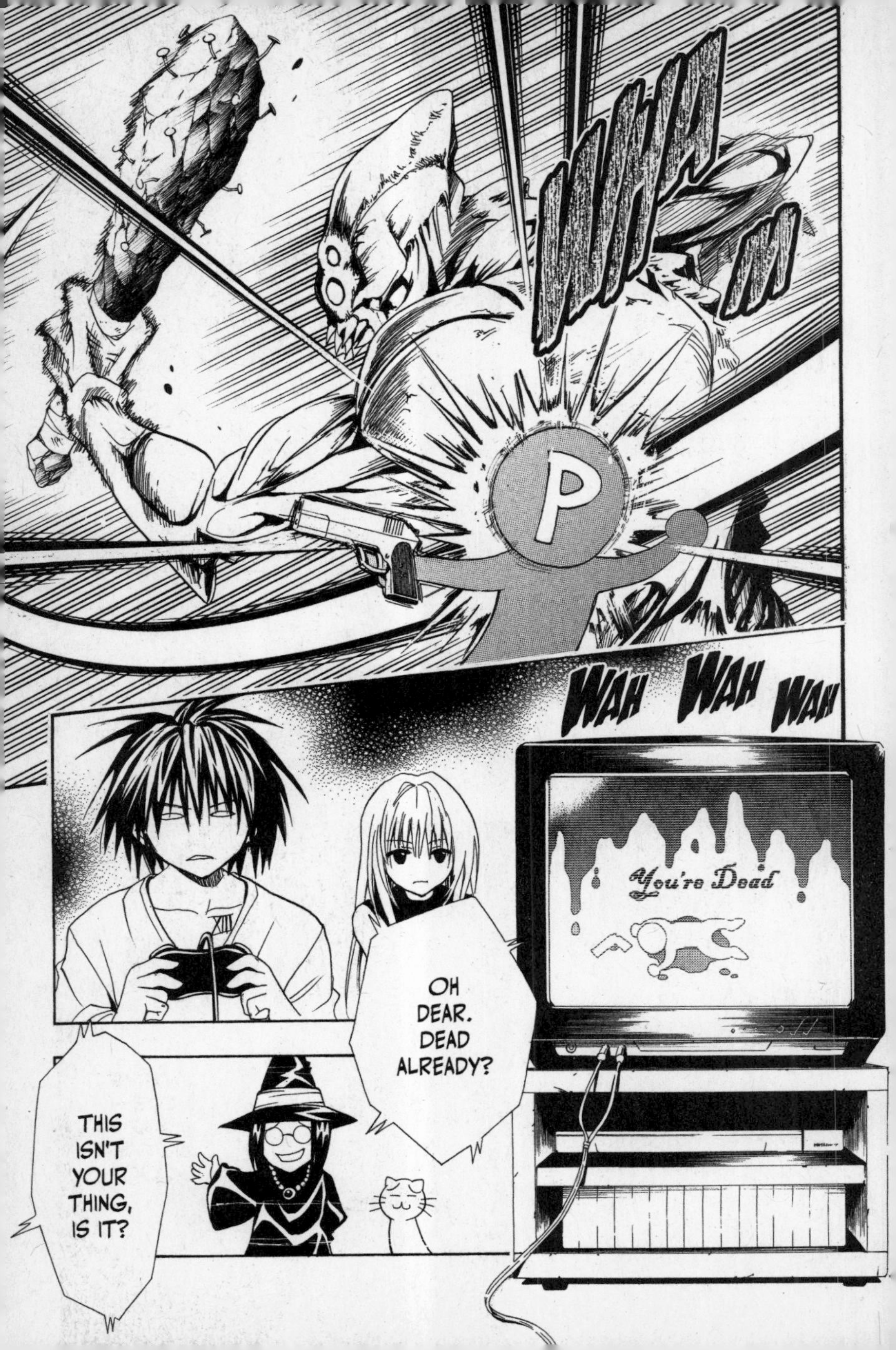
WHA
P
WAH WAH WAH
You're Dead
OH DEAR. DEAD ALREADY?
THIS ISN'T YOUR THING, IS IT?

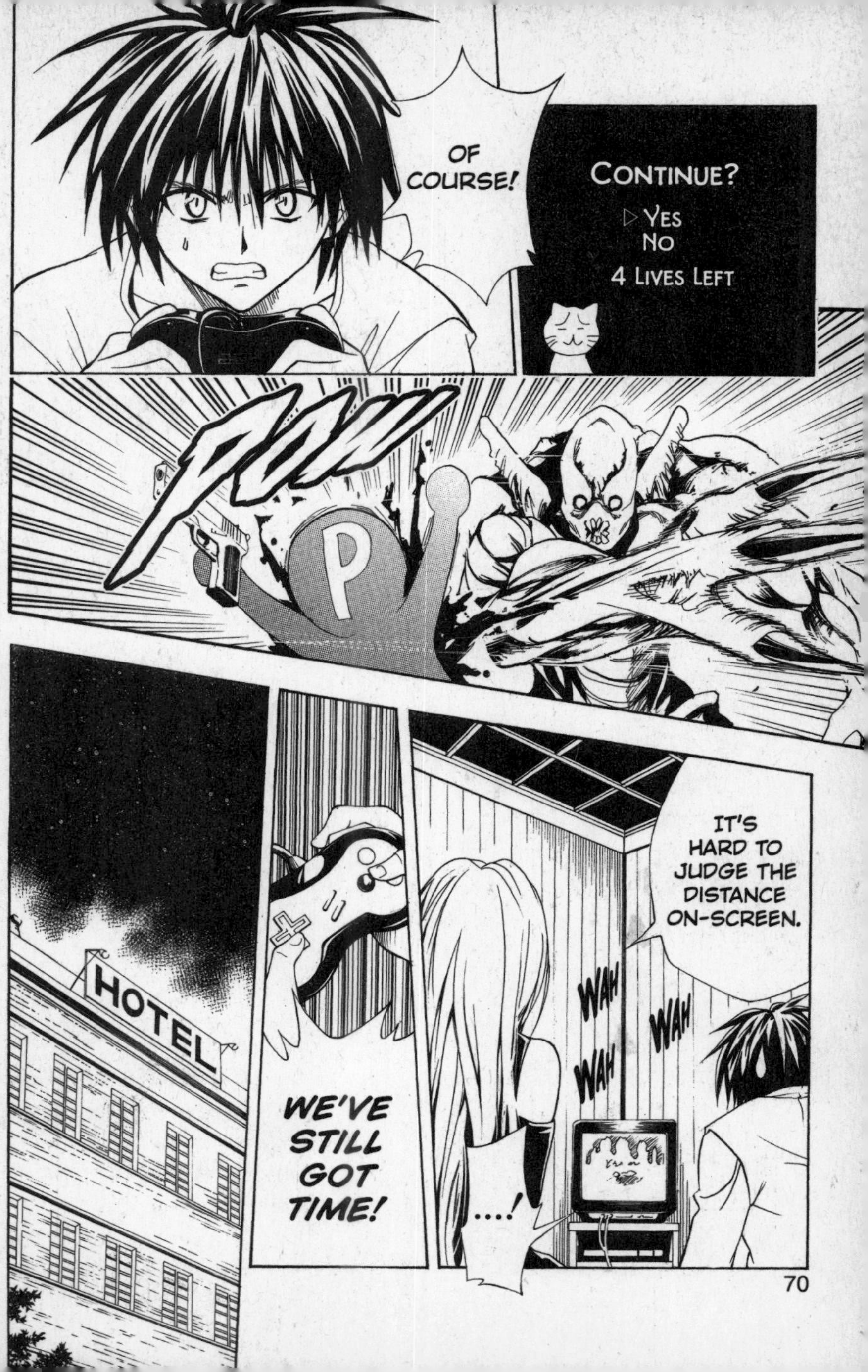
CONTINUE?
▷ YES
NO
4 LIVES LEFT
OF COURSE!
POW
P
IT'S HARD TO JUDGE THE DISTANCE ON-SCREEN.
WAH
WAH
WAH
...!
WE'VE STILL GOT TIME!
HOTEL

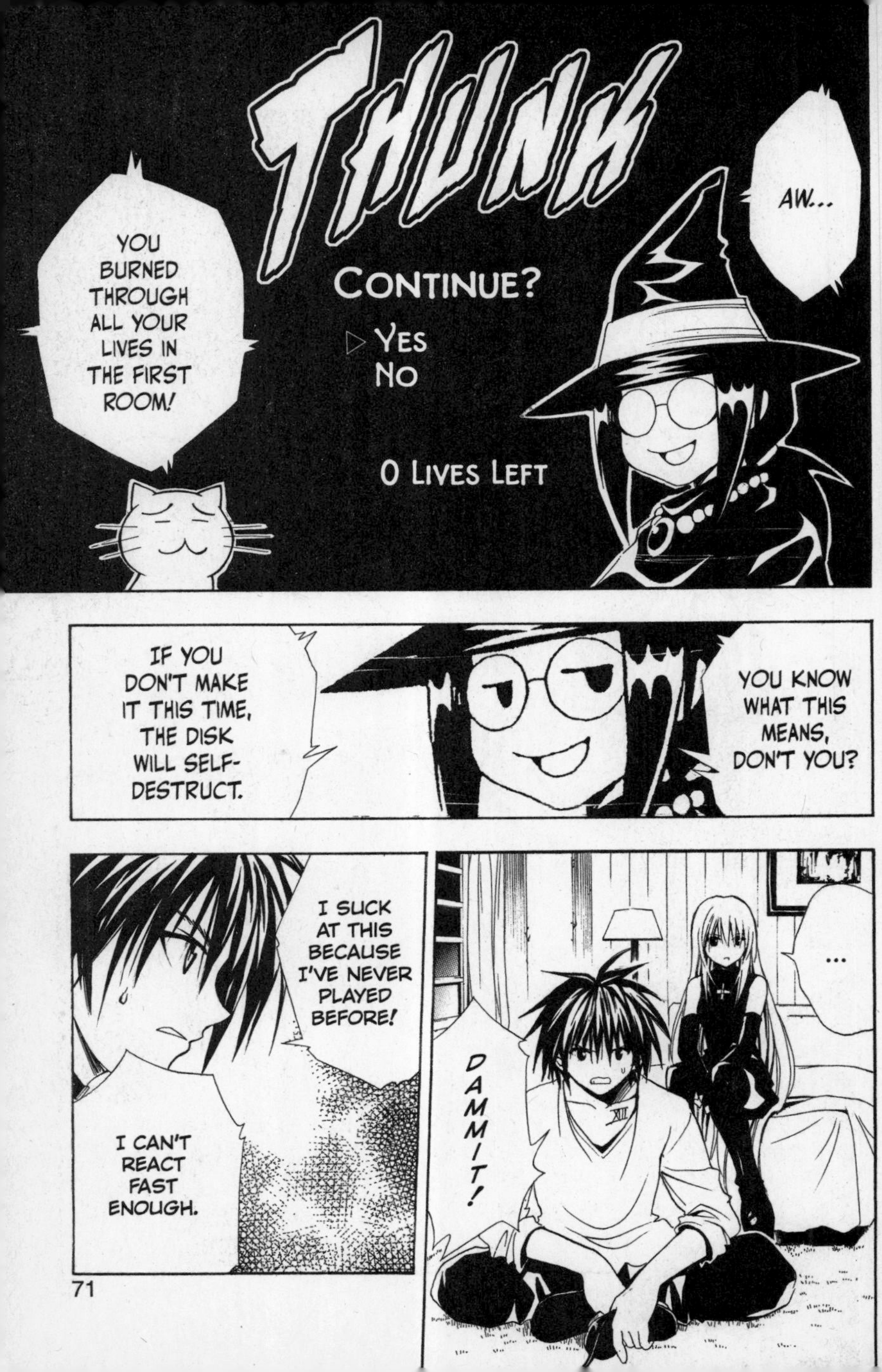
THUNK
AW...
CONTINUE?
▷YES
NO
YOU BURNED THROUGH ALL YOUR LIVES IN THE FIRST ROOM!
0 LIVES LEFT
YOU KNOW WHAT THIS MEANS, DON'T YOU?
IF YOU DON'T MAKE IT THIS TIME, THE DISK WILL SELF-DESTRUCT.
...
DAMMIT!
I SUCK AT THIS BECAUSE I'VE NEVER PLAYED BEFORE!
I CAN'T REACT FAST ENOUGH.

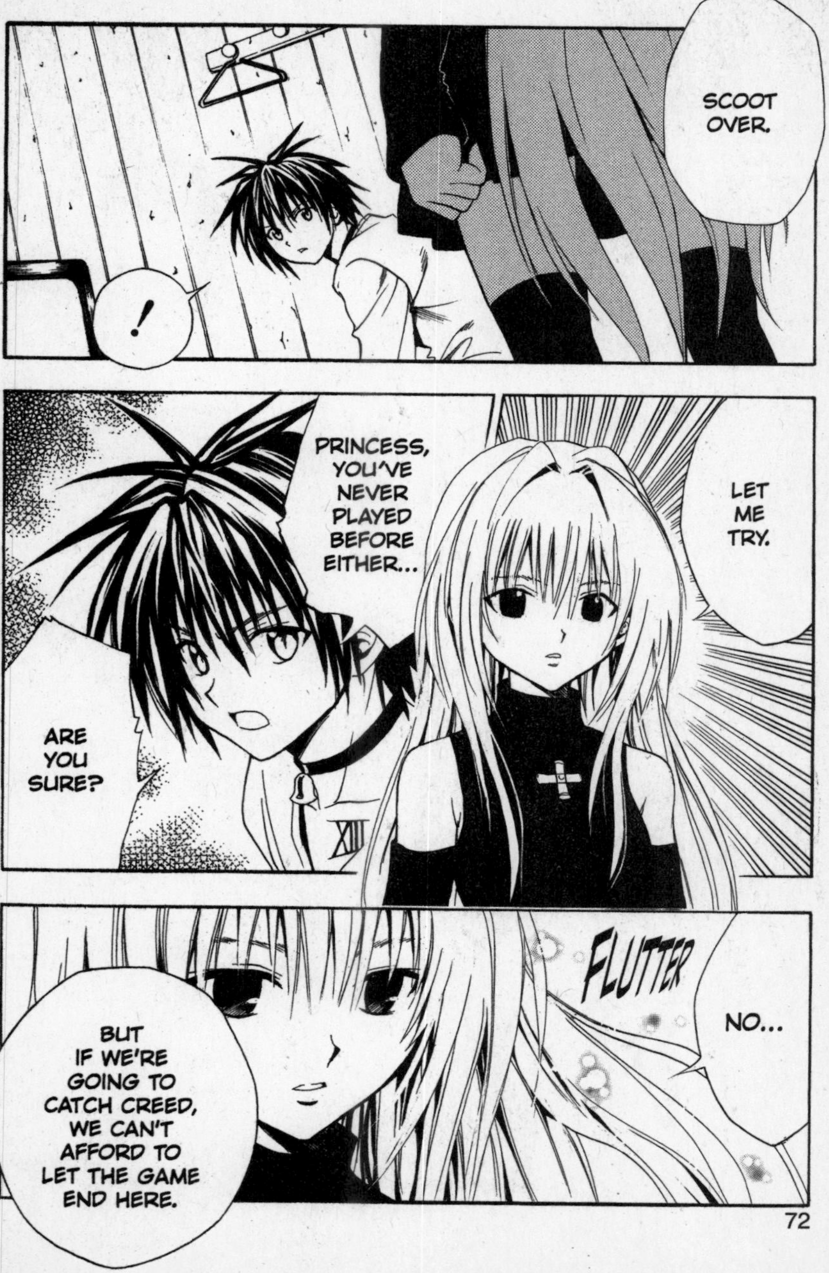
SCOOT OVER.
!
LET ME TRY.
PRINCESS, YOU'VE NEVER PLAYED BEFORE EITHER...
ARE YOU SURE?
FLUTTER
NO...
BUT IF WE'RE GOING TO CATCH CREED, WE CAN'T AFFORD TO LET THE GAME END HERE.

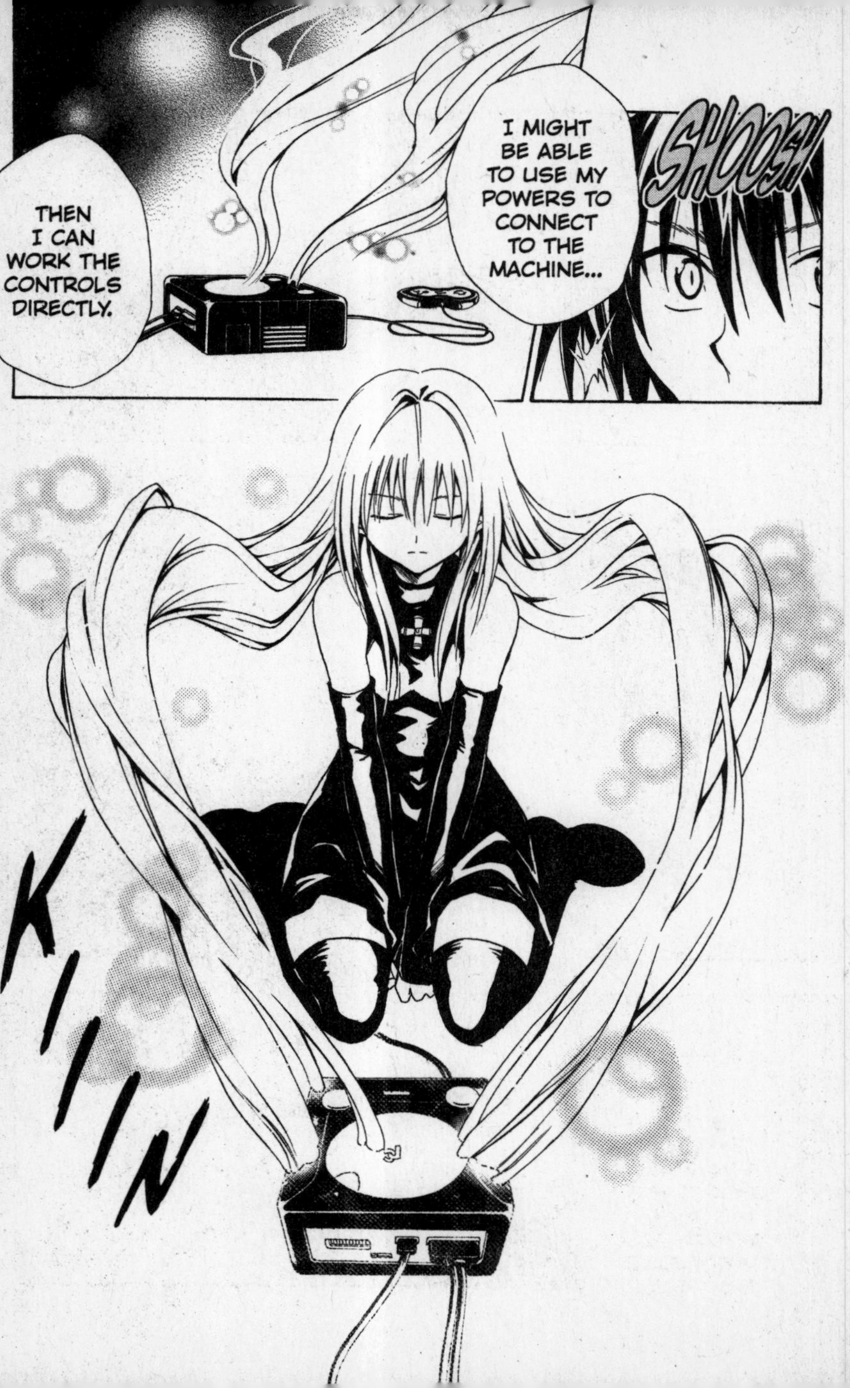
SHOOSH
I MIGHT BE ABLE TO USE MY POWERS TO CONNECT TO THE MACHINE...
THEN I CAN WORK THE CONTROLS DIRECTLY.
KIIIN

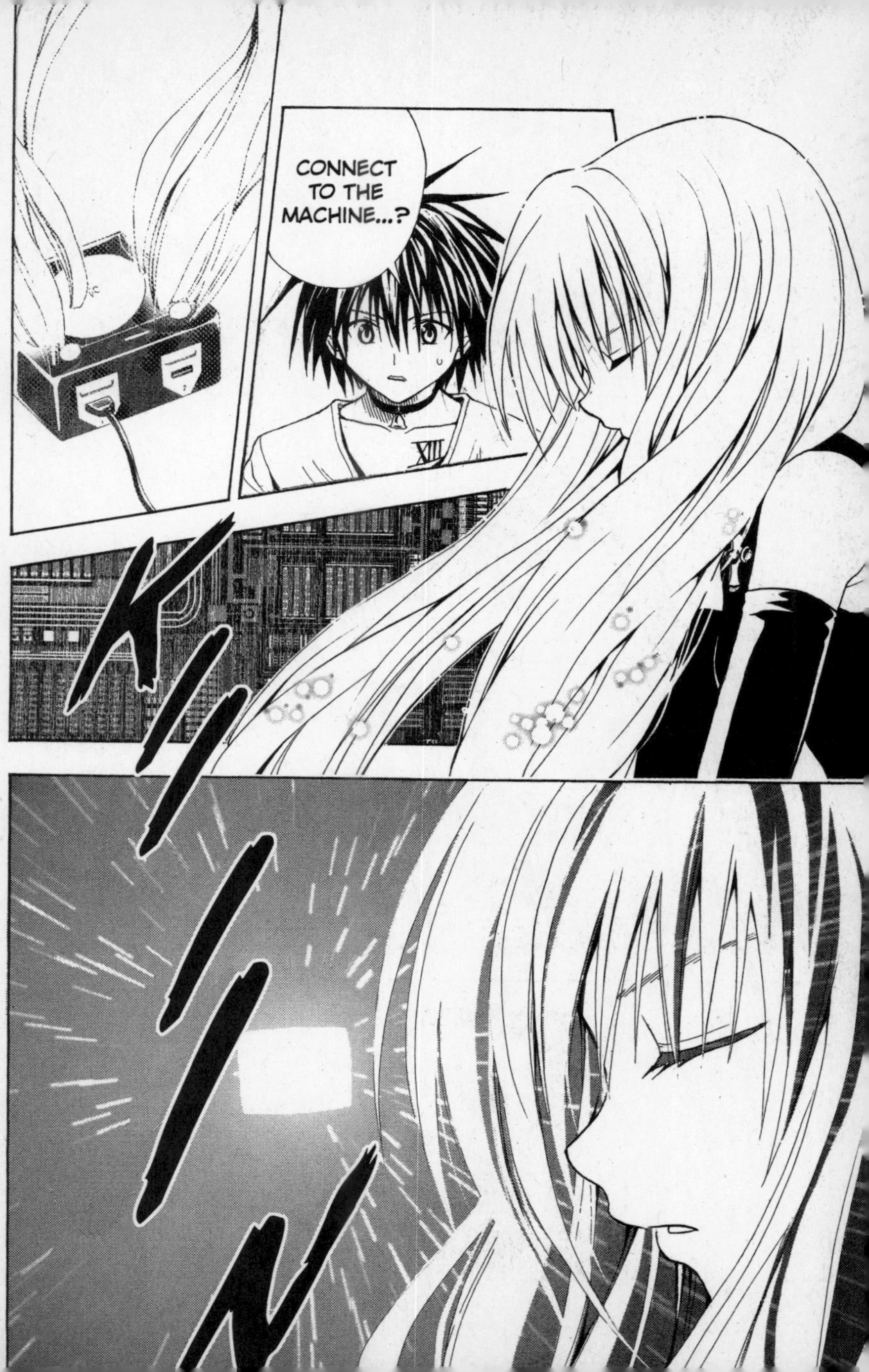
CONNECT TO THE MACHINE...?

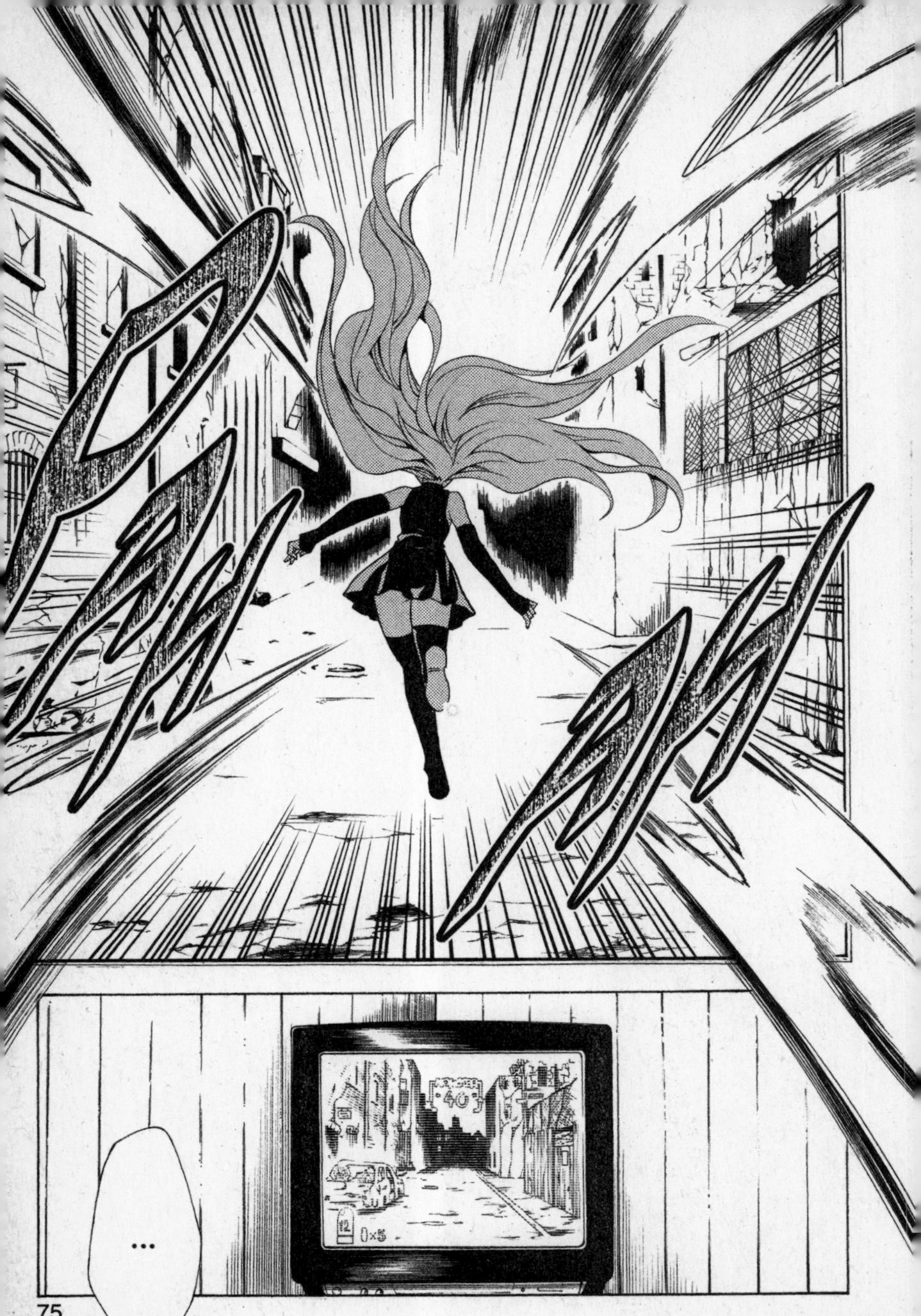
...

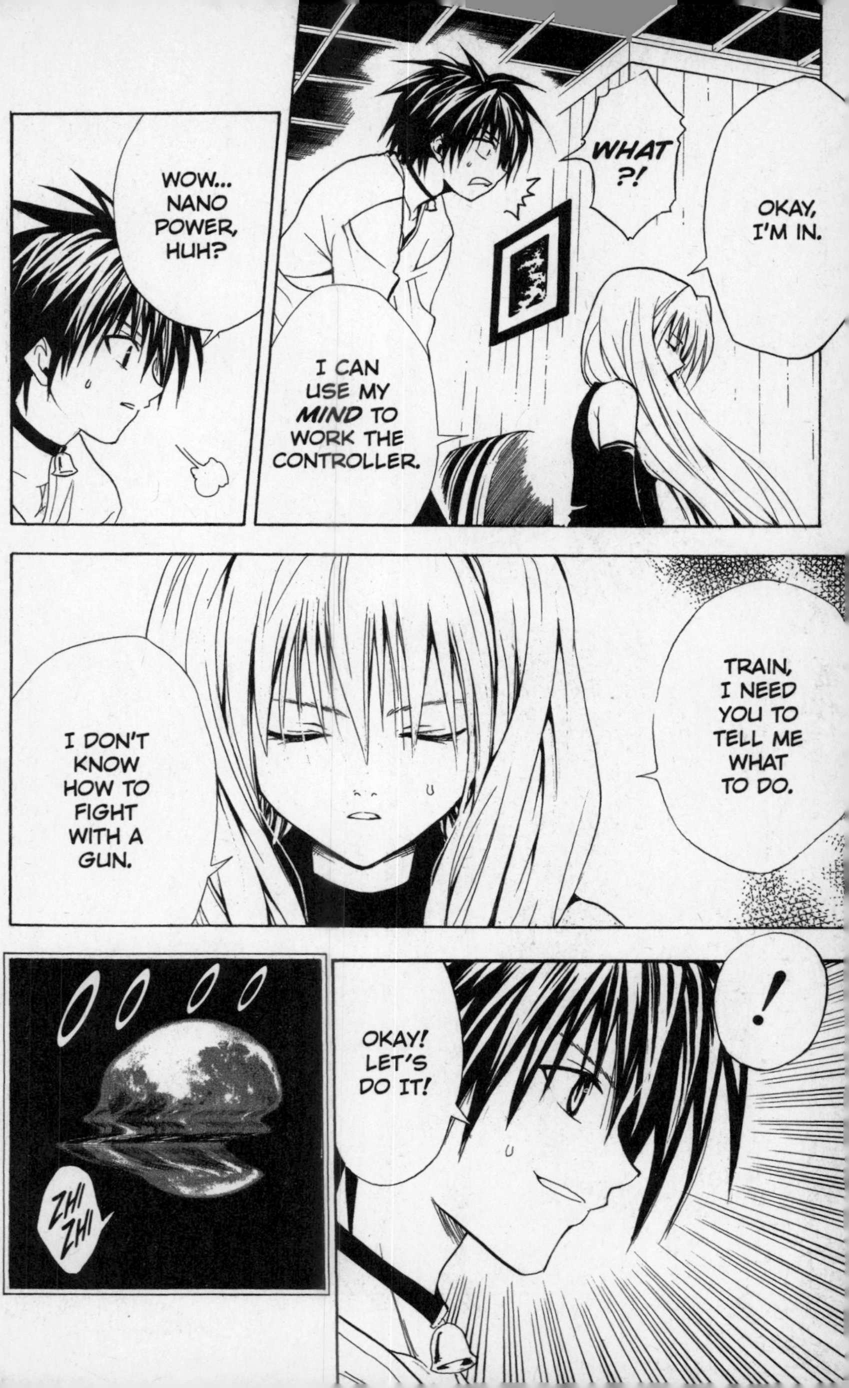
OKAY, I'M IN.
WHAT ?!
I CAN USE MY *MIND* TO WORK THE CONTROLLER.
WOW... NANO POWER, HUH?
TRAIN, I NEED YOU TO TELL ME WHAT TO DO.
I DON'T KNOW HOW TO FIGHT WITH A GUN.
!
OKAY! LET'S DO IT!
ZHI ZHI

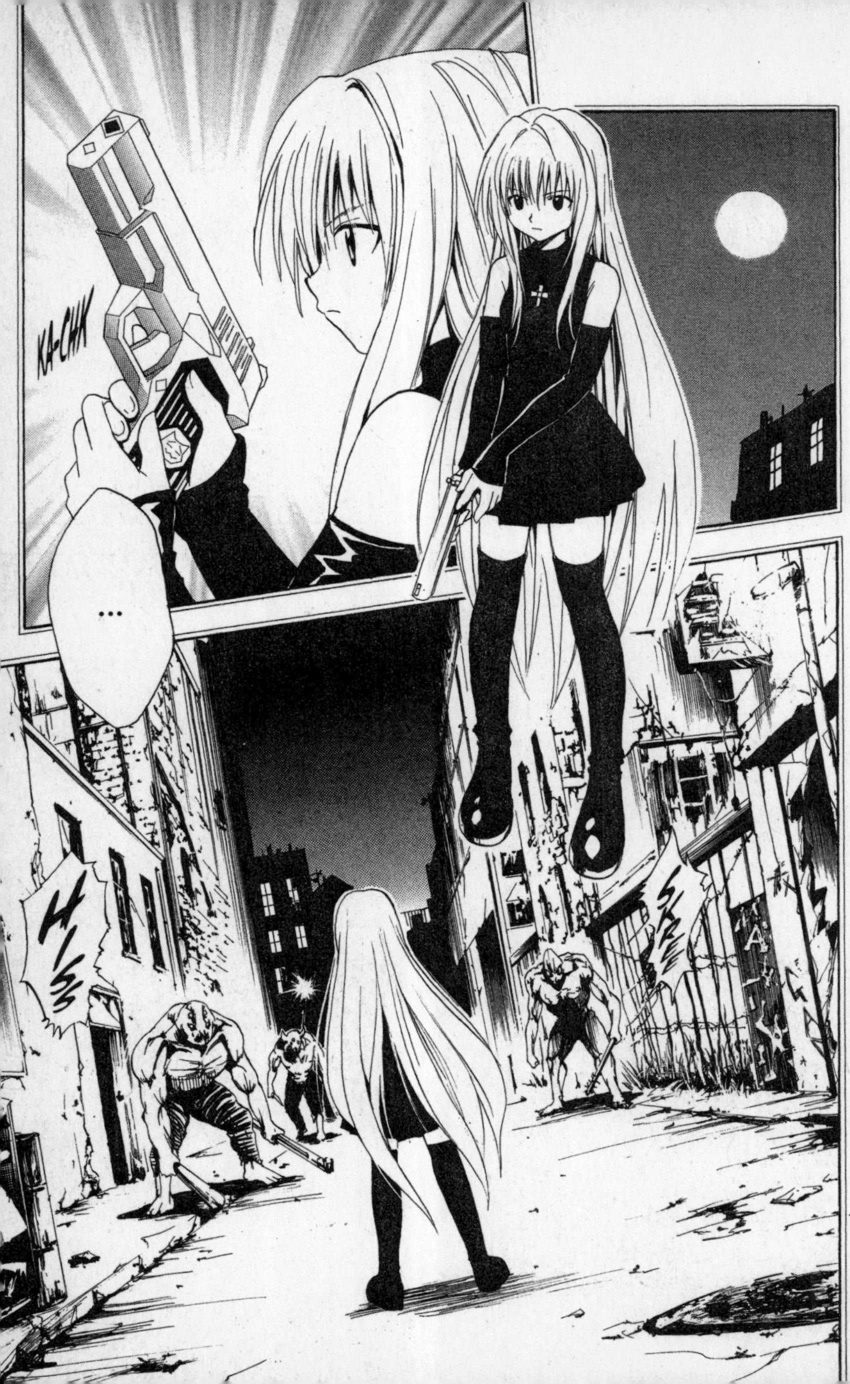
KA-CHK
...
SKREE
HISS

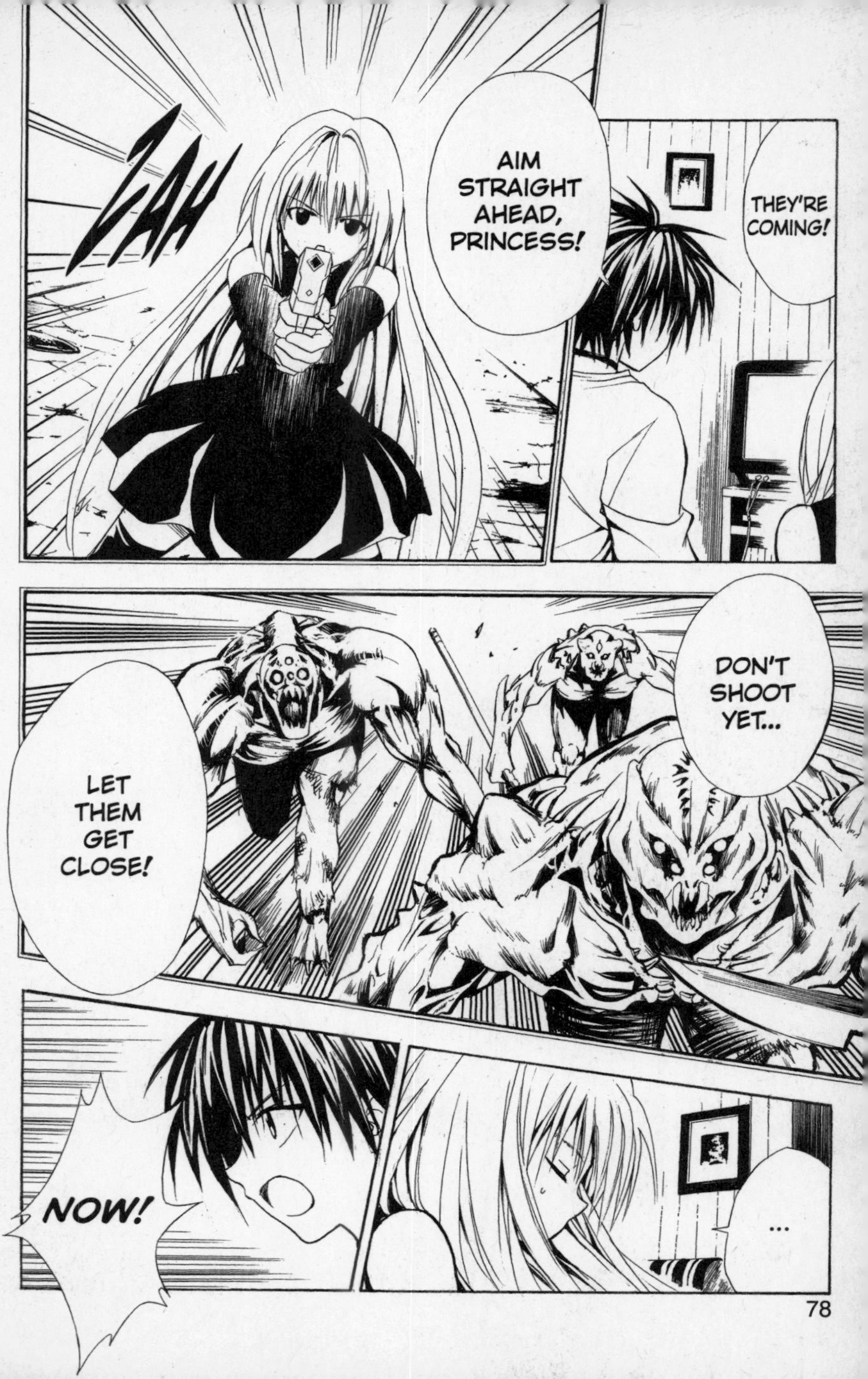
THEY'RE COMING!
AIM STRAIGHT AHEAD, PRINCESS!
ZAH
DON'T SHOOT YET...
LET THEM GET CLOSE!
...
NOW!

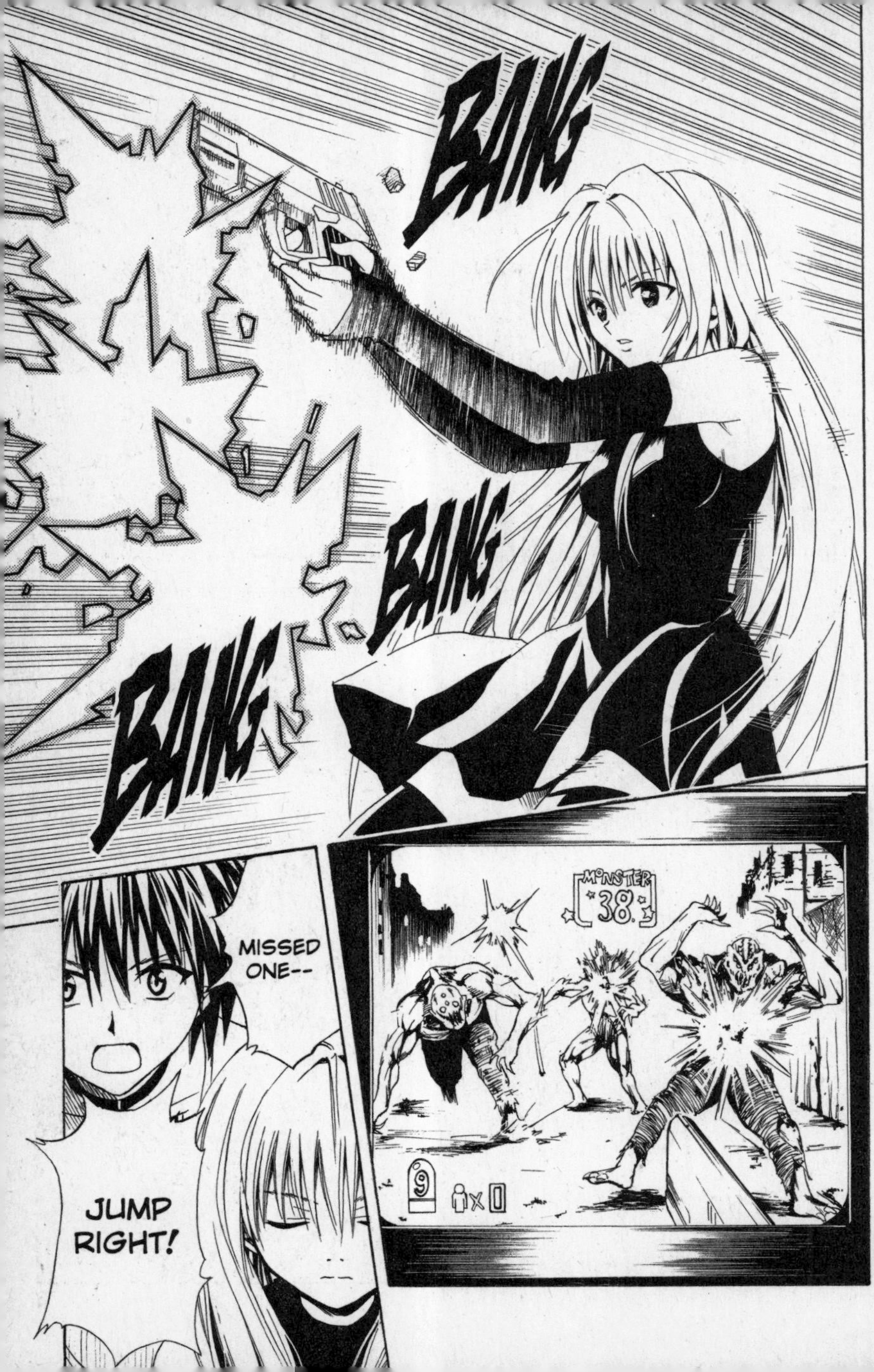
BANG
BANG
BANG
MONSTER
38.
9
x0
MISSED ONE--
JUMP RIGHT!

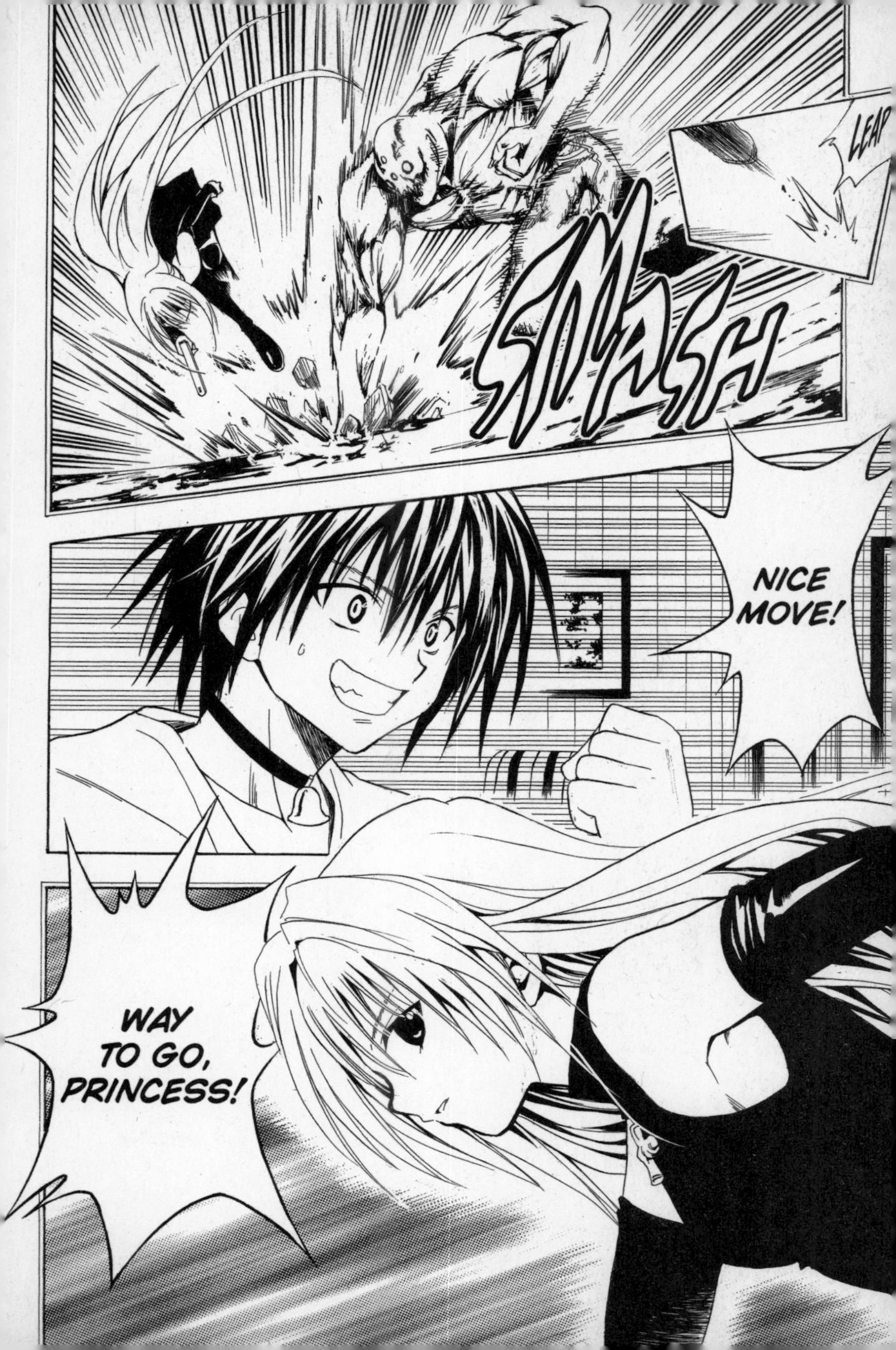
LEAP
SMASH
NICE MOVE!
WAY TO GO, PRINCESS!

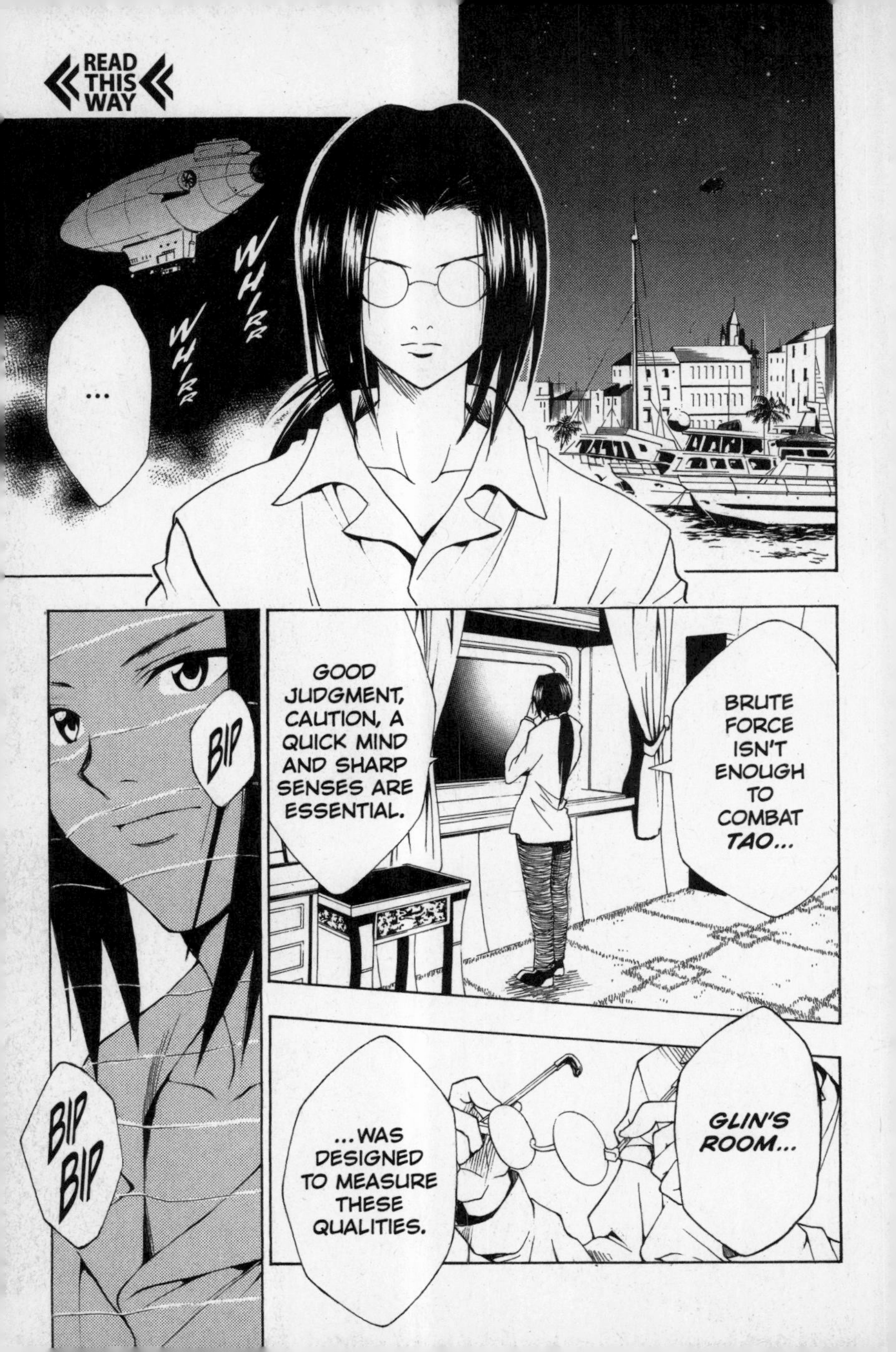
READ THIS WAY
WHIRR
WHIRR
...
BRUTE FORCE ISN'T ENOUGH TO COMBAT *TAO*...
GOOD JUDGMENT, CAUTION, A QUICK MIND AND SHARP SENSES ARE ESSENTIAL.
GLIN'S ROOM...
...WAS DESIGNED TO MEASURE THESE QUALITIES.
BIP
BIP BIP

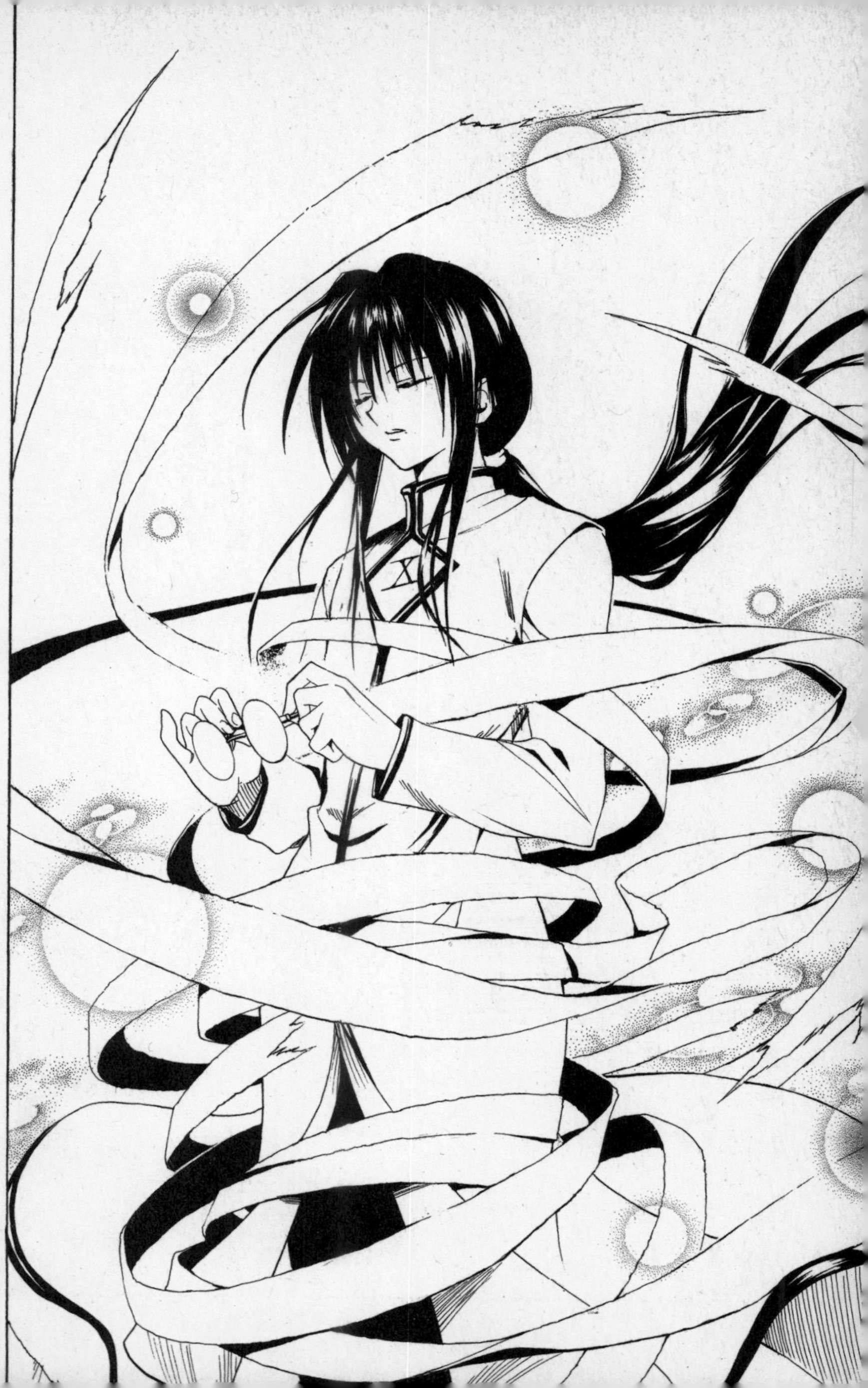

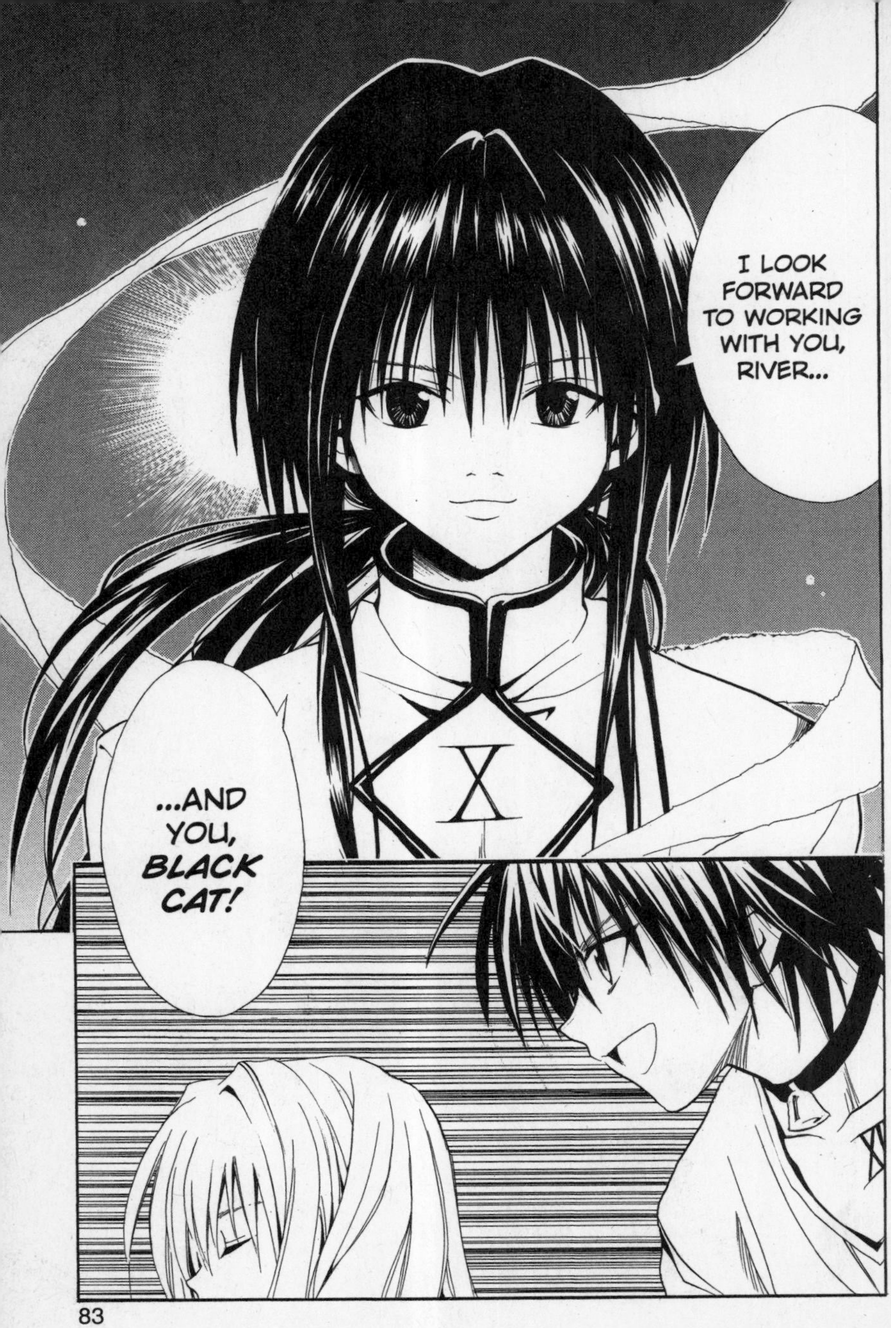
I LOOK FORWARD TO WORKING WITH YOU, RIVER...
...AND YOU, *BLACK CAT!*

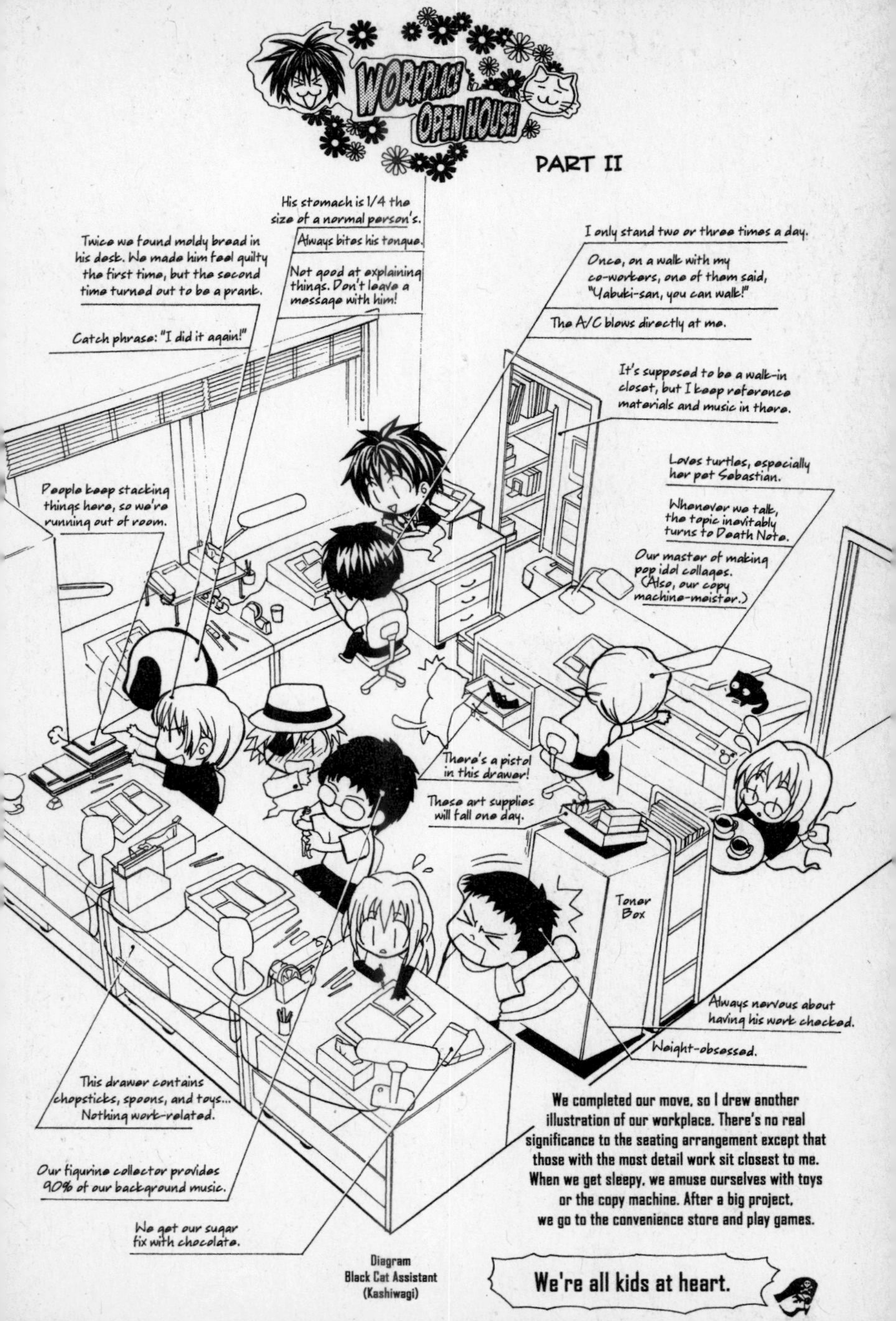
WORKPLACE OPEN HOUSE!
PART II
His stomach is 1/4 the size of a normal person's.
Always bites his tongue.
Not good at explaining things. Don't leave a message with him!
Twice we found moldy bread in his desk. We made him feel guilty the first time, but the second time turned out to be a prank.
Catch phrase: "I did it again!"
I only stand two or three times a day.
Once, on a walk with my co-workers, one of them said, "Yabuki-san, you can walk!"
The A/C blows directly at me.
It's supposed to be a walk-in closet, but I keep reference materials and music in there.
Loves turtles, especially her pet Sebastian.
Whenever we talk, the topic inevitably turns to Death Note.
Our master of making pop idol collages. (Also, our copy machine-meister.)
People keep stacking things here, so we're running out of room.
There's a pistol in this drawer!
These art supplies will fall one day.
Toner Box
Always nervous about having his work checked.
Weight-obsessed.
This drawer contains chopsticks, spoons, and toys... Nothing work-related.
Our figurine collector provides 90% of our background music.
We get our sugar fix with chocolate.
We completed our move, so I drew another illustration of our workplace. There's no real significance to the seating arrangement except that those with the most detail work sit closest to me. When we get sleepy, we amuse ourselves with toys or the copy machine. After a big project, we go to the convenience store and play games.
Diagram
Black Cat Assistant
(Kashiwagi)
We're all kids at heart.

Chapter 127: Test Game

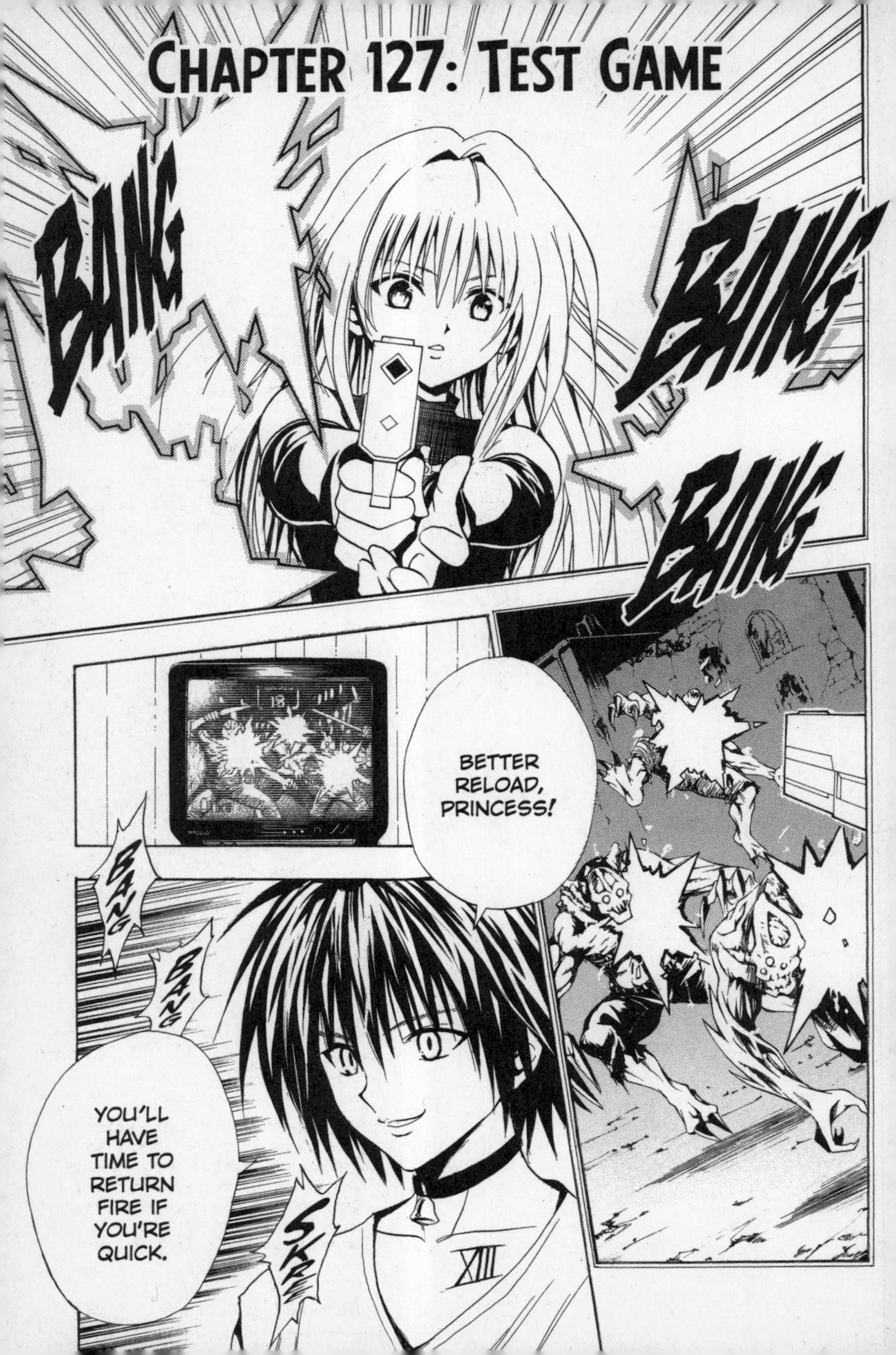

BANG
BANG
BANG
BETTER RELOAD, PRINCESS!
BANG
BANG
YOU'LL HAVE TIME TO RETURN FIRE IF YOU'RE QUICK.
SKREE

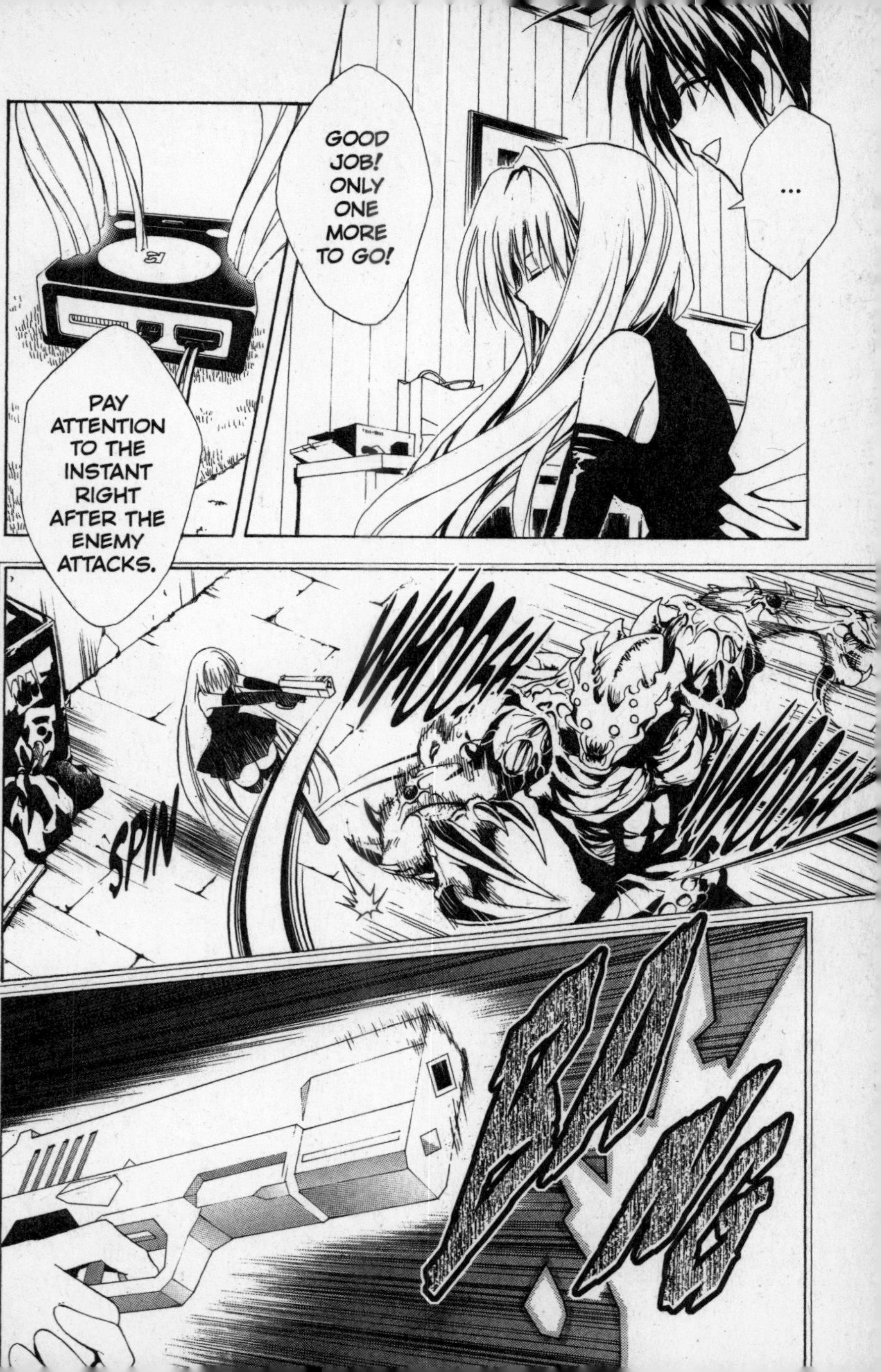
...
GOOD JOB! ONLY ONE MORE TO GO!
PAY ATTENTION TO THE INSTANT RIGHT AFTER THE ENEMY ATTACKS.
WHOOSH
WHOOSH
SPIN
BANG

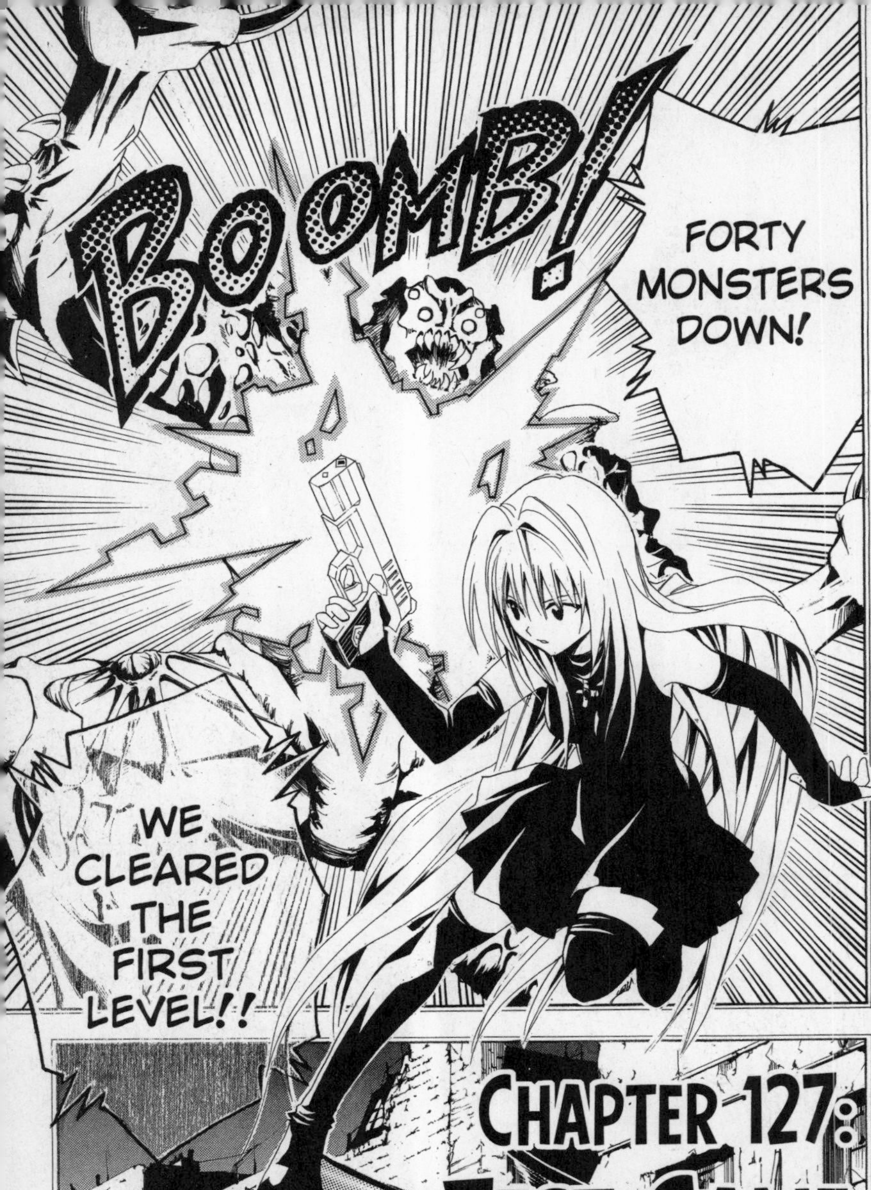
FORTY MONSTERS DOWN!
BOOMB!
WE CLEARED THE FIRST LEVEL!!
CHAPTER 127: TEST GAME

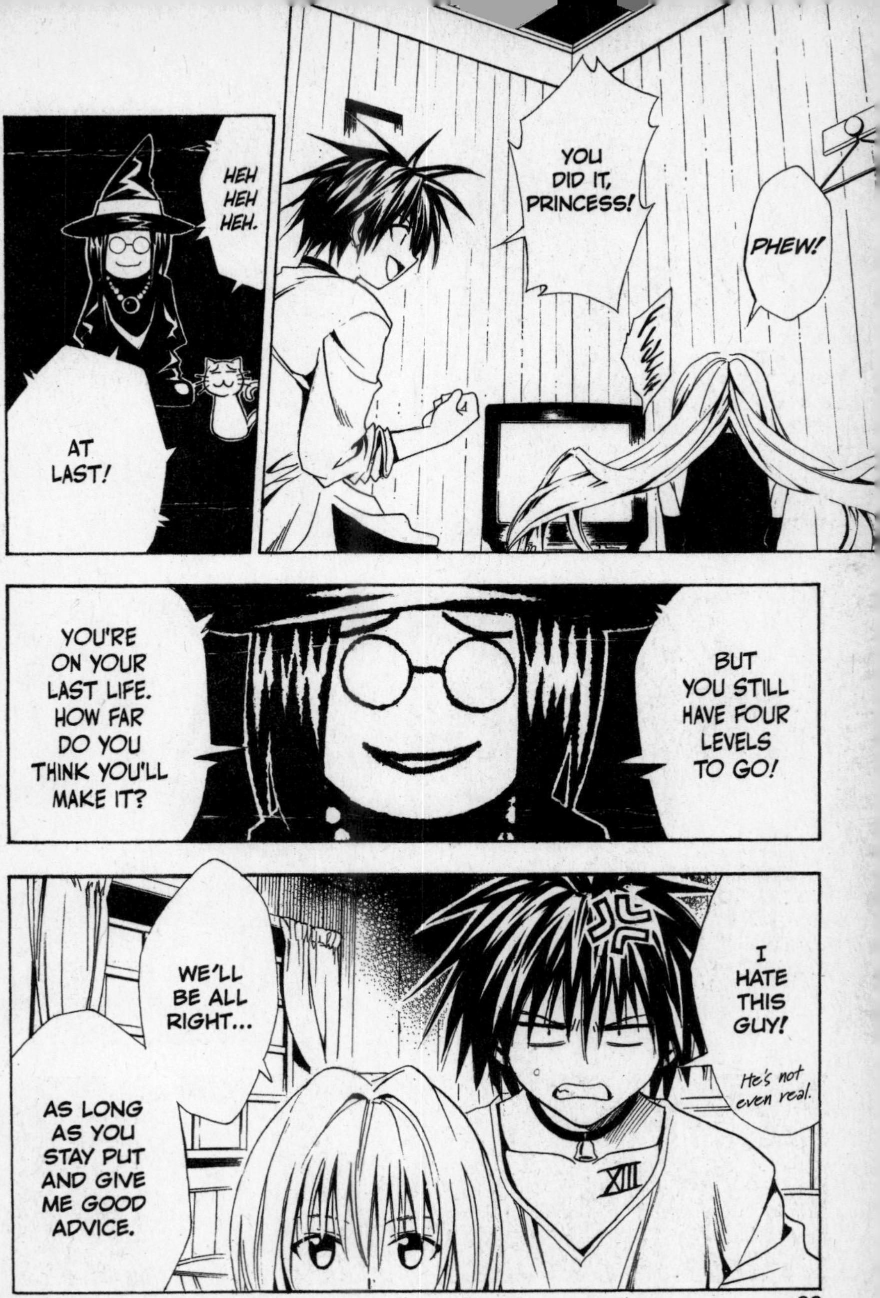
YOU DID IT, PRINCESS!
PHEW!
HEH HEH HEH.
AT LAST!
YOU'RE ON YOUR LAST LIFE. HOW FAR DO YOU THINK YOU'LL MAKE IT?
BUT YOU STILL HAVE FOUR LEVELS TO GO!
I HATE THIS GUY!
He's not even real.
WE'LL BE ALL RIGHT...
AS LONG AS YOU STAY PUT AND GIVE ME GOOD ADVICE.

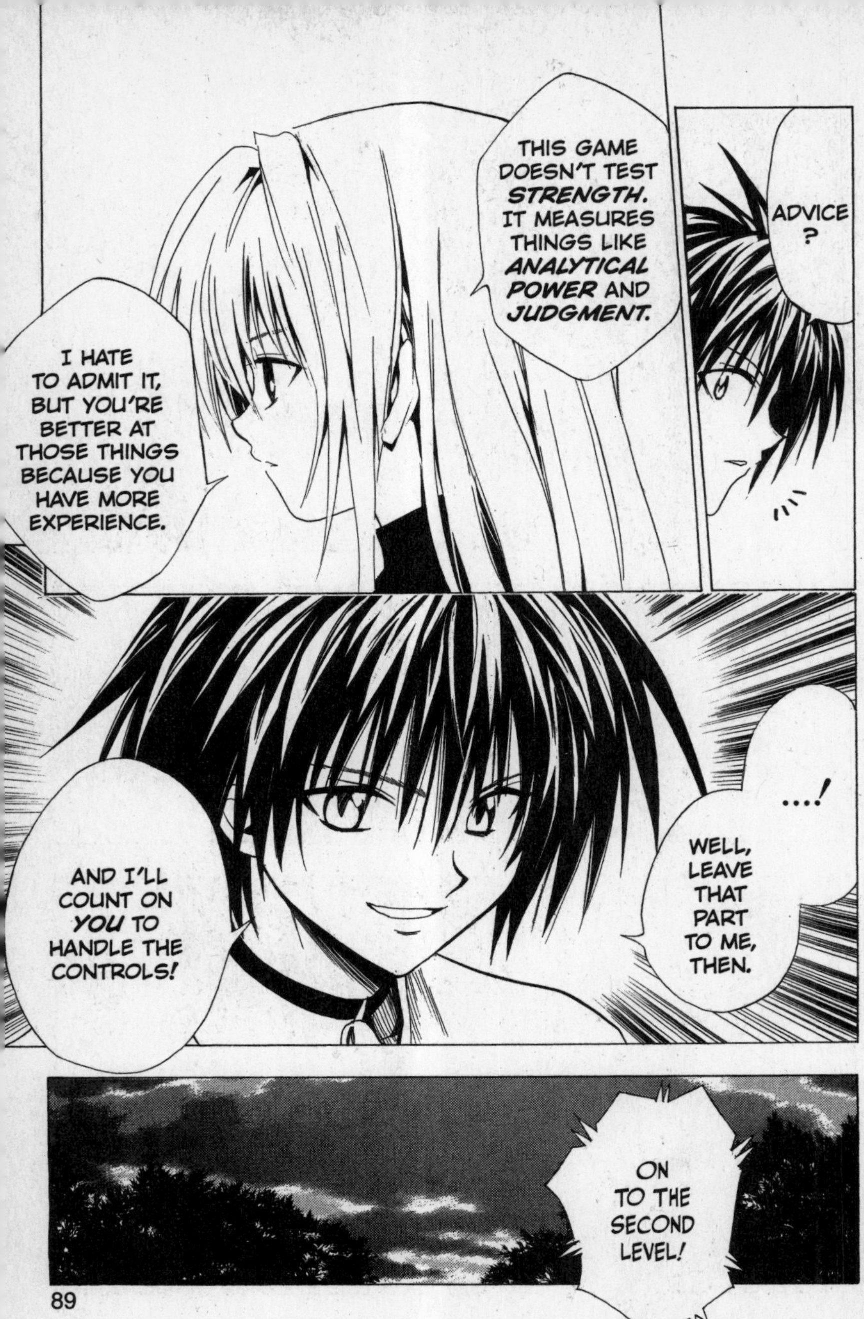
ADVICE ?
THIS GAME DOESN'T TEST STRENGTH. IT MEASURES THINGS LIKE ANALYTICAL POWER AND JUDGMENT.
I HATE TO ADMIT IT, BUT YOU'RE BETTER AT THOSE THINGS BECAUSE YOU HAVE MORE EXPERIENCE.
...!
WELL, LEAVE THAT PART TO ME, THEN.
AND I'LL COUNT ON YOU TO HANDLE THE CONTROLS!
ON TO THE SECOND LEVEL!

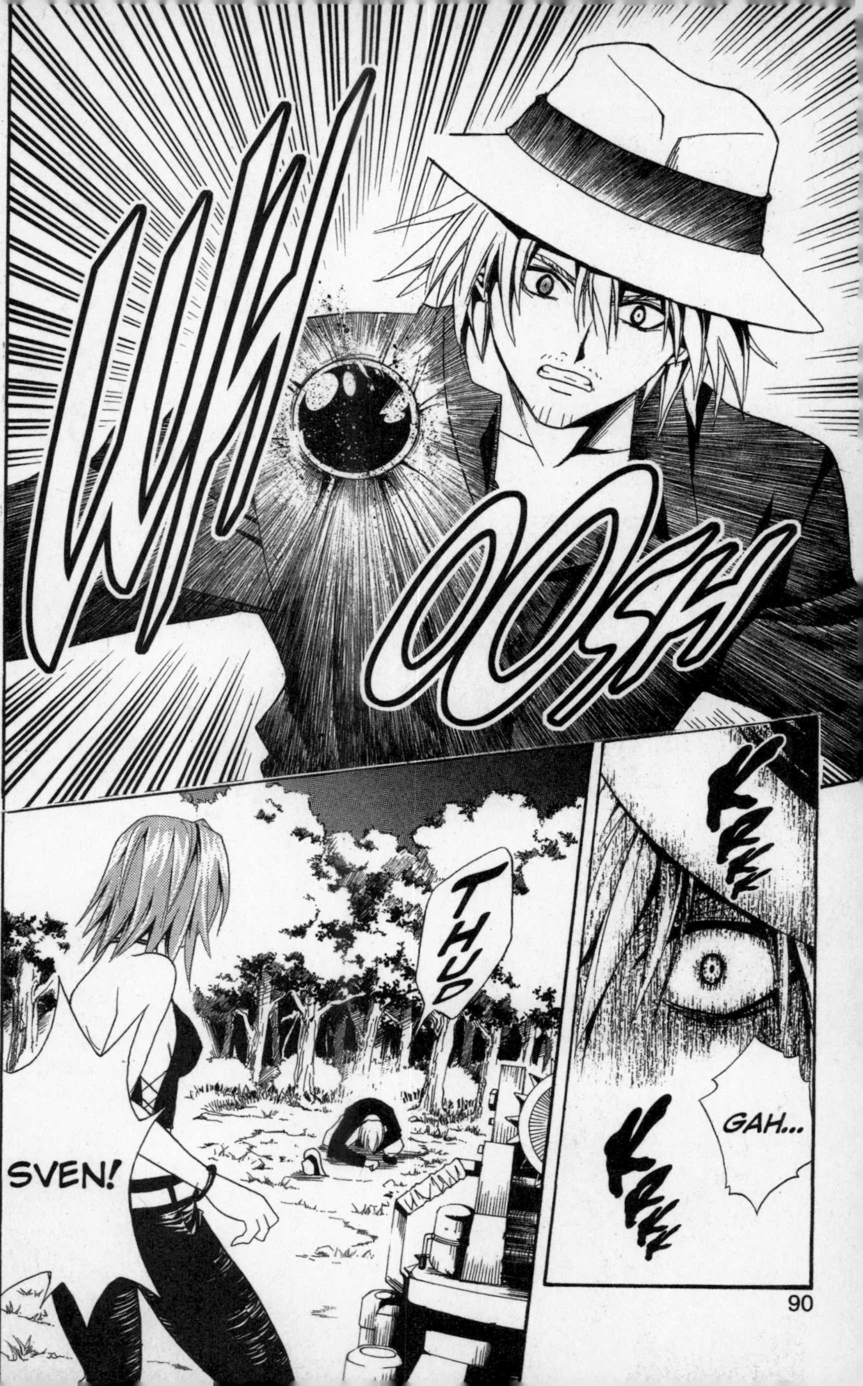
WHOOSH
GAH...
THUD
SVEN!

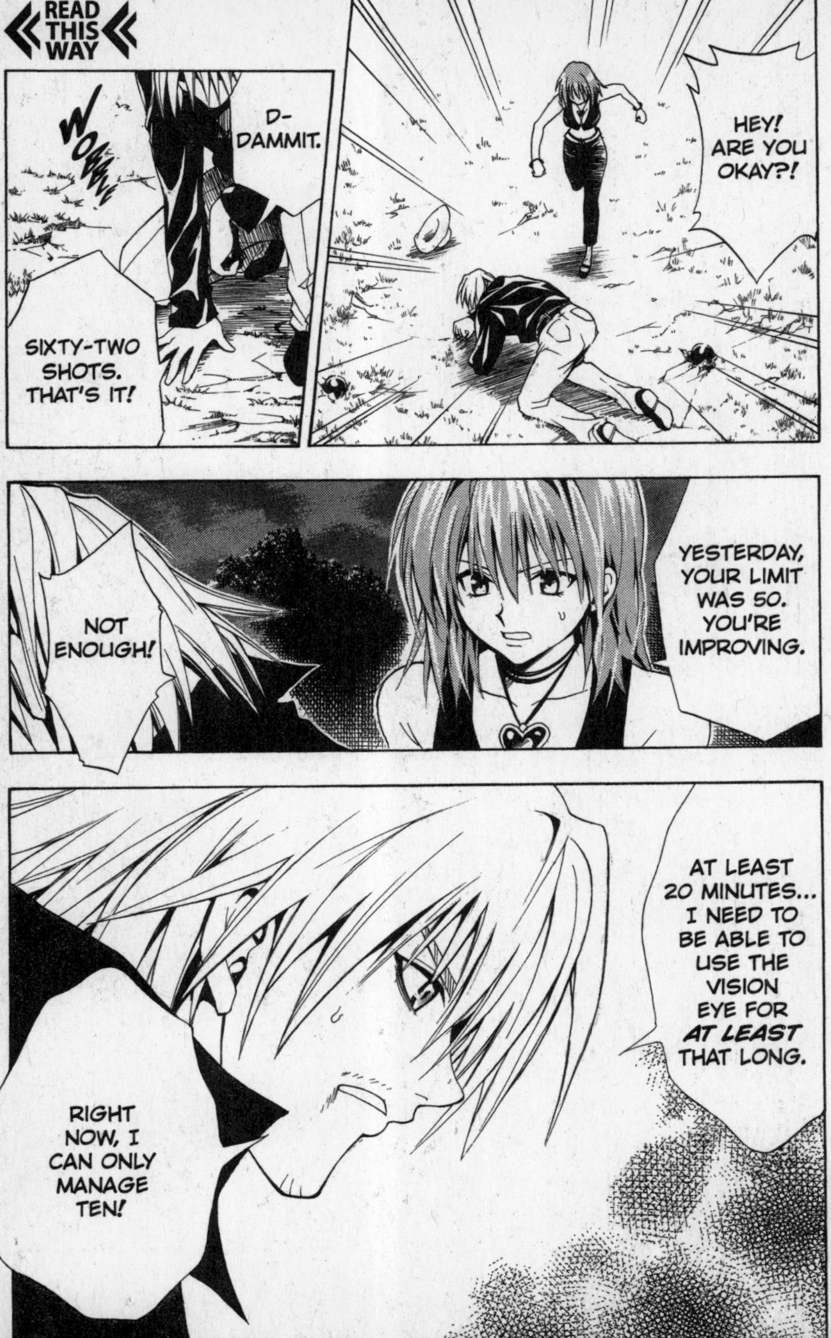
READ THIS WAY
HEY! ARE YOU OKAY?!
D-DAMMIT.
WOWWW
SIXTY-TWO SHOTS. THAT'S IT!
YESTERDAY, YOUR LIMIT WAS 50. YOU'RE IMPROVING.
NOT ENOUGH!
AT LEAST 20 MINUTES... I NEED TO BE ABLE TO USE THE VISION EYE FOR *AT LEAST* THAT LONG.
RIGHT NOW, I CAN ONLY MANAGE TEN!

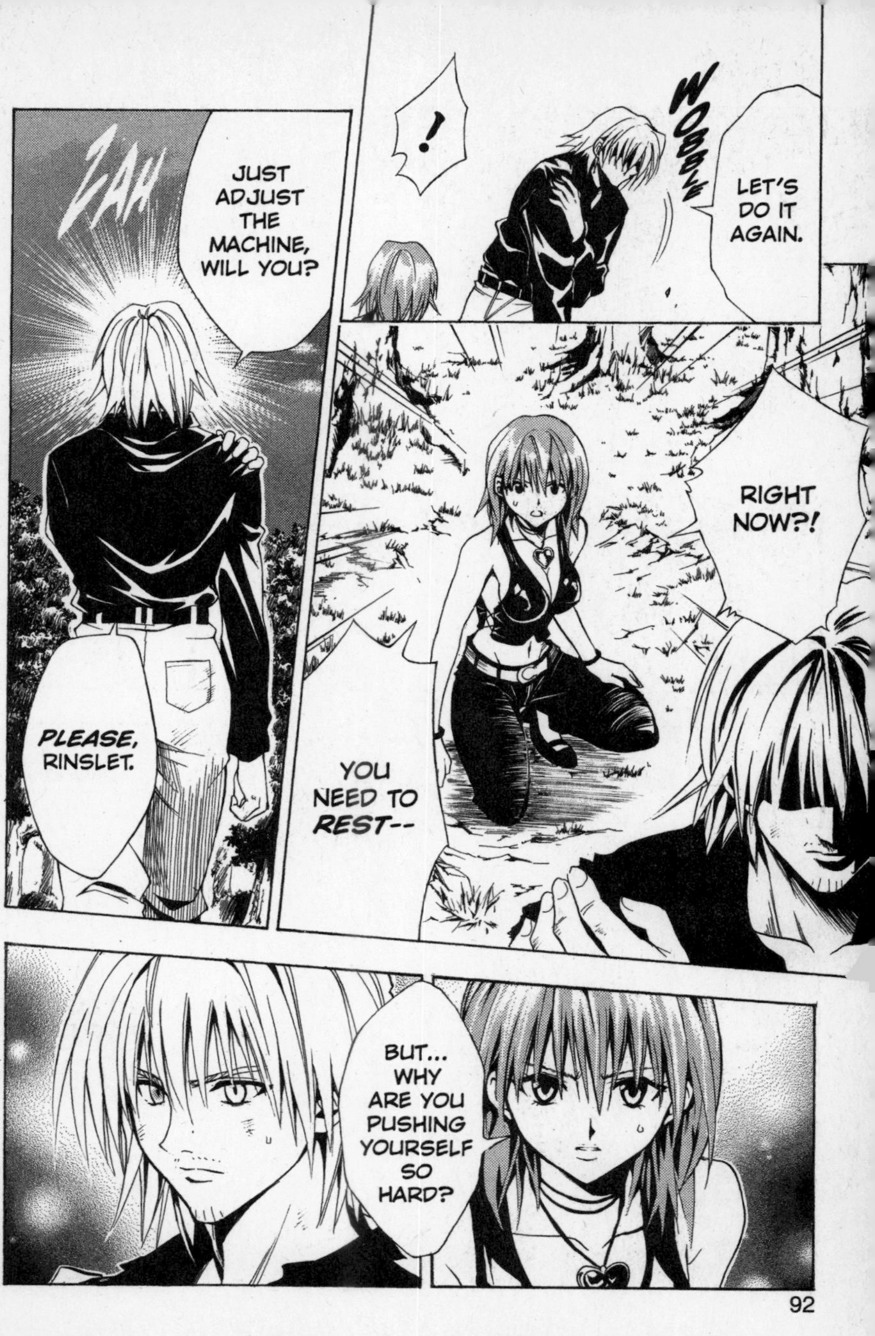

WOBBLE
LET'S DO IT AGAIN.
!
RIGHT NOW?!
YOU NEED TO REST--
ZAH
JUST ADJUST THE MACHINE, WILL YOU?
PLEASE, RINSLET.
BUT... WHY ARE YOU PUSHING YOURSELF SO HARD?

READ THIS WAY

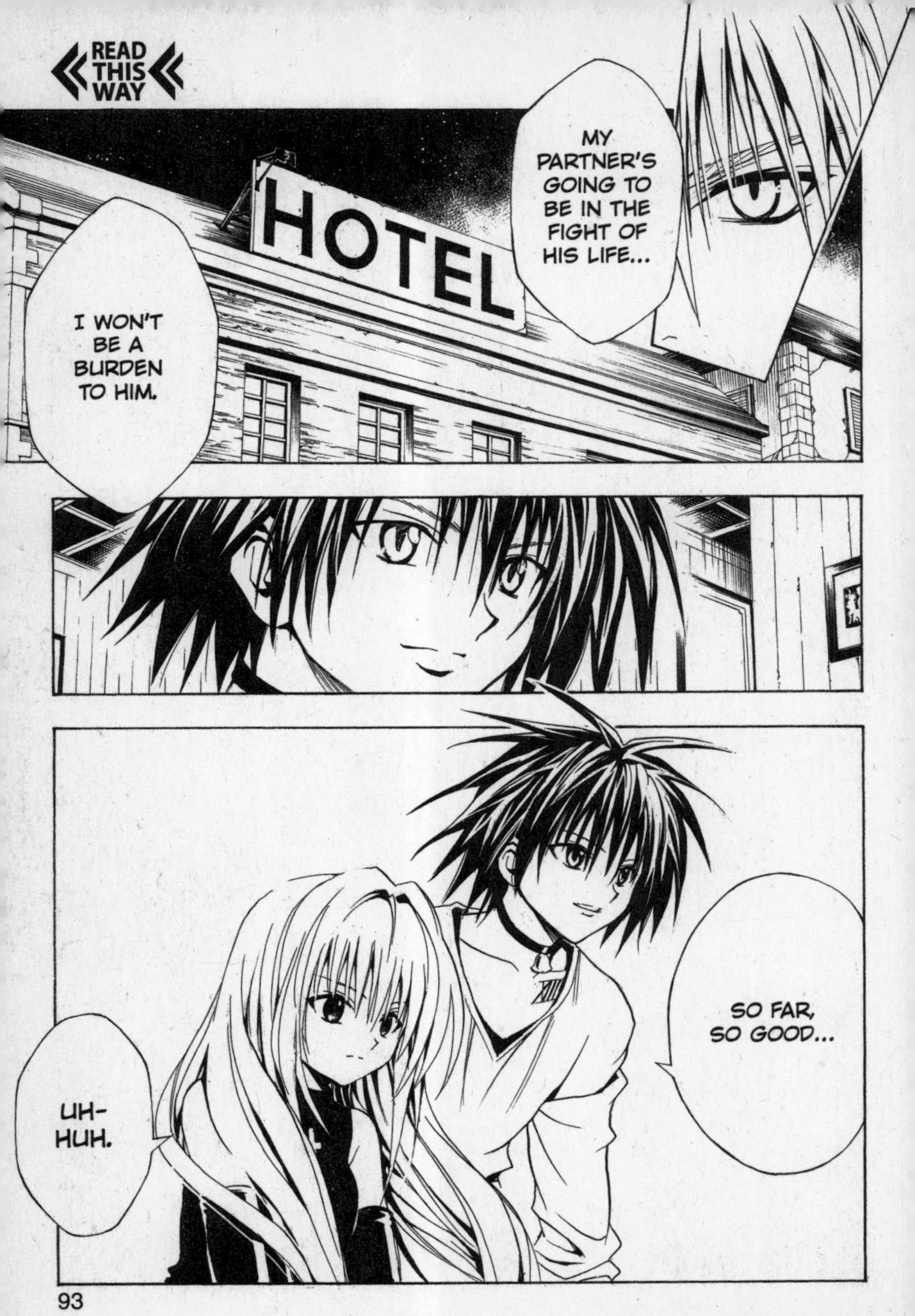
HOTEL
MY PARTNER'S GOING TO BE IN THE FIGHT OF HIS LIFE...
I WON'T BE A BURDEN TO HIM.
SO FAR, SO GOOD...
UH-HUH.

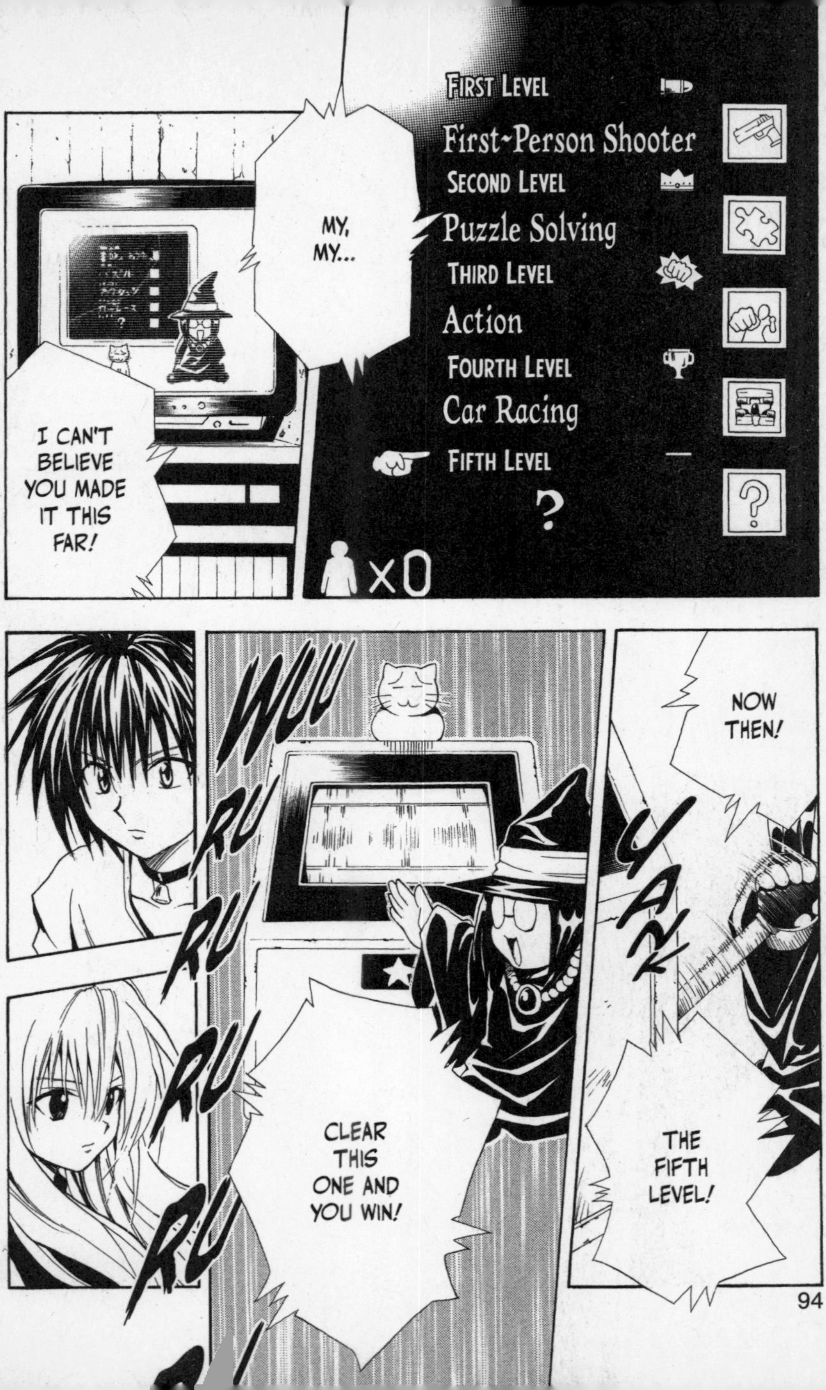

FIRST LEVEL
First-Person Shooter
SECOND LEVEL
Puzzle Solving
THIRD LEVEL
Action
FOURTH LEVEL
Car Racing
FIFTH LEVEL
?
×0
MY, MY...
I CAN'T BELIEVE YOU MADE IT THIS FAR!
NOW THEN!
YANK
THE FIFTH LEVEL!
WURURURU
CLEAR THIS ONE AND YOU WIN!

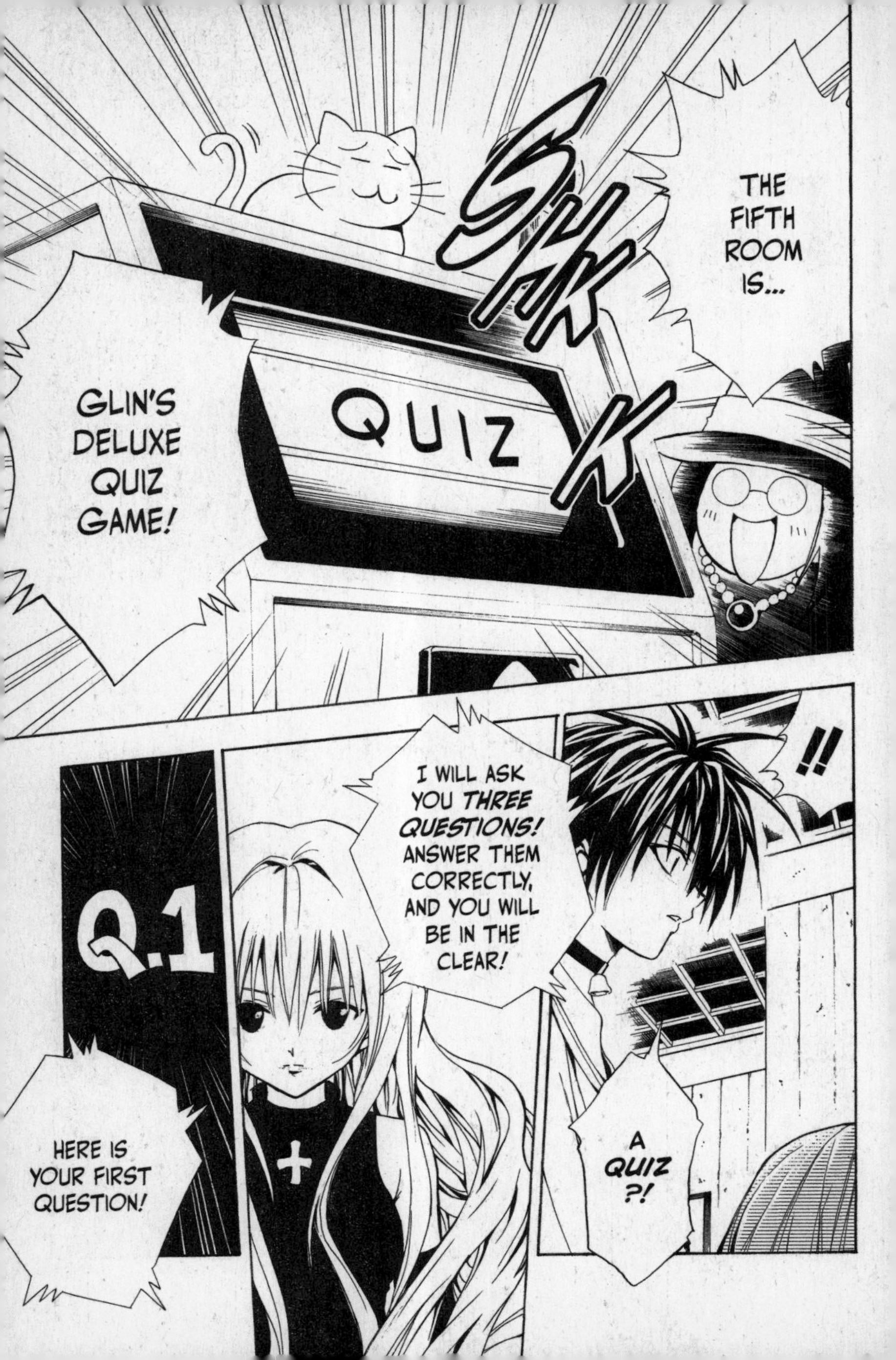
THE FIFTH ROOM IS...
QUIZ
GLIN'S DELUXE QUIZ GAME!
!!
A *QUIZ* ?!
I WILL ASK YOU *THREE QUESTIONS!* ANSWER THEM CORRECTLY, AND YOU WILL BE IN THE CLEAR!
Q.1
HERE IS YOUR FIRST QUESTION!

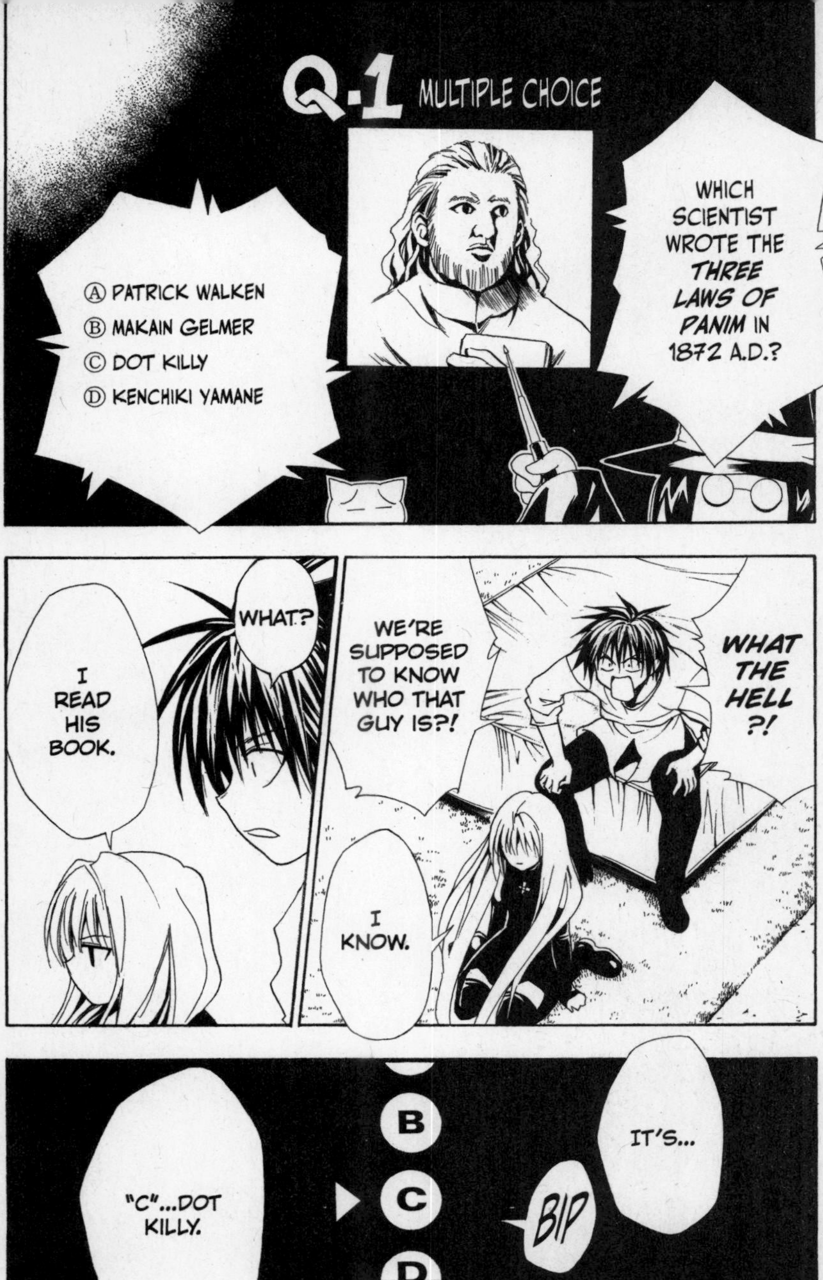
Q.1 MULTIPLE CHOICE
WHICH SCIENTIST WROTE THE *THREE LAWS OF PANIM* IN 1872 A.D.?
Ⓐ PATRICK WALKEN
Ⓑ MAKAIN GELMER
Ⓒ DOT KILLY
Ⓓ KENCHIKI YAMANE
WHAT THE HELL ?!
WE'RE SUPPOSED TO KNOW WHO THAT GUY IS?!
I KNOW.
WHAT?
I READ HIS BOOK.
IT'S...
BIP
B
C
D
"C"...DOT KILLY.

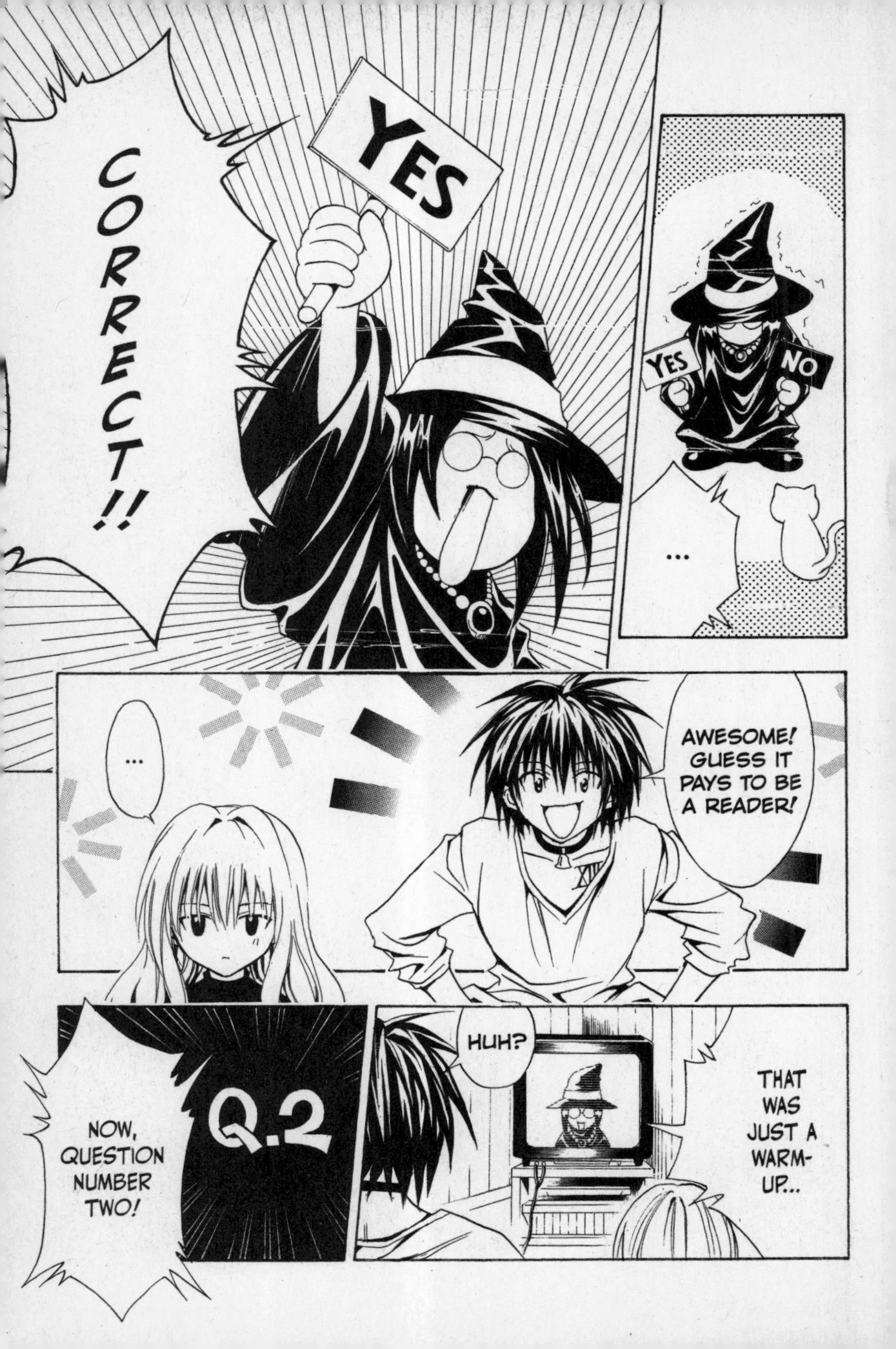
YES
NO
...
YES
CORRECT!!
AWESOME! GUESS IT PAYS TO BE A READER!
...
THAT WAS JUST A WARM-UP...
HUH?
Q.2
NOW, QUESTION NUMBER TWO!

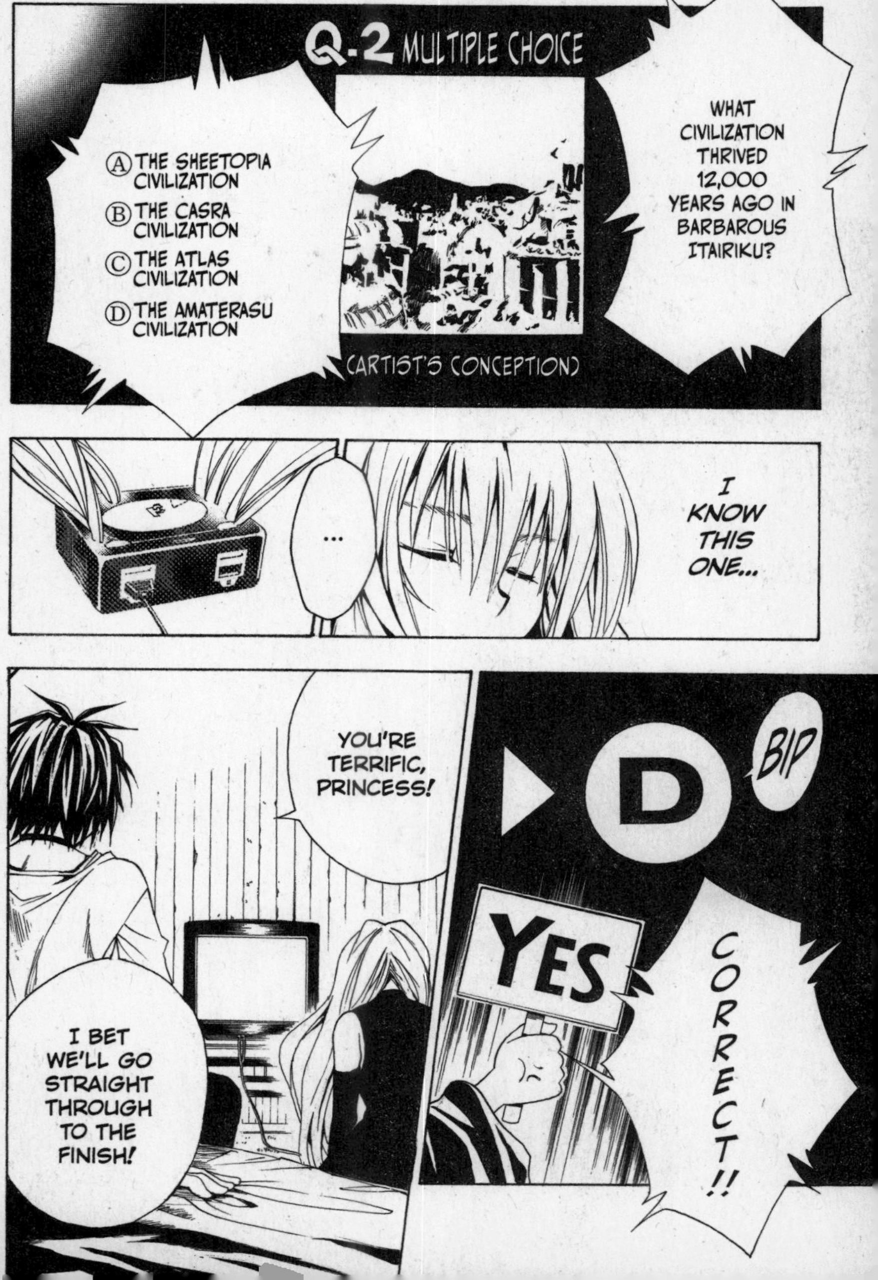
WHAT CIVILIZATION THRIVED 12,000 YEARS AGO IN BARBAROUS ITAIRIKU?
Q-2 MULTIPLE CHOICE
(ARTIST'S CONCEPTION)
Ⓐ THE SHEETOPIA CIVILIZATION
Ⓑ THE CASRA CIVILIZATION
Ⓒ THE ATLAS CIVILIZATION
Ⓓ THE AMATERASU CIVILIZATION
I KNOW THIS ONE...
...
BIP
D
YES
CORRECT!!
YOU'RE TERRIFIC, PRINCESS!
I BET WE'LL GO STRAIGHT THROUGH TO THE FINISH!

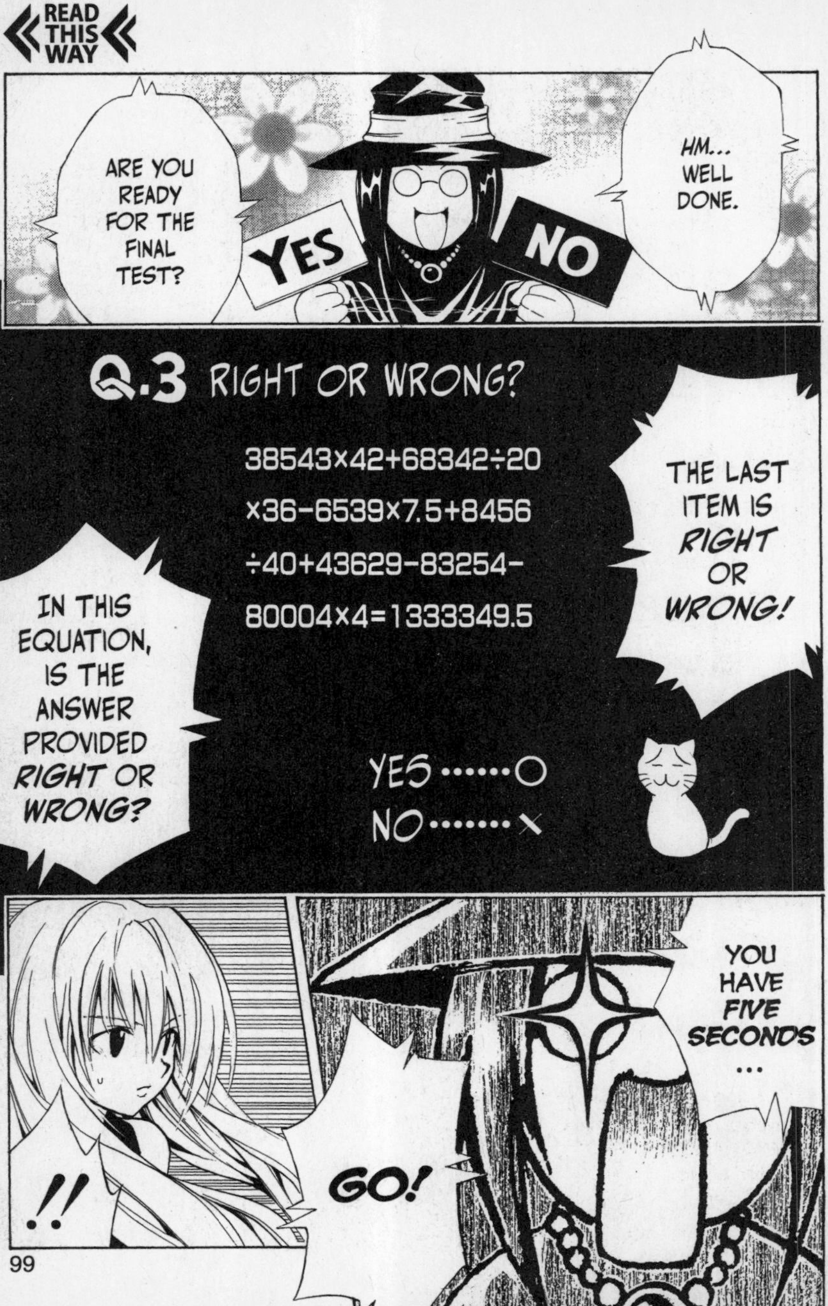
READ THIS WAY
HM... WELL DONE.
NO
YES
ARE YOU READY FOR THE FINAL TEST?
Q.3 RIGHT OR WRONG?
THE LAST ITEM IS RIGHT OR WRONG!
38543×42+68342÷20
×36−6539×7.5+8456
÷40+43629−83254−
80004×4=1333349.5
IN THIS EQUATION, IS THE ANSWER PROVIDED RIGHT OR WRONG?
YES……O
NO……×
YOU HAVE FIVE SECONDS...
GO!
!!

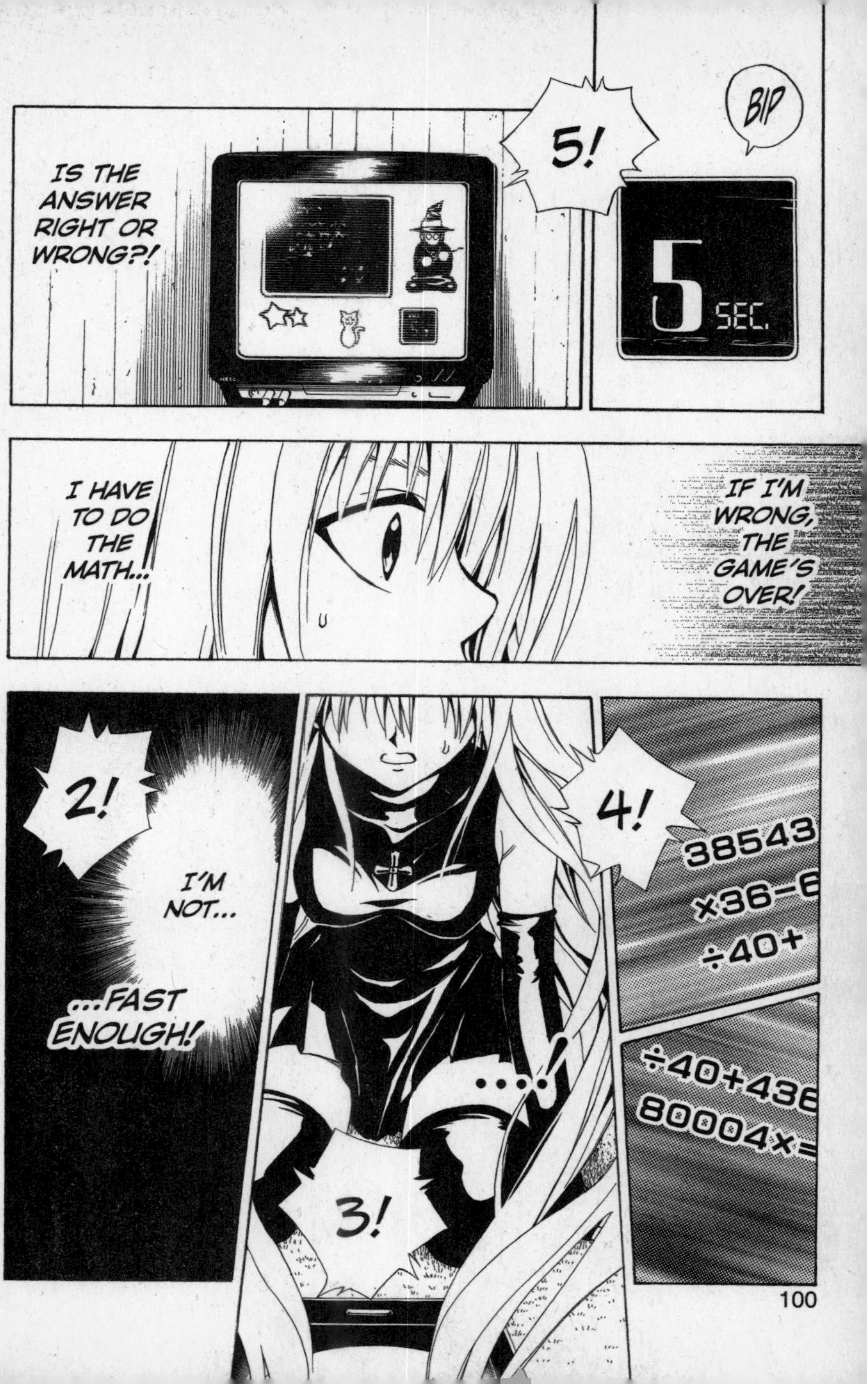
BIP
5!
5 SEC.
IS THE ANSWER RIGHT OR WRONG?!
IF I'M WRONG, THE GAME'S OVER!
I HAVE TO DO THE MATH...
4!
38543 ×36−6 ÷40+
÷40+436 80004×=
...!
3!
2!
I'M NOT...
...FAST ENOUGH!

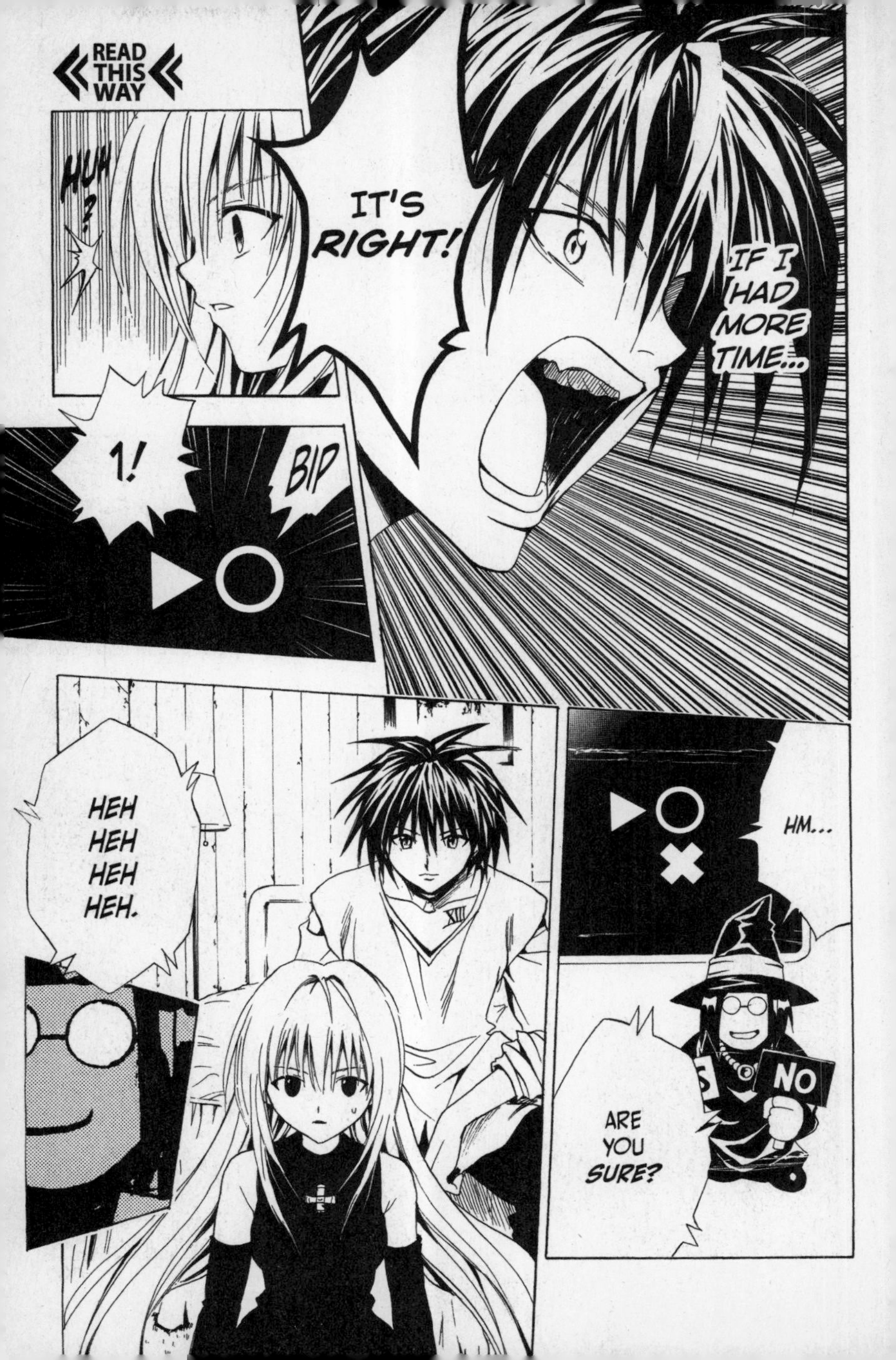
READ THIS WAY
IT'S RIGHT!
IF I HAD MORE TIME...
HUH?
1!
BIP
HM...
NO
ARE YOU SURE?
HEH HEH HEH HEH.

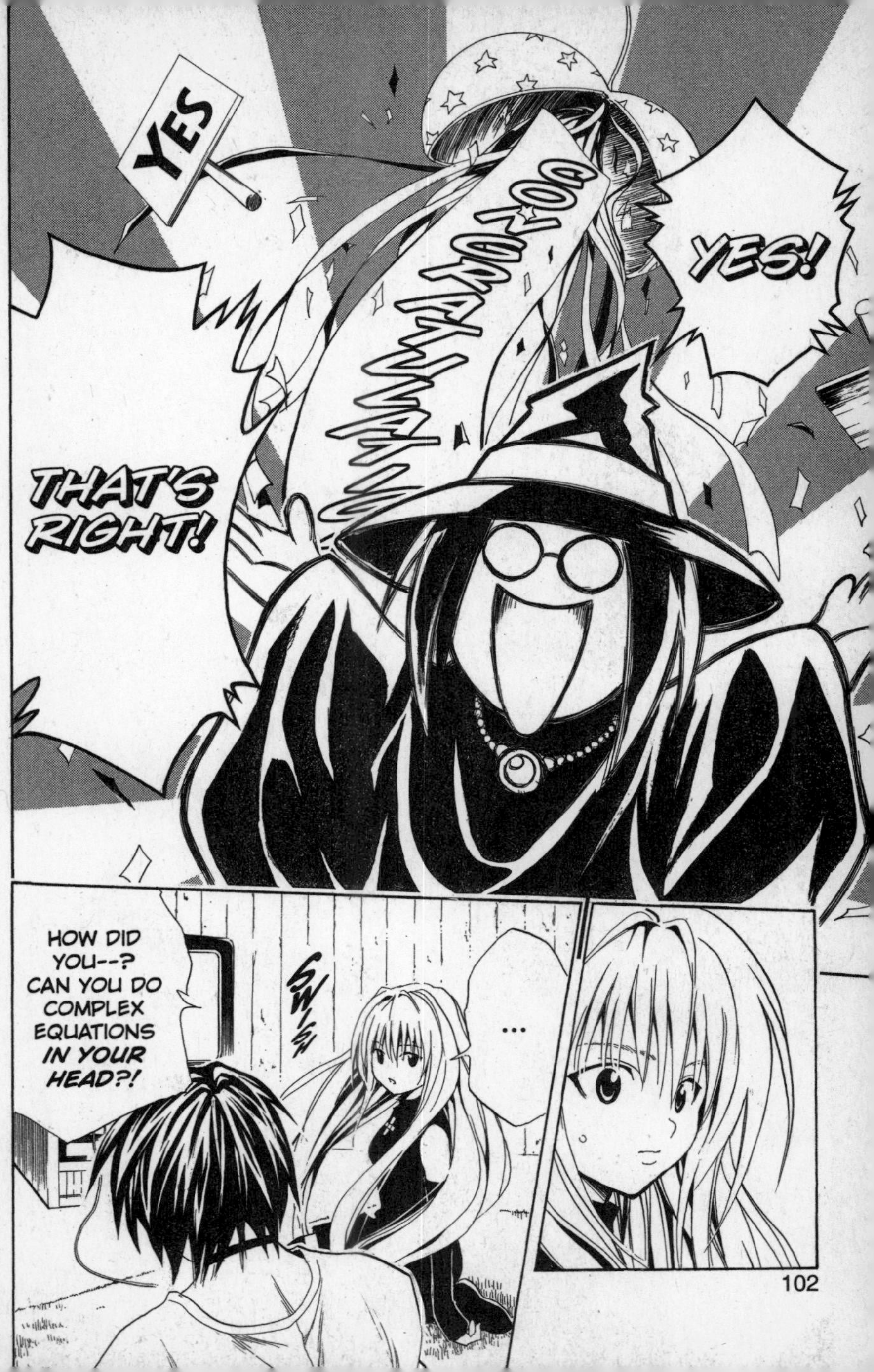
YES
YES!
THAT'S RIGHT!
...
SWISH
HOW DID YOU--? CAN YOU DO COMPLEX EQUATIONS *IN YOUR HEAD?!*

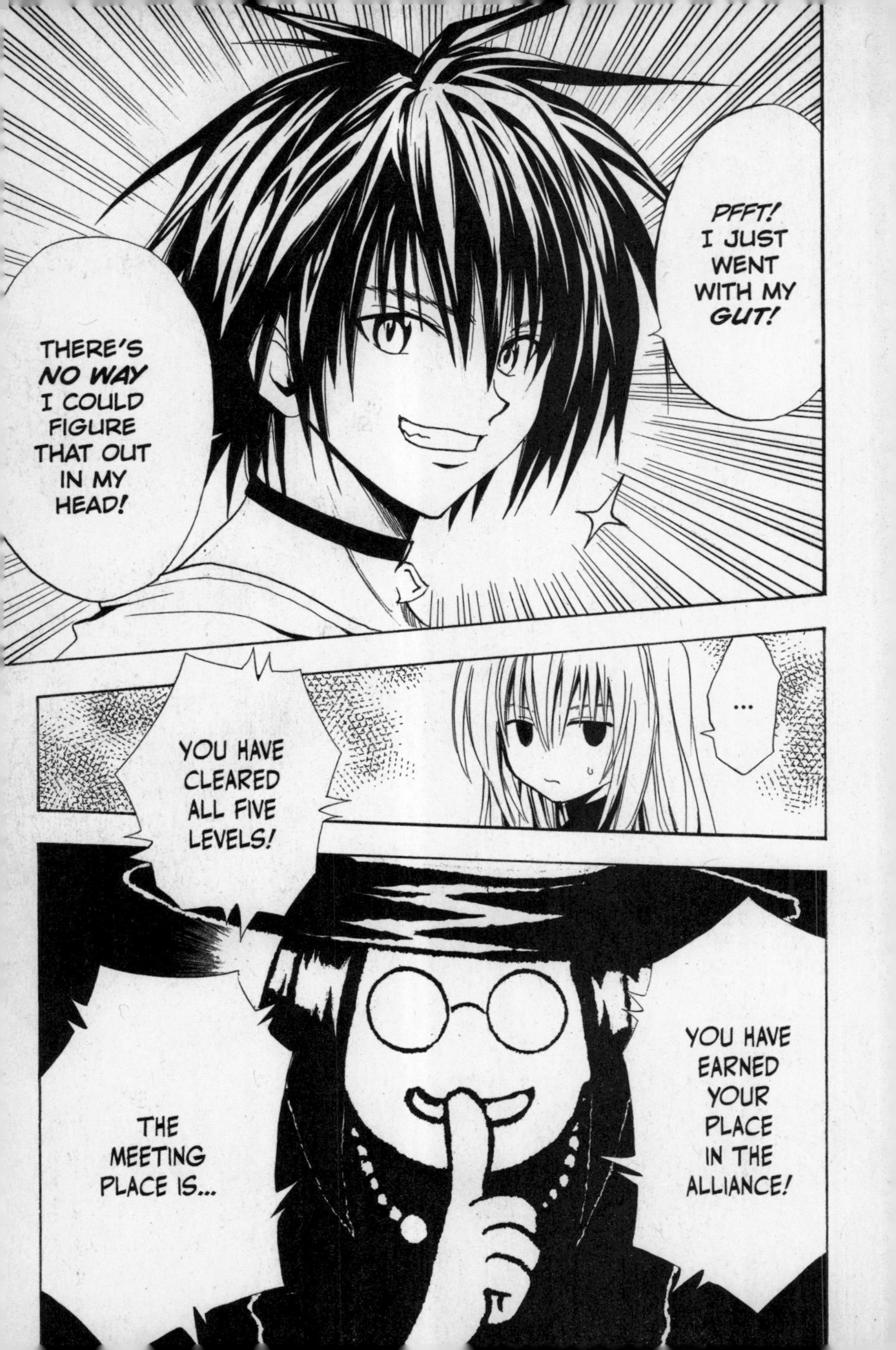
PFFT! I JUST WENT WITH MY GUT!
THERE'S NO WAY I COULD FIGURE THAT OUT IN MY HEAD!
...
YOU HAVE CLEARED ALL FIVE LEVELS!
YOU HAVE EARNED YOUR PLACE IN THE ALLIANCE!
THE MEETING PLACE IS...

NOSTALGIC SERIES

NUMBER 4—DONOVAN

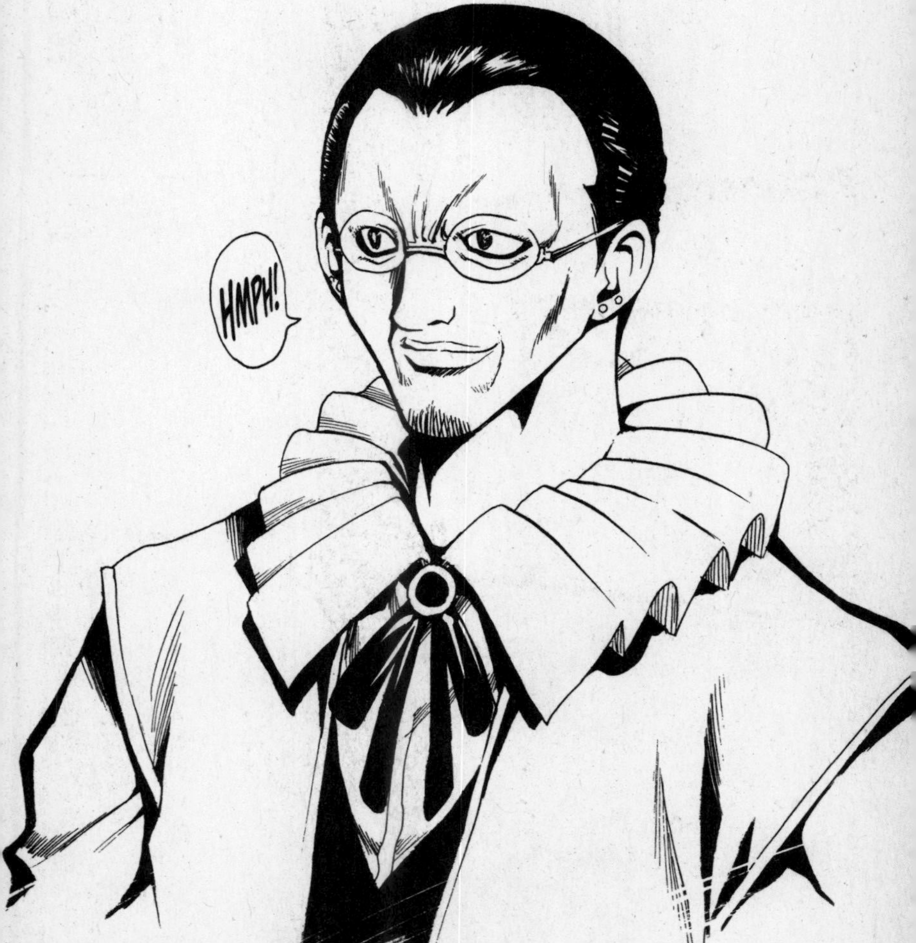
HMPH!

Chapter 128: The Meeting

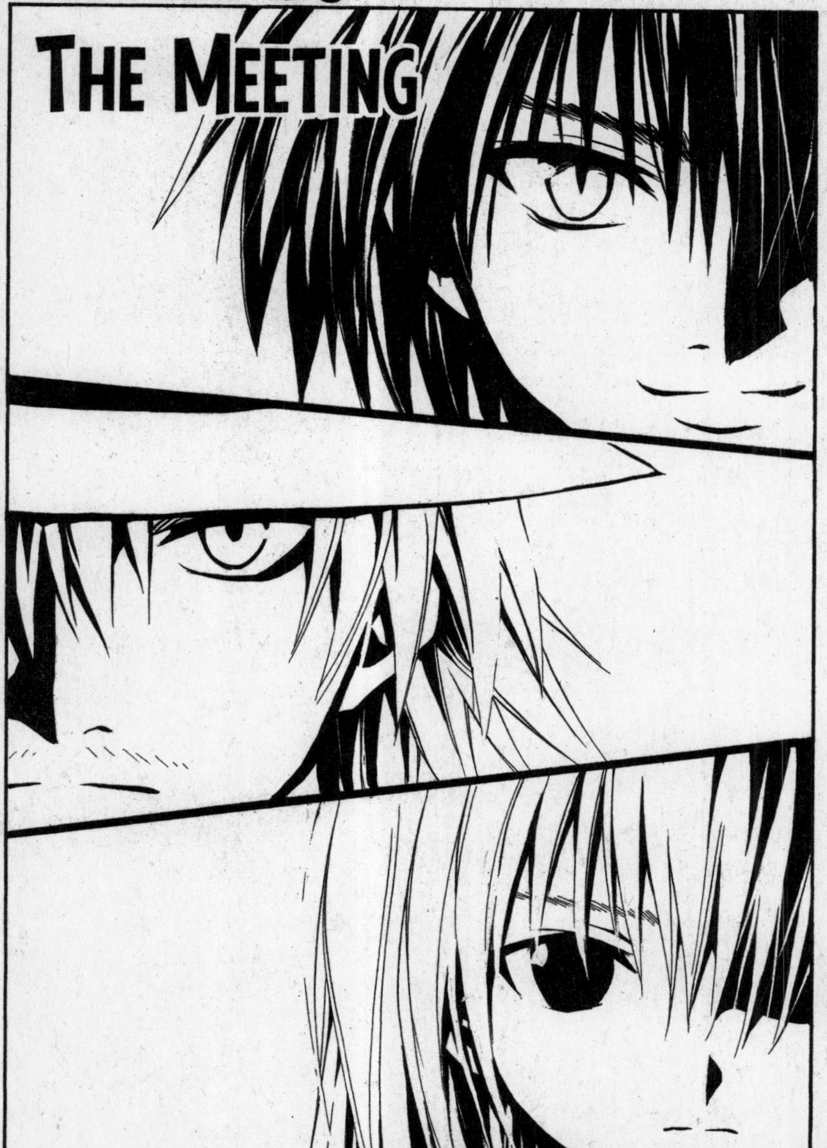

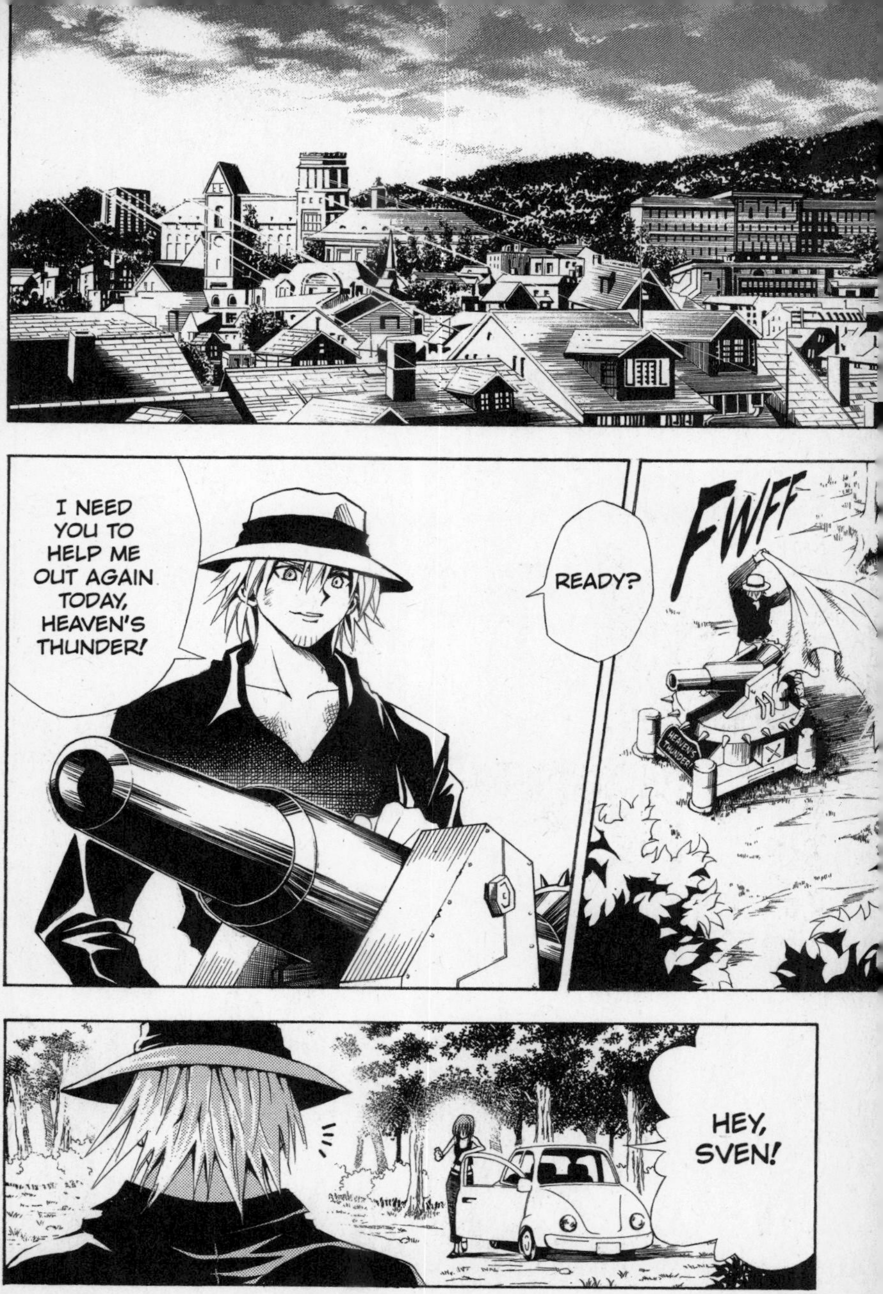
FWFF
READY?
I NEED YOU TO HELP ME OUT AGAIN TODAY, HEAVEN'S THUNDER!
HEY, SVEN!

READ THIS WAY

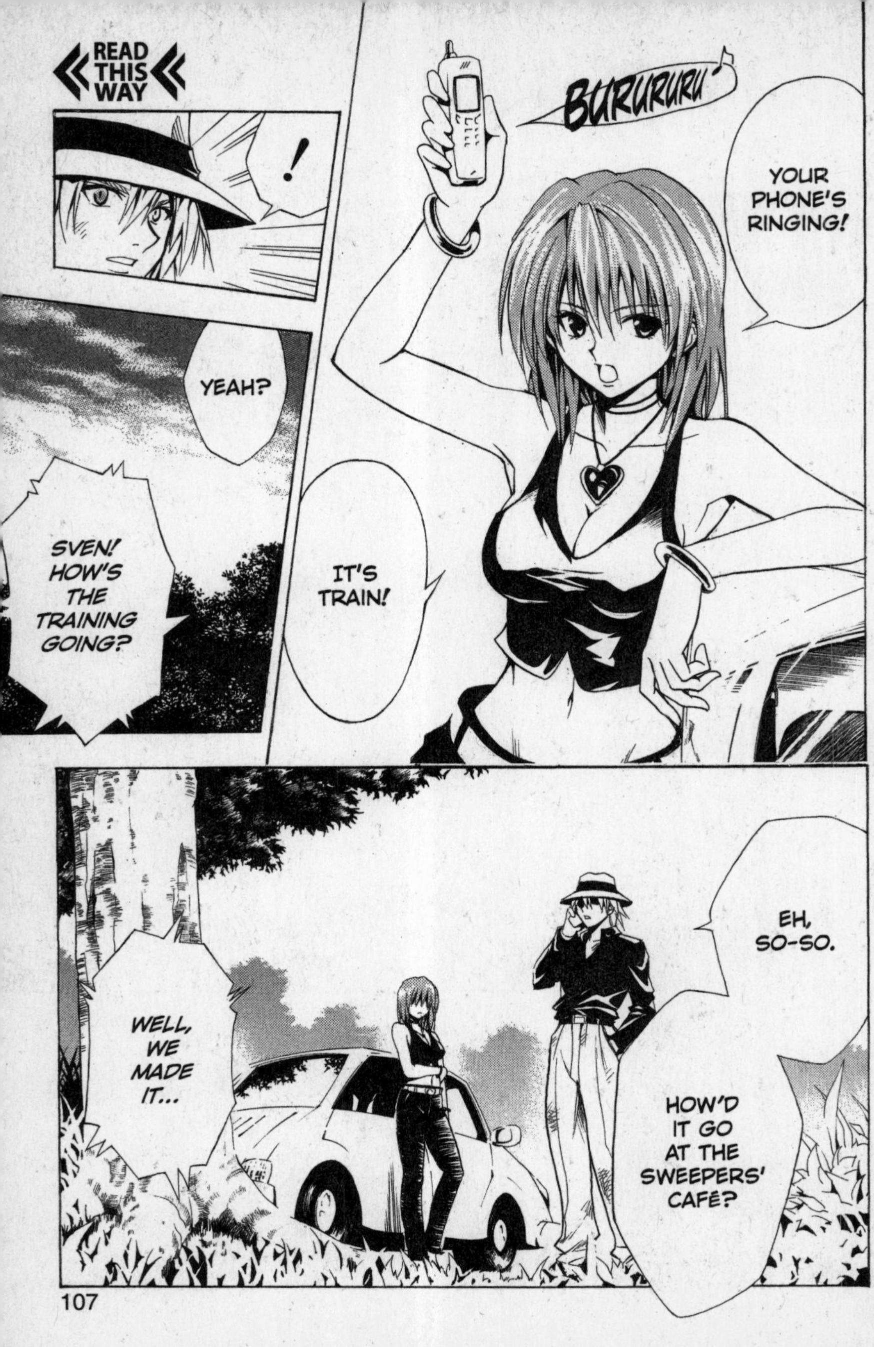

BURURURU
YOUR PHONE'S RINGING!
IT'S TRAIN!
!
YEAH?
SVEN! HOW'S THE TRAINING GOING?
EH, SO-SO.
HOW'D IT GO AT THE SWEEPERS' CAFÉ?
WELL, WE MADE IT...

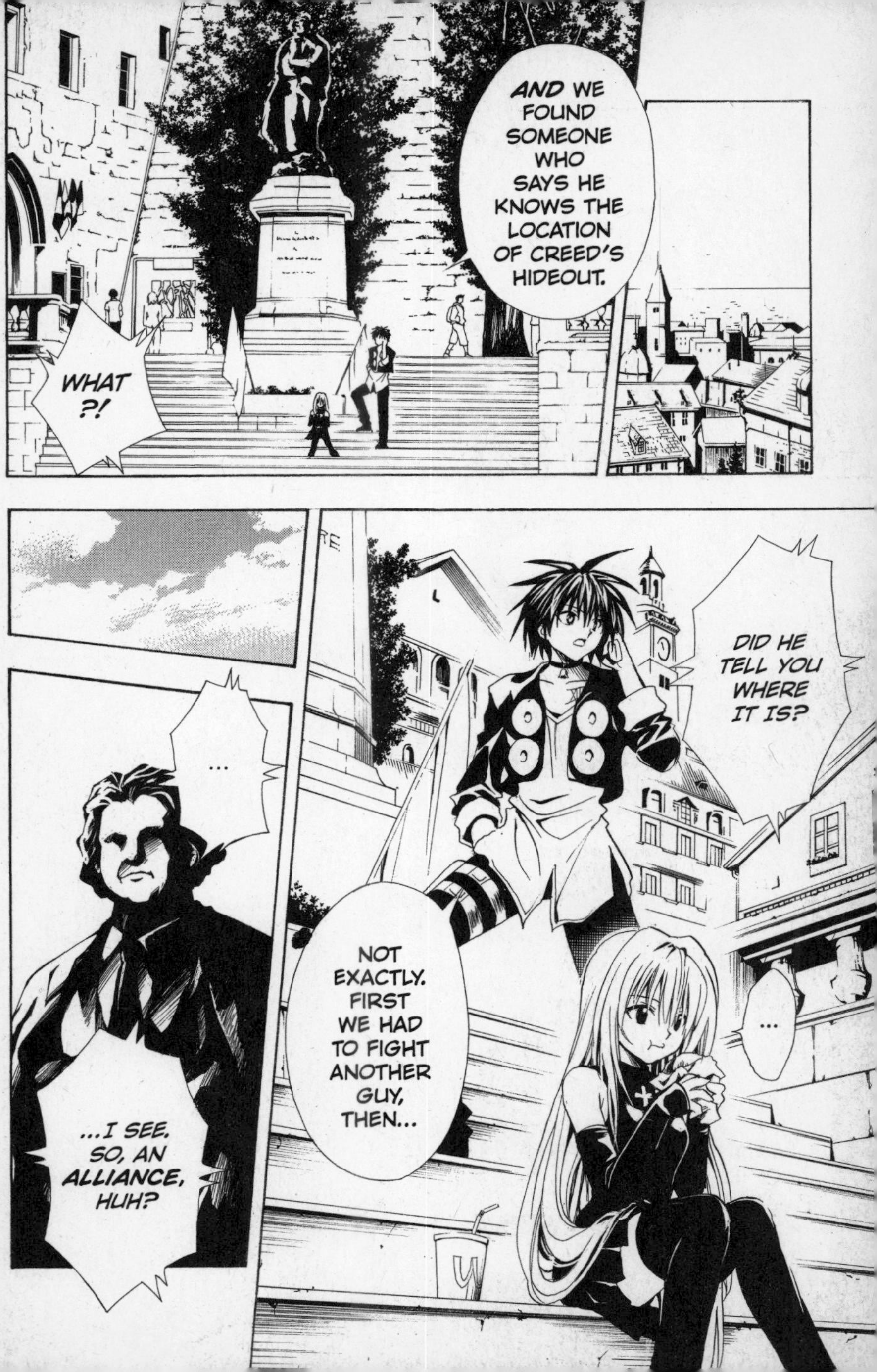
AND WE FOUND SOMEONE WHO SAYS HE KNOWS THE LOCATION OF CREED'S HIDEOUT.
WHAT ?!
DID HE TELL YOU WHERE IT IS?
...
NOT EXACTLY. FIRST WE HAD TO FIGHT ANOTHER GUY, THEN...
...
...I SEE. SO, AN ALLIANCE, HUH?

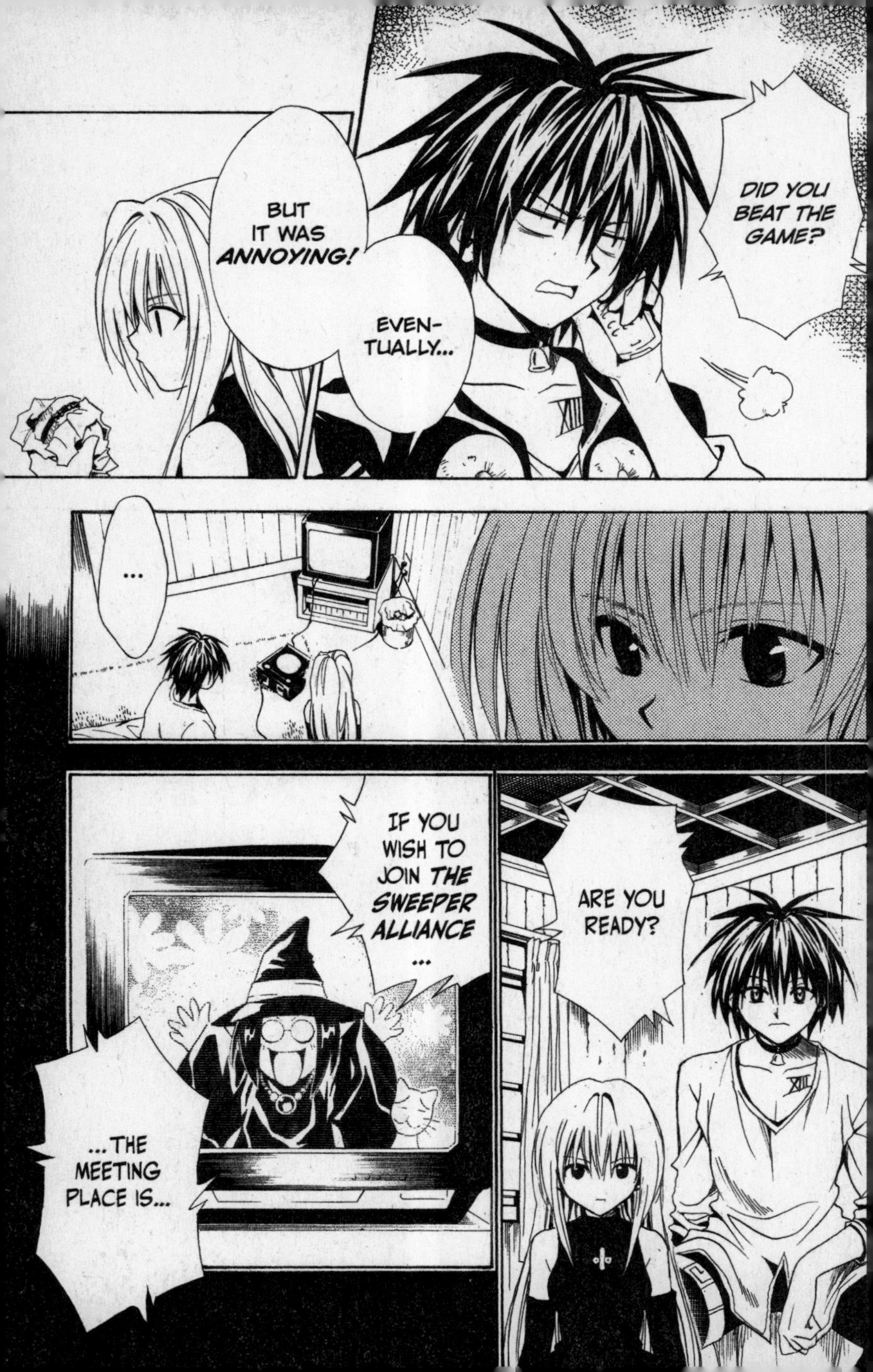
DID YOU BEAT THE GAME?
EVEN-TUALLY...
BUT IT WAS ANNOYING!
...
ARE YOU READY?
IF YOU WISH TO JOIN THE SWEEPER ALLIANCE ...
...THE MEETING PLACE IS...

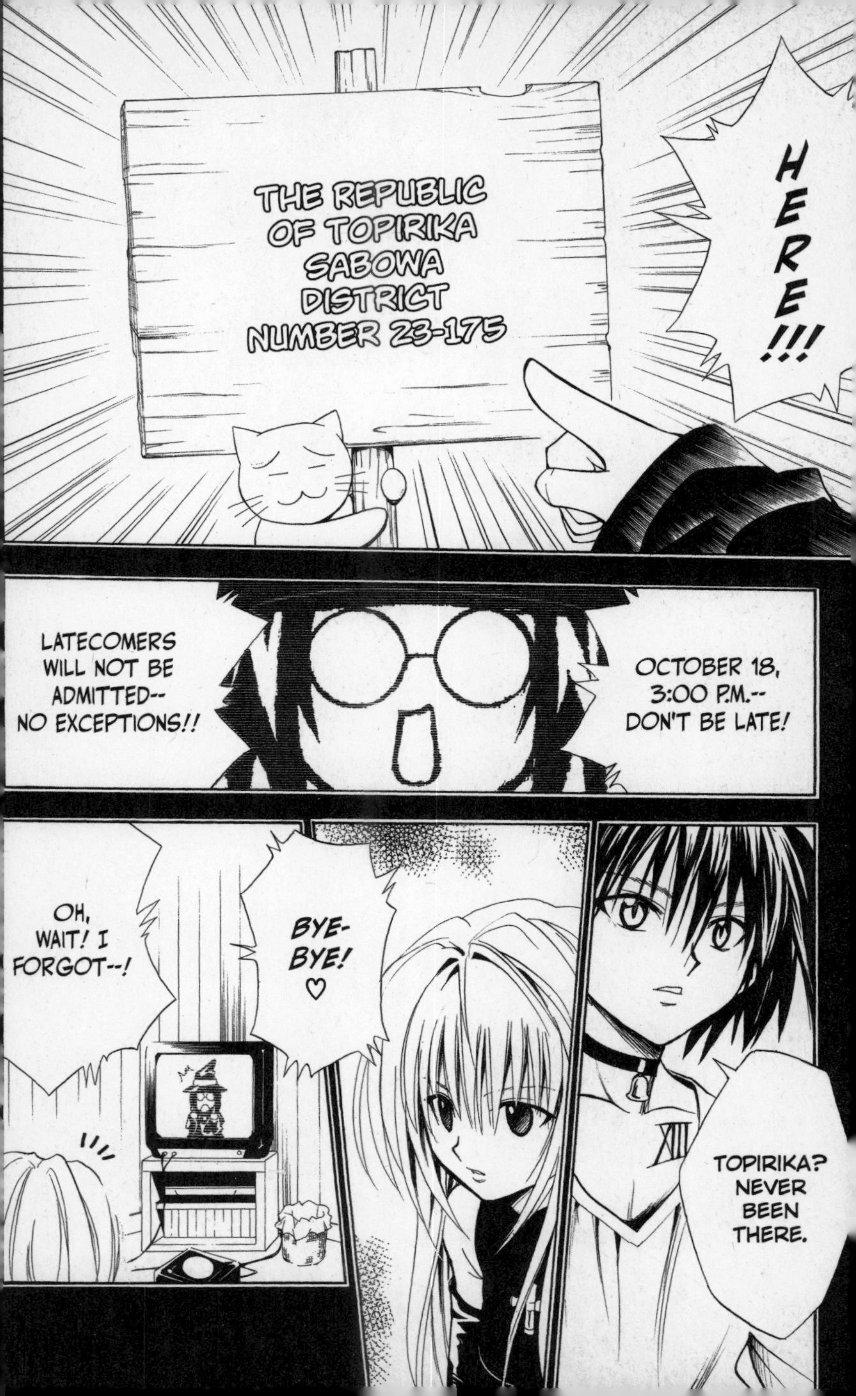
HERE!!!
THE REPUBLIC OF TOPIRIKA SABOWA DISTRICT NUMBER 23-175
OCTOBER 18, 3:00 P.M.-- DON'T BE LATE!
LATECOMERS WILL NOT BE ADMITTED-- NO EXCEPTIONS!!
TOPIRIKA? NEVER BEEN THERE.
BYE-BYE! ♡
OH, WAIT! I FORGOT--!

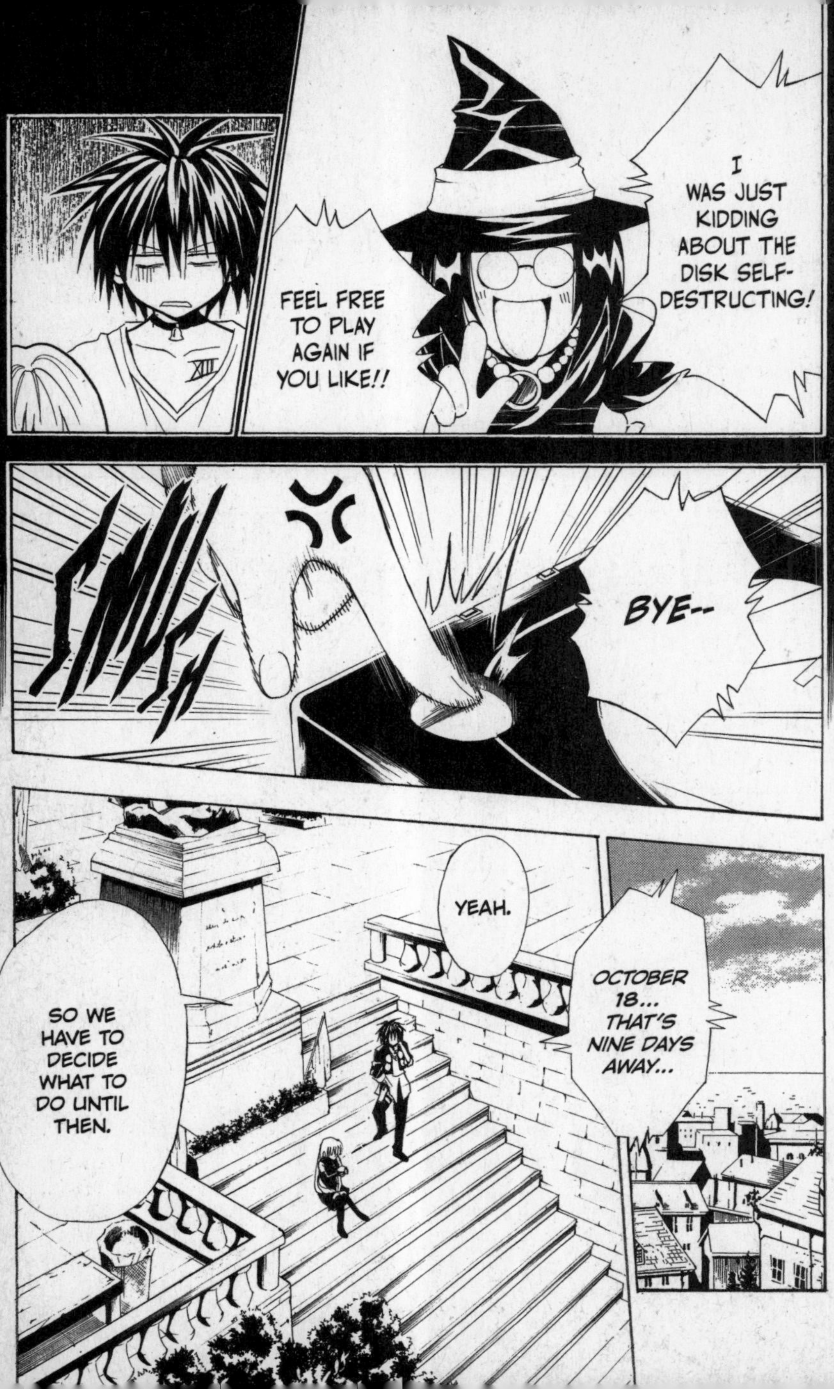
I WAS JUST KIDDING ABOUT THE DISK SELF-DESTRUCTING!
FEEL FREE TO PLAY AGAIN IF YOU LIKE!!
BYE--
OCTOBER 18... THAT'S NINE DAYS AWAY...
YEAH.
SO WE HAVE TO DECIDE WHAT TO DO UNTIL THEN.

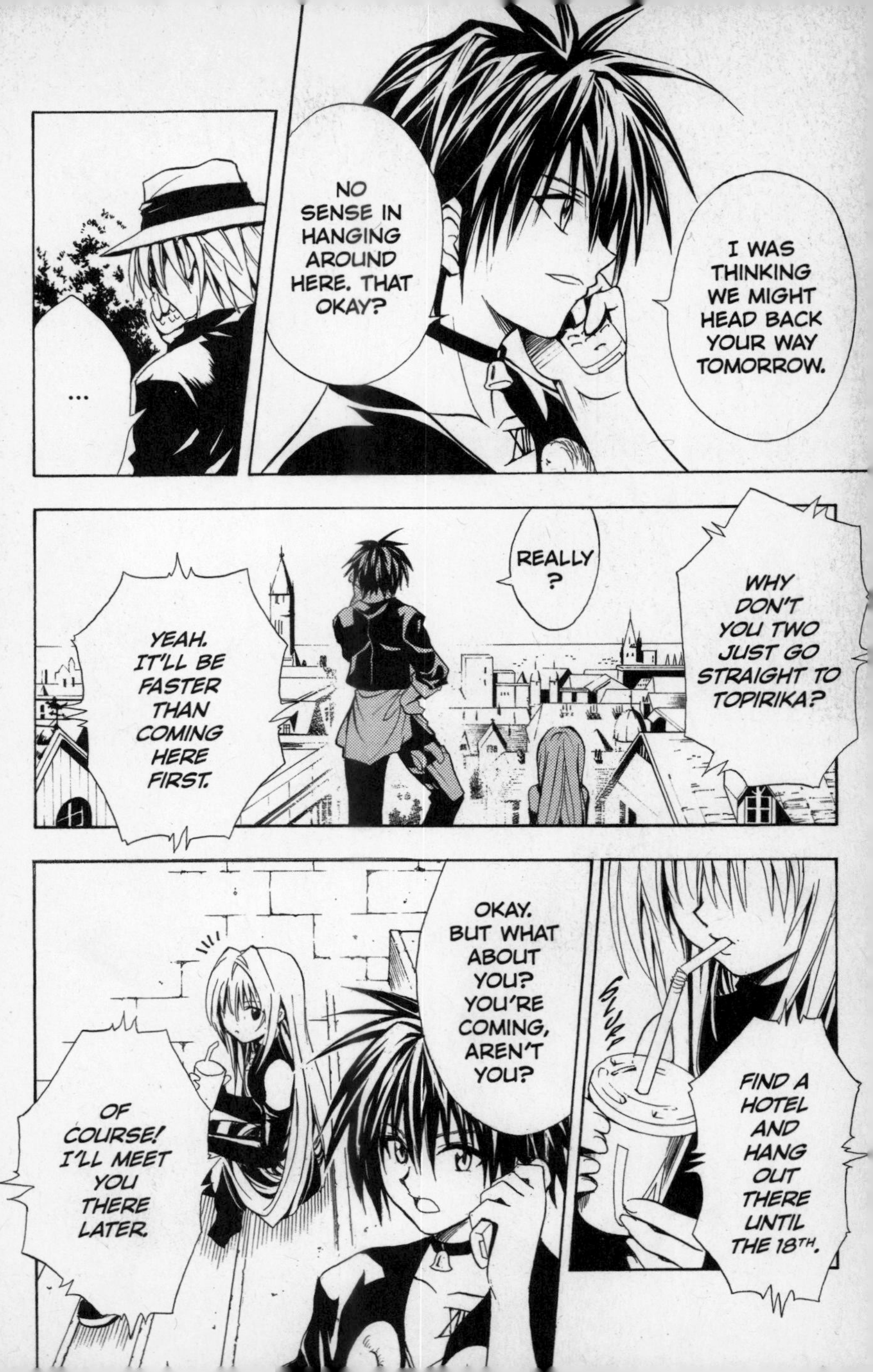
I WAS THINKING WE MIGHT HEAD BACK YOUR WAY TOMORROW.
NO SENSE IN HANGING AROUND HERE. THAT OKAY?
...
WHY DON'T YOU TWO JUST GO STRAIGHT TO TOPIRIKA?
REALLY?
YEAH. IT'LL BE FASTER THAN COMING HERE FIRST.
FIND A HOTEL AND HANG OUT THERE UNTIL THE 18TH.
OKAY. BUT WHAT ABOUT YOU? YOU'RE COMING, AREN'T YOU?
OF COURSE! I'LL MEET YOU THERE LATER.

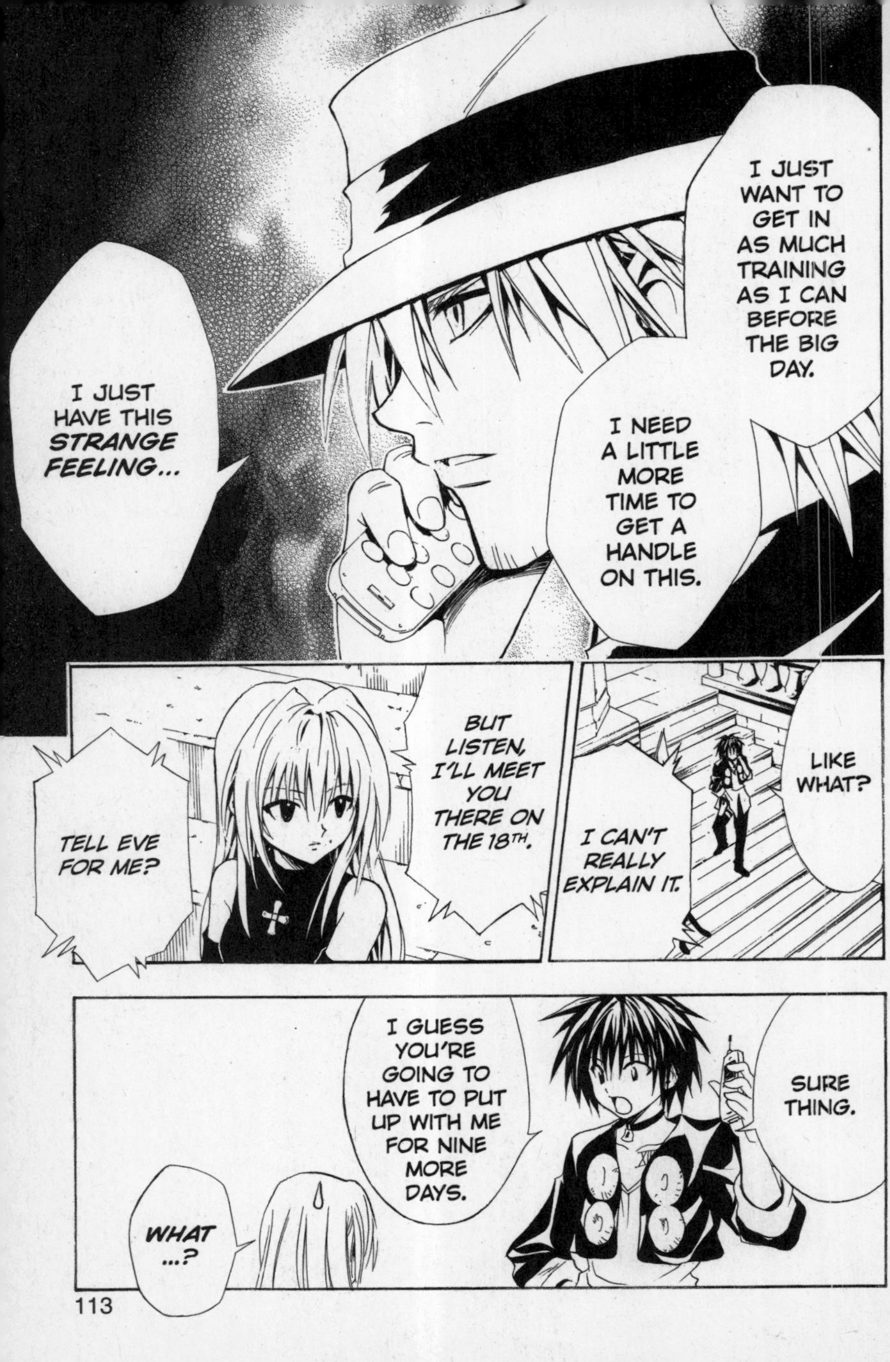
I JUST WANT TO GET IN AS MUCH TRAINING AS I CAN BEFORE THE BIG DAY.
I NEED A LITTLE MORE TIME TO GET A HANDLE ON THIS.
I JUST HAVE THIS *STRANGE FEELING...*
LIKE WHAT?
I CAN'T REALLY EXPLAIN IT.
BUT LISTEN, I'LL MEET YOU THERE ON THE 18TH.
TELL EVE FOR ME?
SURE THING.
I GUESS YOU'RE GOING TO HAVE TO PUT UP WITH ME FOR NINE MORE DAYS.
WHAT ...?

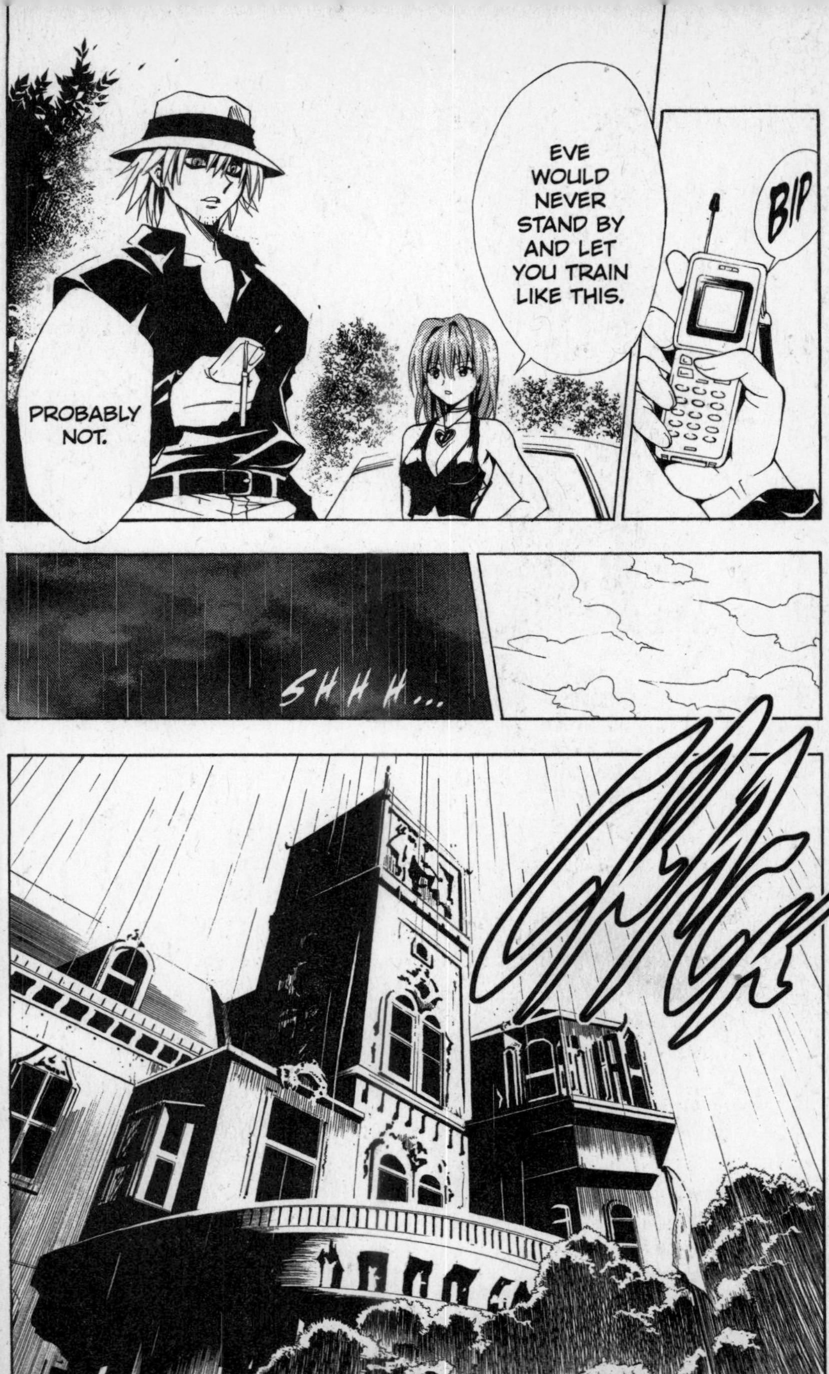
BIP
EVE WOULD NEVER STAND BY AND LET YOU TRAIN LIKE THIS.
PROBABLY NOT.
SHHH...

READ THIS WAY

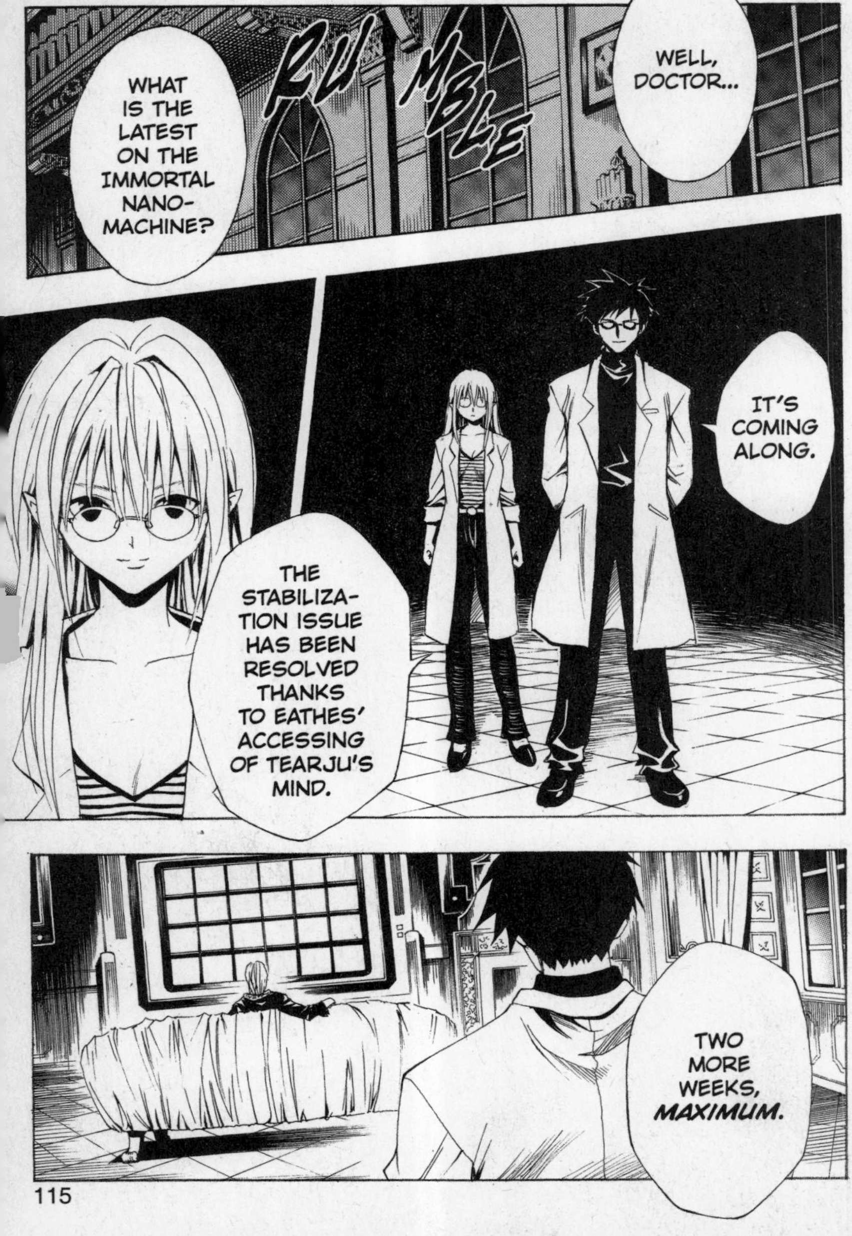

WELL, DOCTOR...
RUMBLE
WHAT IS THE LATEST ON THE IMMORTAL NANO-MACHINE?
IT'S COMING ALONG.
THE STABILIZATION ISSUE HAS BEEN RESOLVED THANKS TO EATHES' ACCESSING OF TEARJU'S MIND.
TWO MORE WEEKS, *MAXIMUM.*

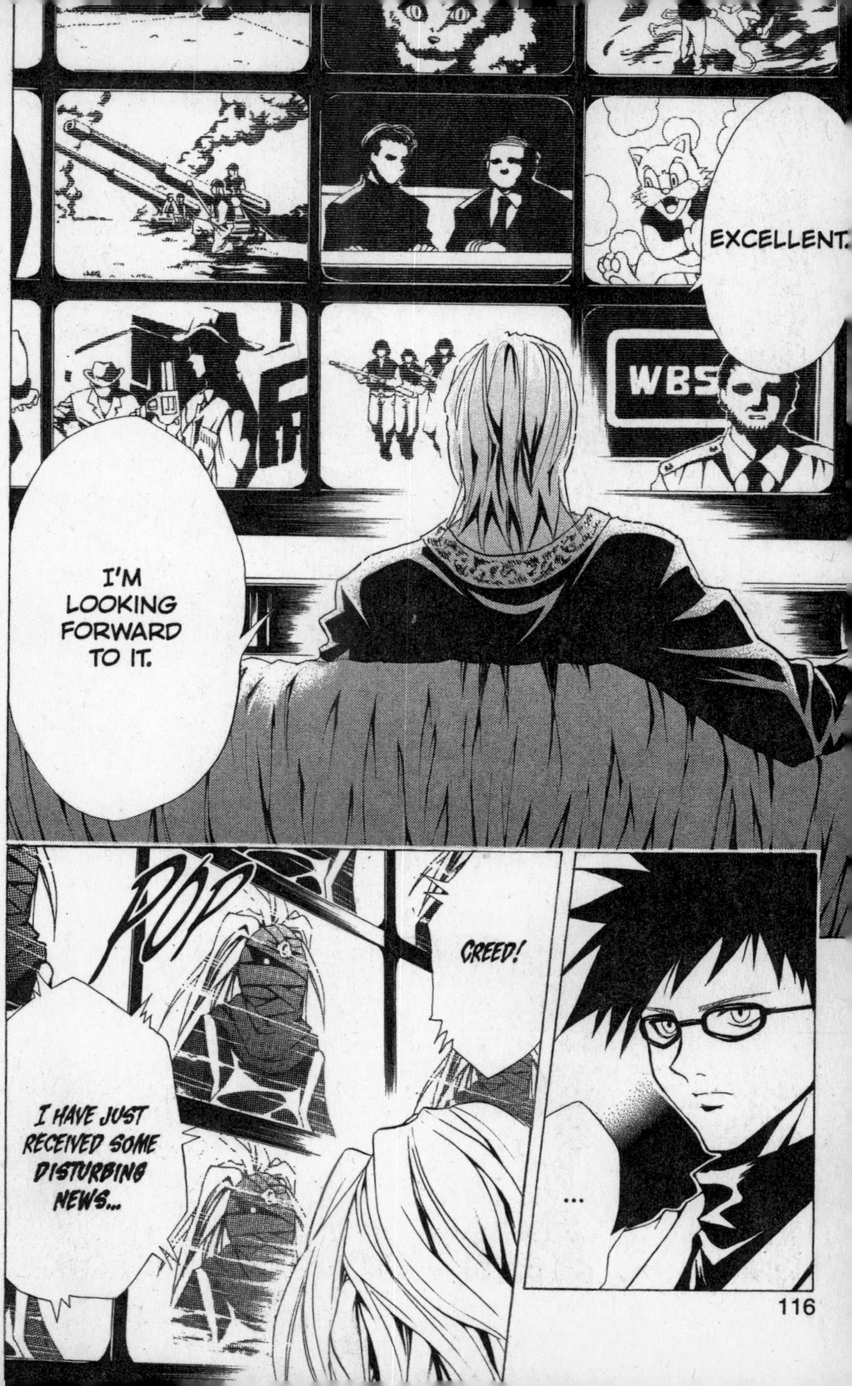
WBS
EXCELLENT.
I'M LOOKING FORWARD TO IT.
...
CREED!
POP
I HAVE JUST RECEIVED SOME DISTURBING NEWS...

READ THIS WAY

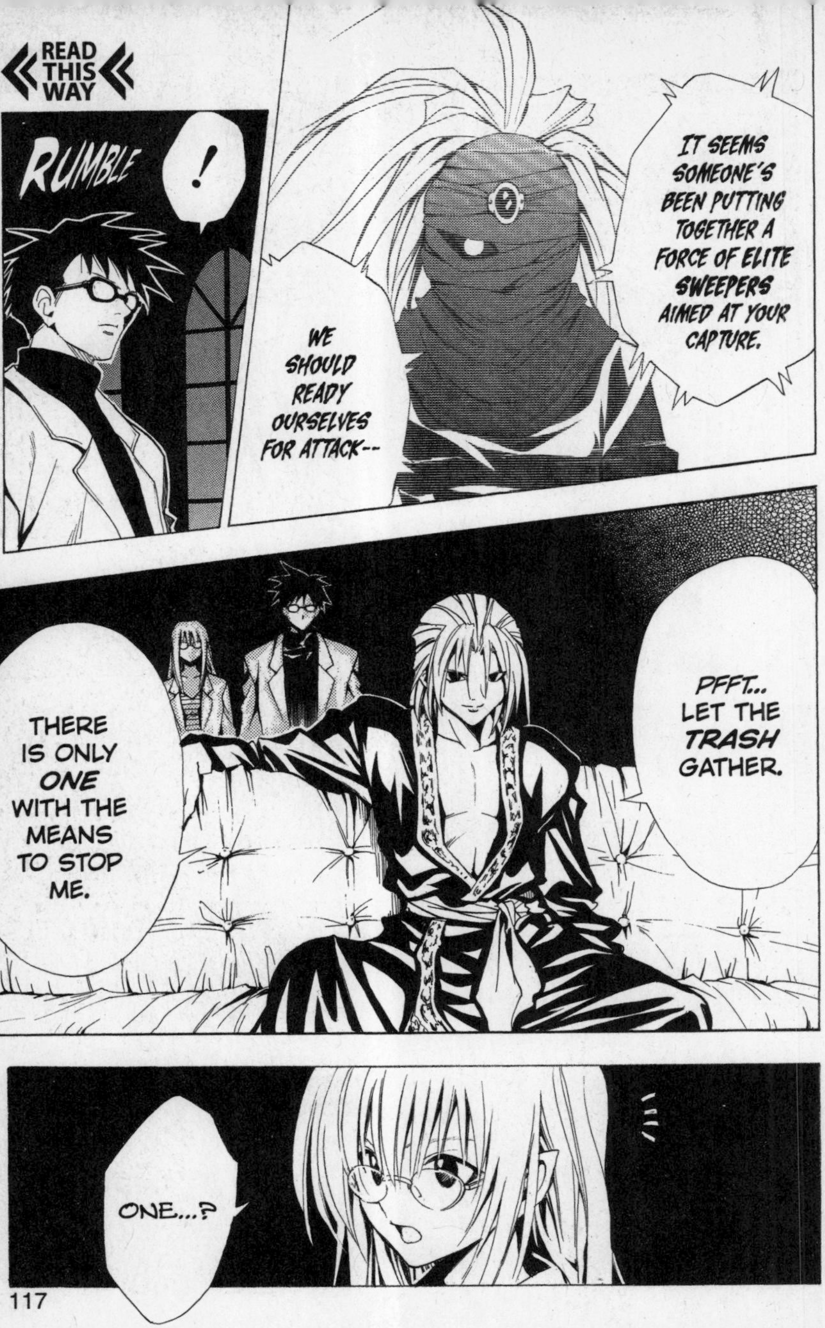

IT SEEMS SOMEONE'S BEEN PUTTING TOGETHER A FORCE OF ELITE SWEEPERS AIMED AT YOUR CAPTURE.
WE SHOULD READY OURSELVES FOR ATTACK--
RUMBLE
!
PFFT... LET THE *TRASH* GATHER.
THERE IS ONLY *ONE* WITH THE MEANS TO STOP ME.
ONE...?

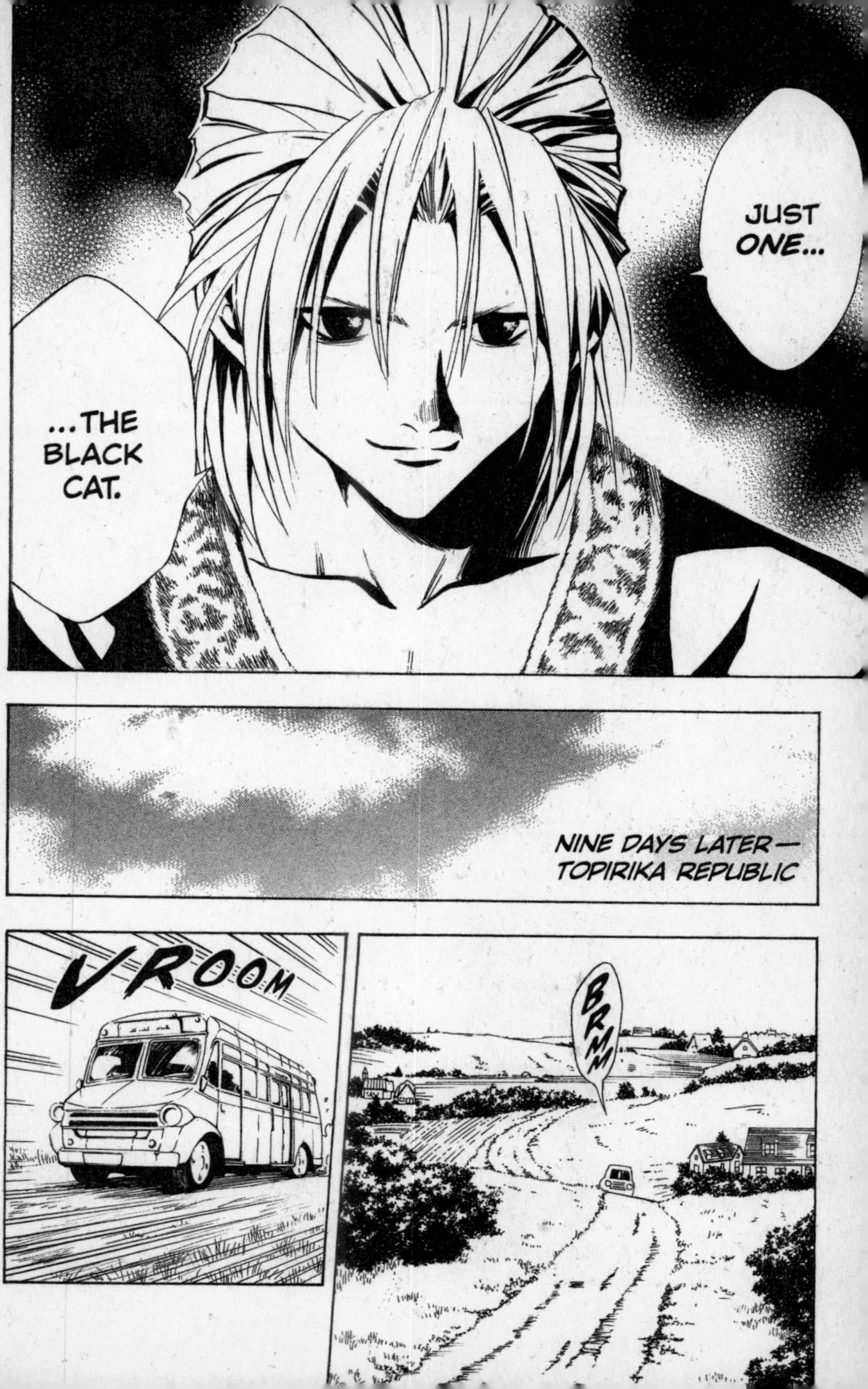
JUST ONE...
...THE BLACK CAT.
NINE DAYS LATER—
TOPIRIKA REPUBLIC
BRMM
VROOM

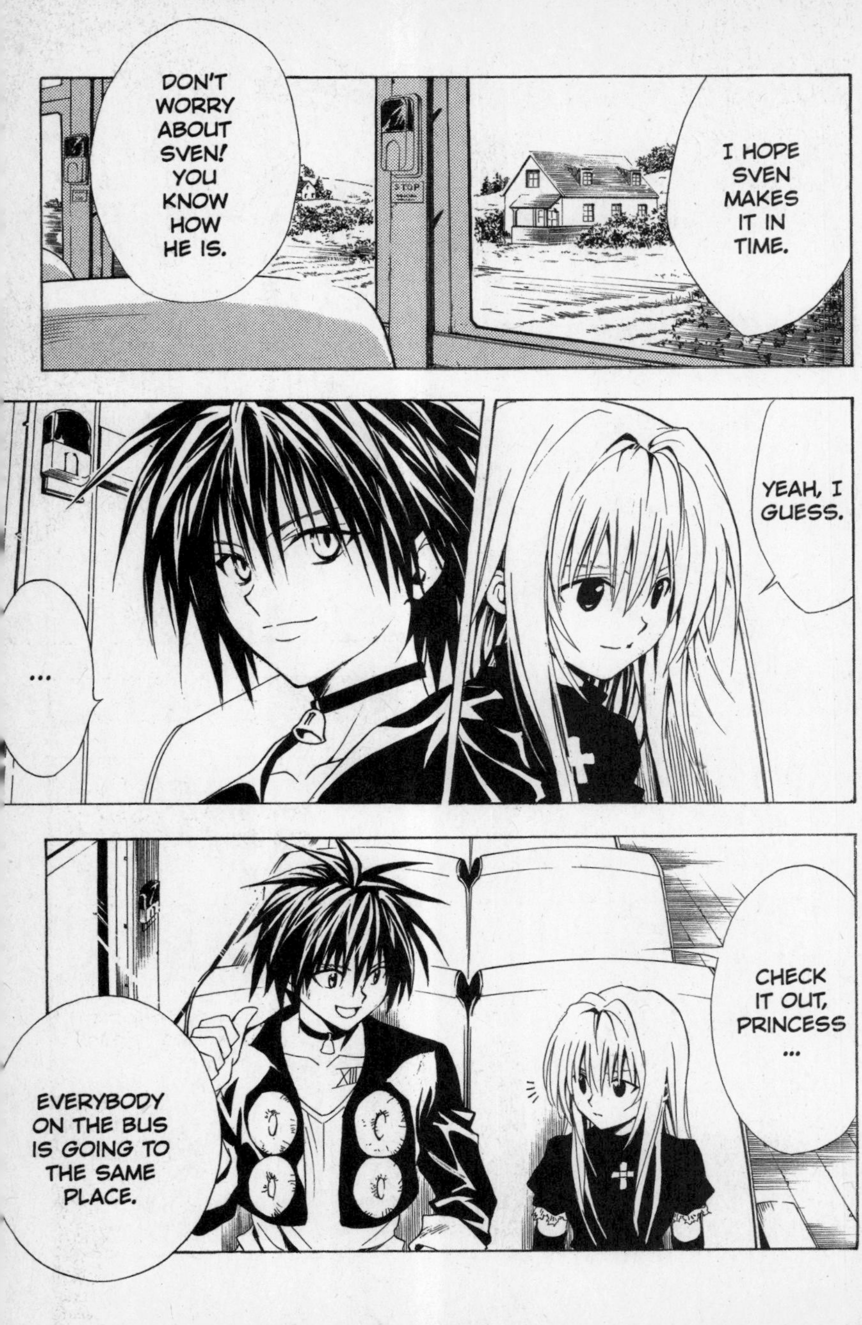
I HOPE SVEN MAKES IT IN TIME.
DON'T WORRY ABOUT SVEN! YOU KNOW HOW HE IS.
YEAH, I GUESS.
...
CHECK IT OUT, PRINCESS ...
EVERYBODY ON THE BUS IS GOING TO THE SAME PLACE.

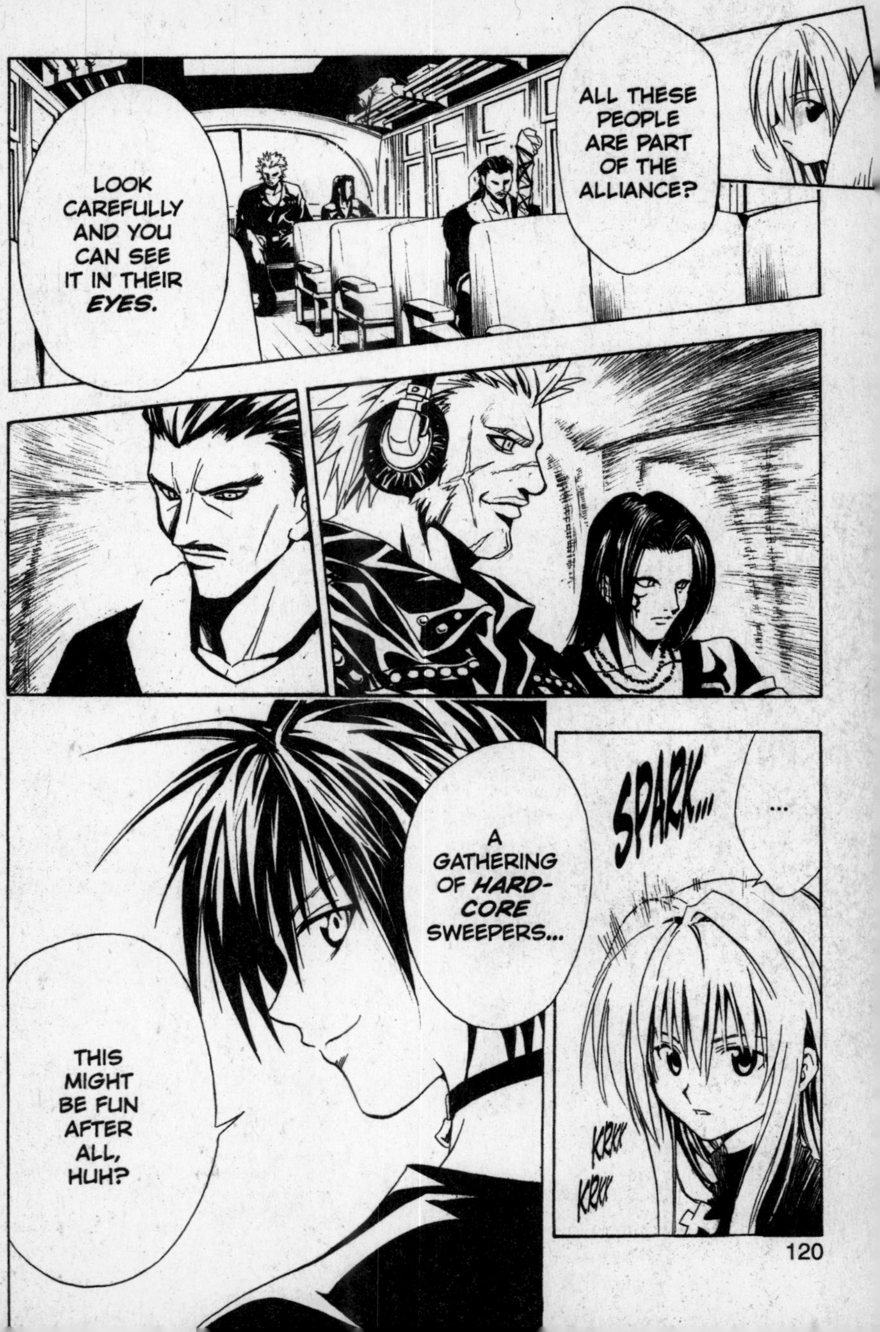
ALL THESE PEOPLE ARE PART OF THE ALLIANCE?
LOOK CAREFULLY AND YOU CAN SEE IT IN THEIR EYES.
SPARK...
...
KRKK KRKK
A GATHERING OF HARD-CORE SWEEPERS...
THIS MIGHT BE FUN AFTER ALL, HUH?

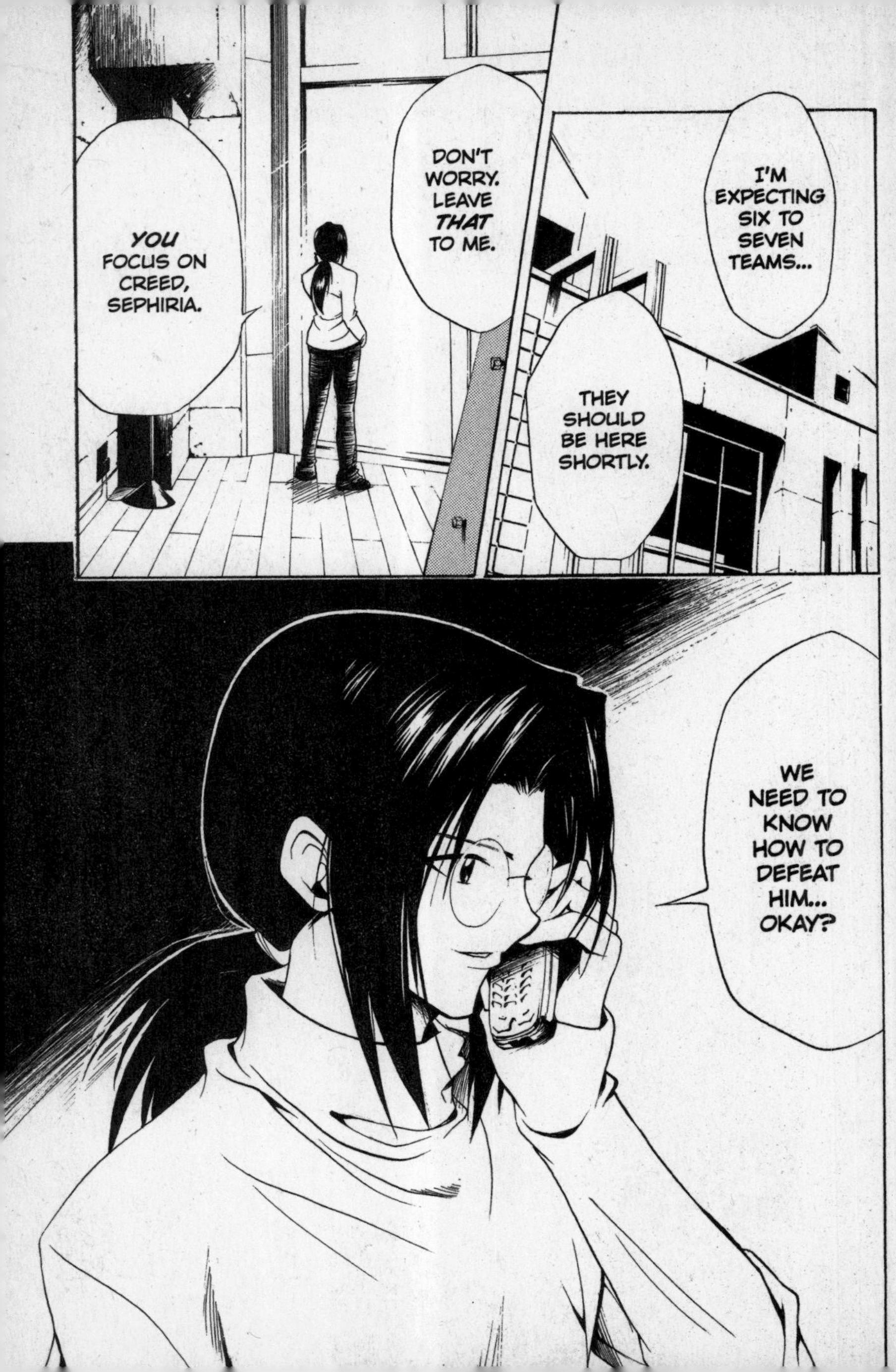
I'M EXPECTING SIX TO SEVEN TEAMS...
THEY SHOULD BE HERE SHORTLY.
DON'T WORRY. LEAVE *THAT* TO ME.
YOU FOCUS ON CREED, SEPHIRIA.
WE NEED TO KNOW HOW TO DEFEAT HIM... OKAY?

NOSTALGIC SERIES

NUMBER 5—MAYOR KARL

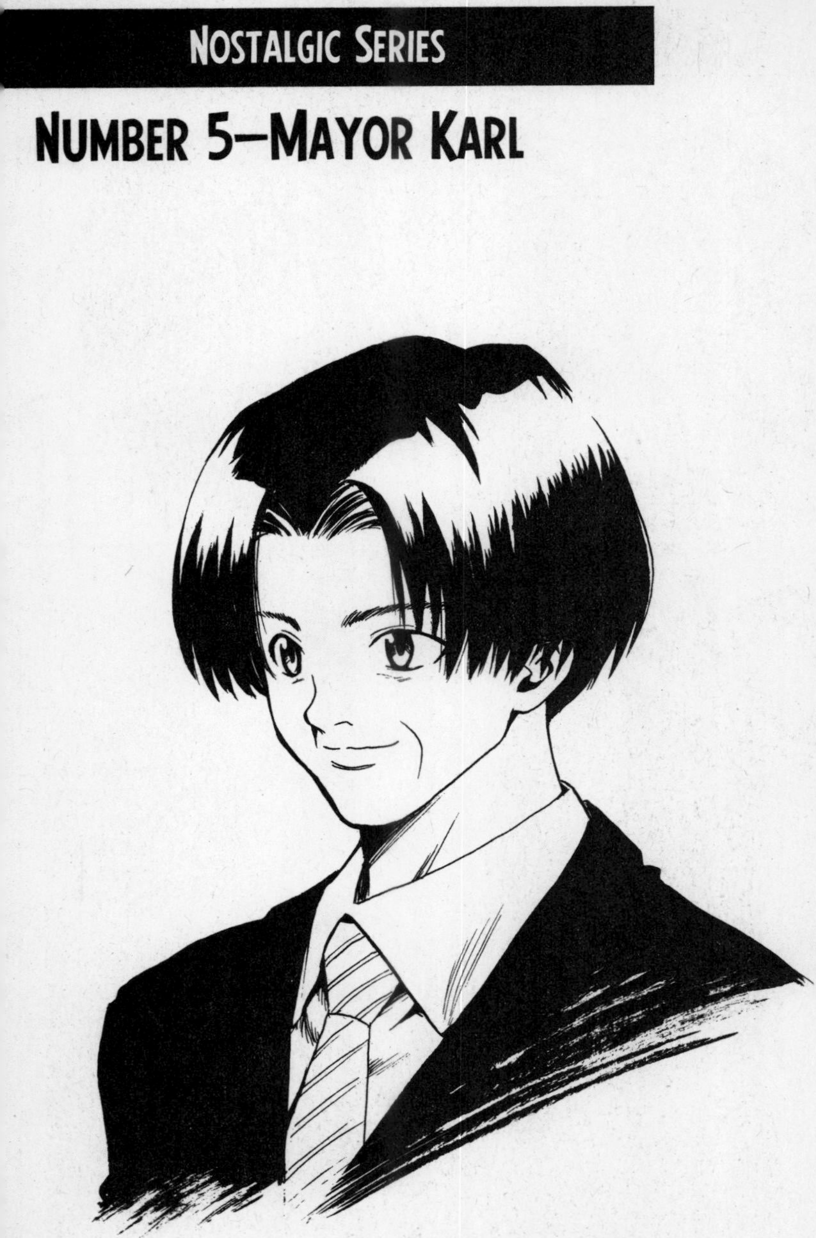

Chapter 129: Alliance

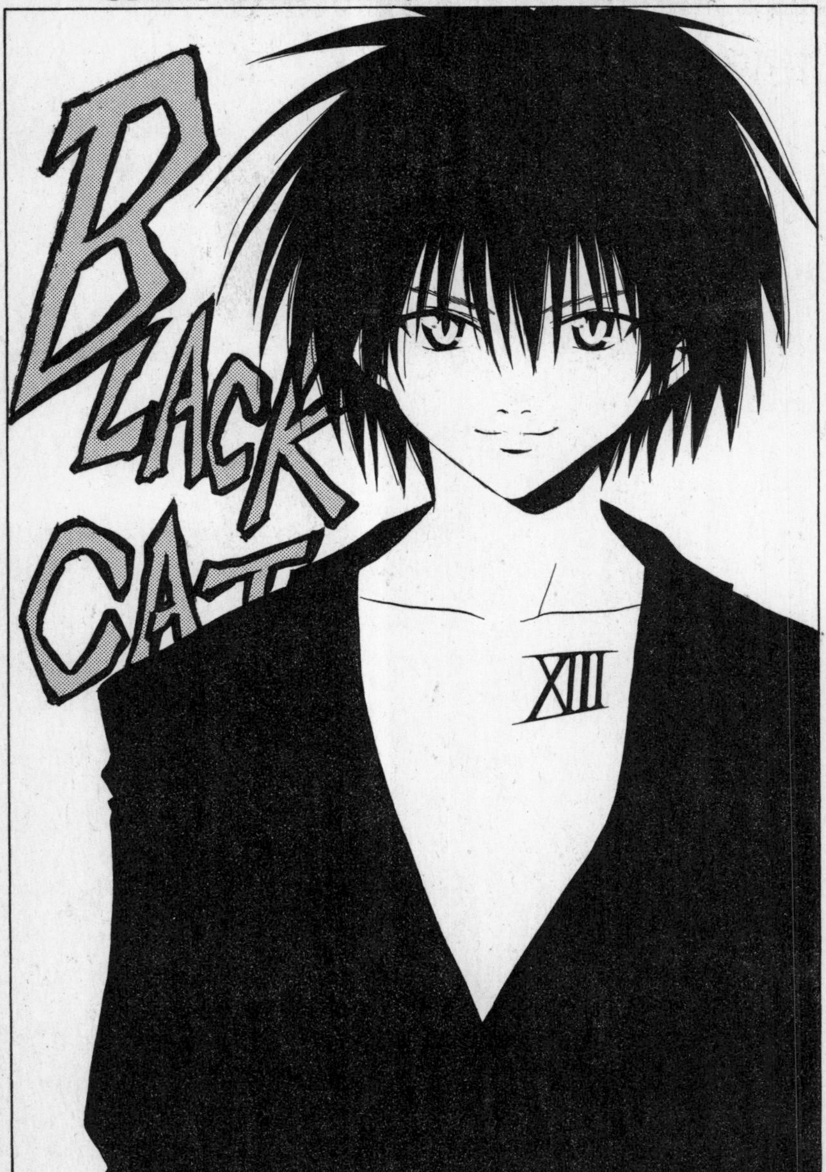

BLACK CAT
XIII

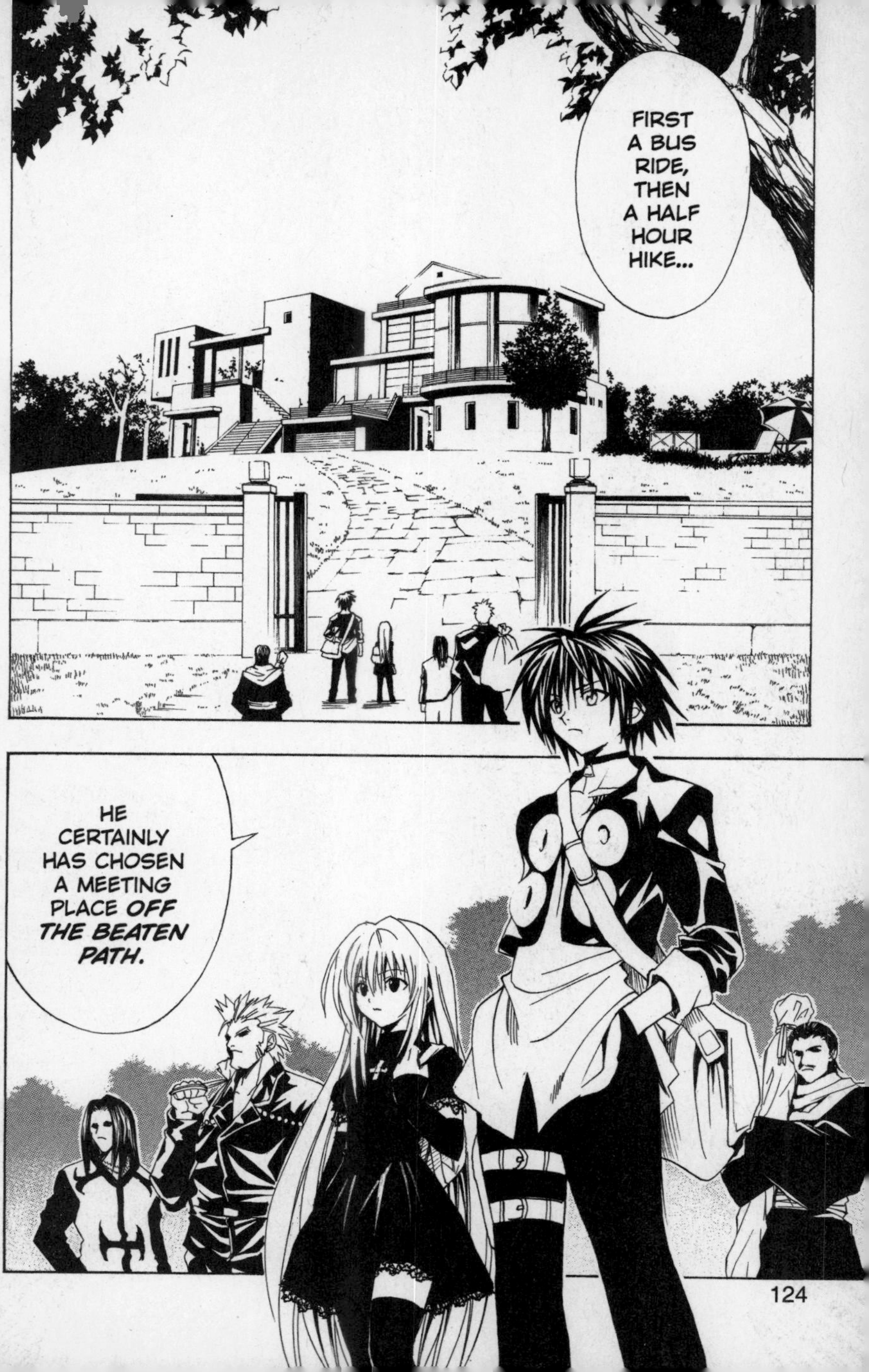
FIRST A BUS RIDE, THEN A HALF HOUR HIKE...
HE CERTAINLY HAS CHOSEN A MEETING PLACE OFF THE BEATEN PATH.

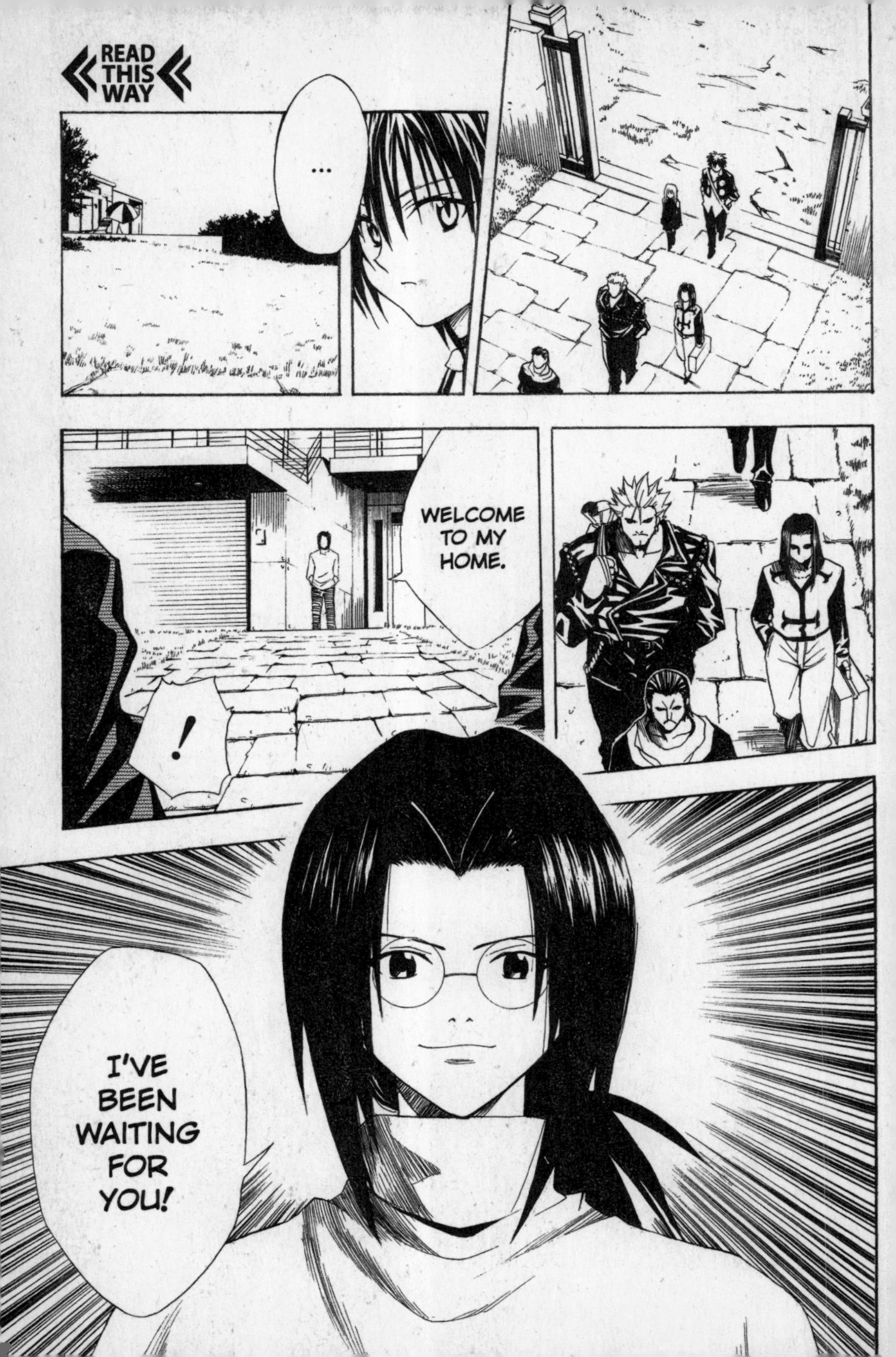
READ THIS WAY
...
WELCOME TO MY HOME.
!
I'VE BEEN WAITING FOR YOU!

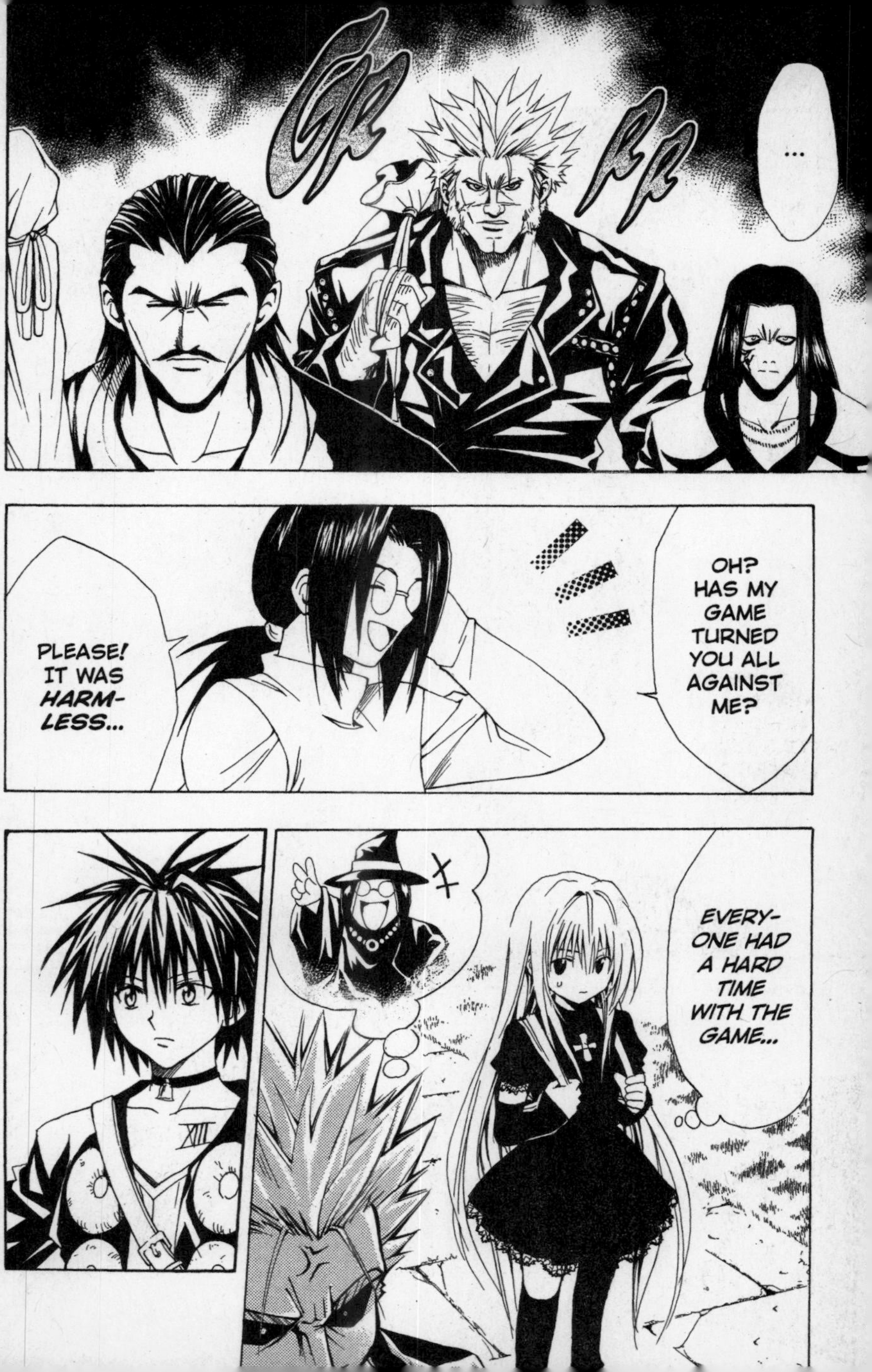
...
OH? HAS MY GAME TURNED YOU ALL AGAINST ME?
PLEASE! IT WAS HARMLESS...
EVERYONE HAD A HARD TIME WITH THE GAME...

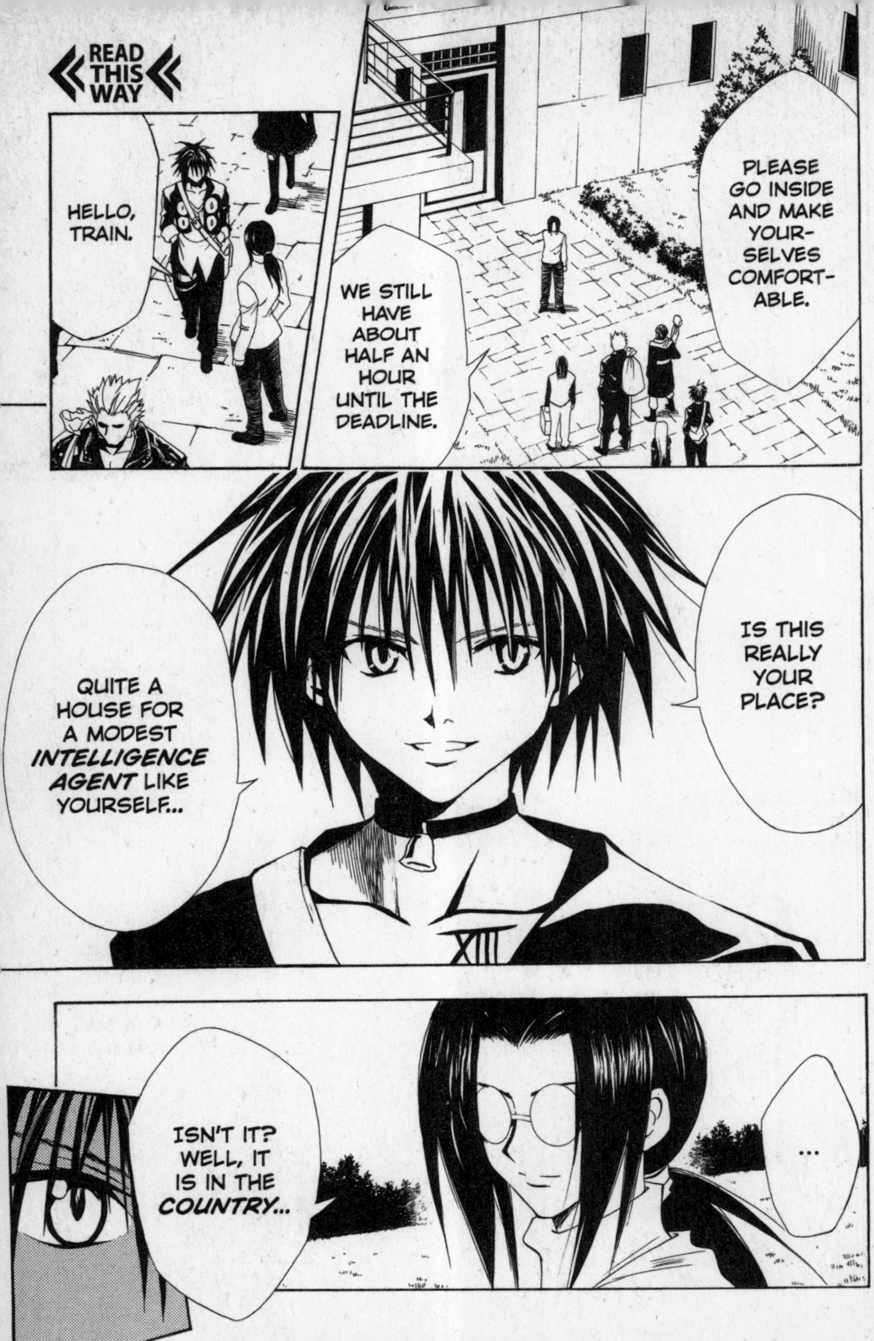
READ THIS WAY
PLEASE GO INSIDE AND MAKE YOURSELVES COMFORTABLE.
WE STILL HAVE ABOUT HALF AN HOUR UNTIL THE DEADLINE.
HELLO, TRAIN.
IS THIS REALLY YOUR PLACE?
QUITE A HOUSE FOR A MODEST INTELLIGENCE AGENT LIKE YOURSELF...
...
ISN'T IT? WELL, IT IS IN THE COUNTRY...

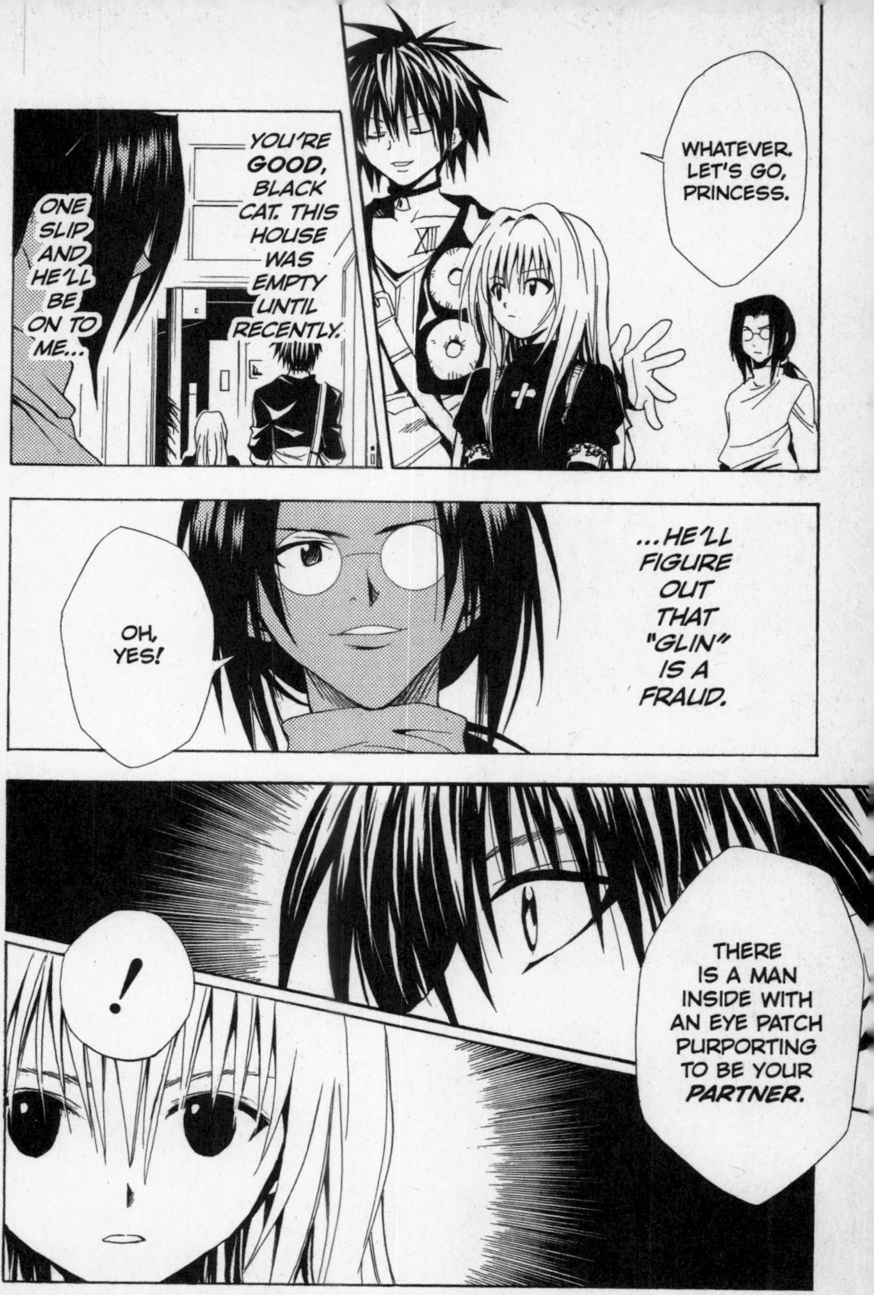
WHATEVER. LET'S GO, PRINCESS.
YOU'RE GOOD, BLACK CAT. THIS HOUSE WAS EMPTY UNTIL RECENTLY.
ONE SLIP AND HE'LL BE ON TO ME...
...HE'LL FIGURE OUT THAT "GLIN" IS A FRAUD.
OH, YES!
THERE IS A MAN INSIDE WITH AN EYE PATCH PURPORTING TO BE YOUR PARTNER.
!

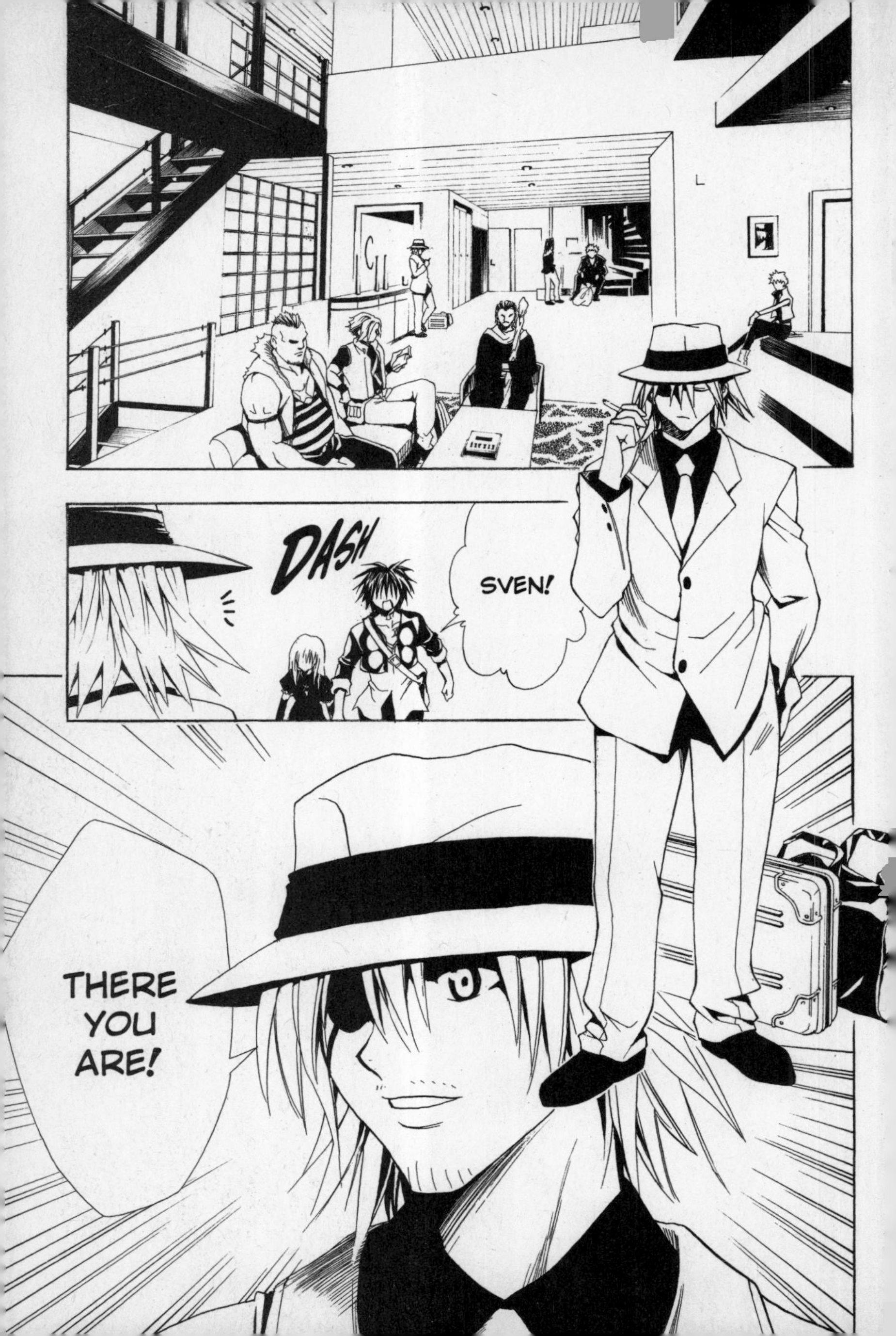
SVEN!
DASH
THERE YOU ARE!

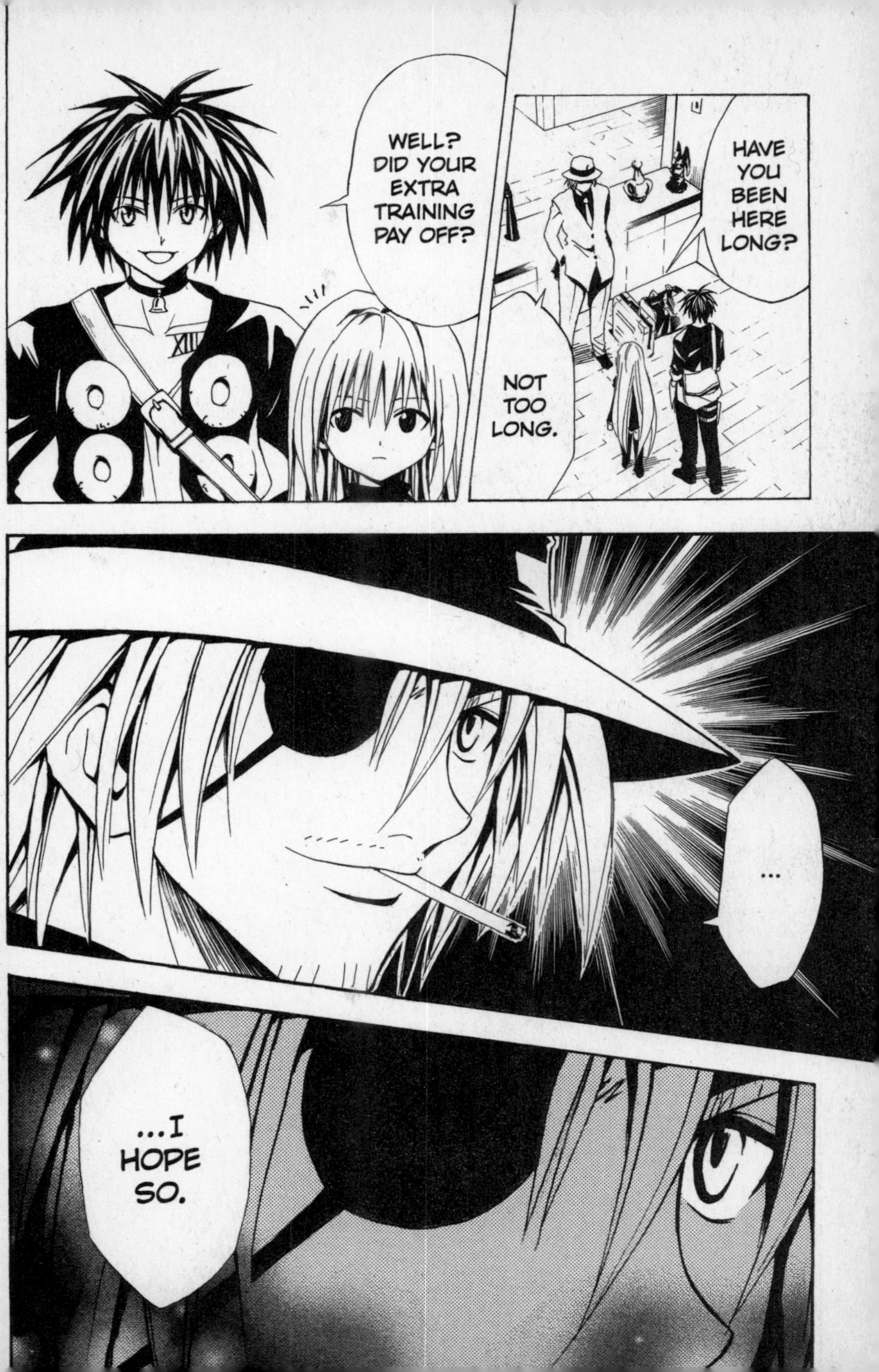
HAVE YOU BEEN HERE LONG?
NOT TOO LONG.
WELL? DID YOUR EXTRA TRAINING PAY OFF?
...
...I HOPE SO.

READ THIS WAY

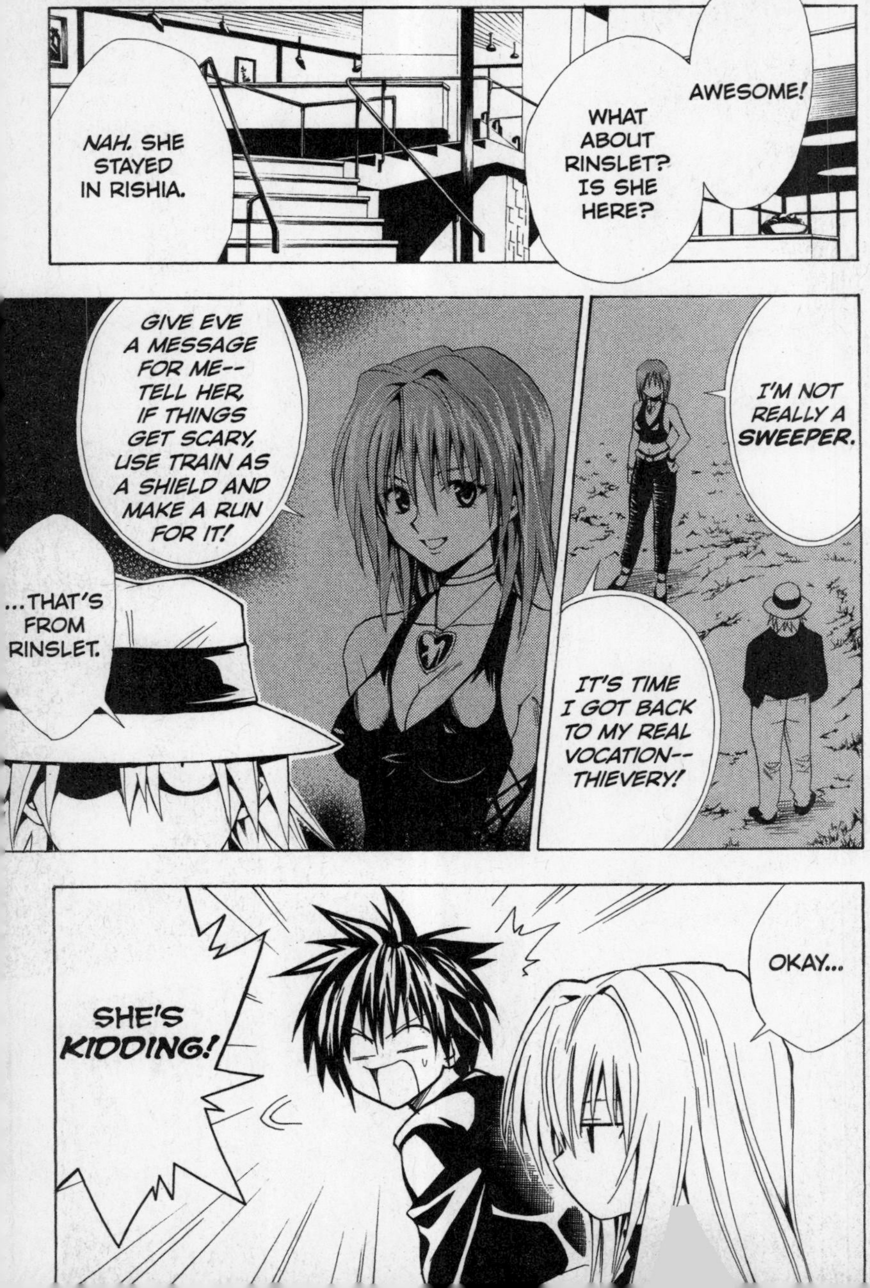

AWESOME!
WHAT ABOUT RINSLET? IS SHE HERE?
NAH. SHE STAYED IN RISHIA.
I'M NOT REALLY A SWEEPER.
IT'S TIME I GOT BACK TO MY REAL VOCATION--THIEVERY!
GIVE EVE A MESSAGE FOR ME--TELL HER, IF THINGS GET SCARY, USE TRAIN AS A SHIELD AND MAKE A RUN FOR IT!
...THAT'S FROM RINSLET.
OKAY...
SHE'S KIDDING!

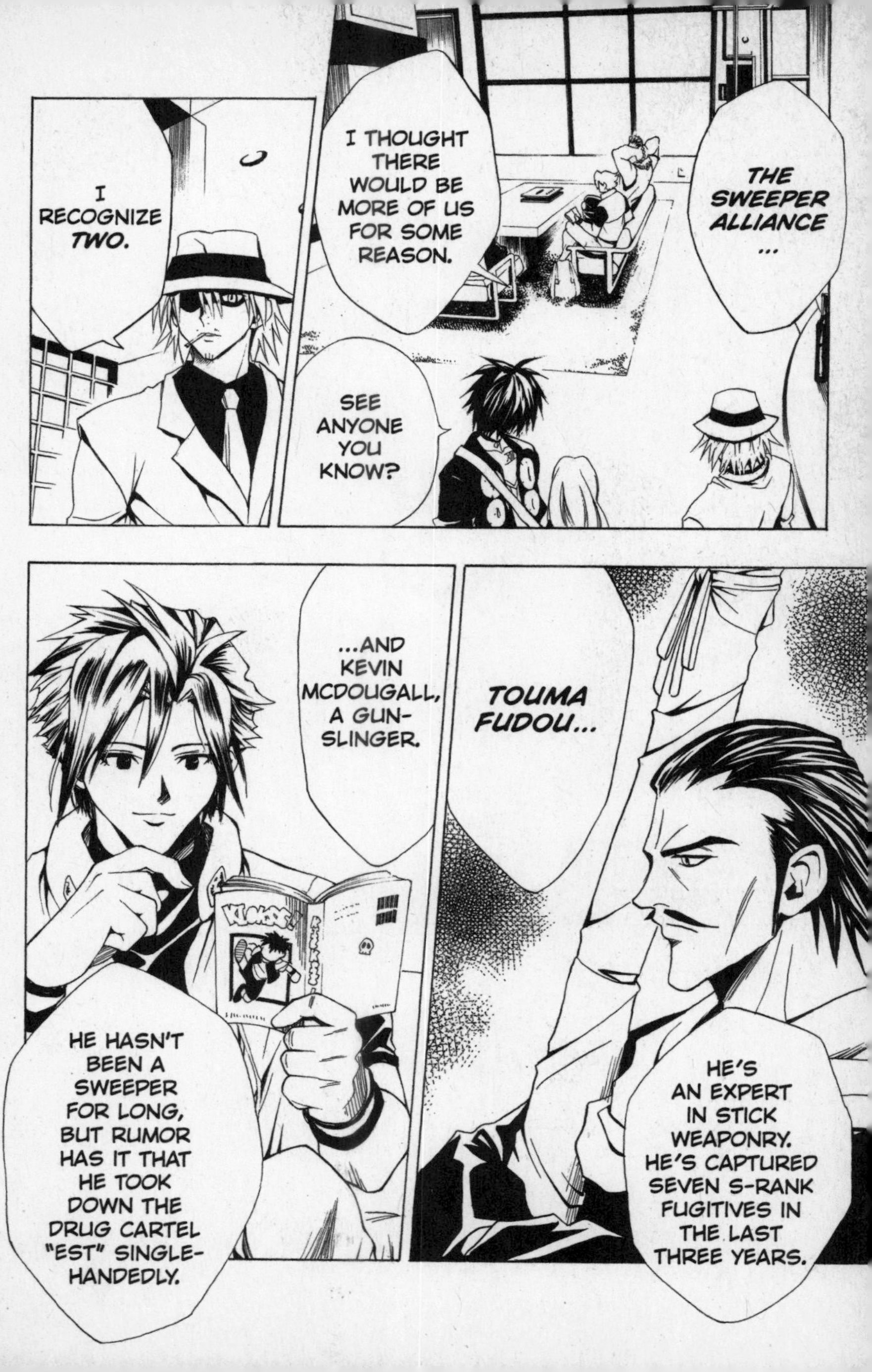
THE SWEEPER ALLIANCE ...
I THOUGHT THERE WOULD BE MORE OF US FOR SOME REASON.
SEE ANYONE YOU KNOW?
I RECOGNIZE TWO.
TOUMA FUDOU...
HE'S AN EXPERT IN STICK WEAPONRY. HE'S CAPTURED SEVEN S-RANK FUGITIVES IN THE LAST THREE YEARS.
...AND KEVIN MCDOUGALL, A GUN-SLINGER.
HE HASN'T BEEN A SWEEPER FOR LONG, BUT RUMOR HAS IT THAT HE TOOK DOWN THE DRUG CARTEL "EST" SINGLE-HANDEDLY.

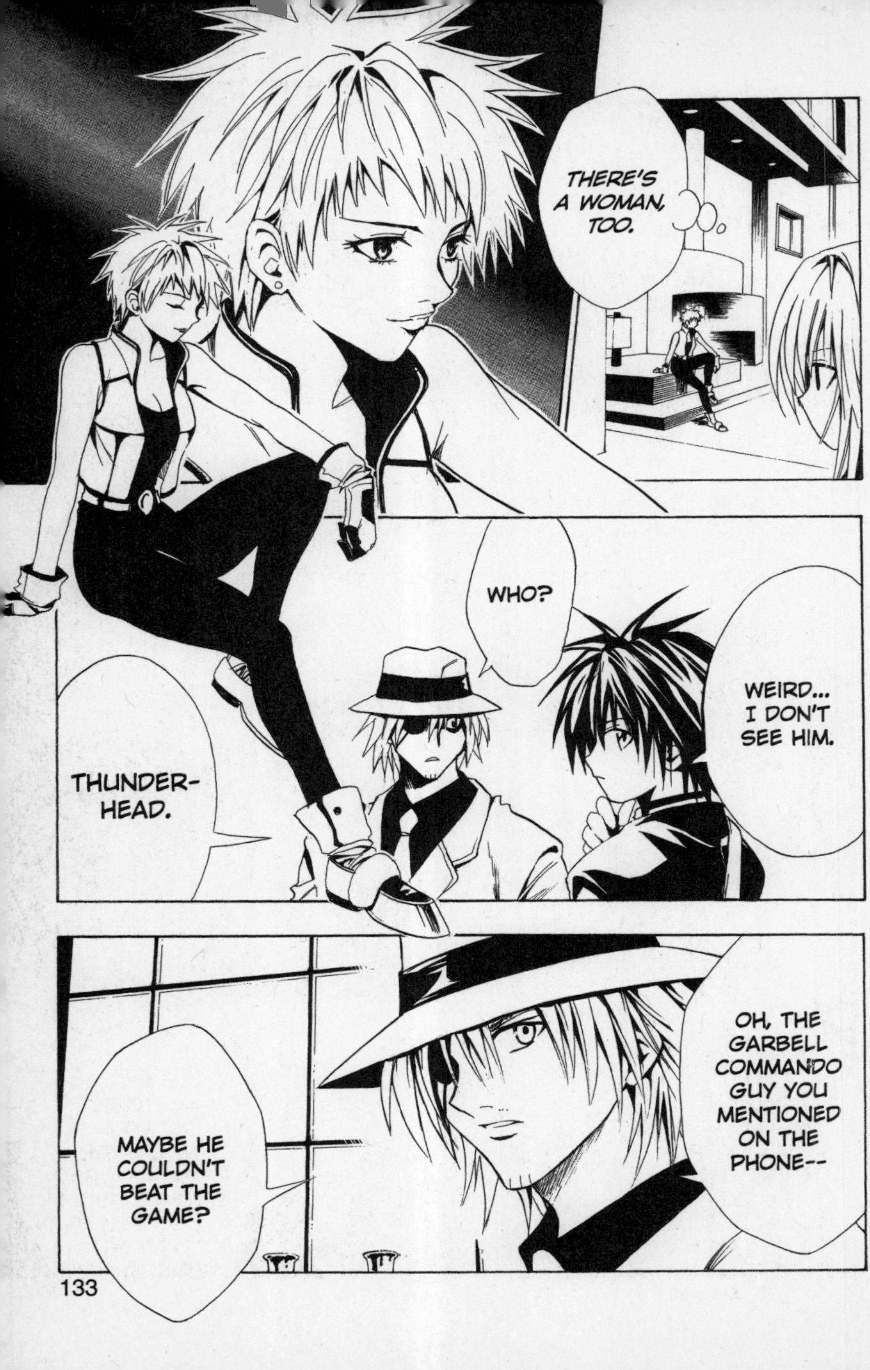
THERE'S A WOMAN, TOO.
WEIRD... I DON'T SEE HIM.
WHO?
THUNDER-HEAD.
OH, THE GARBELL COMMANDO GUY YOU MENTIONED ON THE PHONE--
MAYBE HE COULDN'T BEAT THE GAME?

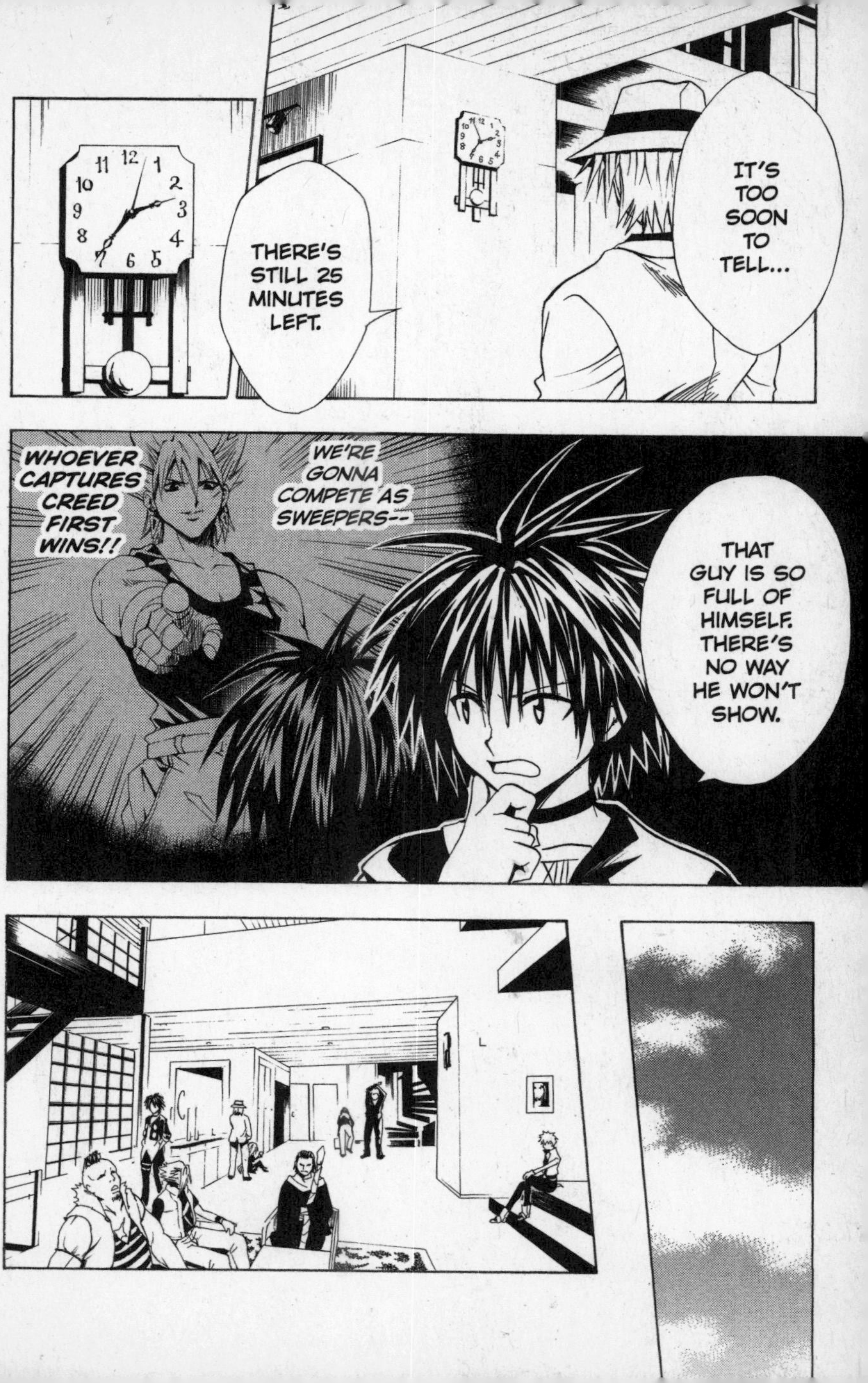
IT'S TOO SOON TO TELL...
THERE'S STILL 25 MINUTES LEFT.
THAT GUY IS SO FULL OF HIMSELF. THERE'S NO WAY HE WON'T SHOW.
WE'RE GONNA COMPETE AS SWEEPERS--
WHOEVER CAPTURES CREED FIRST WINS!!

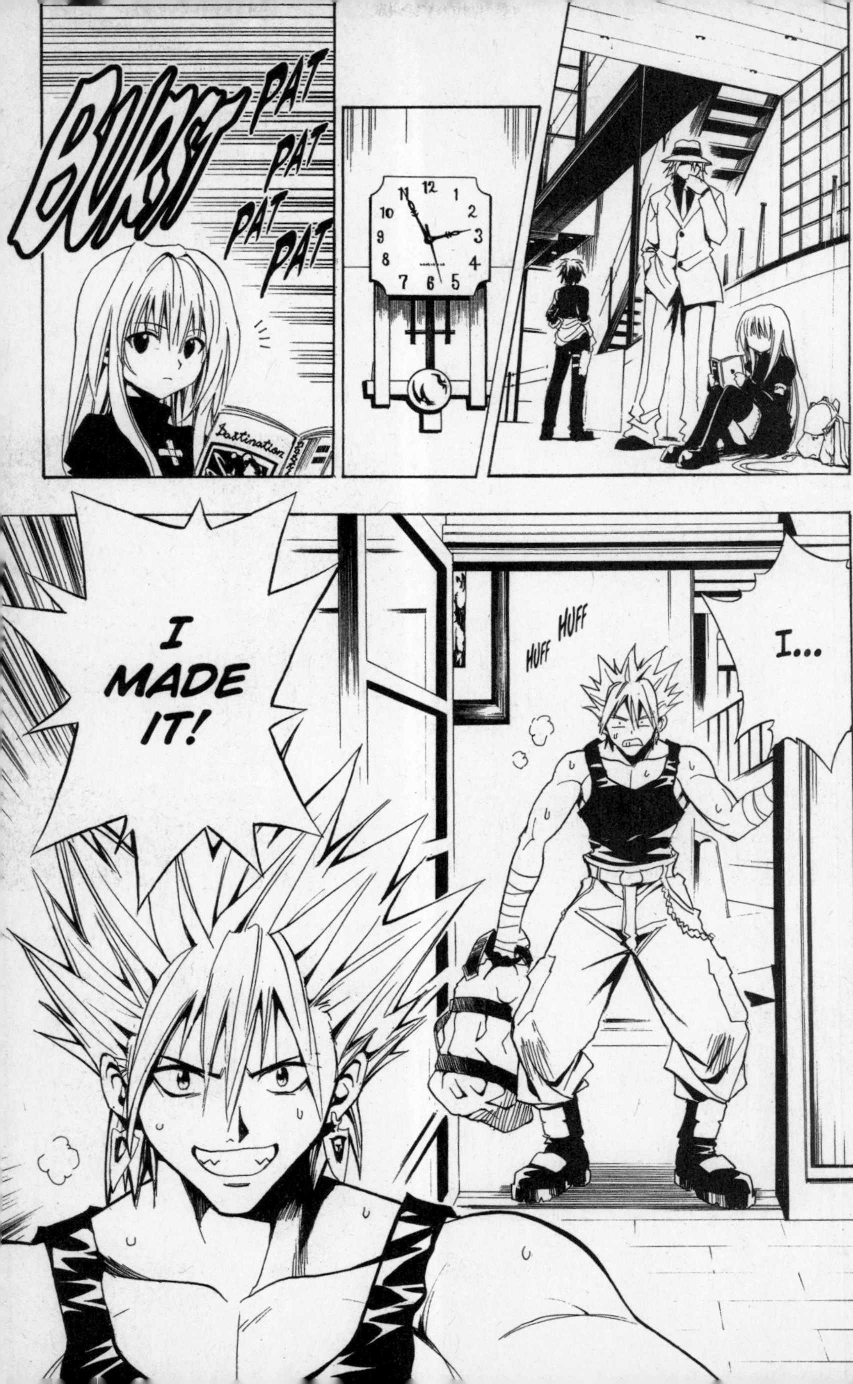
PAT PAT PAT PAT
HUFF HUFF
I...
I MADE IT!

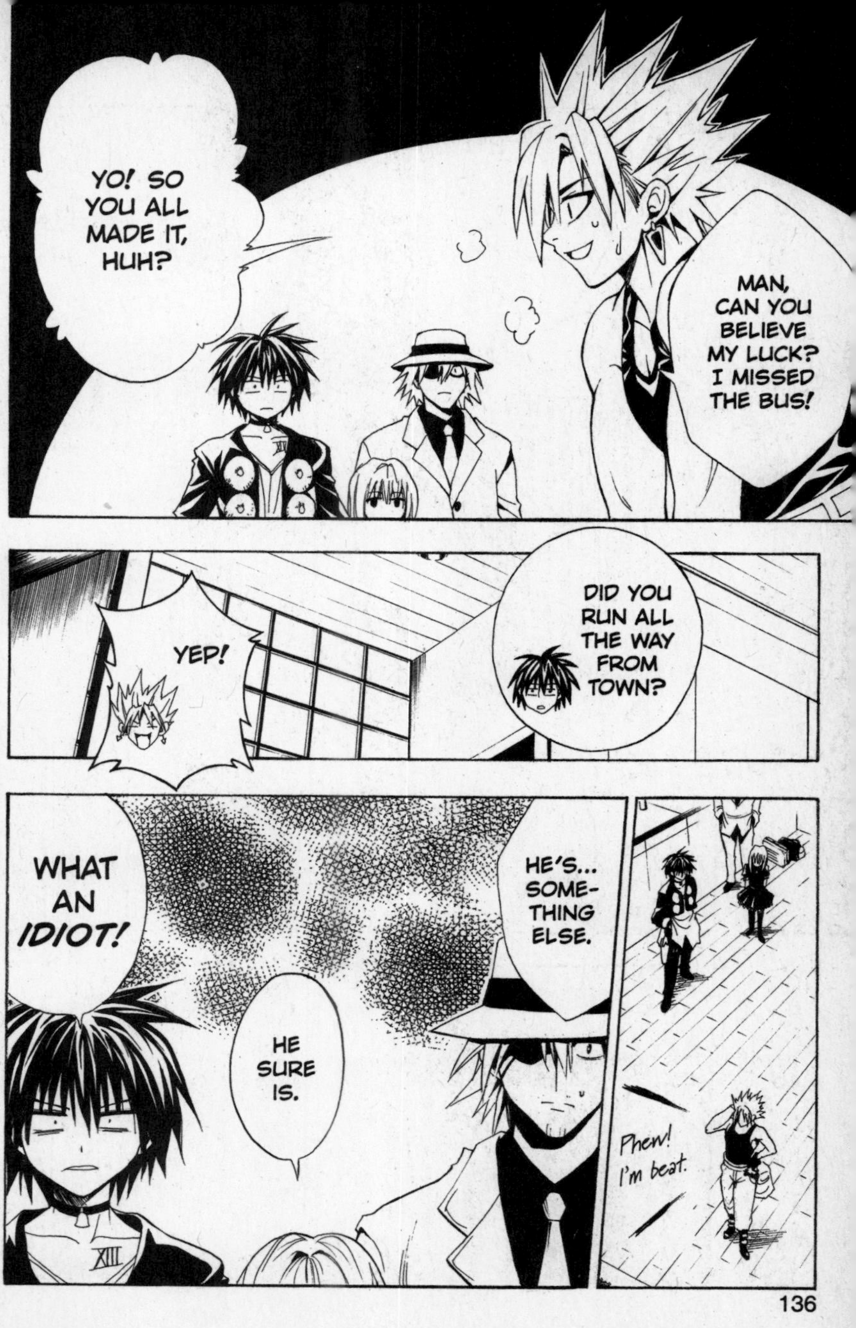
YO! SO YOU ALL MADE IT, HUH?
MAN, CAN YOU BELIEVE MY LUCK? I MISSED THE BUS!
DID YOU RUN ALL THE WAY FROM TOWN?
YEP!
Phew! I'm beat.
HE'S... SOME-THING ELSE.
HE SURE IS.
WHAT AN *IDIOT!*

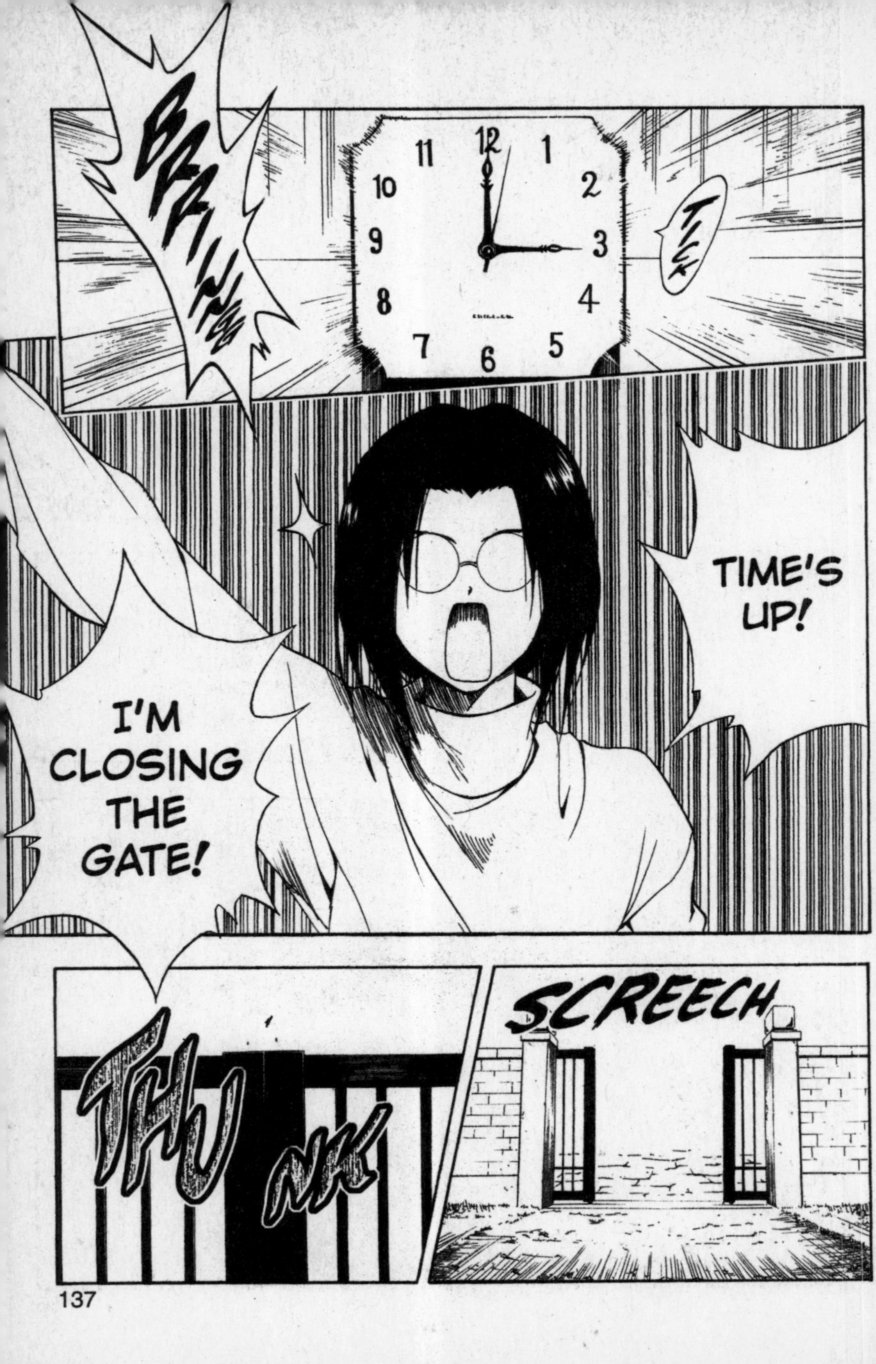
TICK
TIME'S UP!
I'M CLOSING THE GATE!
SCREECH
THUNK

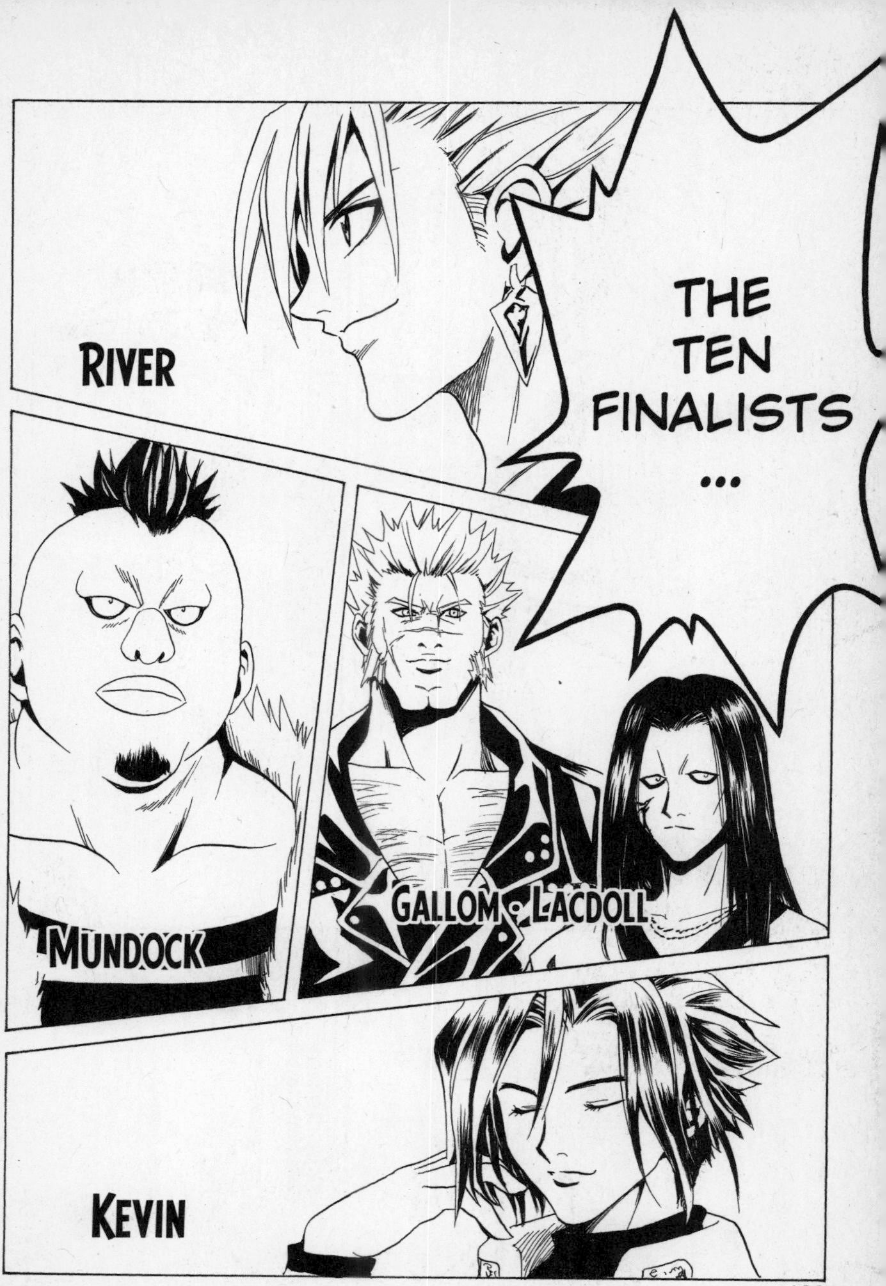
THE TEN FINALISTS ...
RIVER
GALLOM
LACDOLL
MUNDOCK
KEVIN

READ THIS WAY

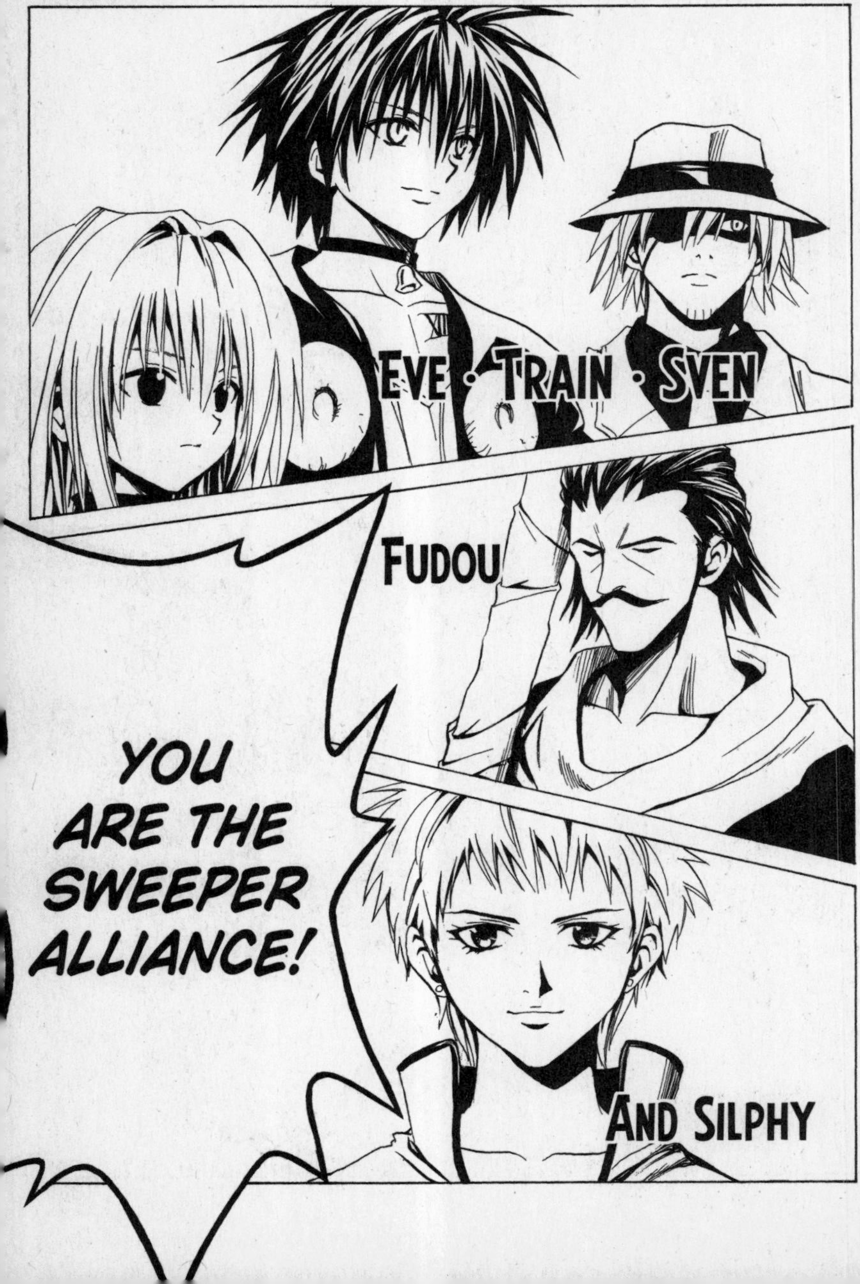
EVE · TRAIN · SVEN
FUDOU
AND SILPHY
YOU ARE THE SWEEPER ALLIANCE!

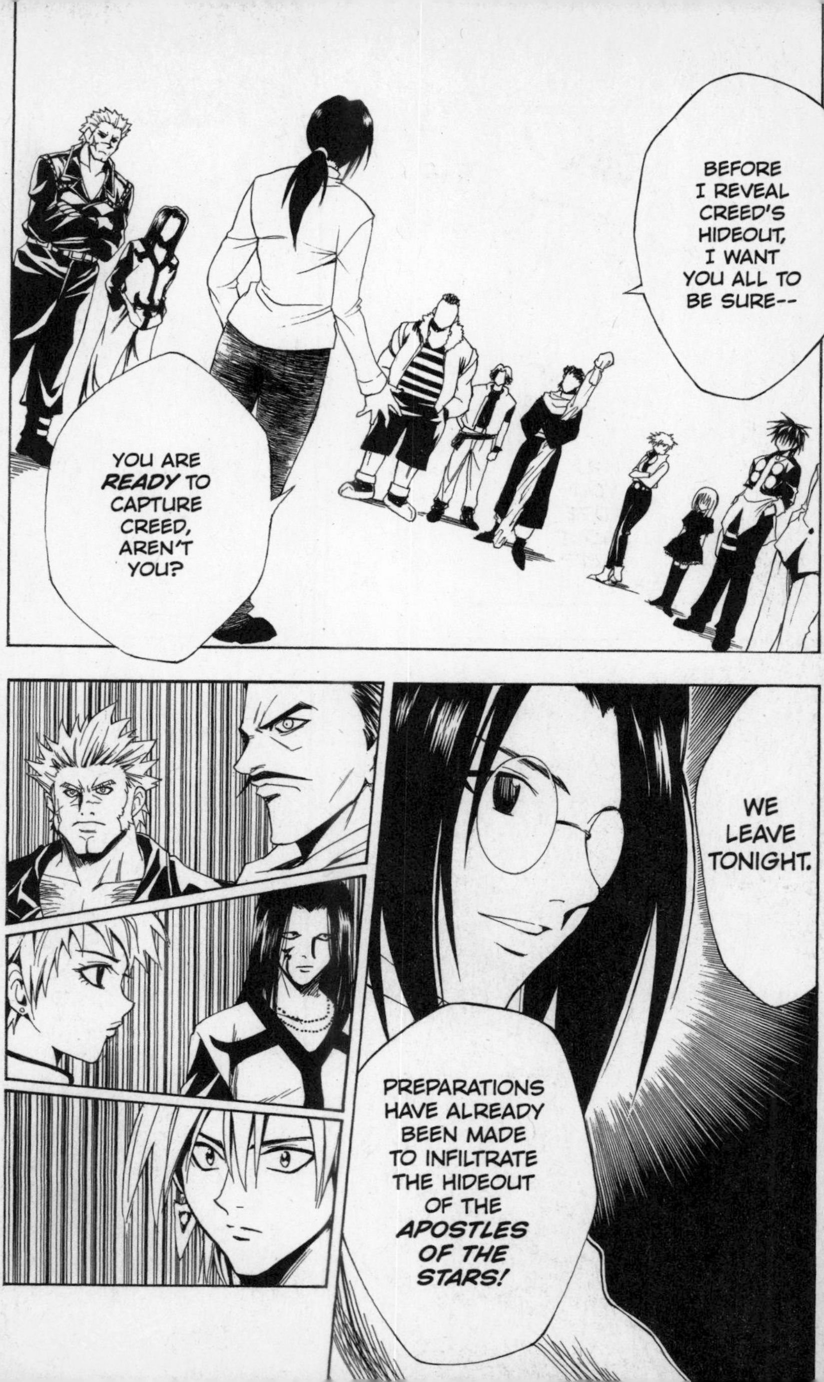
BEFORE I REVEAL CREED'S HIDEOUT, I WANT YOU ALL TO BE SURE--
YOU ARE *READY* TO CAPTURE CREED, AREN'T YOU?
WE LEAVE TONIGHT.
PREPARATIONS HAVE ALREADY BEEN MADE TO INFILTRATE THE HIDEOUT OF THE *APOSTLES OF THE STARS!*

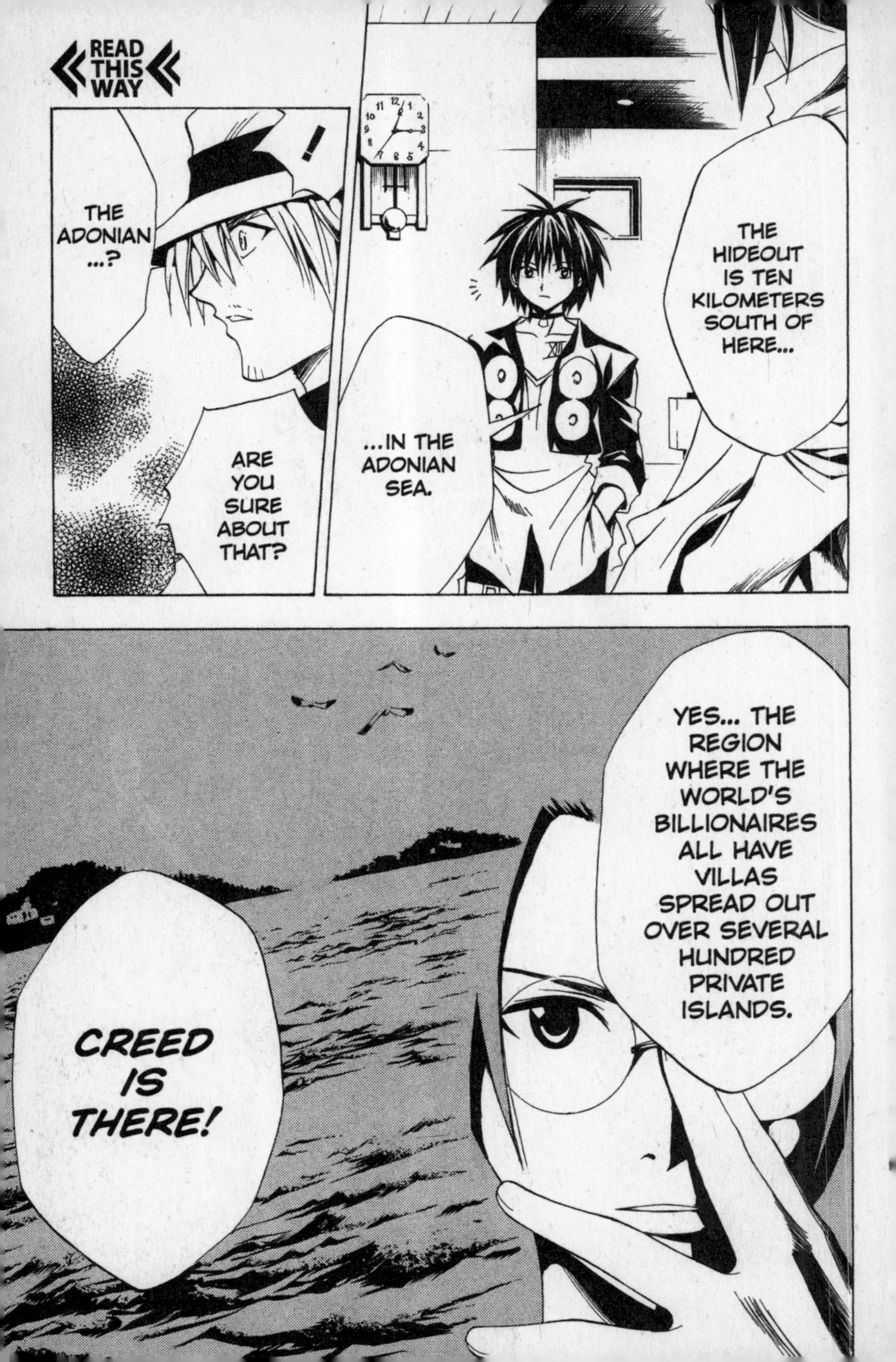
READ THIS WAY
THE HIDEOUT IS TEN KILOMETERS SOUTH OF HERE...
...IN THE ADONIAN SEA.
!
THE ADONIAN ...?
ARE YOU SURE ABOUT THAT?
YES... THE REGION WHERE THE WORLD'S BILLIONAIRES ALL HAVE VILLAS SPREAD OUT OVER SEVERAL HUNDRED PRIVATE ISLANDS.
CREED IS THERE!

Nostalgic Series

Number 6—Lugart Won

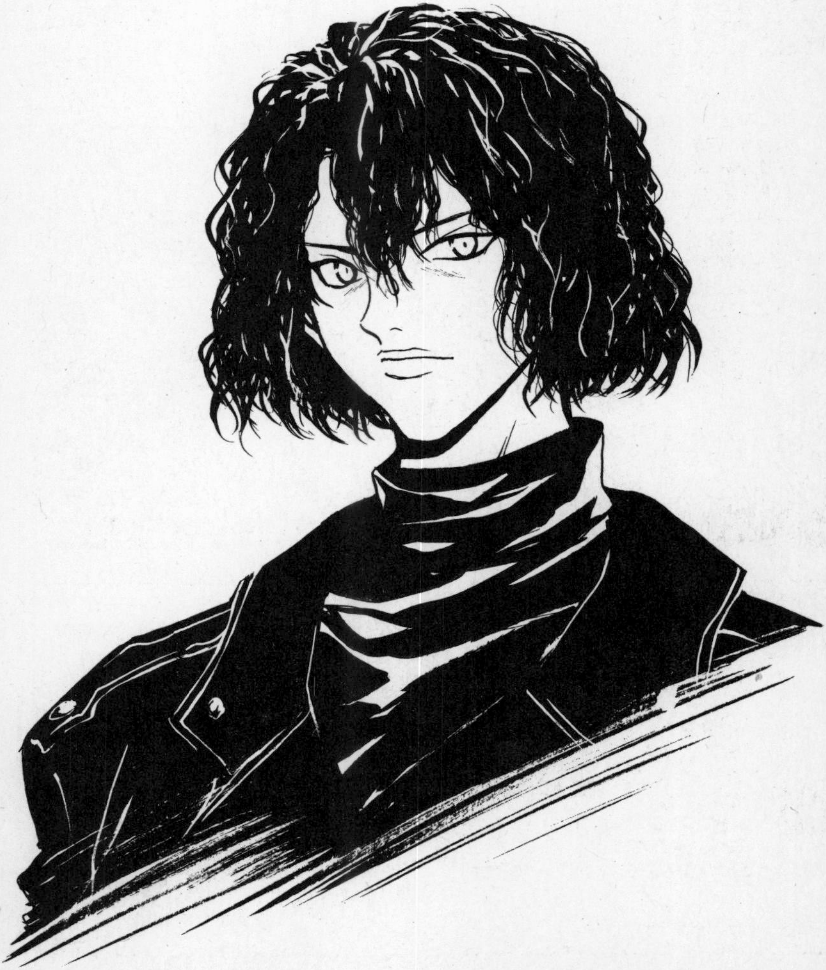

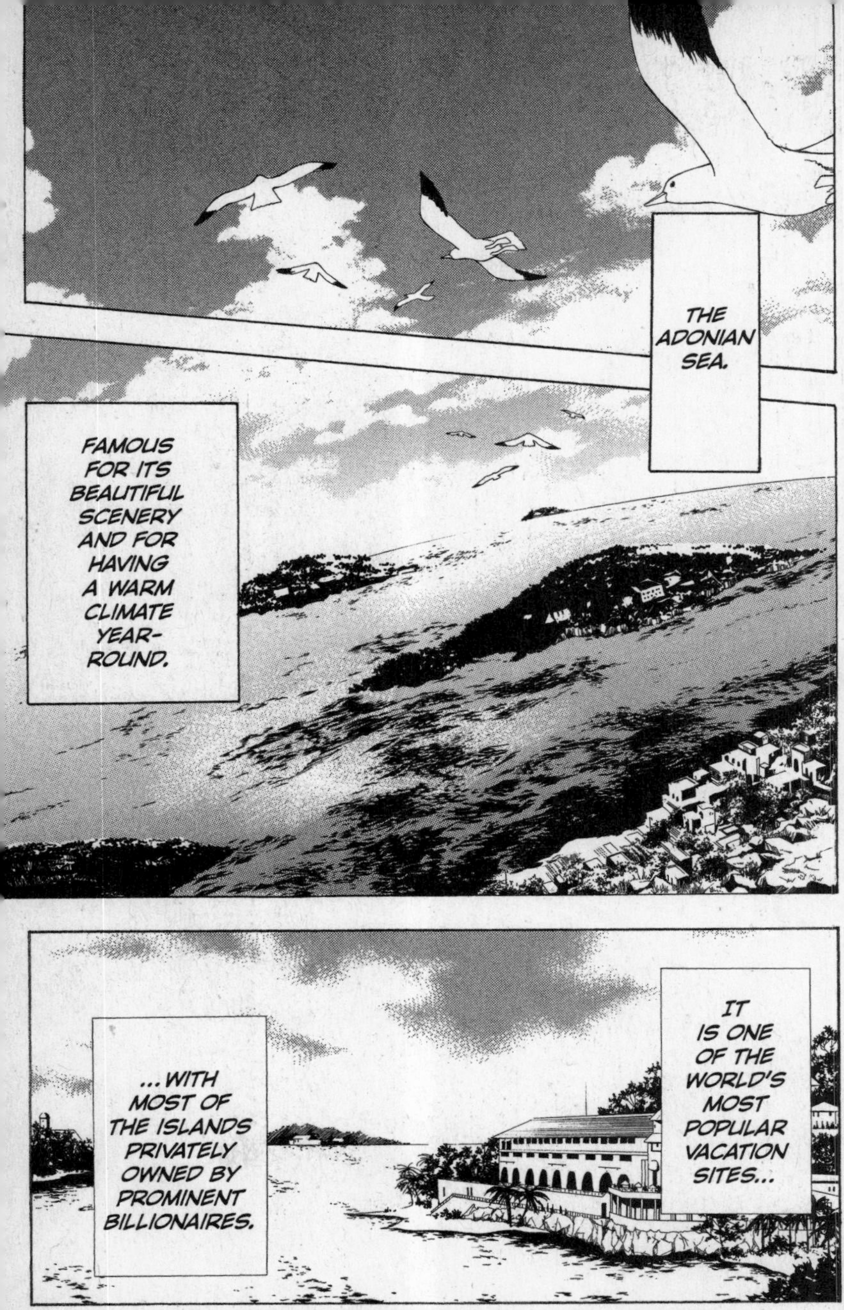
THE ADONIAN SEA.
FAMOUS FOR ITS BEAUTIFUL SCENERY AND FOR HAVING A WARM CLIMATE YEAR-ROUND.
IT IS ONE OF THE WORLD'S MOST POPULAR VACATION SITES...
...WITH MOST OF THE ISLANDS PRIVATELY OWNED BY PROMINENT BILLIONAIRES.

Chapter 130: Danger at Sea!!

Chapter 130: Danger at Sea!!

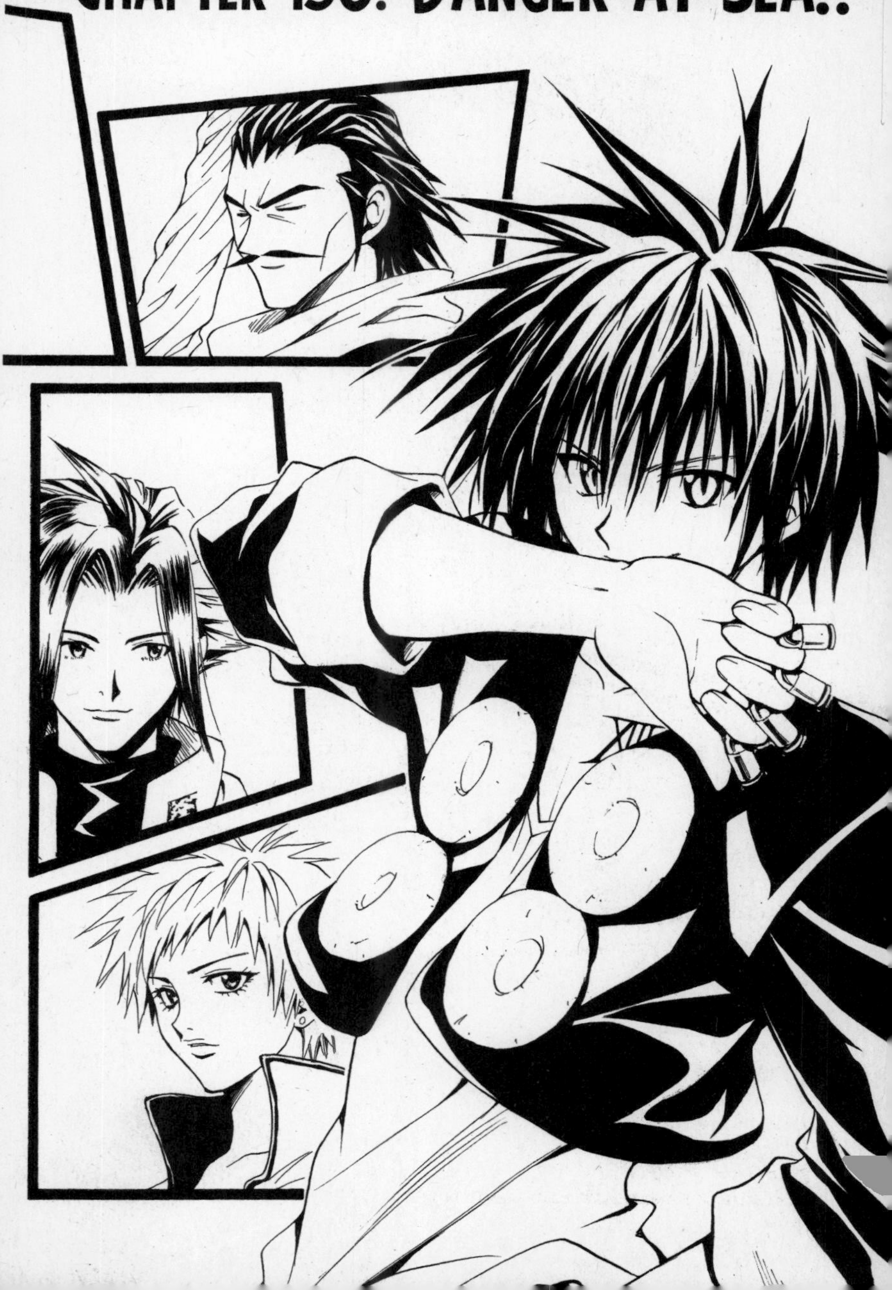

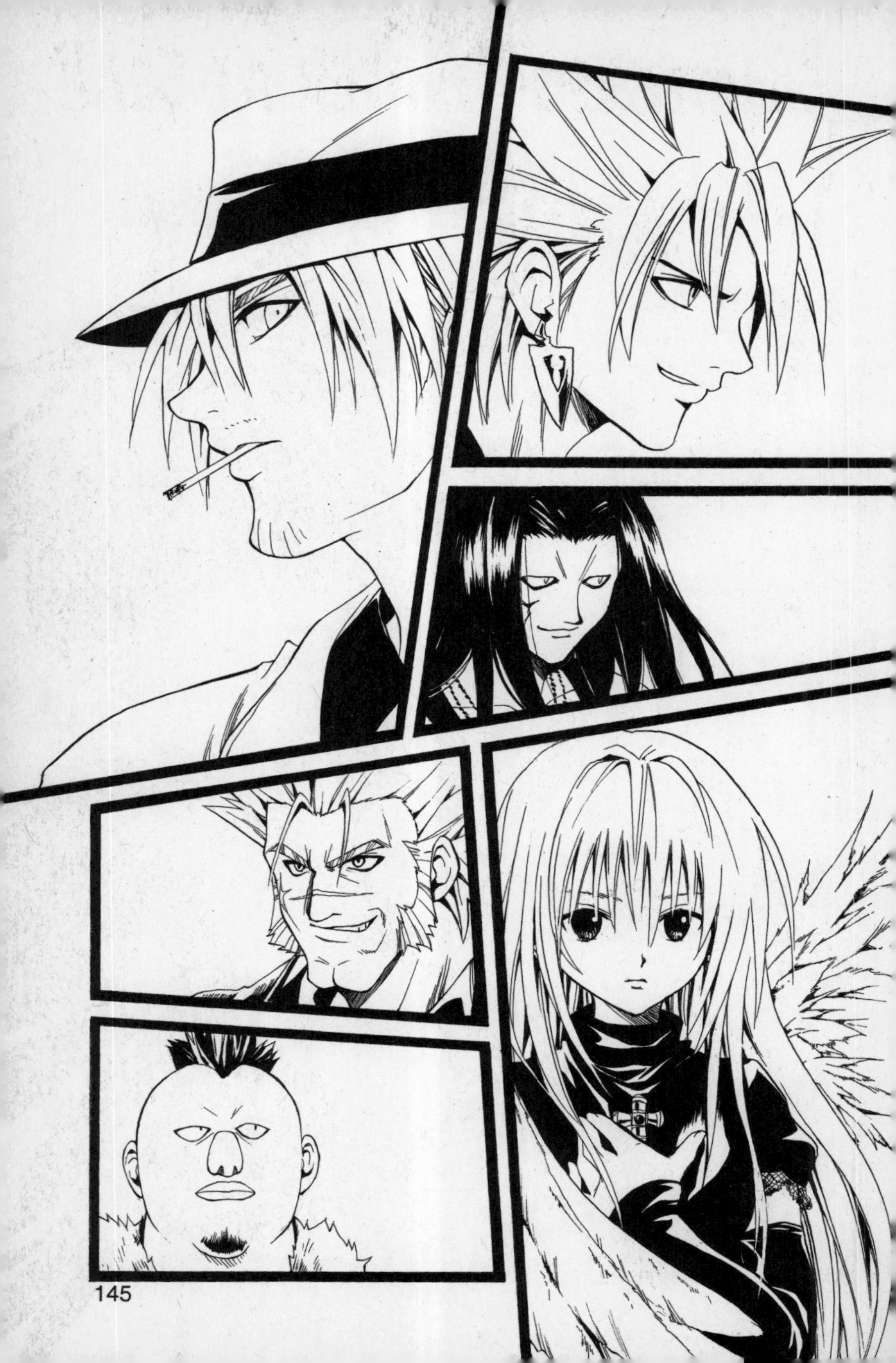

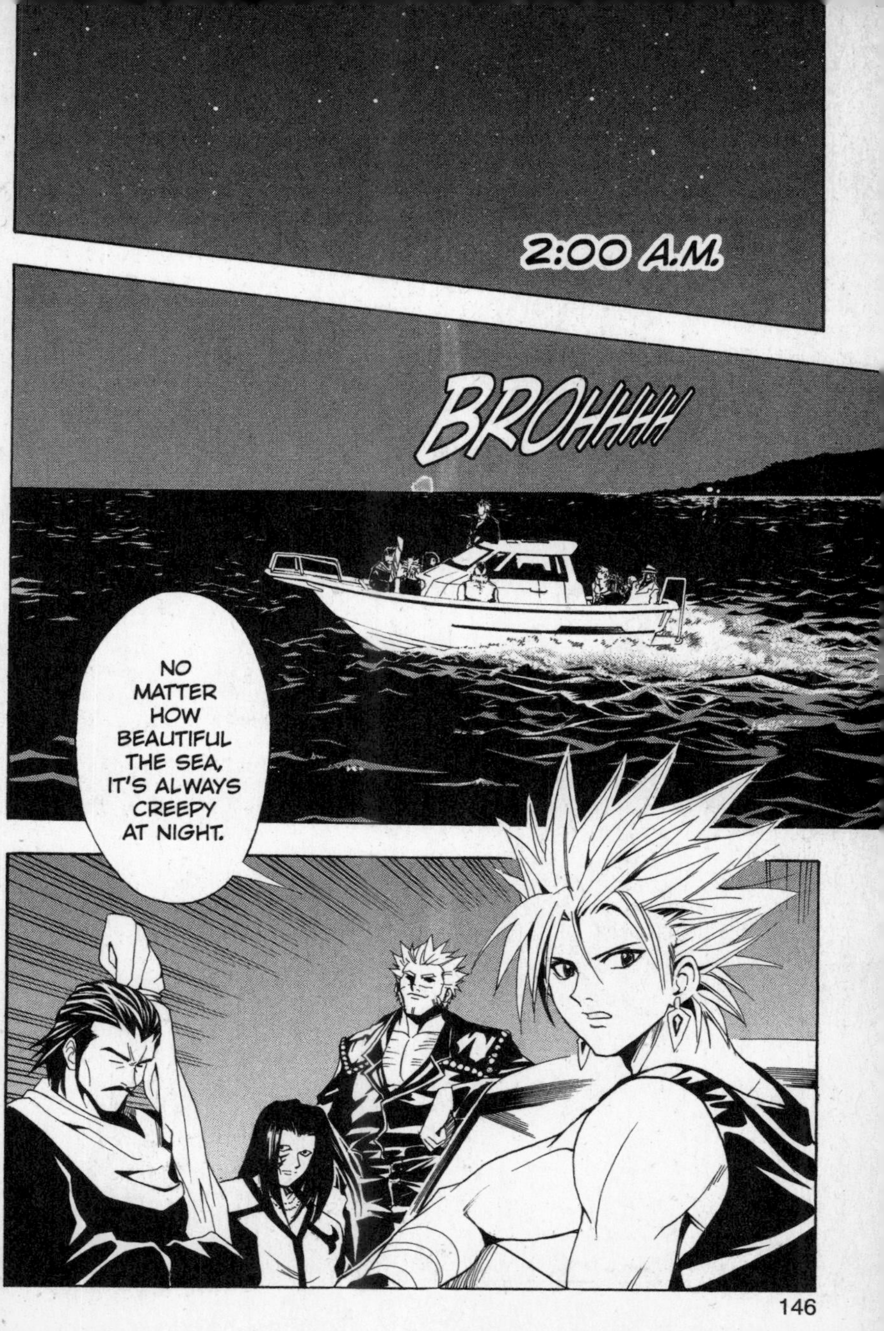
2:00 A.M.
BROHHHH
NO MATTER HOW BEAUTIFUL THE SEA, IT'S ALWAYS CREEPY AT NIGHT.

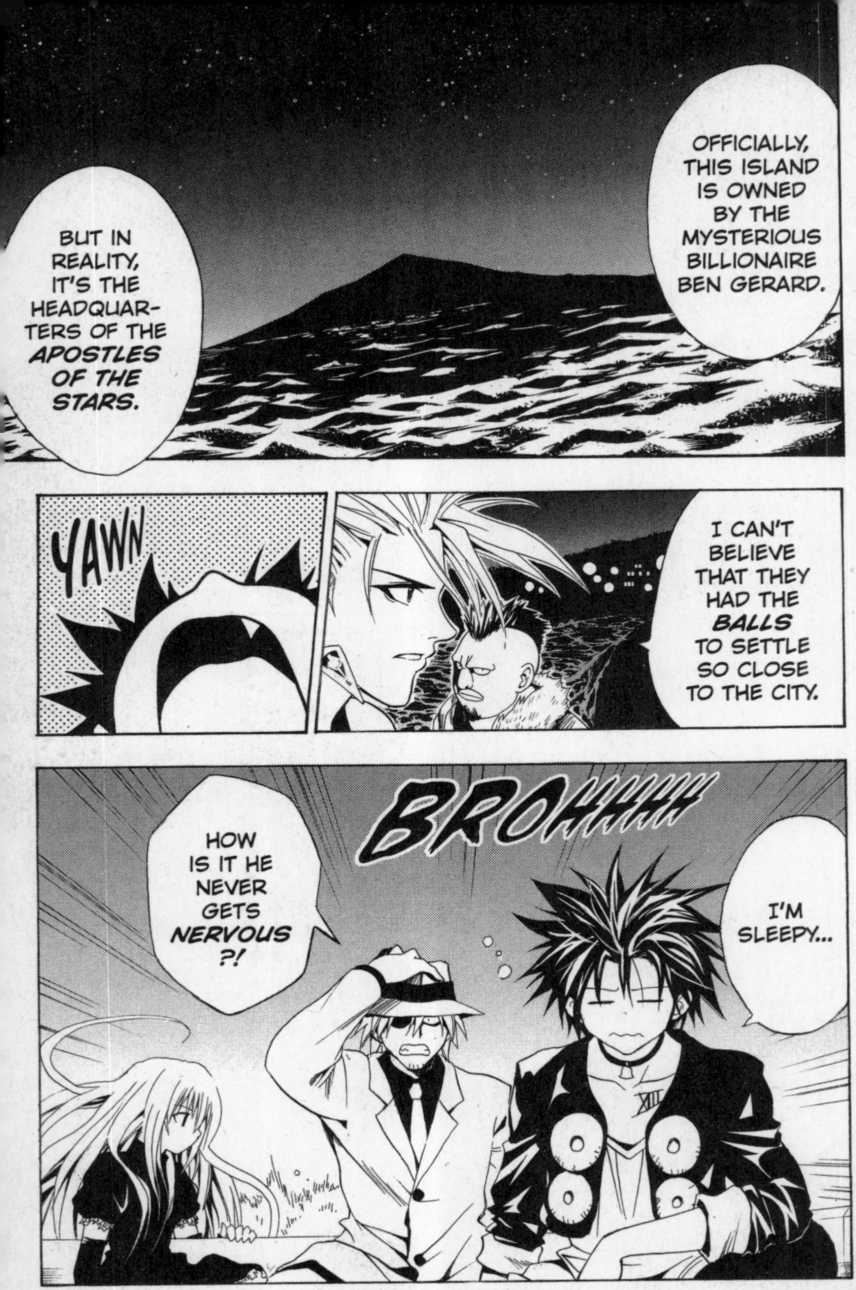
OFFICIALLY, THIS ISLAND IS OWNED BY THE MYSTERIOUS BILLIONAIRE BEN GERARD.
BUT IN REALITY, IT'S THE HEADQUARTERS OF THE *APOSTLES OF THE STARS.*
I CAN'T BELIEVE THAT THEY HAD THE *BALLS* TO SETTLE SO CLOSE TO THE CITY.
YAWN
BROHHHH
I'M SLEEPY...
HOW IS IT HE NEVER GETS *NERVOUS* ?!

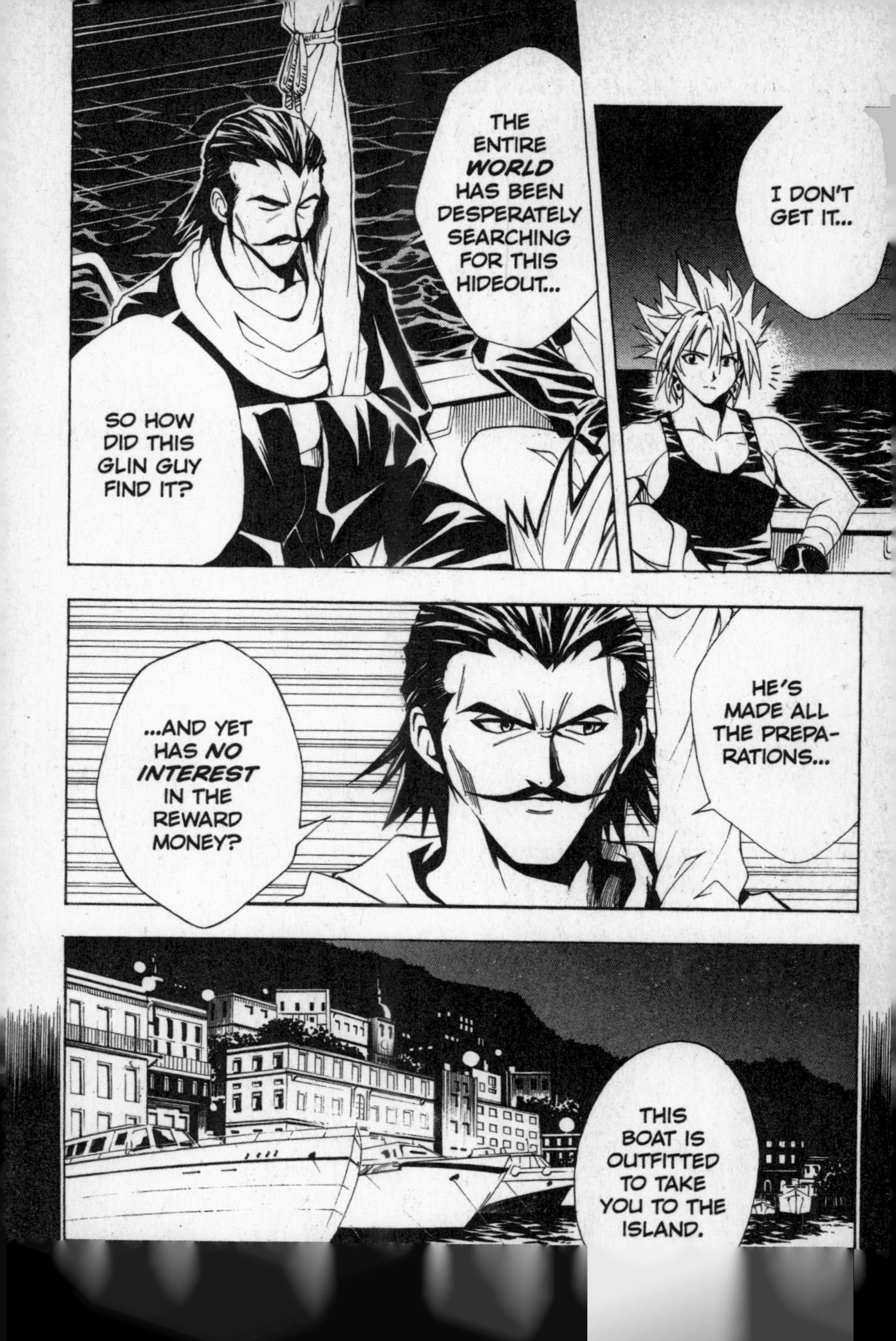
I DON'T GET IT...
THE ENTIRE WORLD HAS BEEN DESPERATELY SEARCHING FOR THIS HIDEOUT...
SO HOW DID THIS GLIN GUY FIND IT?
HE'S MADE ALL THE PREPARATIONS...
...AND YET HAS NO INTEREST IN THE REWARD MONEY?
THIS BOAT IS OUTFITTED TO TAKE YOU TO THE ISLAND.

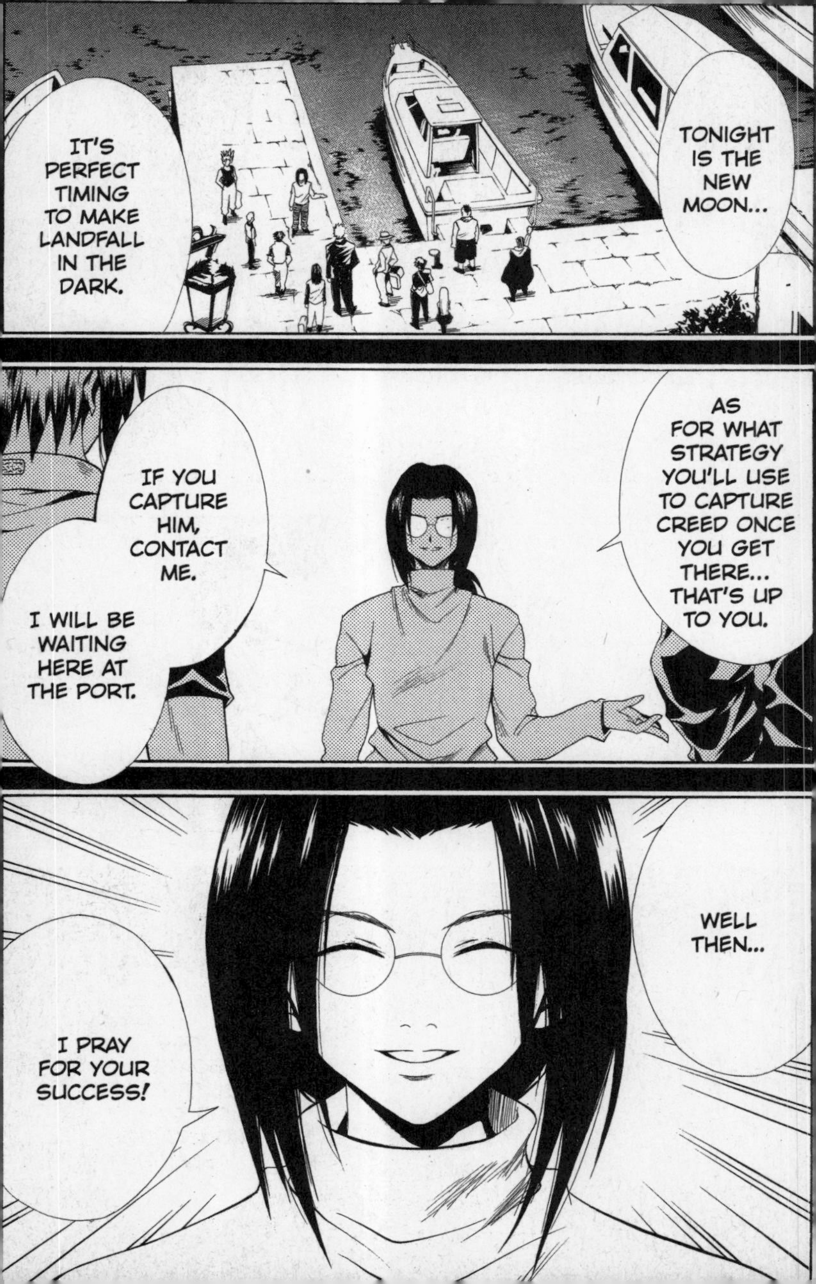
TONIGHT IS THE NEW MOON...
IT'S PERFECT TIMING TO MAKE LANDFALL IN THE DARK.
AS FOR WHAT STRATEGY YOU'LL USE TO CAPTURE CREED ONCE YOU GET THERE... THAT'S UP TO YOU.
IF YOU CAPTURE HIM, CONTACT ME.
I WILL BE WAITING HERE AT THE PORT.
WELL THEN...
I PRAY FOR YOUR SUCCESS!

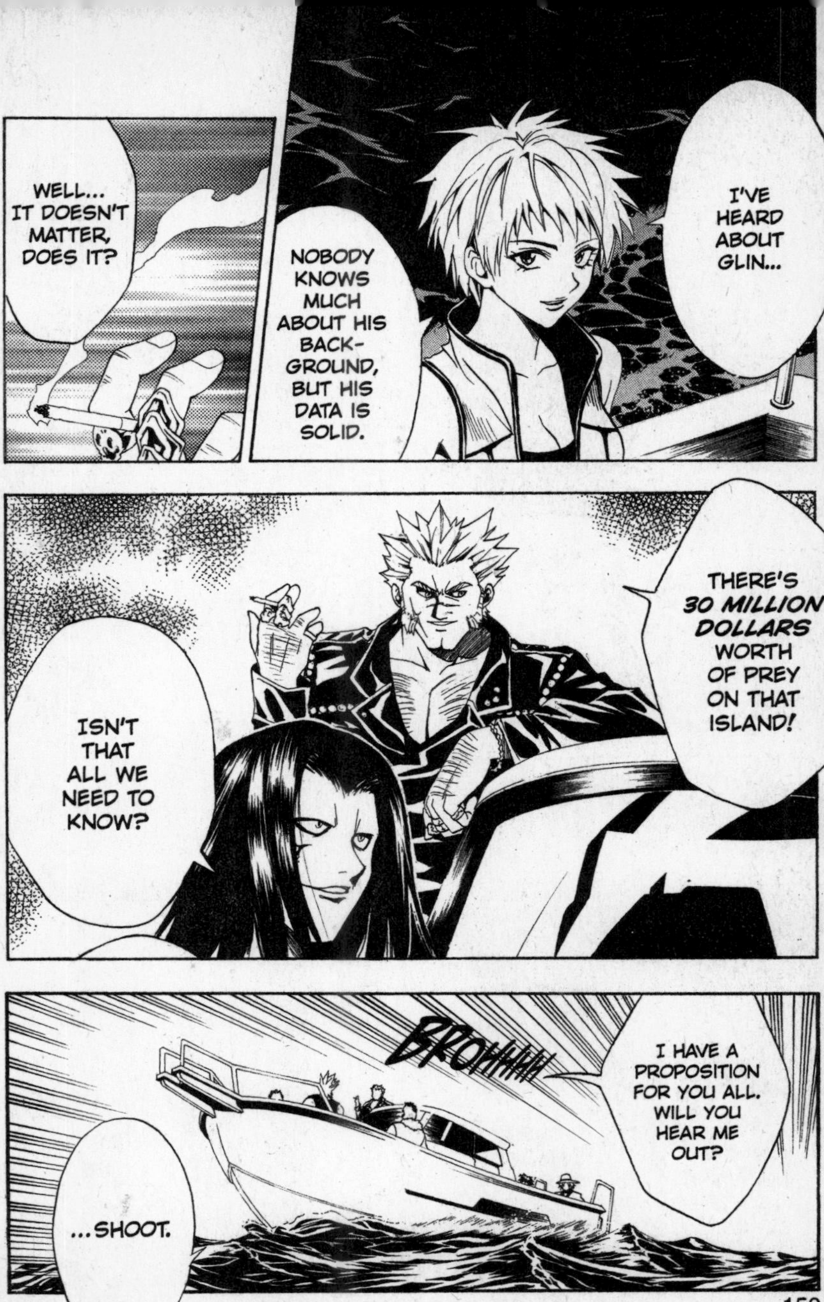
I'VE HEARD ABOUT GLIN...
NOBODY KNOWS MUCH ABOUT HIS BACK-GROUND, BUT HIS DATA IS SOLID.
WELL... IT DOESN'T MATTER, DOES IT?
THERE'S *30 MILLION DOLLARS* WORTH OF PREY ON THAT ISLAND!
ISN'T THAT ALL WE NEED TO KNOW?
BROHHHH
I HAVE A PROPOSITION FOR YOU ALL. WILL YOU HEAR ME OUT?
...SHOOT.

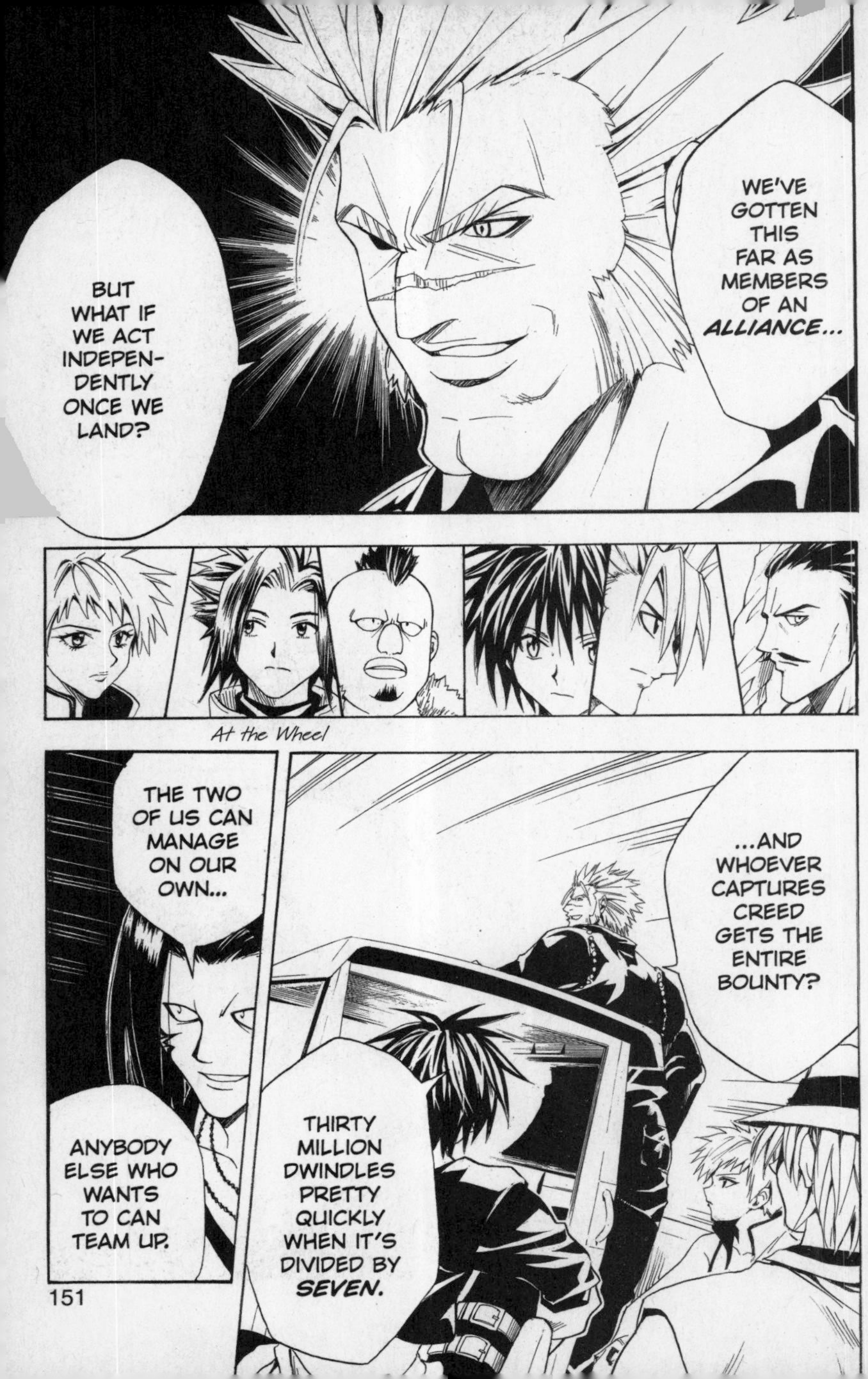
WE'VE GOTTEN THIS FAR AS MEMBERS OF AN ***ALLIANCE...***
BUT WHAT IF WE ACT INDEPENDENTLY ONCE WE LAND?
At the Wheel
...AND WHOEVER CAPTURES CREED GETS THE ENTIRE BOUNTY?
THIRTY MILLION DWINDLES PRETTY QUICKLY WHEN IT'S DIVIDED BY ***SEVEN.***
THE TWO OF US CAN MANAGE ON OUR OWN...
ANYBODY ELSE WHO WANTS TO CAN TEAM UP.

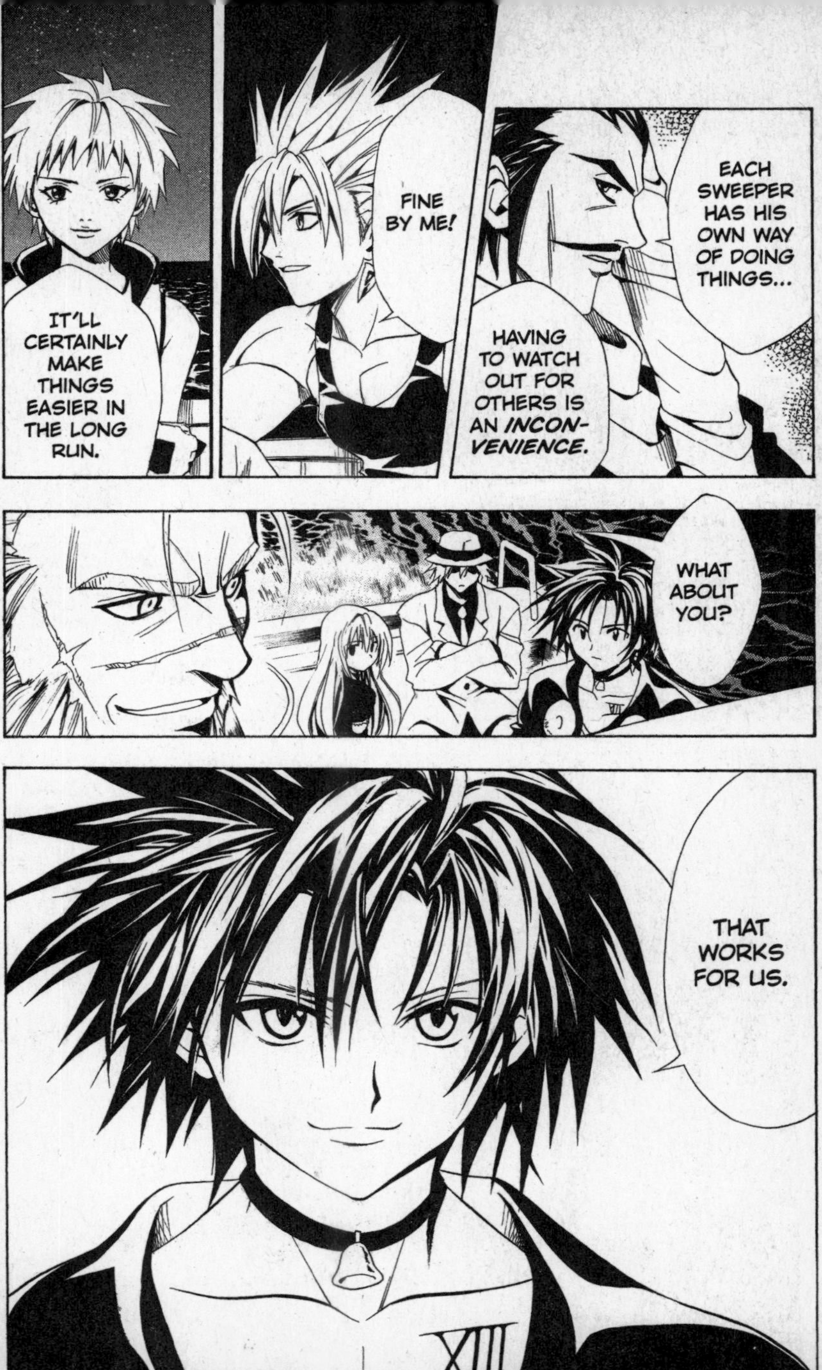
EACH SWEEPER HAS HIS OWN WAY OF DOING THINGS...
HAVING TO WATCH OUT FOR OTHERS IS AN *INCONVENIENCE*.
FINE BY ME!
IT'LL CERTAINLY MAKE THINGS EASIER IN THE LONG RUN.
WHAT ABOUT YOU?
THAT WORKS FOR US.

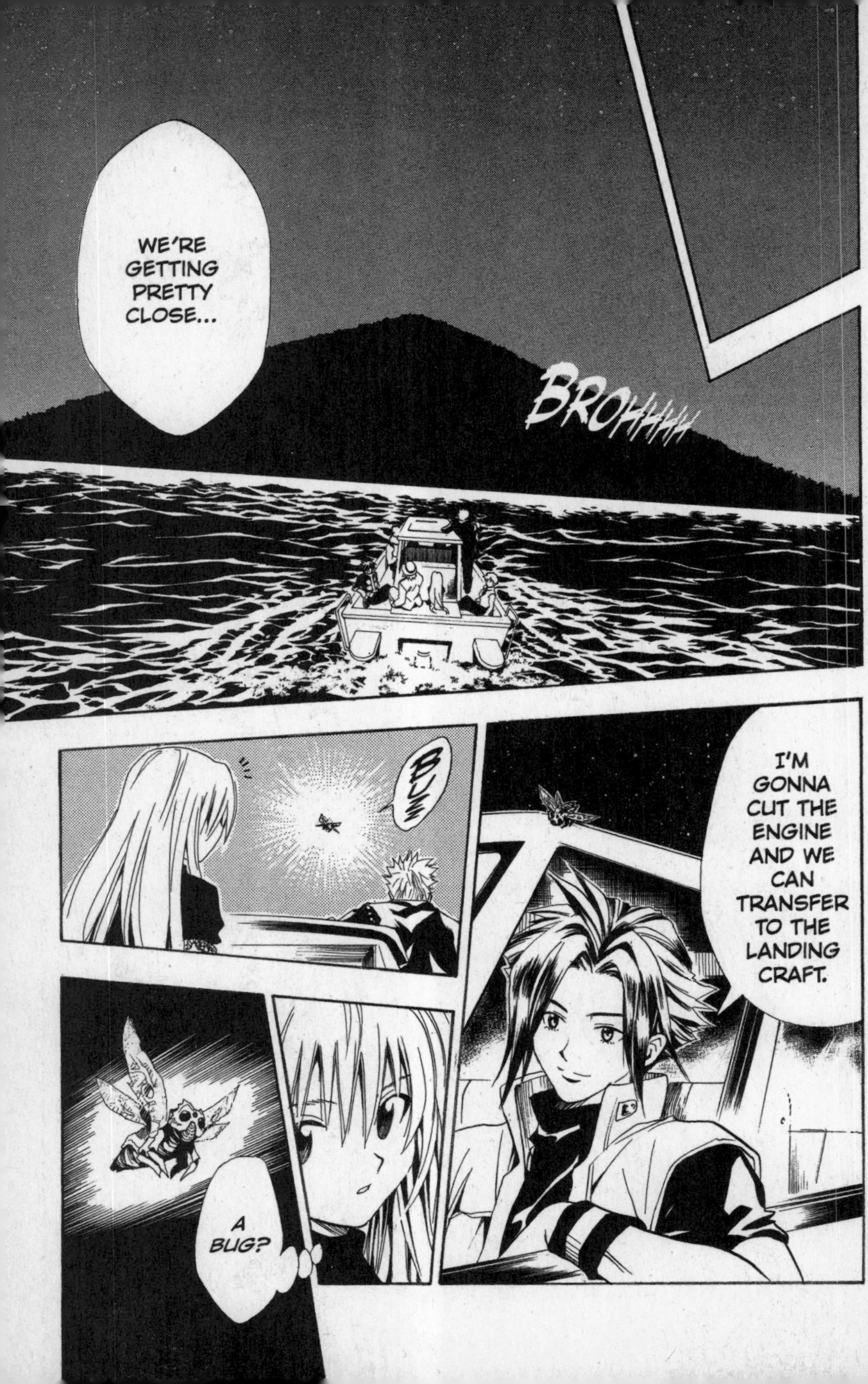
WE'RE GETTING PRETTY CLOSE...
BROHHHH
I'M GONNA CUT THE ENGINE AND WE CAN TRANSFER TO THE LANDING CRAFT.
BUZZ
A BUG?

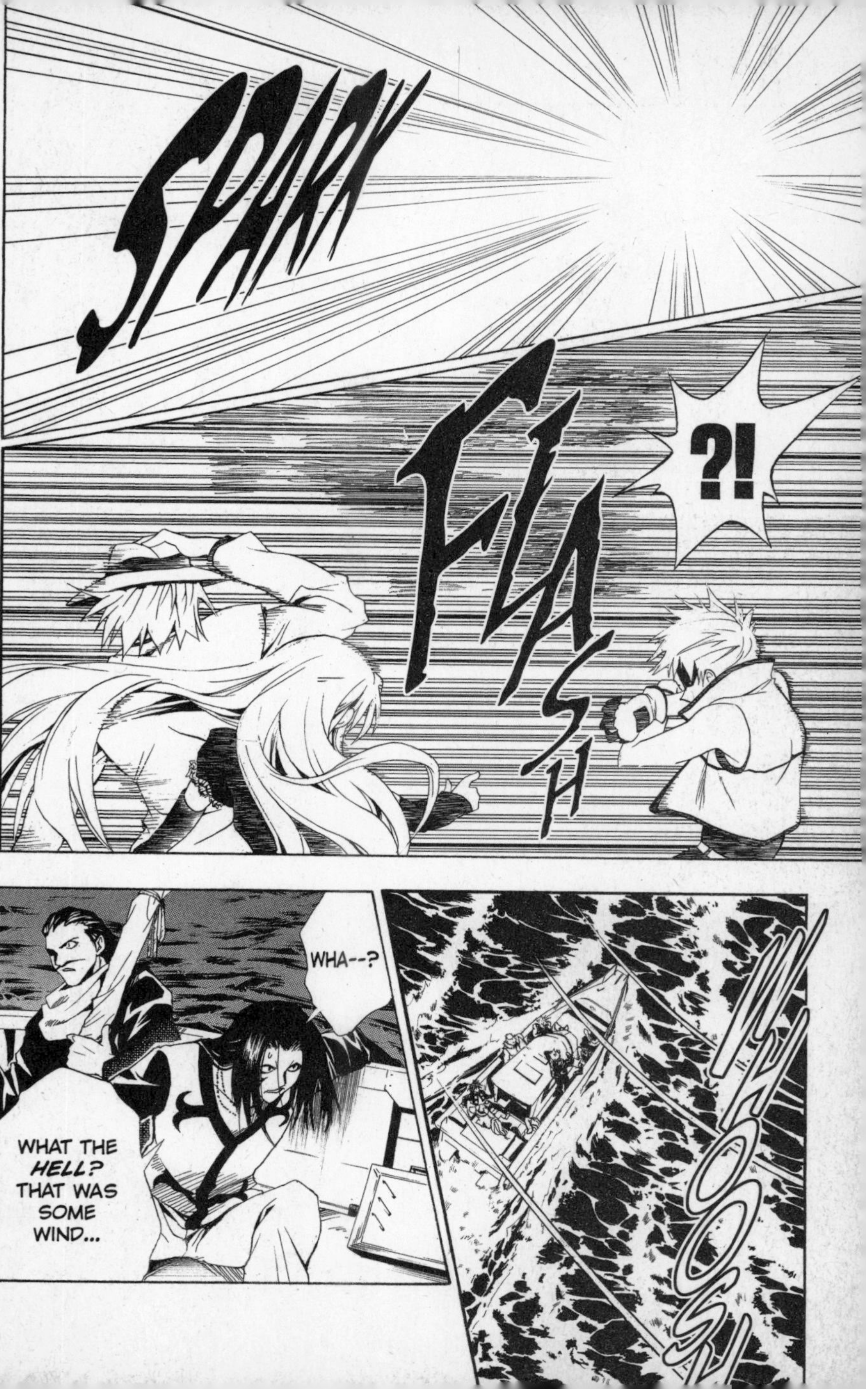
SPARK
FLASH
?!
WHA--?
WHAT THE *HELL?* THAT WAS SOME WIND...

READ THIS WAY

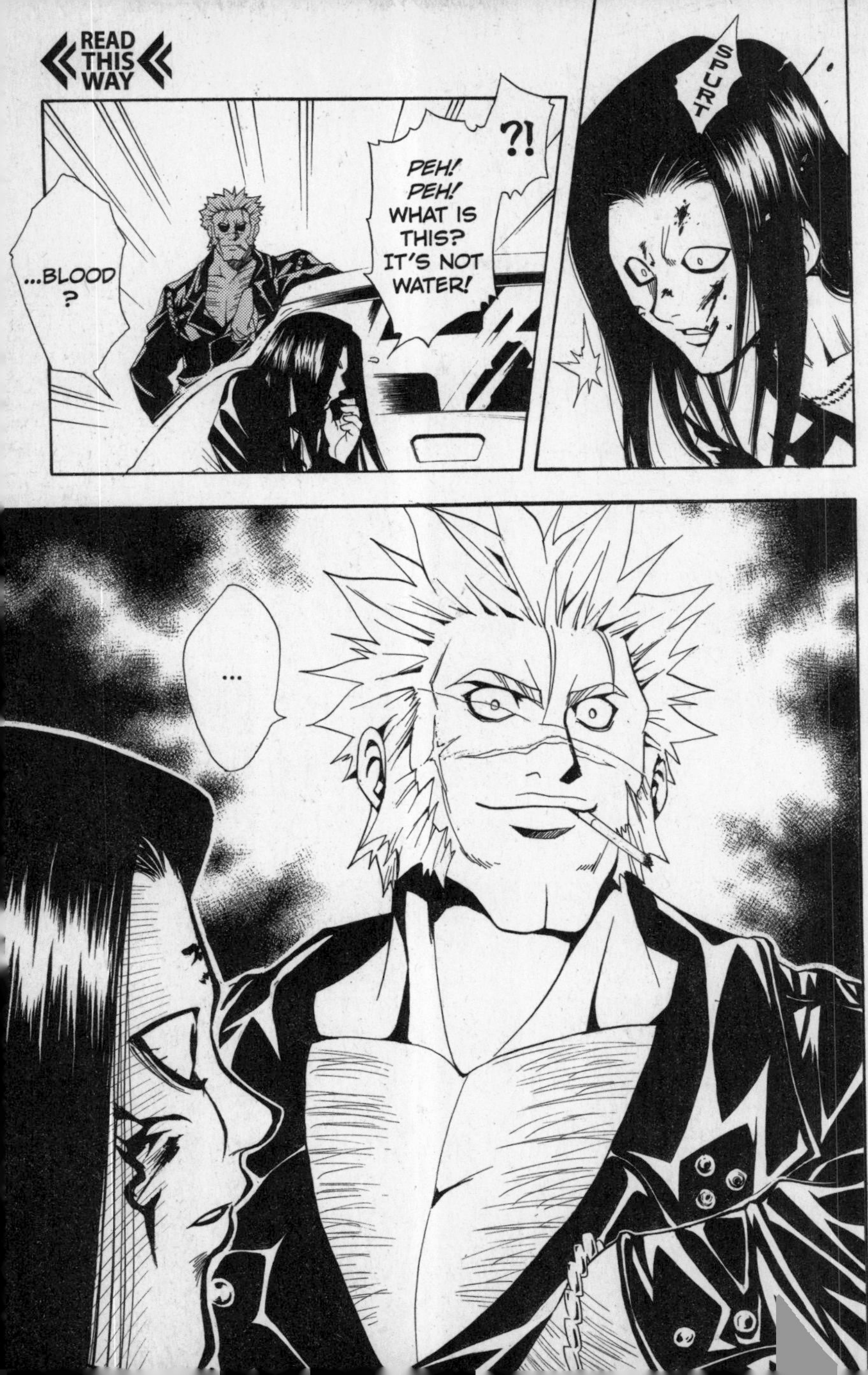
SPURT
?!
PEH! PEH! WHAT IS THIS? IT'S NOT WATER!
...BLOOD ?
...

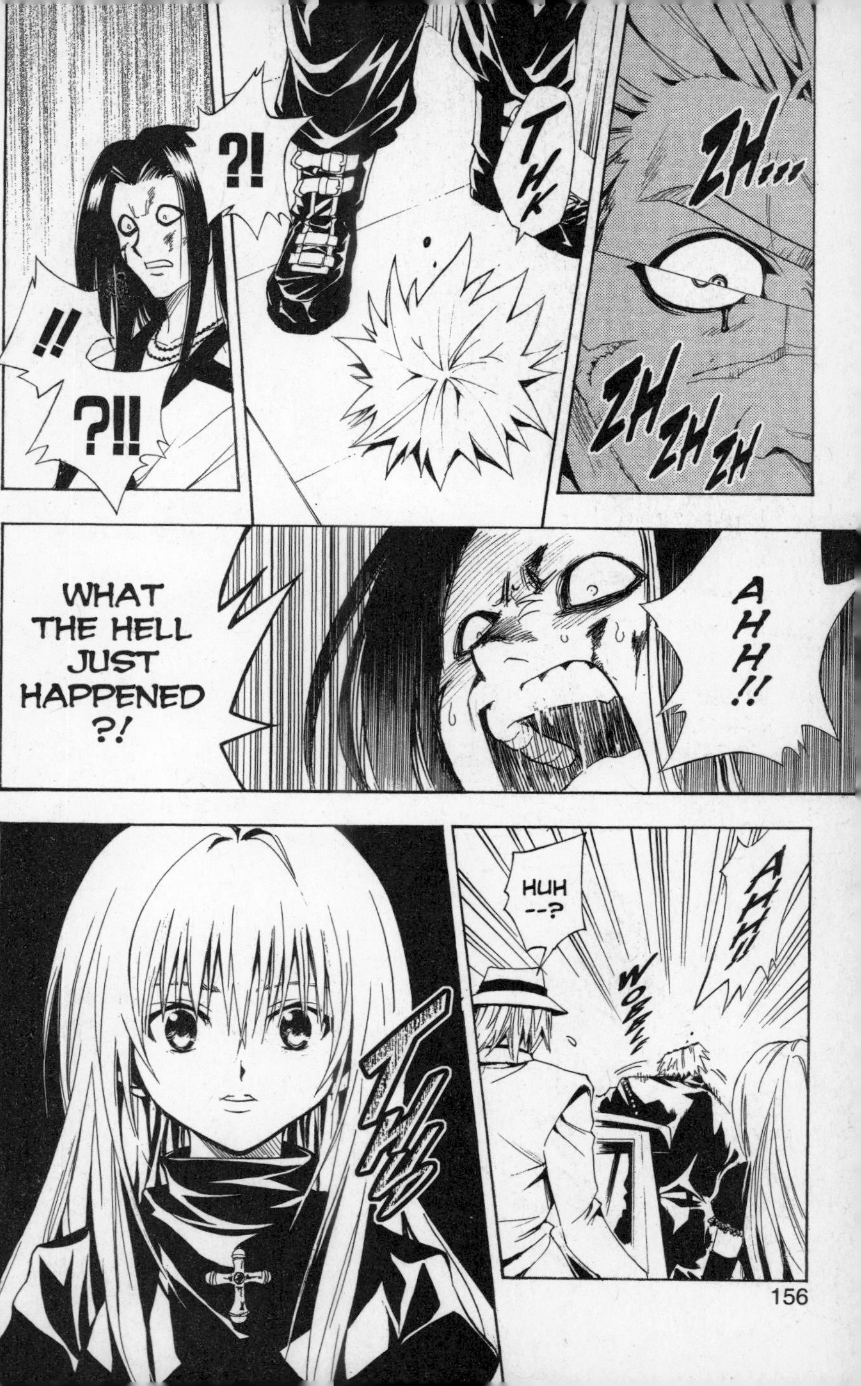
ZH...
ZH ZH ZH
THK
?!
!!
?!!
AHH!!
WHAT THE HELL JUST HAPPENED ?!
AHH!!
HUH --?

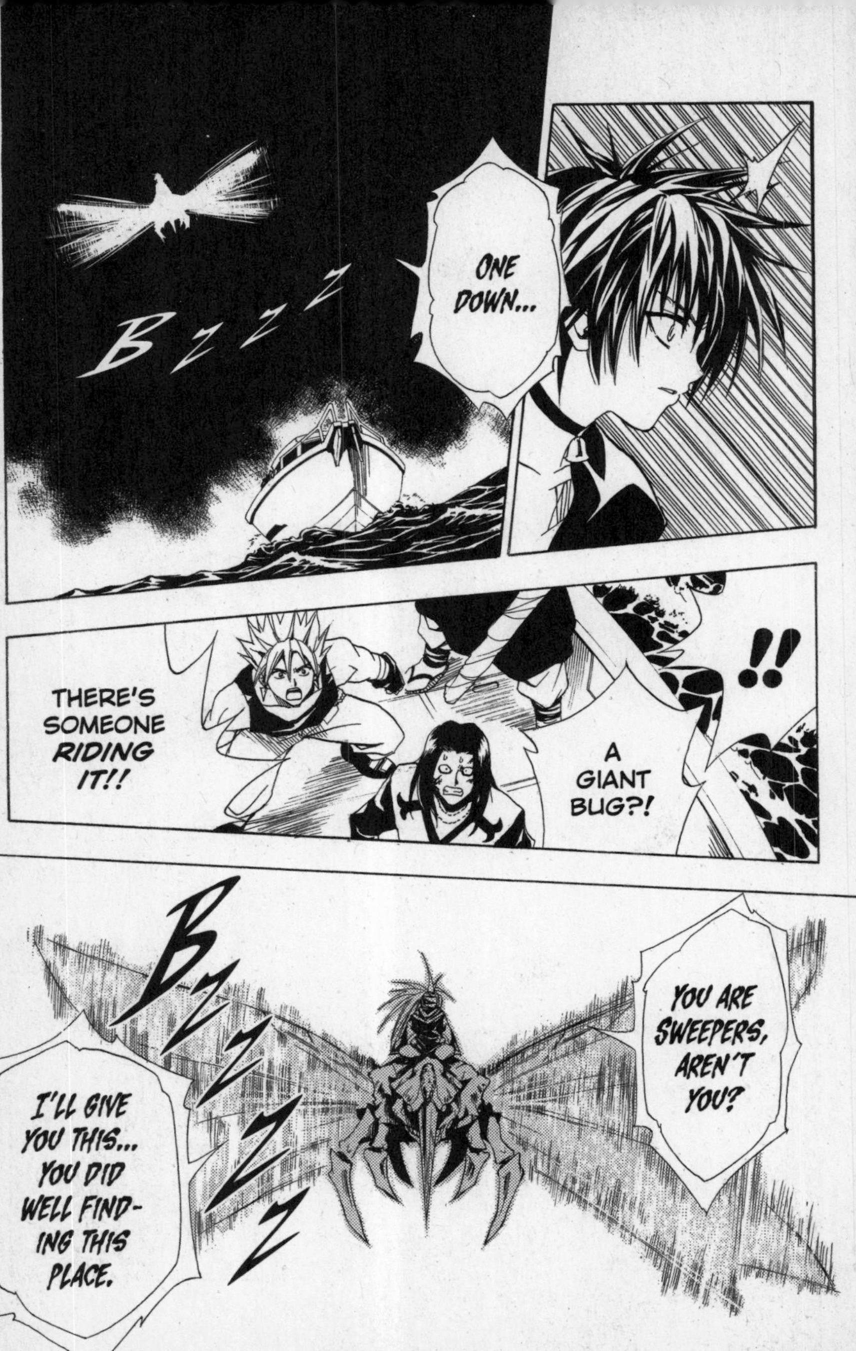
ONE DOWN...
BZZZ
!!
A GIANT BUG?!
THERE'S SOMEONE RIDING IT!!
YOU ARE SWEEPERS, AREN'T YOU?
BZZZZ
I'LL GIVE YOU THIS... YOU DID WELL FINDING THIS PLACE.

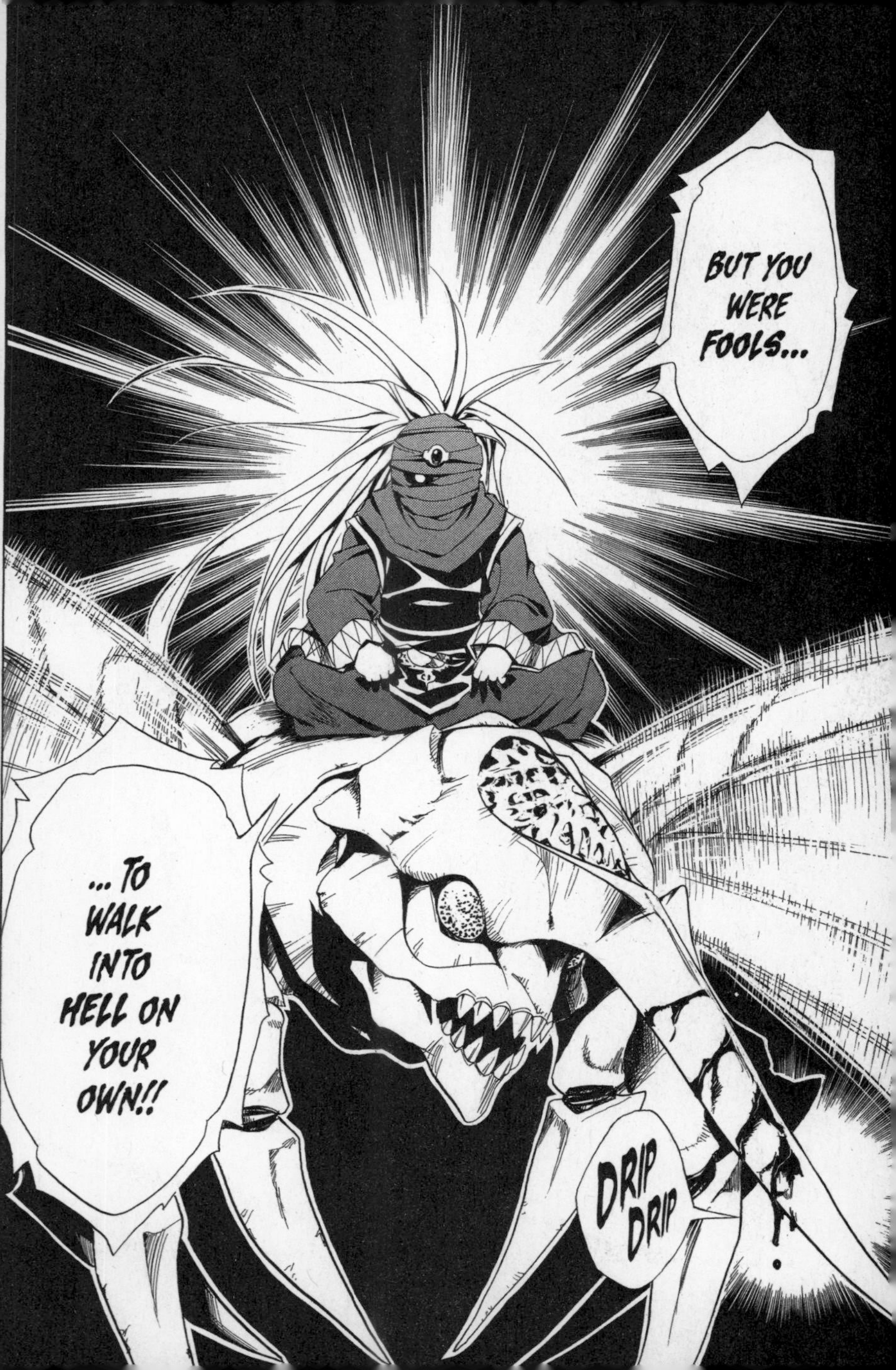
BUT YOU WERE FOOLS...
...TO WALK INTO HELL ON YOUR OWN!!
DRIP DRIP

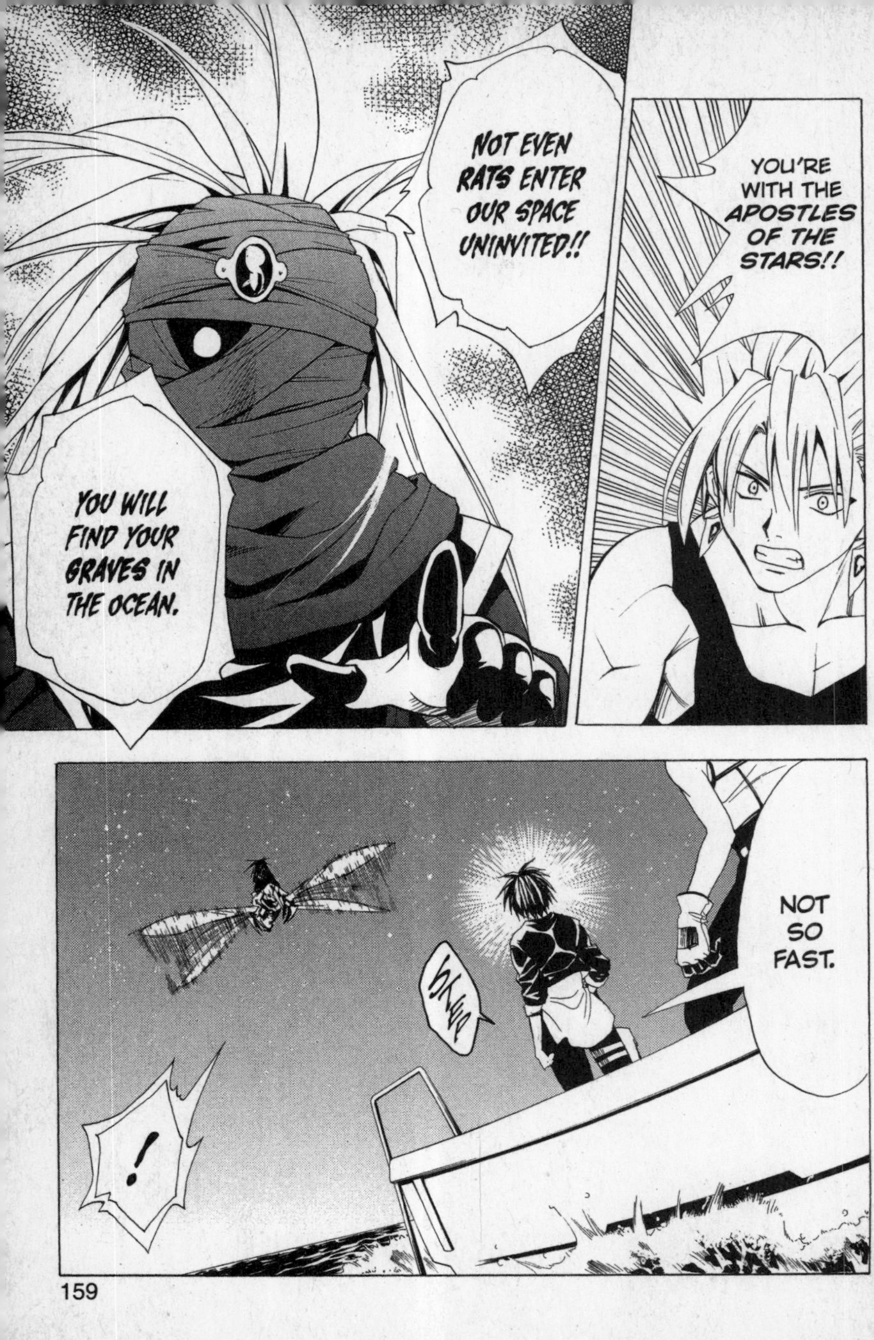
YOU'RE WITH THE APOSTLES OF THE STARS!!
NOT EVEN RATS ENTER OUR SPACE UNINVITED!!
YOU WILL FIND YOUR GRAVES IN THE OCEAN.
NOT SO FAST.
!

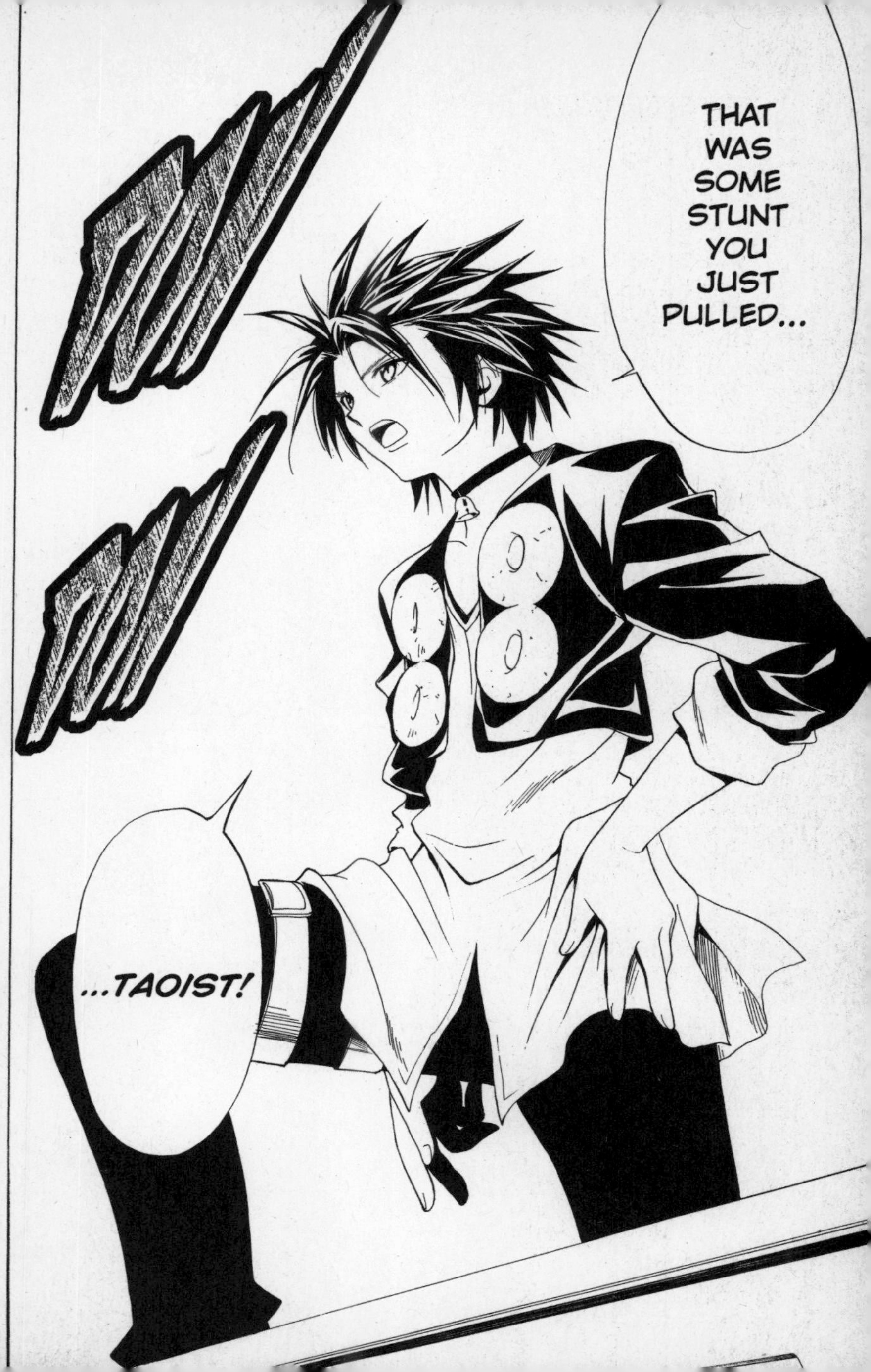
THAT WAS SOME STUNT YOU JUST PULLED...
...TAOIST!

READ THIS WAY

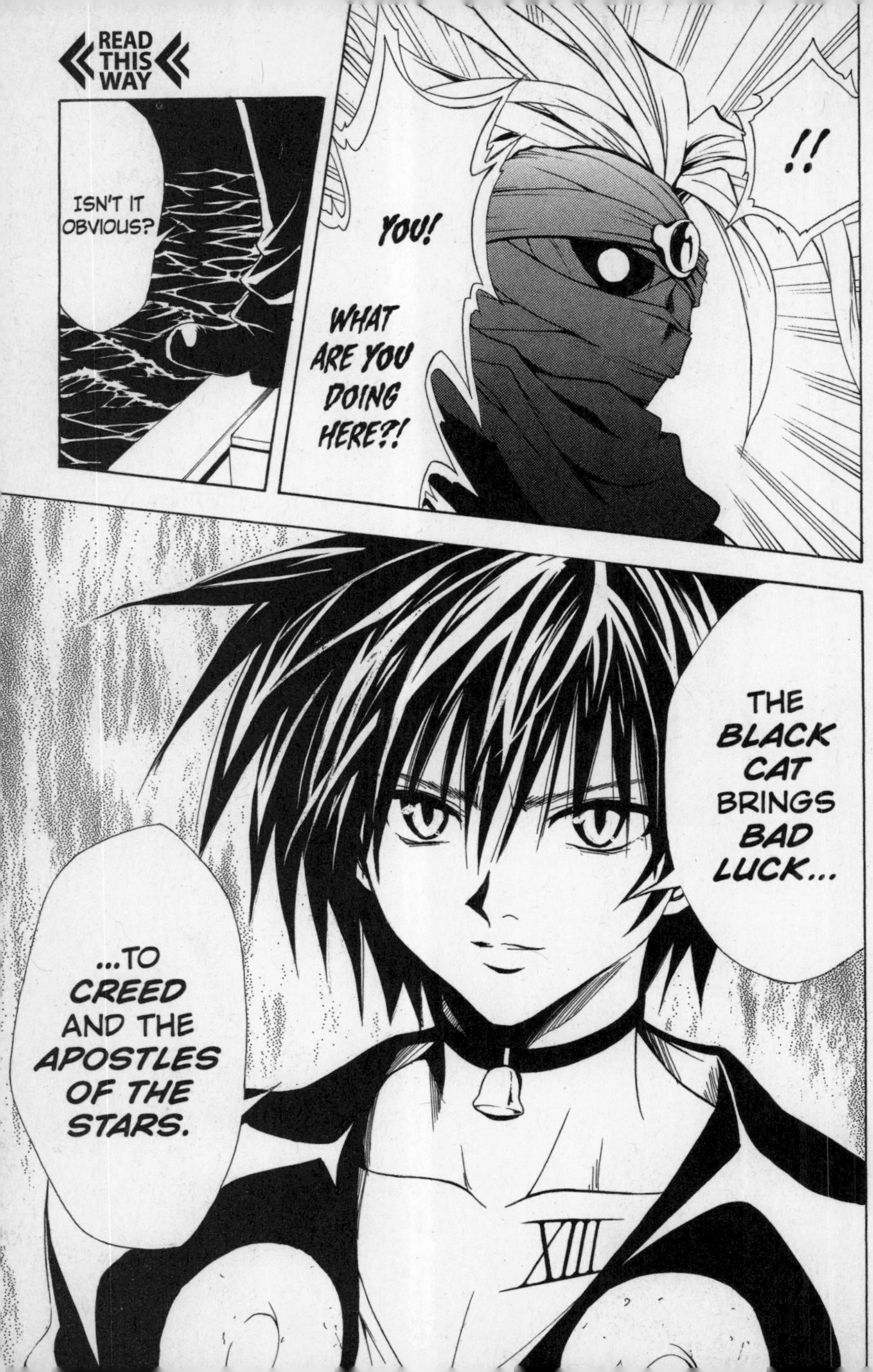
!!
YOU!
WHAT ARE YOU DOING HERE?!
ISN'T IT OBVIOUS?
THE BLACK CAT BRINGS BAD LUCK...
...TO CREED AND THE APOSTLES OF THE STARS.

NOSTALGIC SERIES

NUMBER 7—TIM

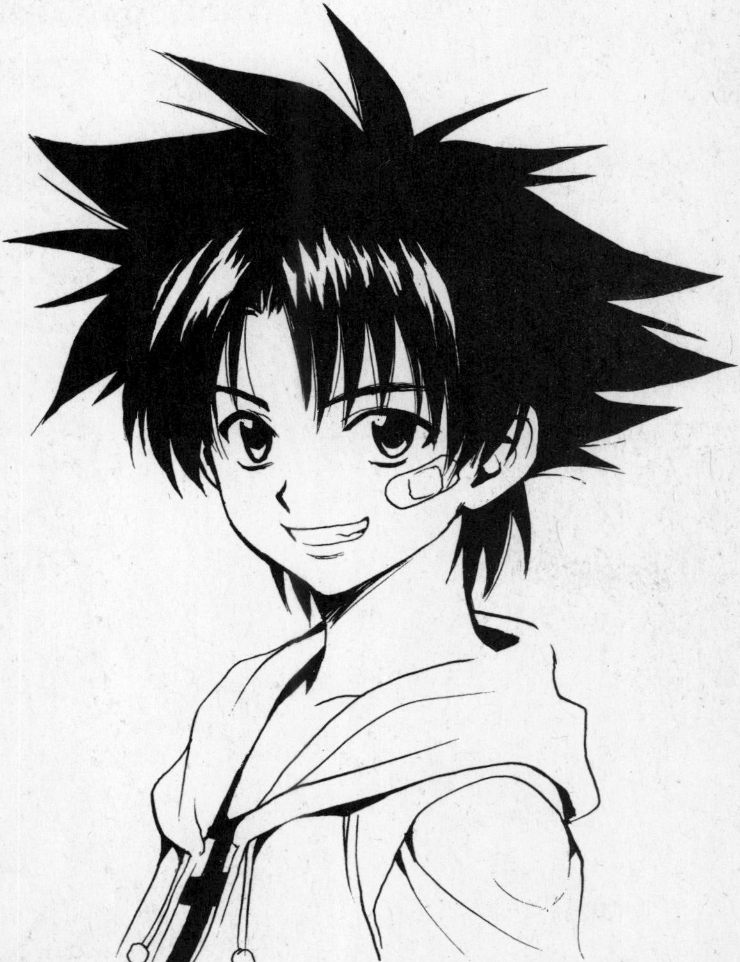

Chapter 131: Aerial Enemy!

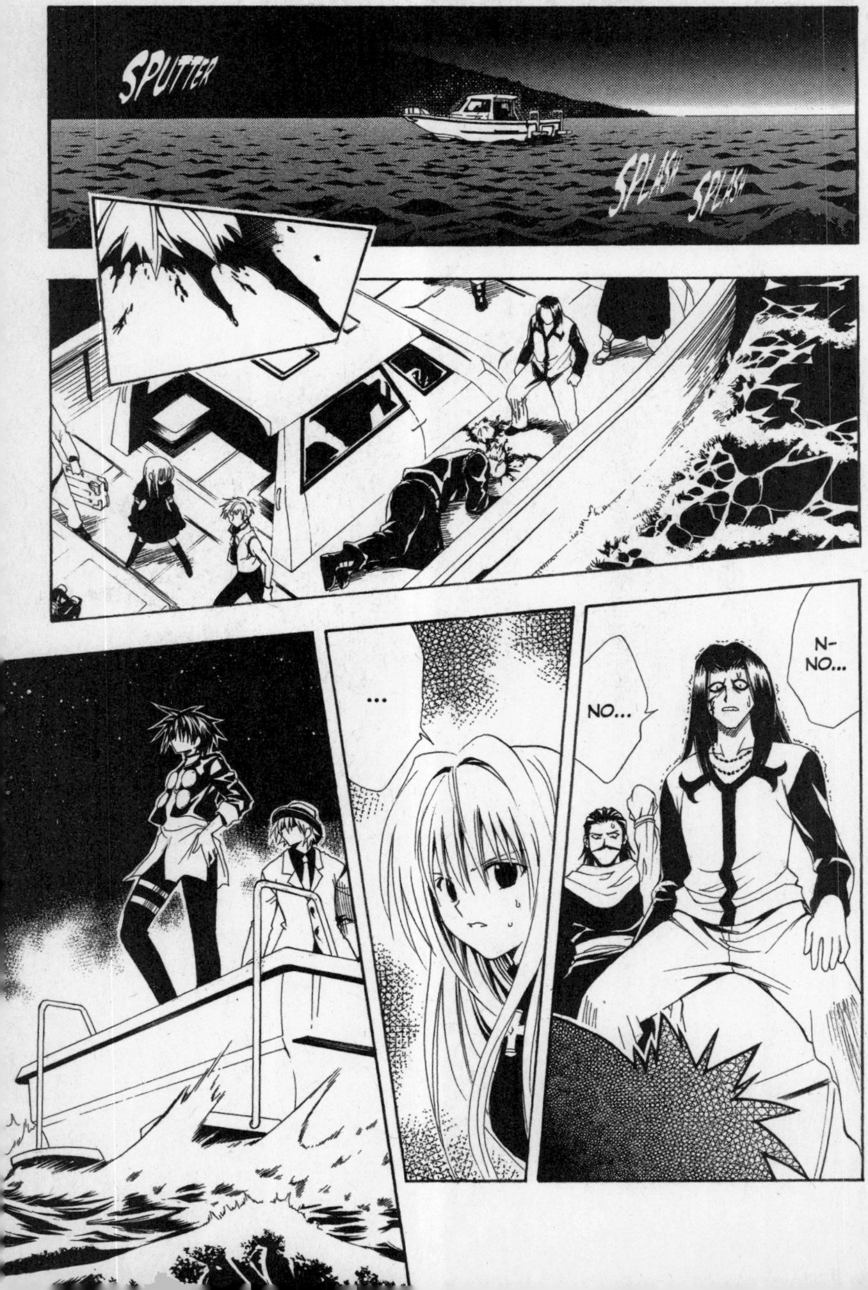
SPUTTER
SPLASH SPLASH
N- NO...
NO...
...

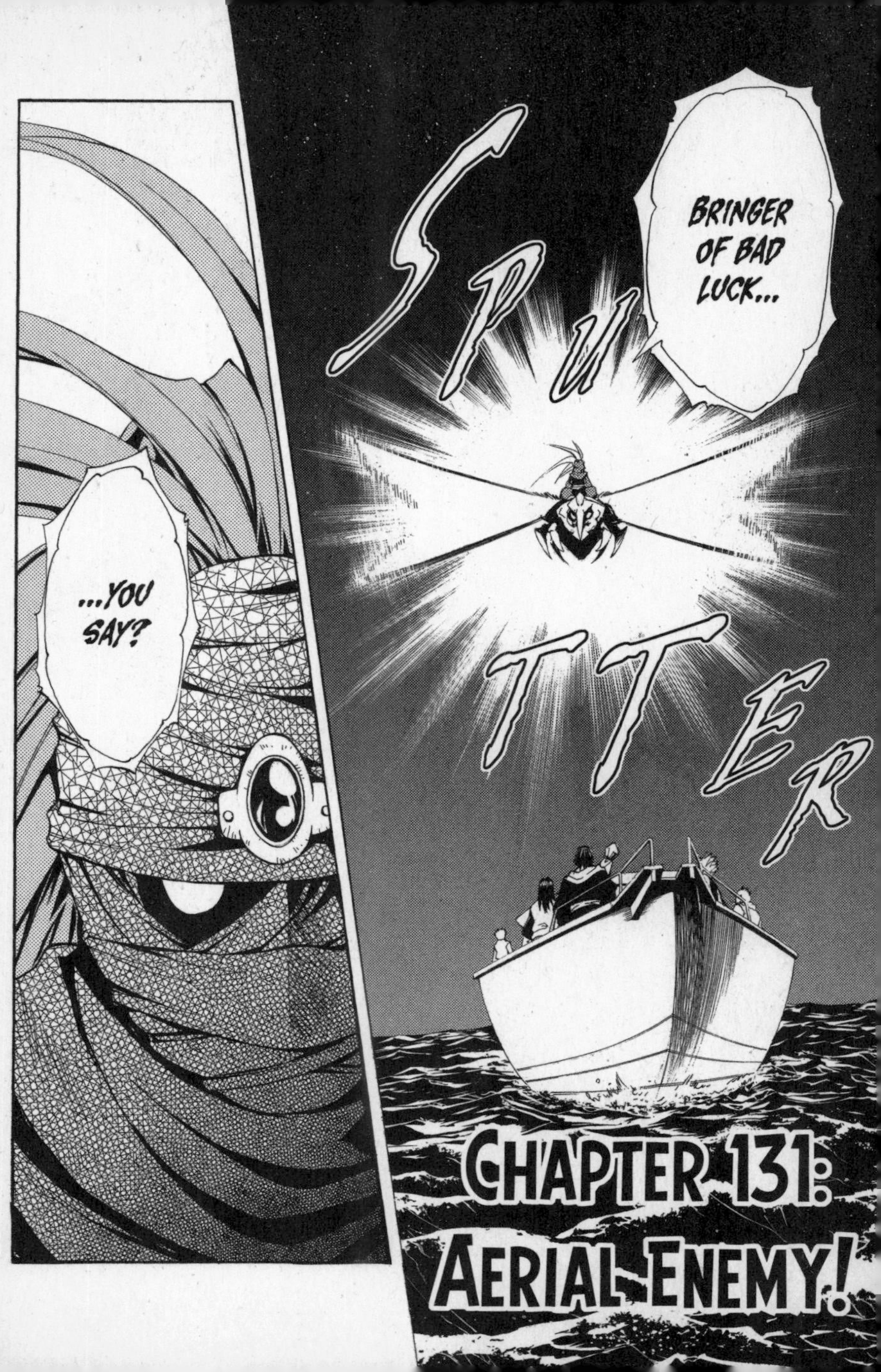
BRINGER OF BAD LUCK...
SPUTTER
CHAPTER 131:
AERIAL ENEMY!
...YOU SAY?

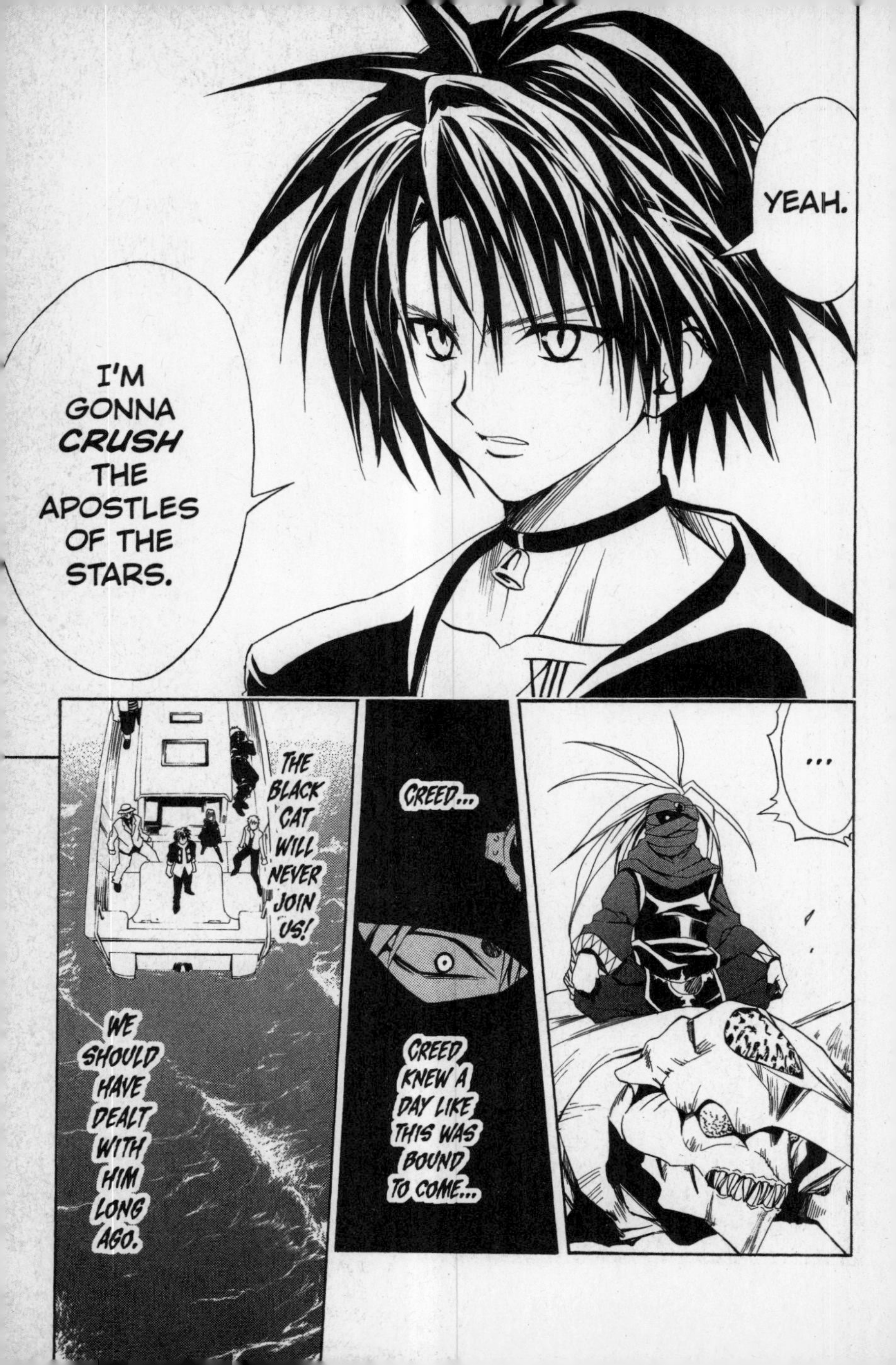
YEAH.
I'M GONNA *CRUSH* THE APOSTLES OF THE STARS.
...
CREED...
CREED KNEW A DAY LIKE THIS WAS BOUND TO COME...
THE BLACK CAT WILL NEVER JOIN US!
WE SHOULD HAVE DEALT WITH HIM LONG AGO.

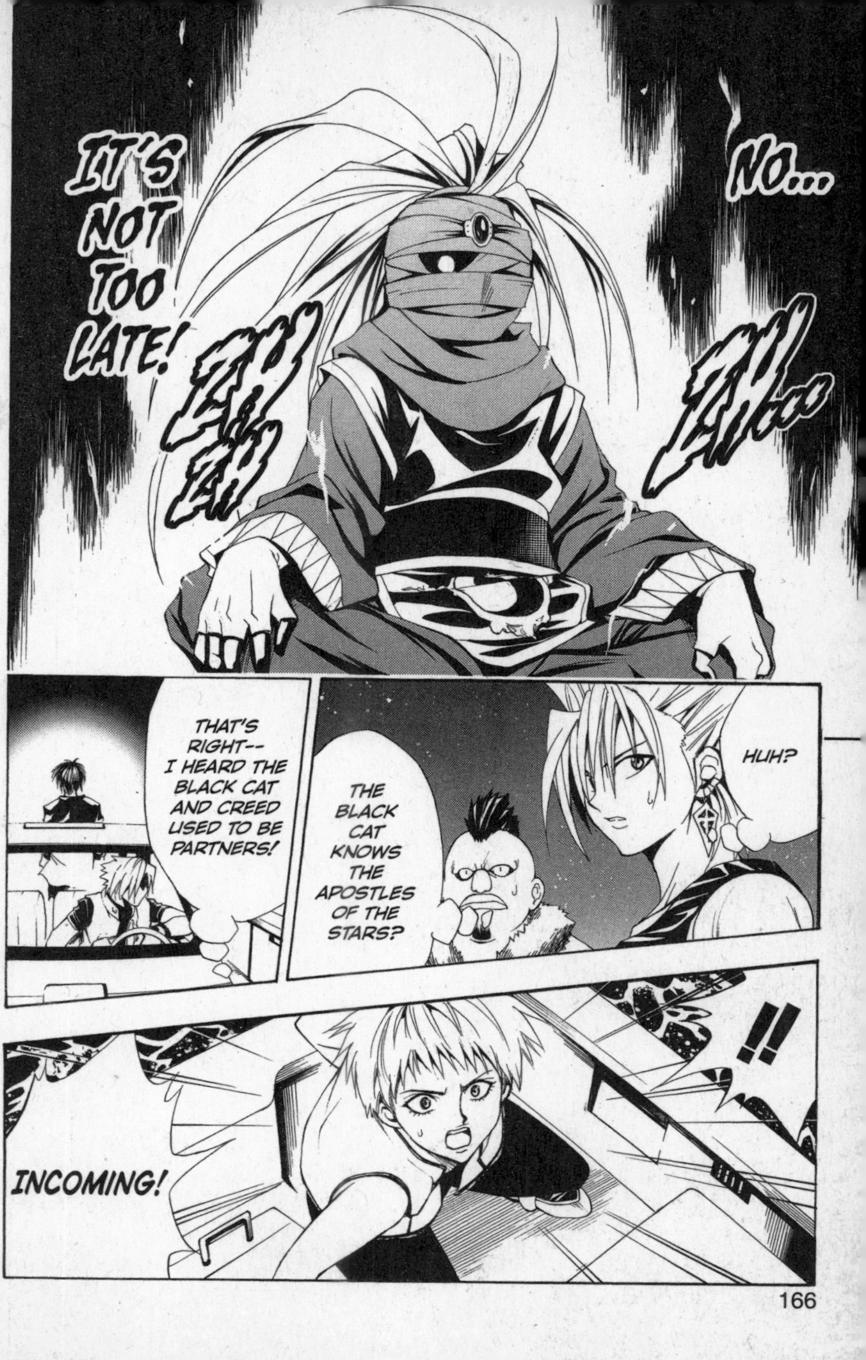
NO...
IT'S NOT TOO LATE!
HUH?
THE BLACK CAT KNOWS THE APOSTLES OF THE STARS?
THAT'S RIGHT-- I HEARD THE BLACK CAT AND CREED USED TO BE PARTNERS!
!!
INCOMING!

READ THIS WAY

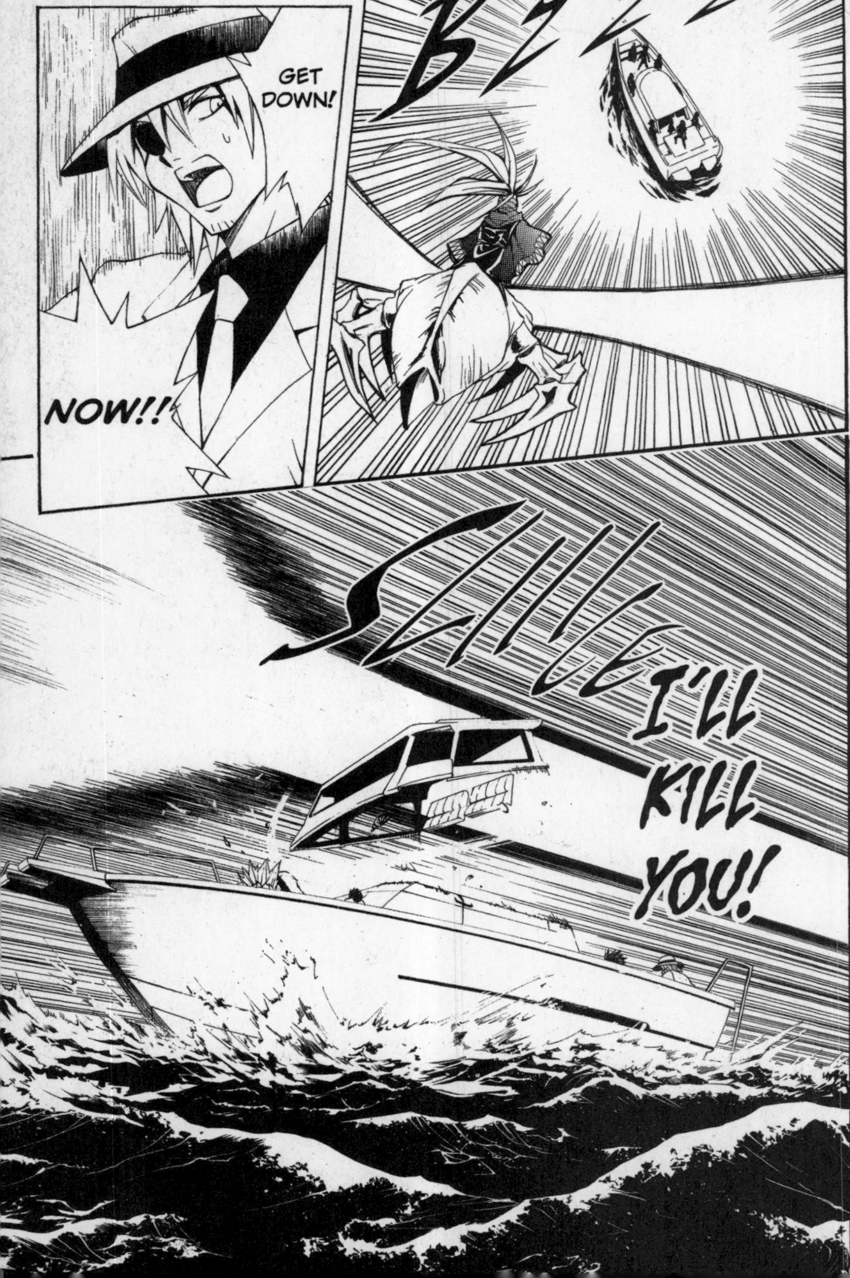
BZZZ
GET DOWN!
NOW!!
I'LL KILL YOU!

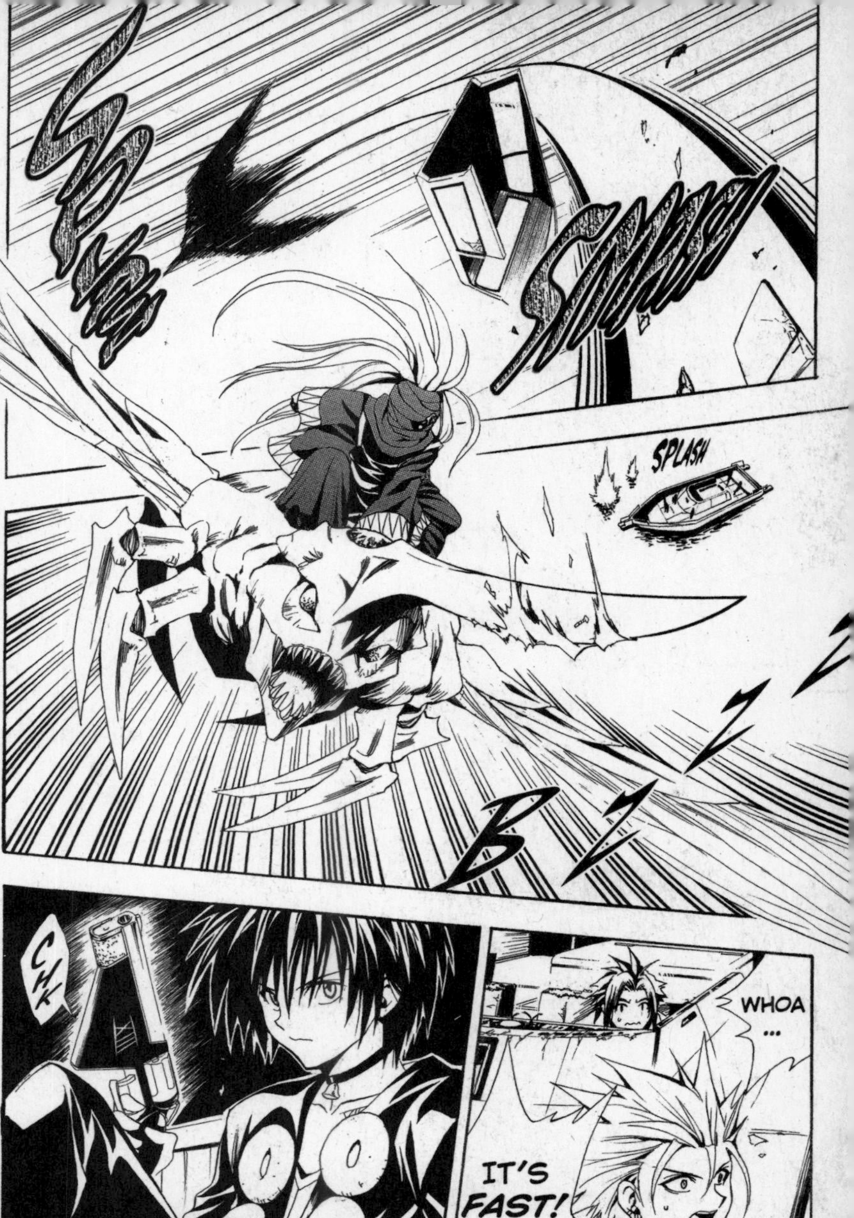
SPLASH
WHOA ...
IT'S FAST!
CHK

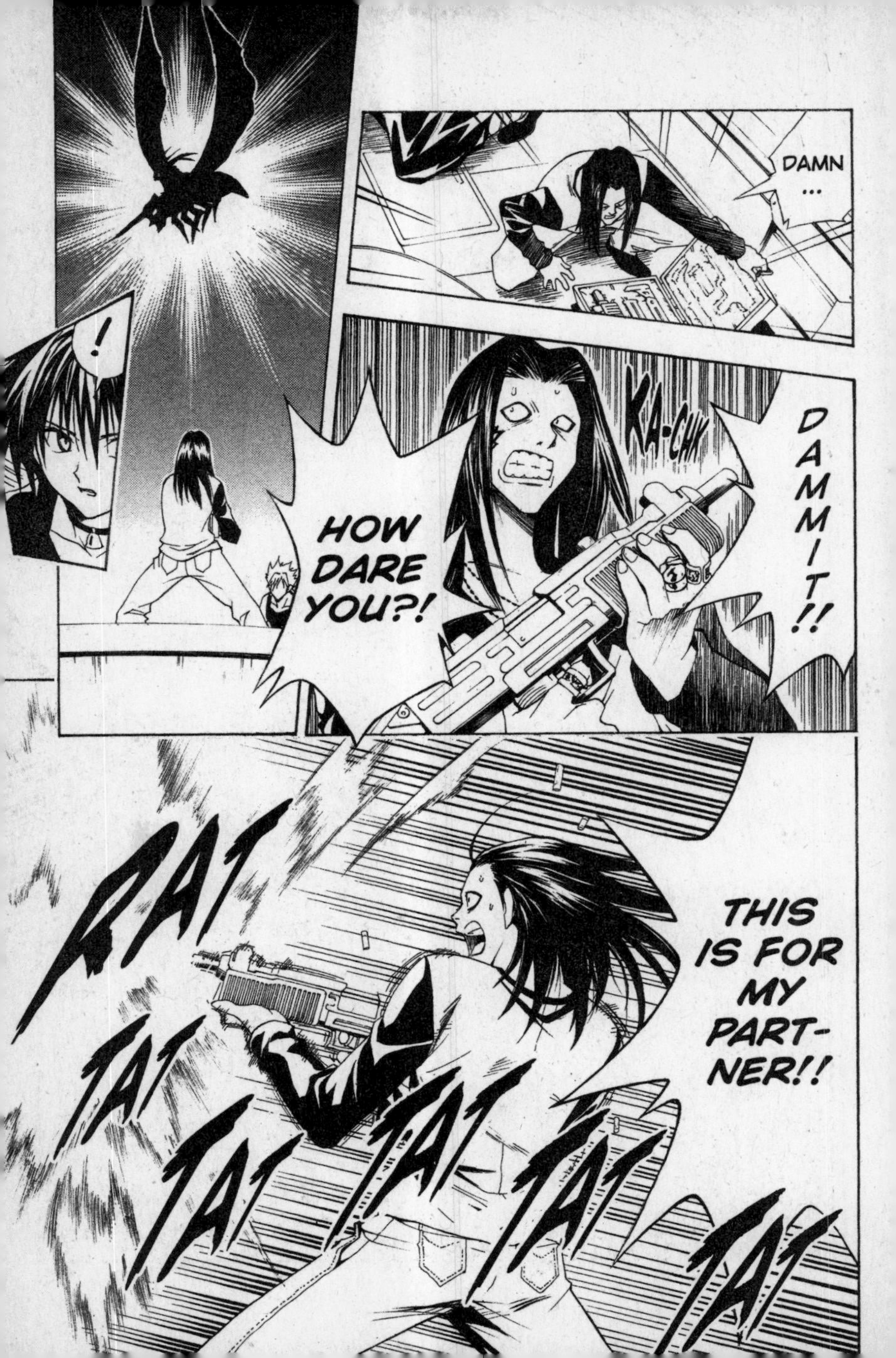

DAMN ...
KA-CHK
DAMMIT!!
HOW DARE YOU?!
!
THIS IS FOR MY PART-NER!!
RAT TAT TAT TAT TAT TAT

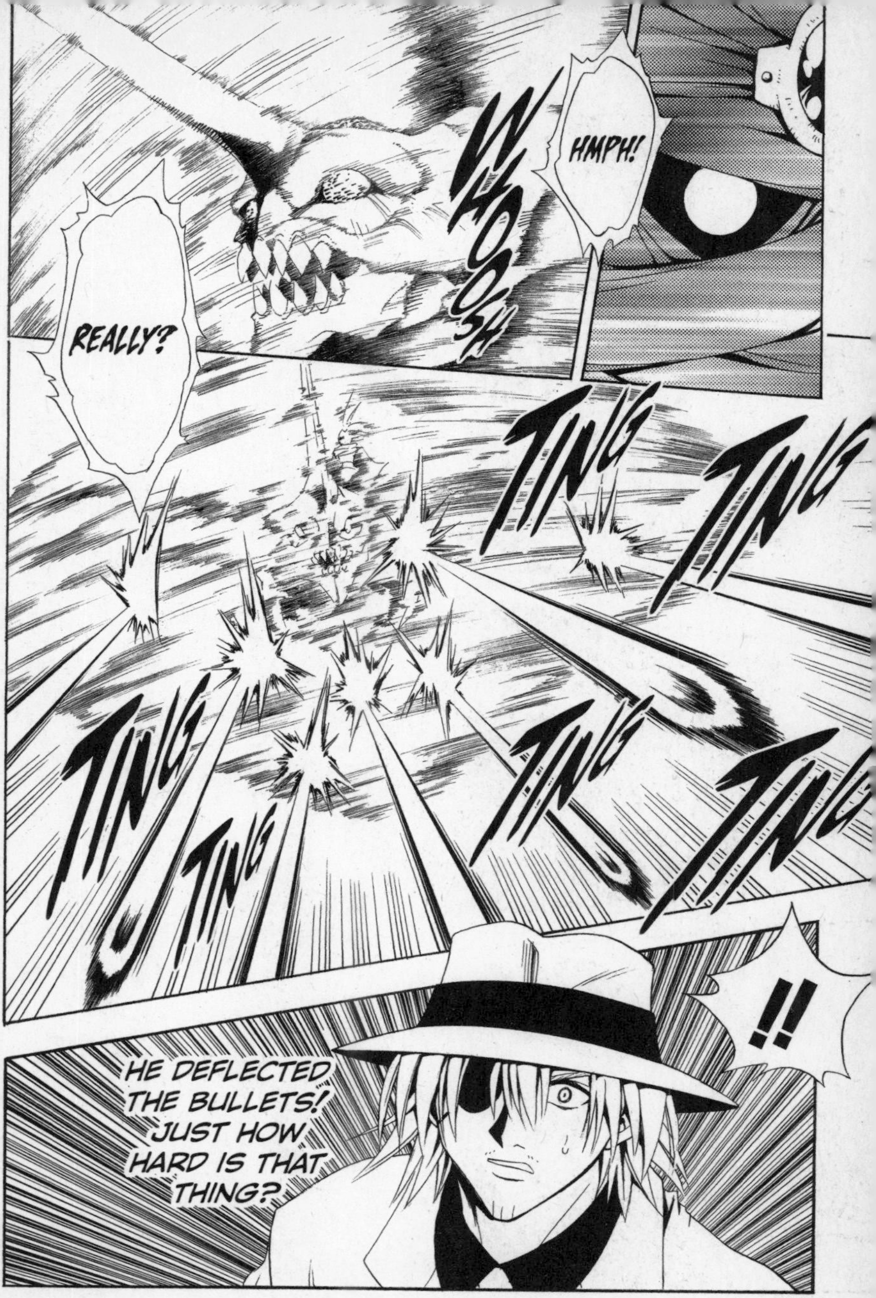
HMPH!
WHOOOSH
REALLY?
TING
TING
TING
TING
TING
TING
!!
HE DEFLECTED THE BULLETS! JUST HOW HARD IS THAT THING?

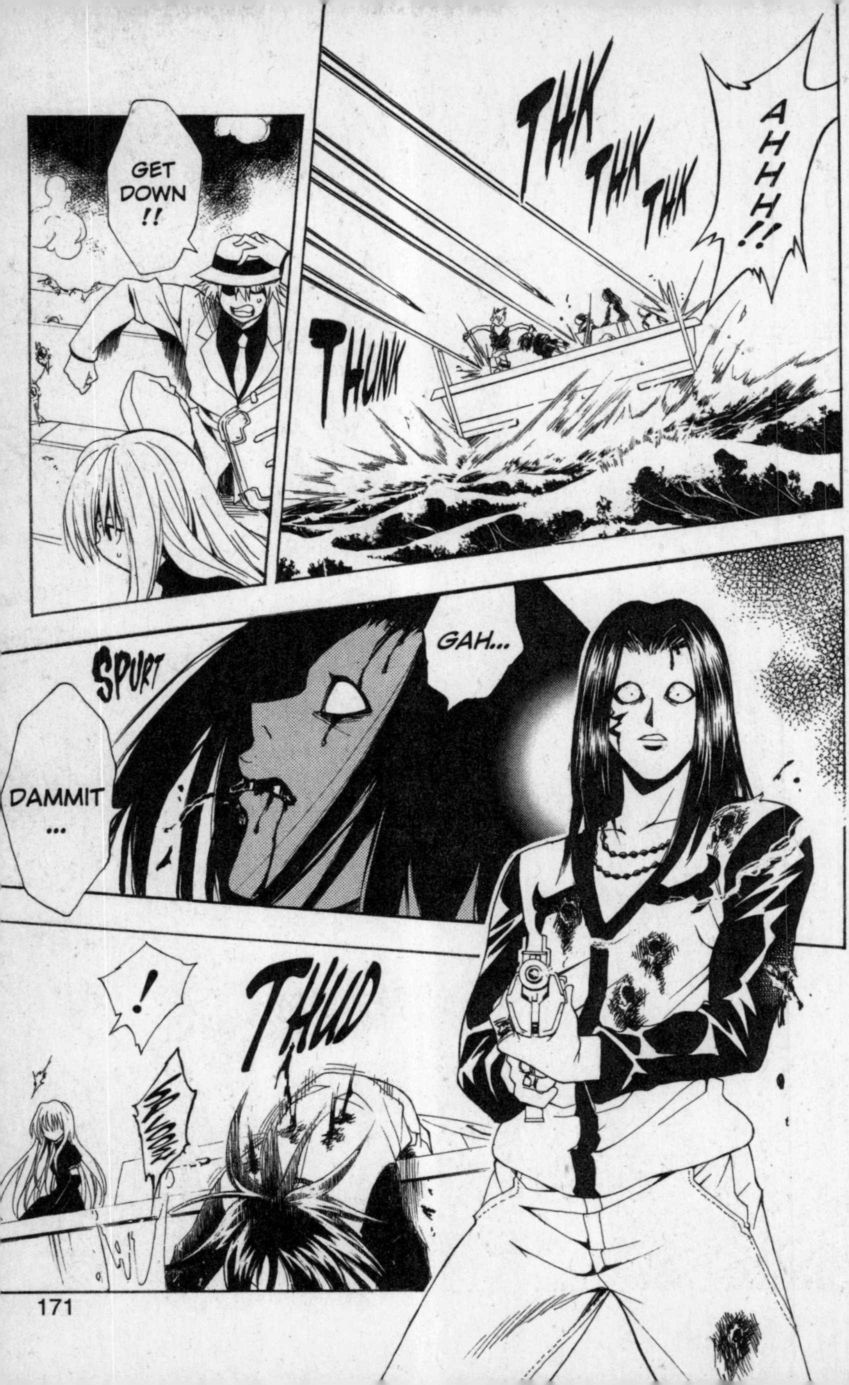
THK
THK
THK
AHHHH!!
THUNK
GET DOWN!!
GAH...
SPURT
DAMMIT...
!
THUD

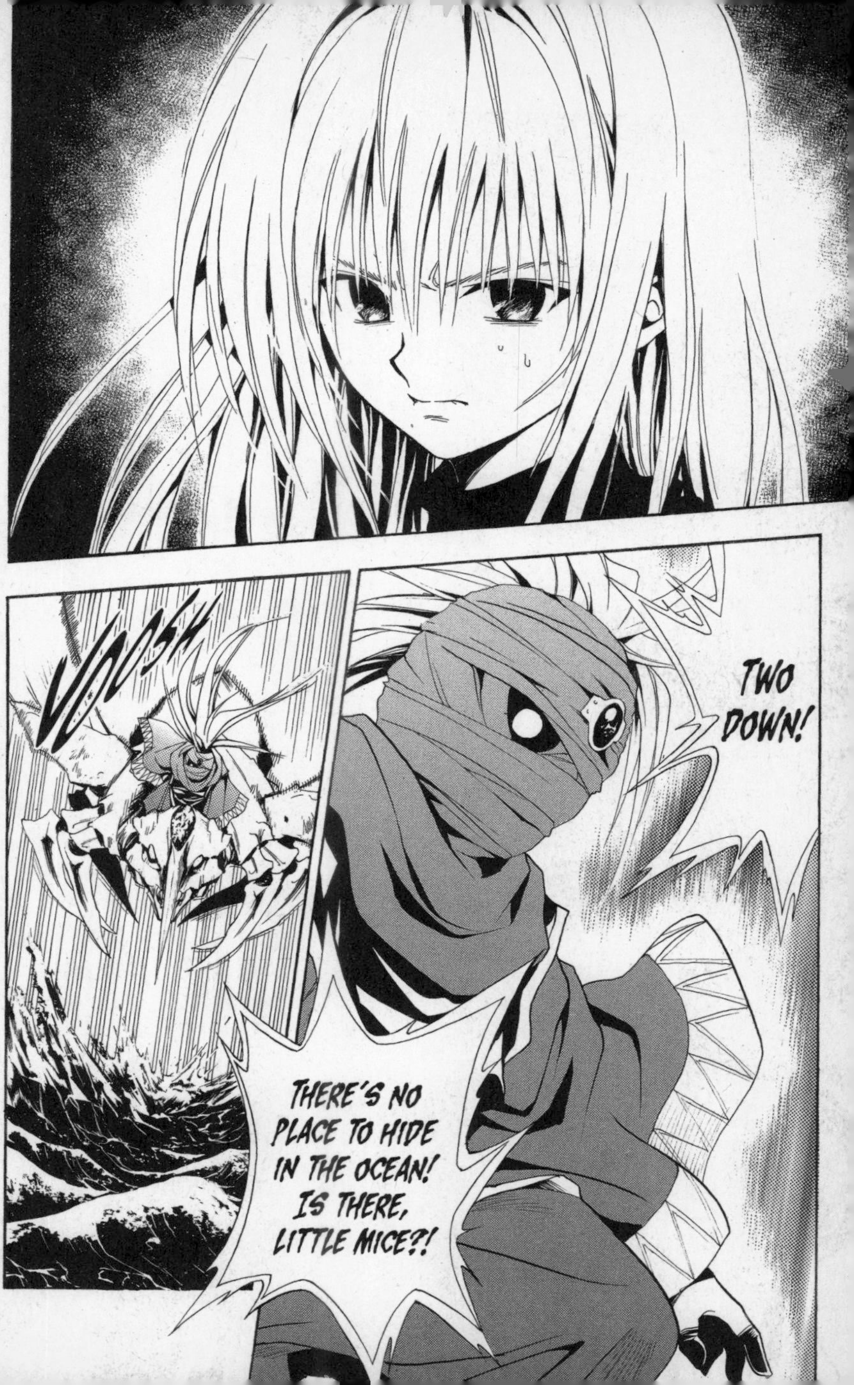
TWO DOWN!
THERE'S NO PLACE TO HIDE IN THE OCEAN! IS THERE, LITTLE MICE?!
VOOSH

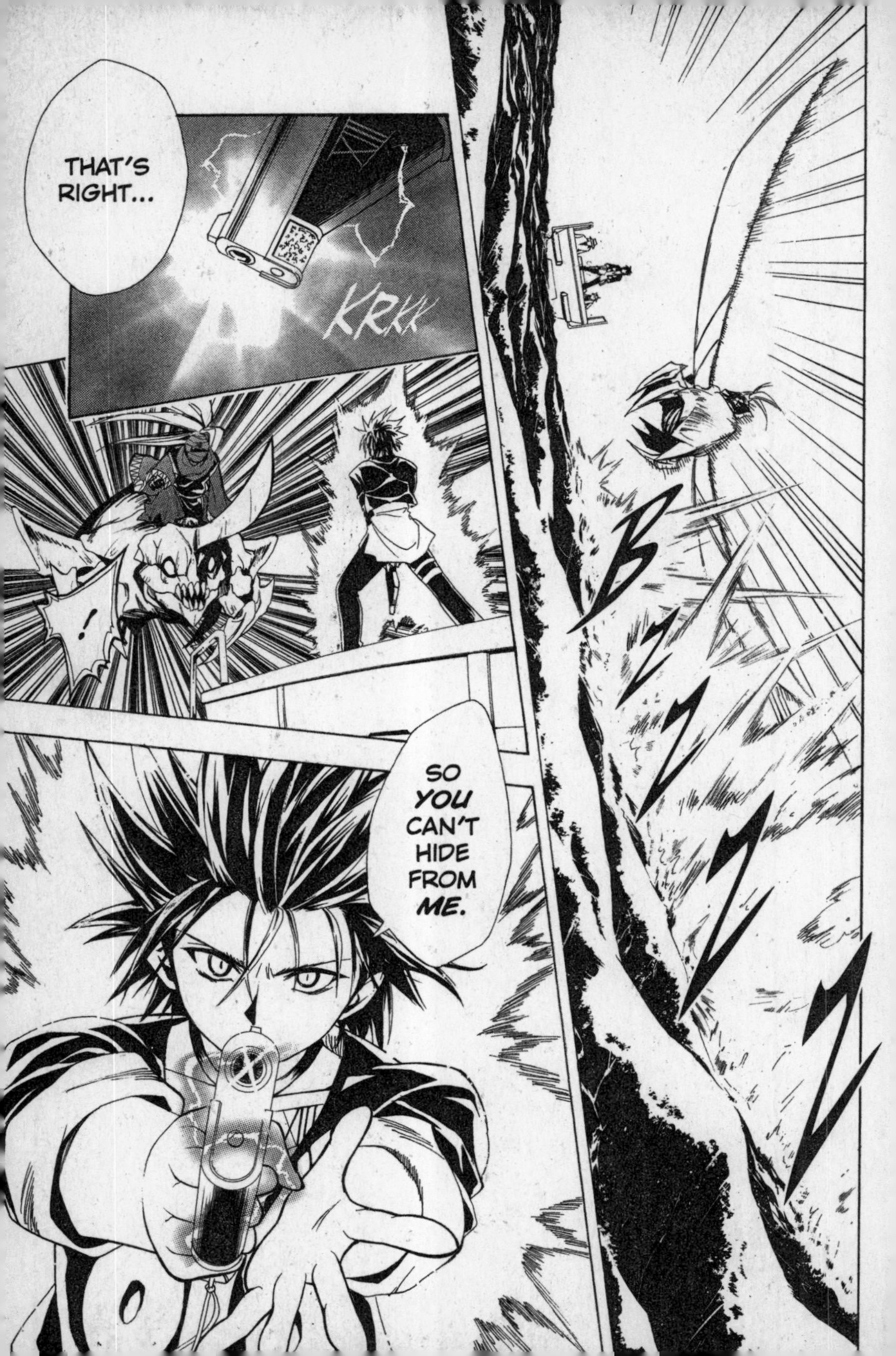
THAT'S RIGHT...
KRKK
!
SO YOU CAN'T HIDE FROM ME.

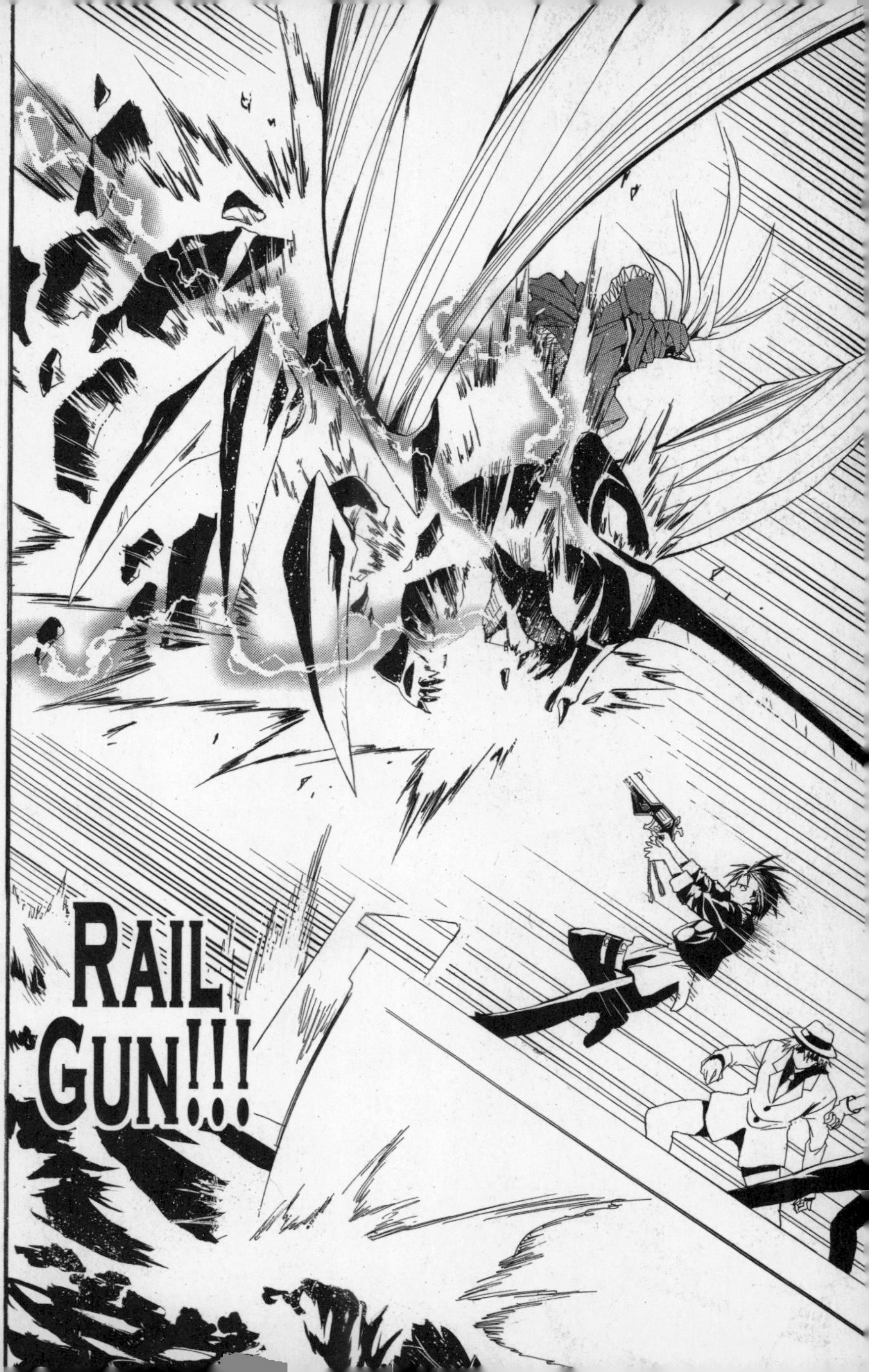
RAIL GUN!!!

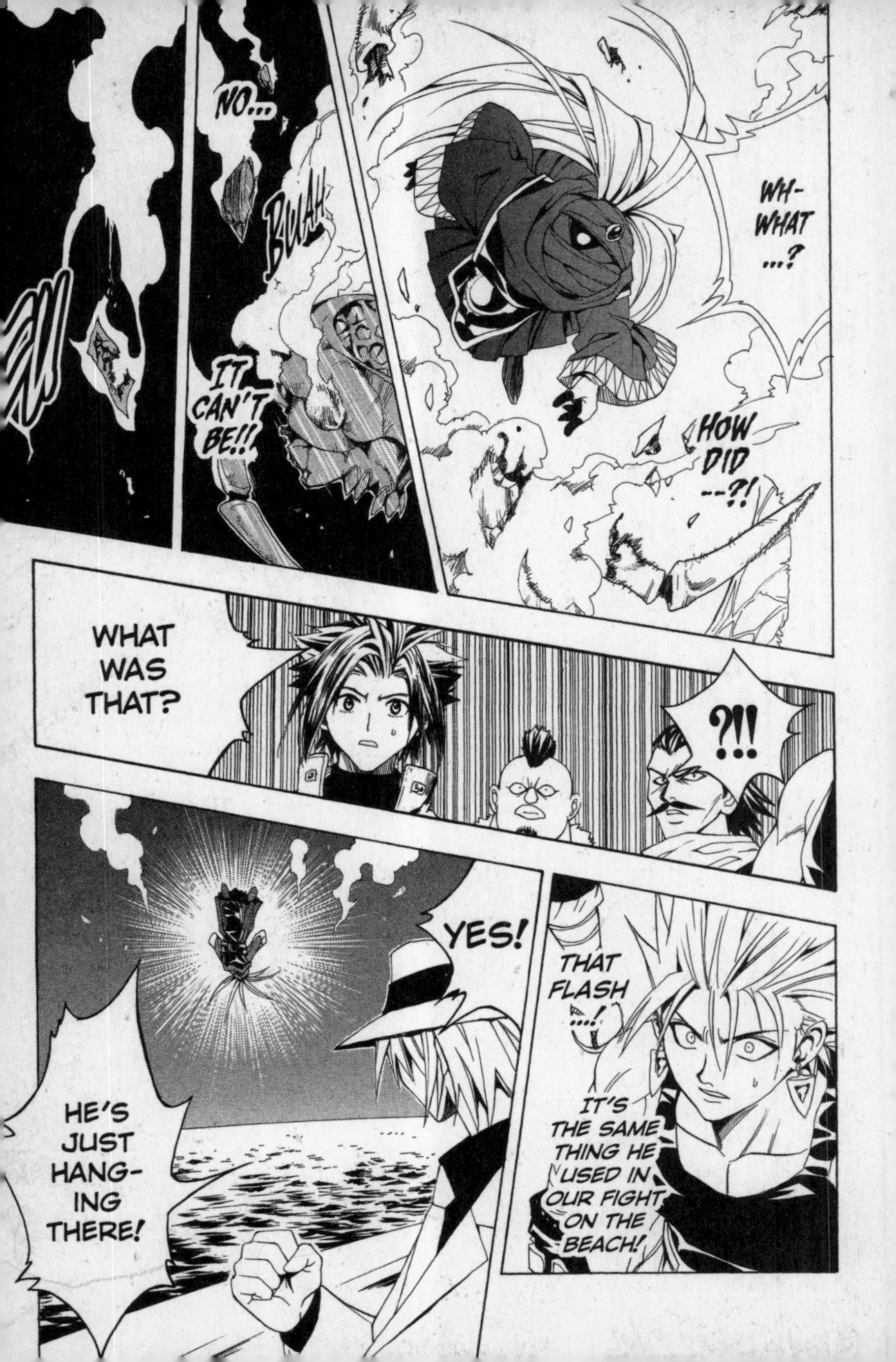
WH-WHAT ...?
HOW DID --?!
NO...
BUAH
IT CAN'T BE!!
WHAT WAS THAT?
?!!
THAT FLASH ...!
IT'S THE SAME THING HE USED IN OUR FIGHT ON THE BEACH!
YES!
HE'S JUST HANG-ING THERE!

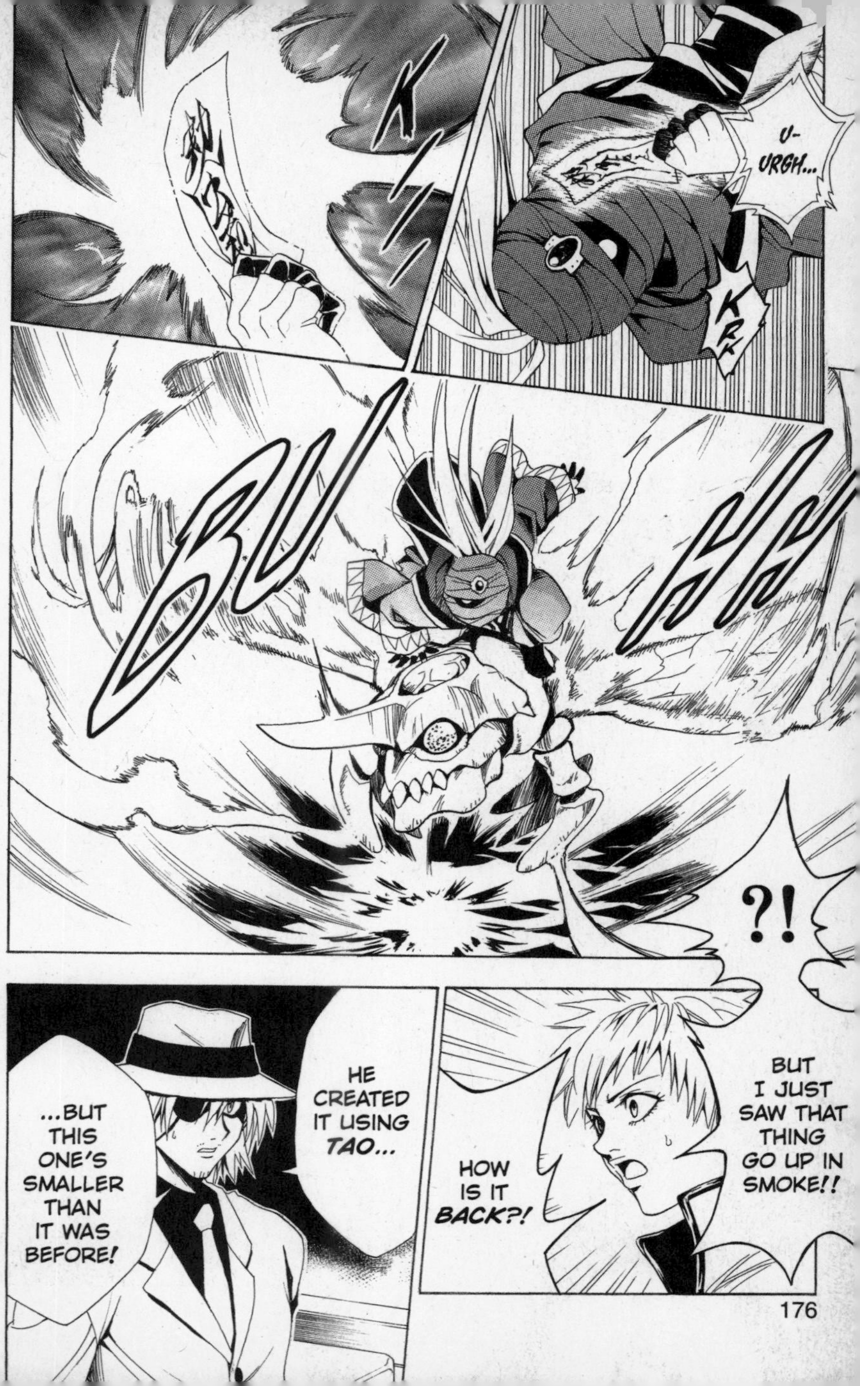
U-URGH...
BUHH
?!
BUT I JUST SAW THAT THING GO UP IN SMOKE!!
HOW IS IT *BACK*?!
HE CREATED IT USING *TAO*...
...BUT THIS ONE'S SMALLER THAN IT WAS BEFORE!

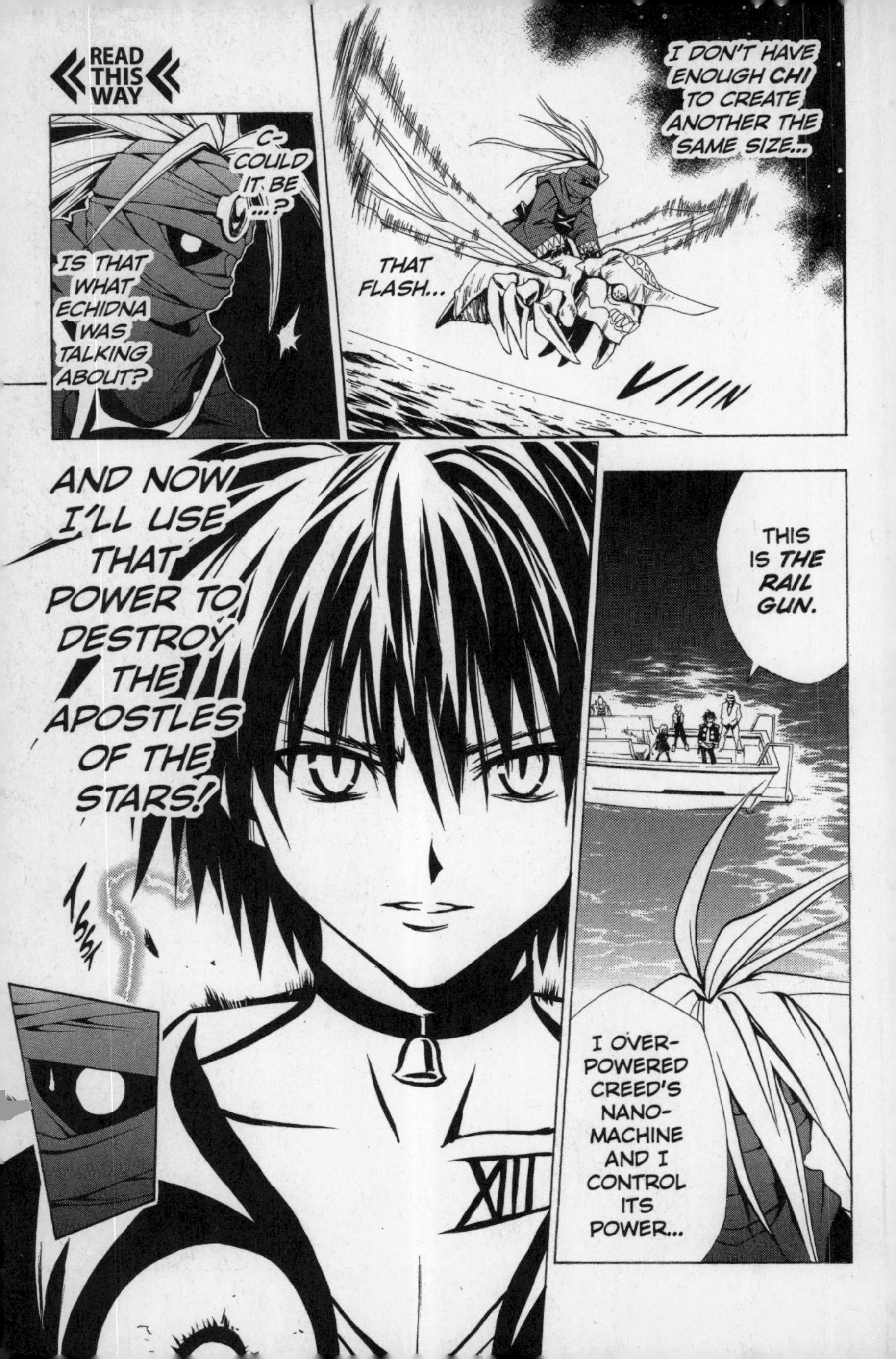
READ THIS WAY
I DON'T HAVE ENOUGH CHI TO CREATE ANOTHER THE SAME SIZE...
THAT FLASH...
VIIIN
C-COULD IT BE ...?
IS THAT WHAT ECHIDNA WAS TALKING ABOUT?
THIS IS THE RAIL GUN.
I OVER-POWERED CREED'S NANO-MACHINE AND I CONTROL ITS POWER...
AND NOW I'LL USE THAT POWER TO DESTROY THE APOSTLES OF THE STARS!

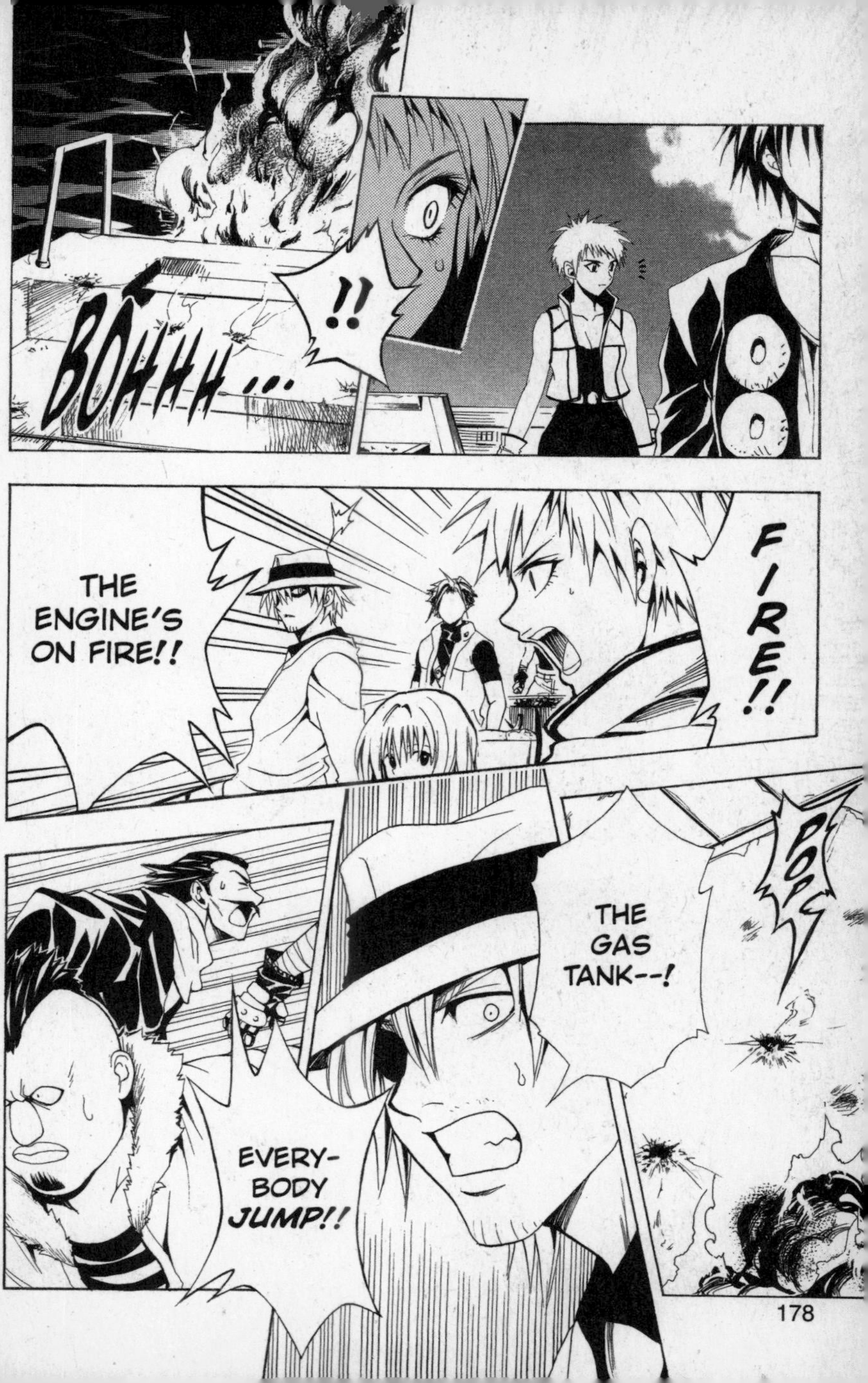
!!
BOHHH...
FIRE!!
THE ENGINE'S ON FIRE!!
POP
THE GAS TANK--!
EVERY-BODY JUMP!!

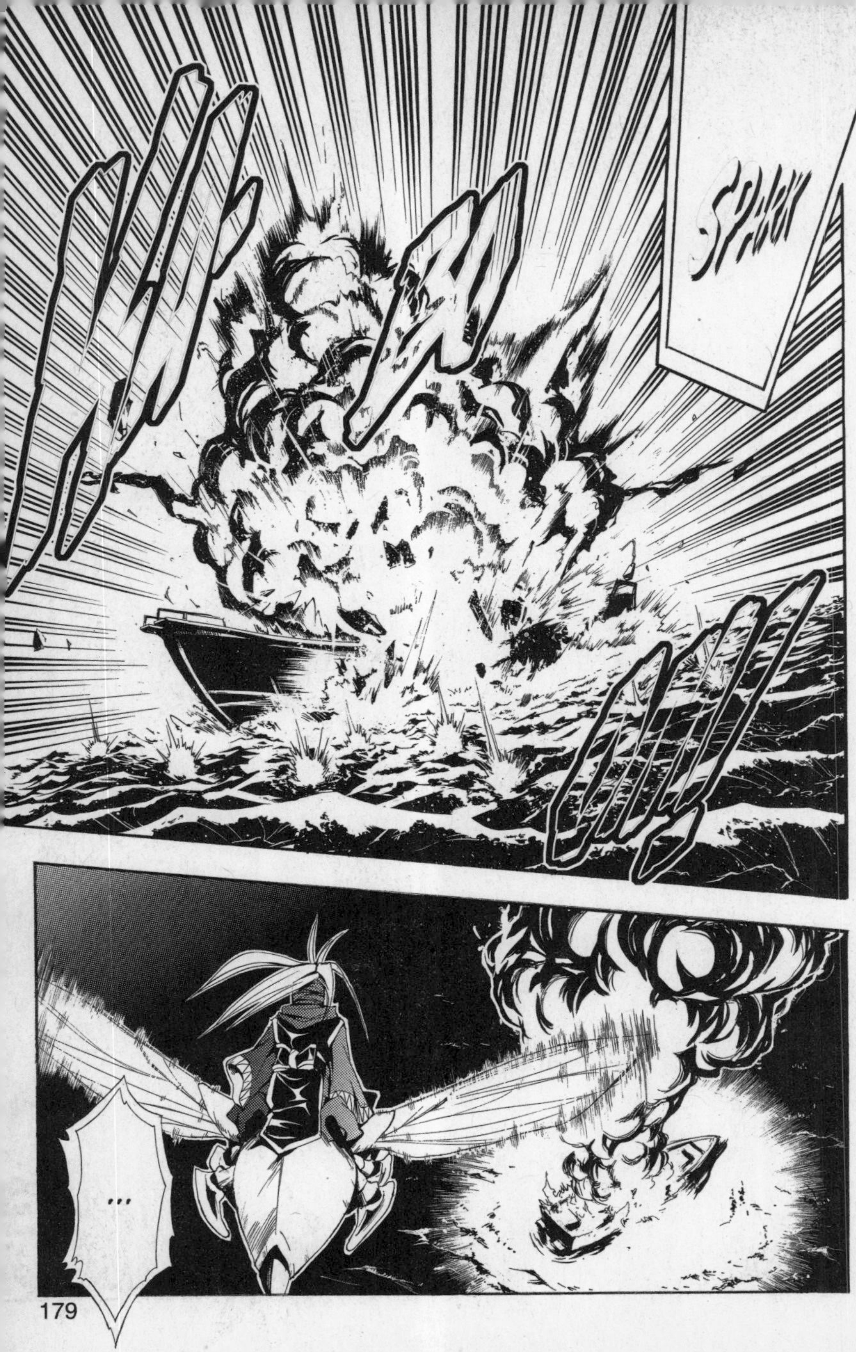
...

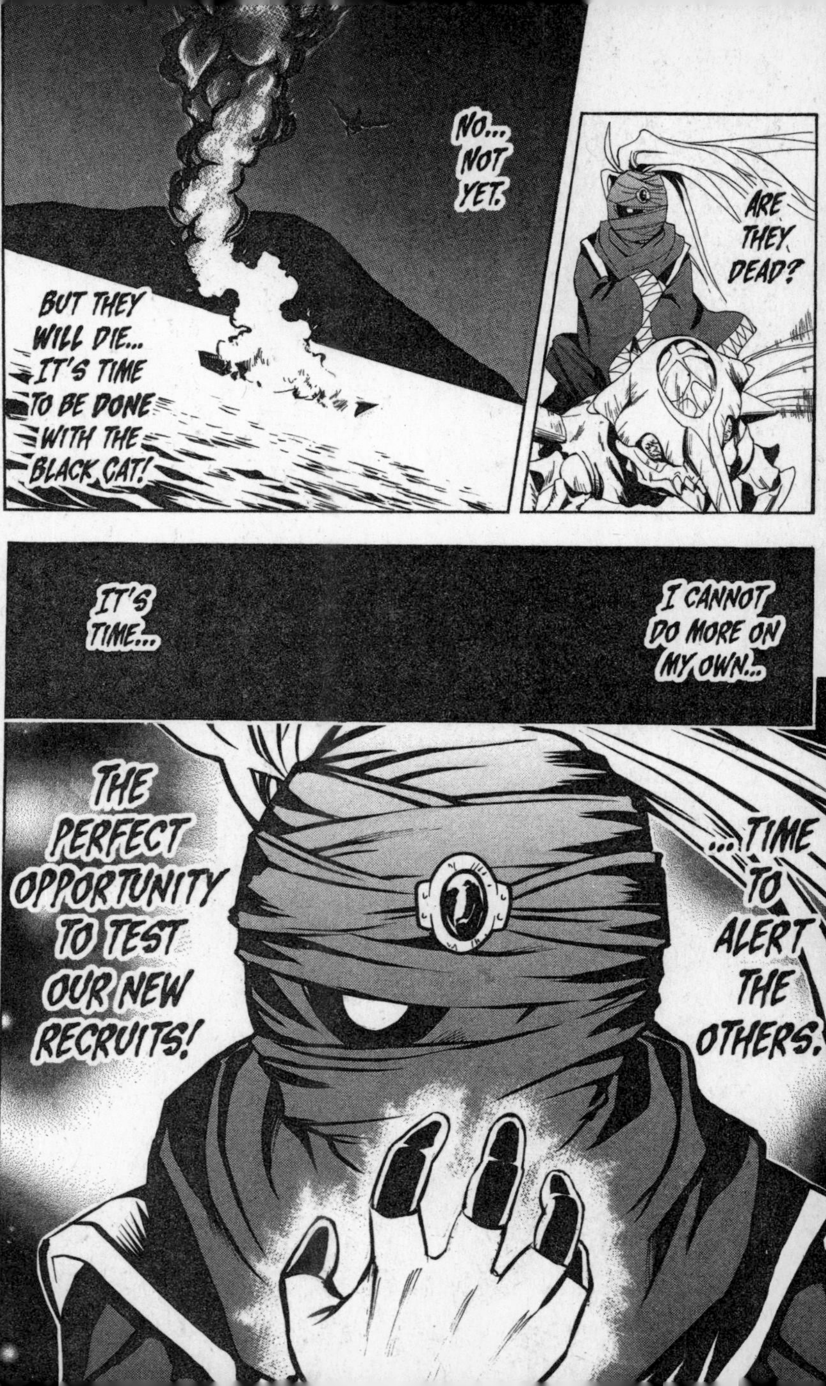
ARE THEY DEAD?
NO... NOT YET.
BUT THEY WILL DIE... IT'S TIME TO BE DONE WITH THE BLACK CAT!
I CANNOT DO MORE ON MY OWN...
IT'S TIME...
...TIME TO ALERT THE OTHERS.
THE PERFECT OPPORTUNITY TO TEST OUR NEW RECRUITS!

READ THIS WAY

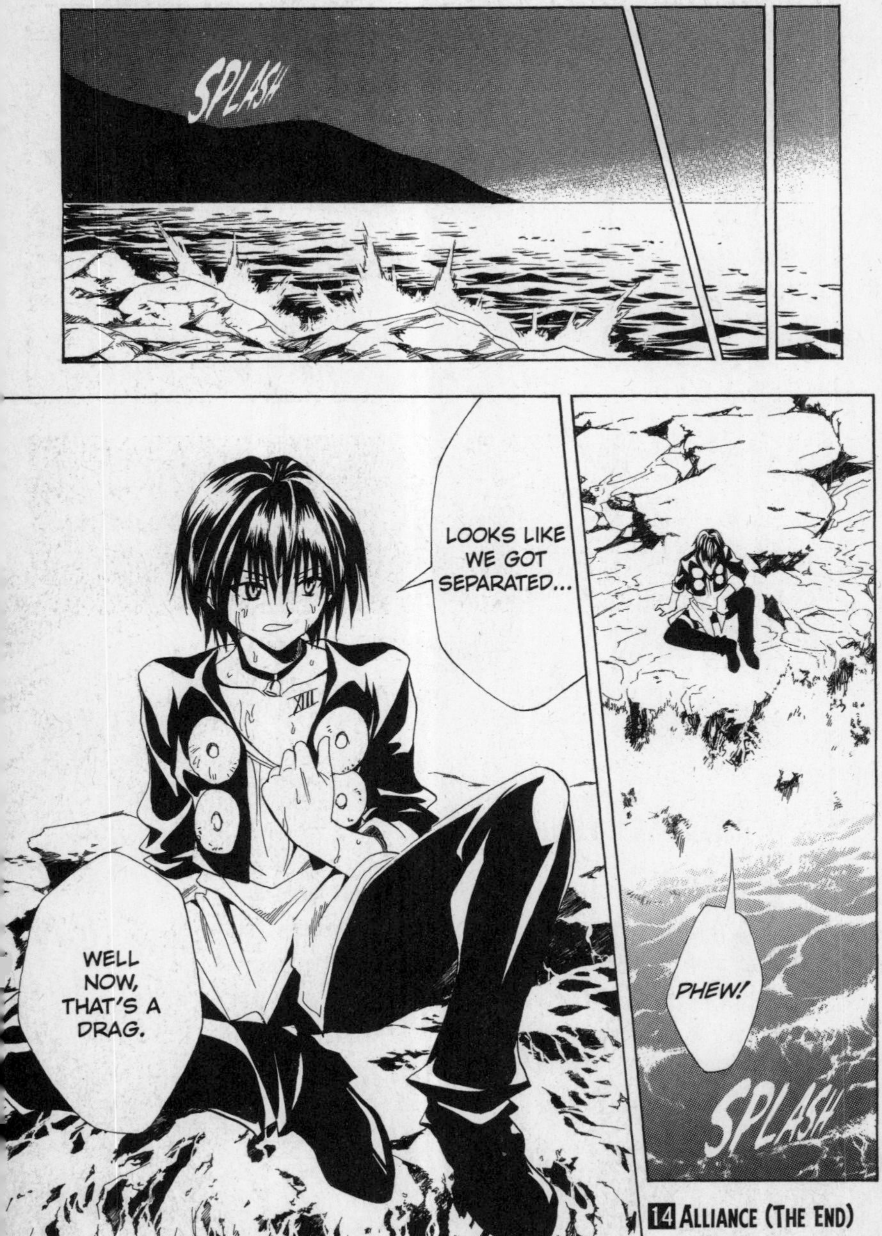
SPLASH
PHEW!
SPLASH
LOOKS LIKE WE GOT SEPARATED...
WELL NOW, THAT'S A DRAG.

14 ALLIANCE (THE END)

IN THE NEXT VOLUME...

Separated from the others, Train and River forge an uneasy partnership as they find themselves confronting Maro and Preta Ghoul. On another part of the island, Eve and the wounded Kevin McDougall must take on Leon Elliot. Will any of the Sweeper Alliance survive to face Creed?

AVAILABLE JULY 2008!

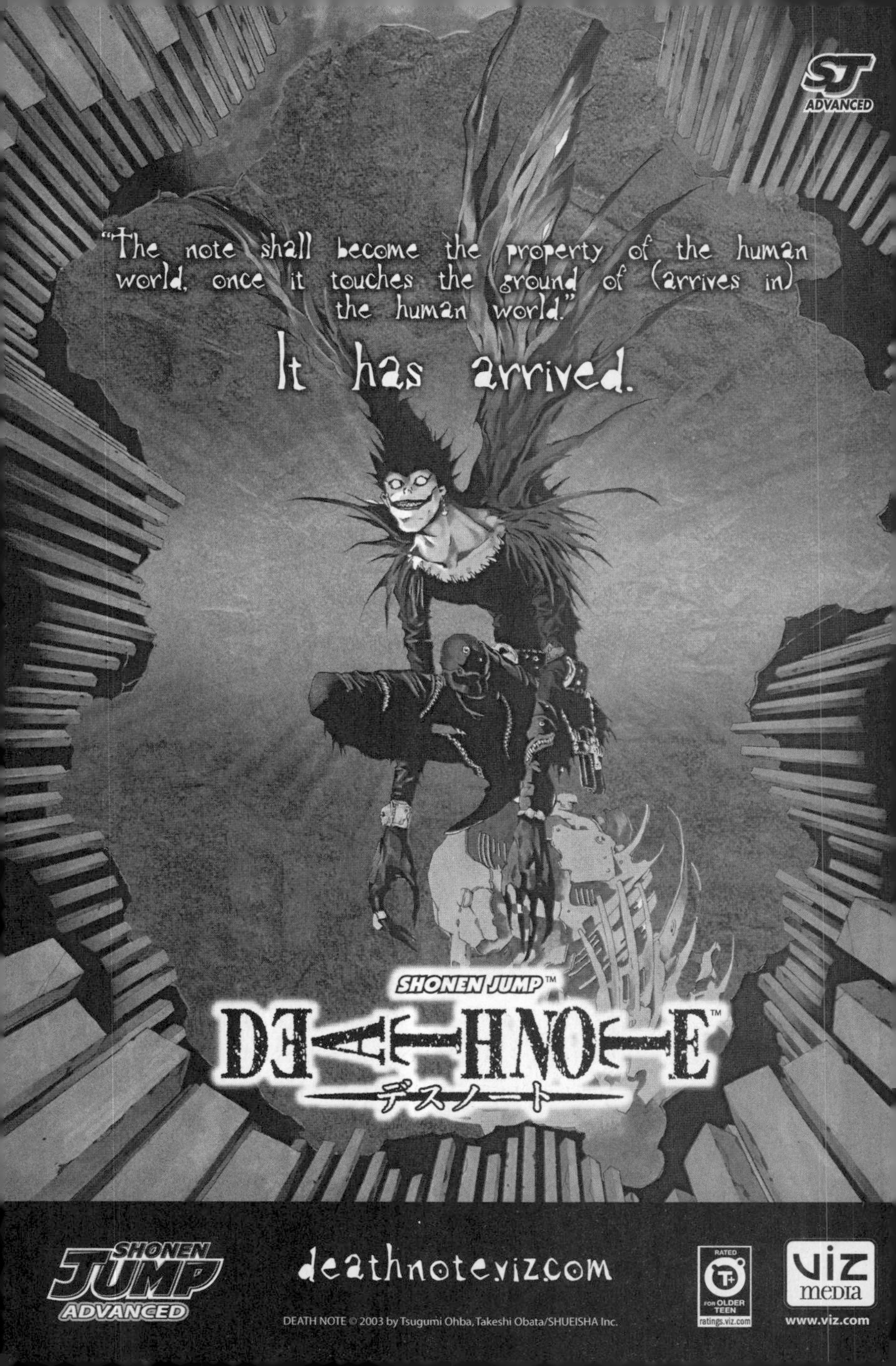
SJ ADVANCED
"The note shall become the property of the human world, once it touches the ground of (arrives in) the human world."
It has arrived.
SHONEN JUMP™
DEATH NOTE™
デスノート
SHONEN JUMP ADVANCED
deathnote.viz.com
DEATH NOTE © 2003 by Tsugumi Ohba, Takeshi Obata/SHUEISHA Inc.
RATED T+ FOR OLDER TEEN
ratings.viz.com
viz media
www.viz.com

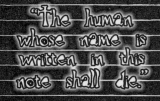

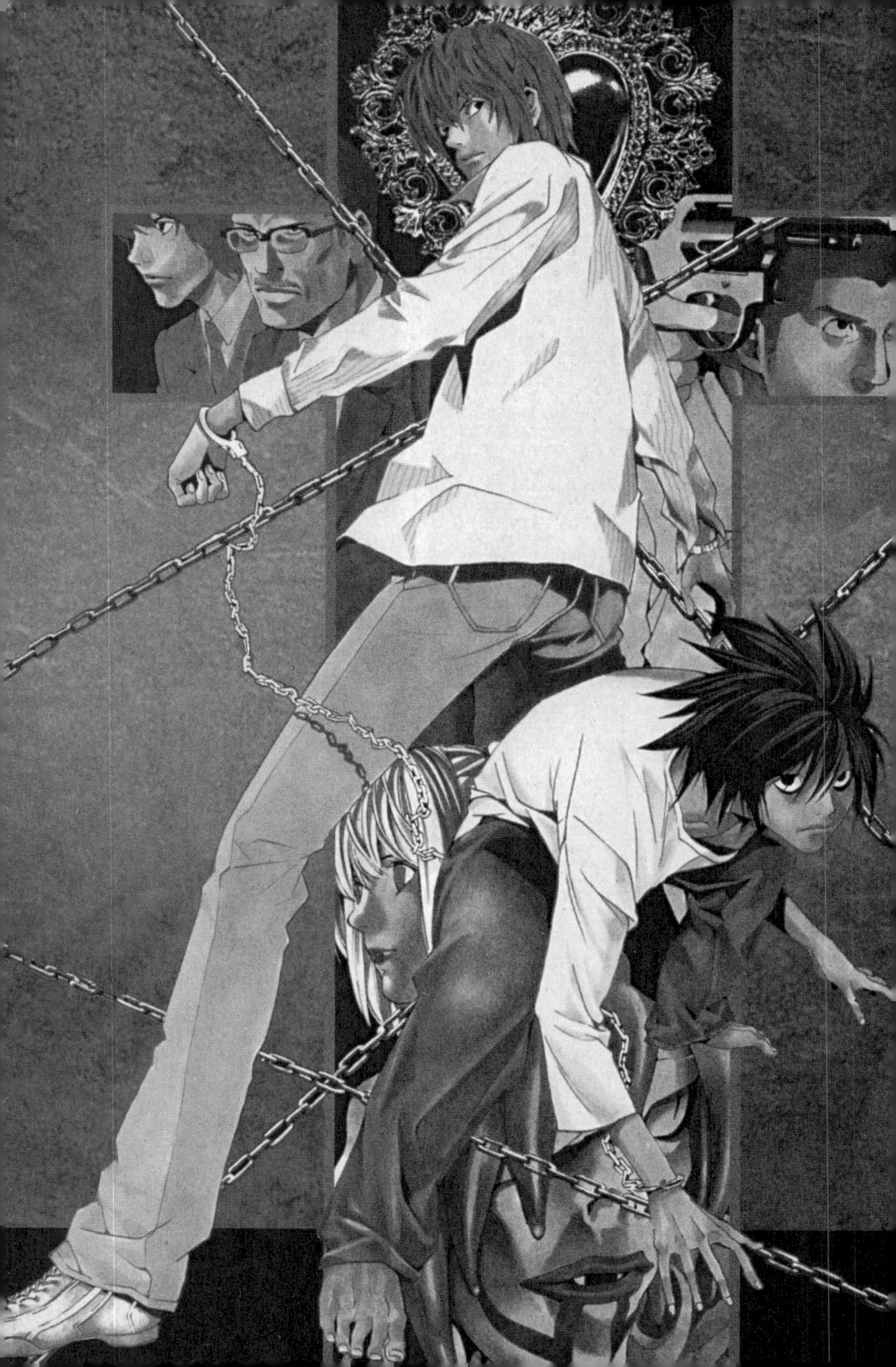

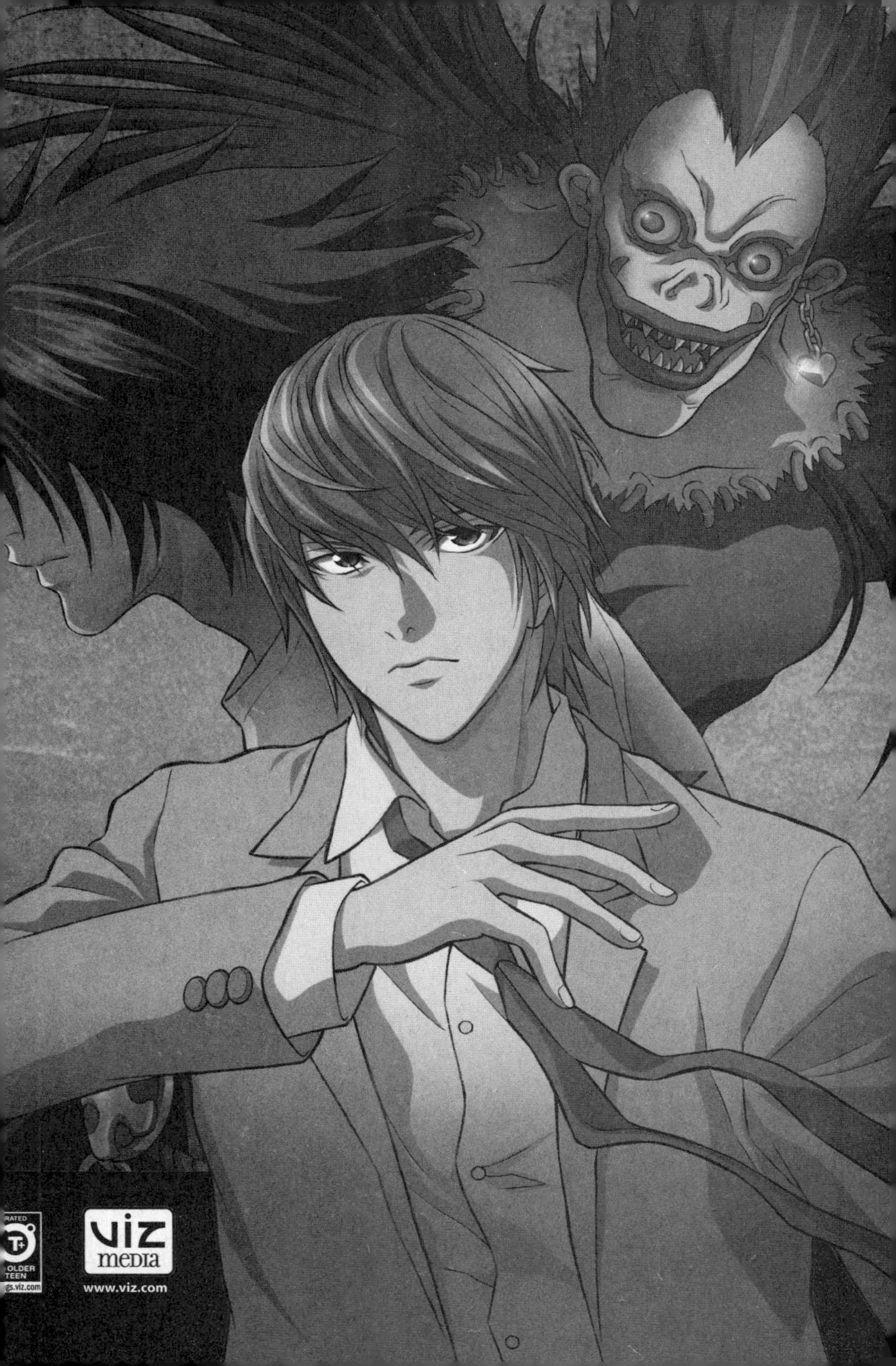
RATED
T+
OLDER TEEN
viz media
www.viz.com

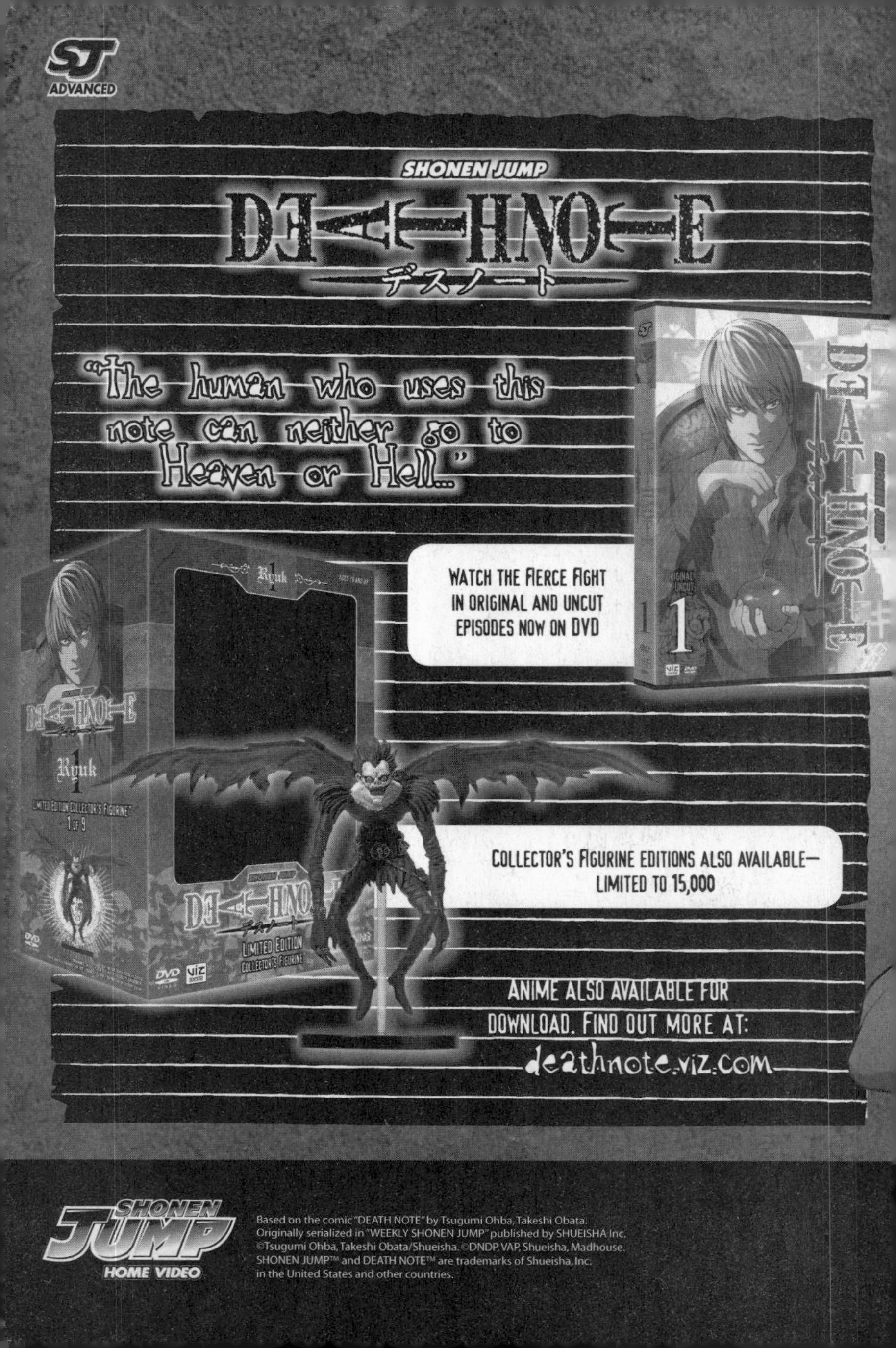
SJ ADVANCED
SHONEN JUMP
DEATH NOTE
デスノート
"The human who uses this note can neither go to Heaven or Hell..."
WATCH THE FIERCE FIGHT IN ORIGINAL AND UNCUT EPISODES NOW ON DVD
COLLECTOR'S FIGURINE EDITIONS ALSO AVAILABLE— LIMITED TO 15,000
ANIME ALSO AVAILABLE FOR DOWNLOAD. FIND OUT MORE AT:
deathnote.viz.com
SHONEN JUMP HOME VIDEO
Based on the comic "DEATH NOTE" by Tsugumi Ohba, Takeshi Obata.
Originally serialized in "WEEKLY SHONEN JUMP" published by SHUEISHA Inc.
©Tsugumi Ohba, Takeshi Obata/Shueisha. ©DNDP, VAP, Shueisha, Madhouse.
SHONEN JUMP™ and DEATH NOTE™ are trademarks of Shueisha, Inc.
in the United States and other countries.

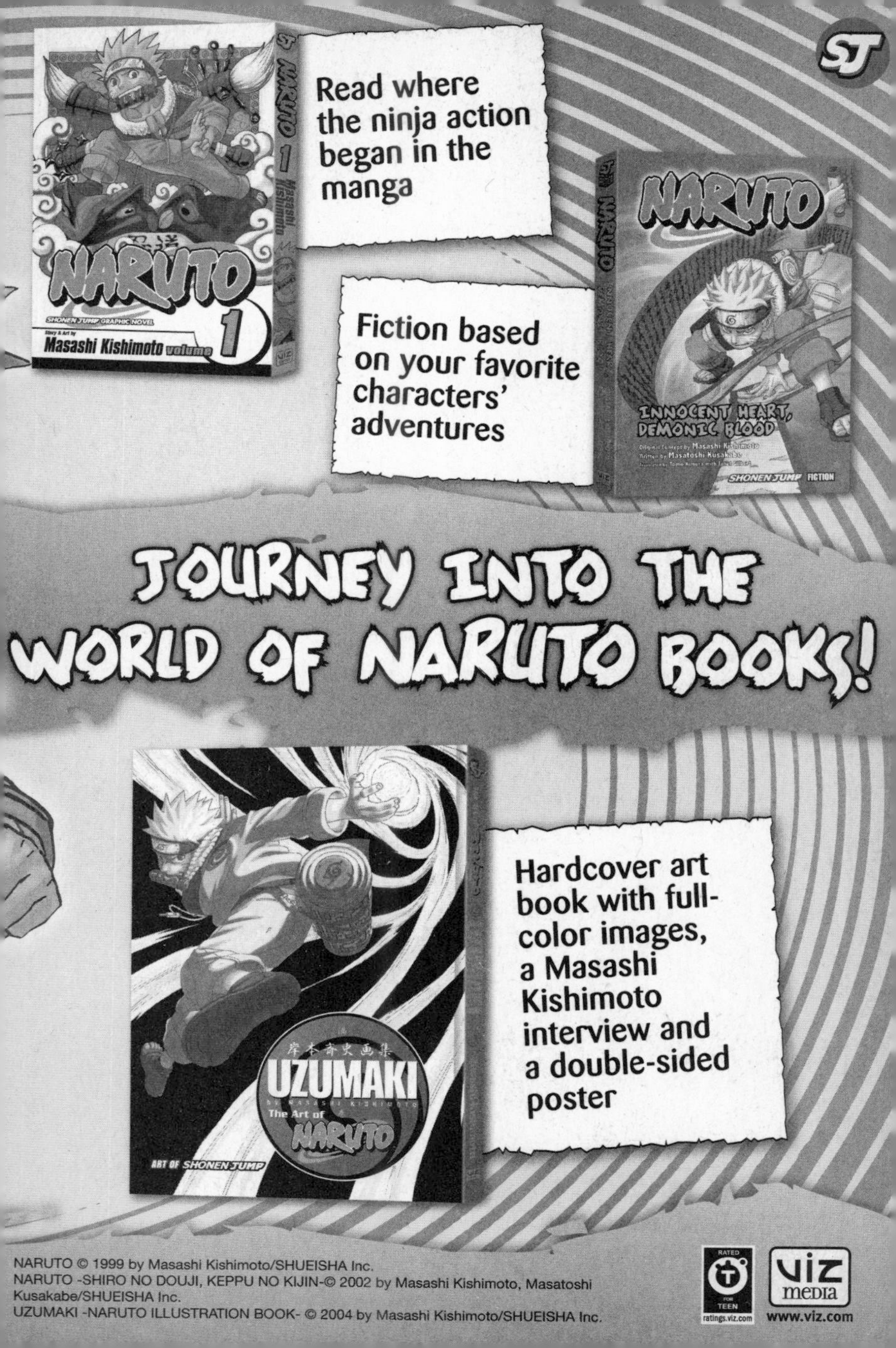
SJ
NARUTO
SHONEN JUMP GRAPHIC NOVEL
Story & Art by
Masashi Kishimoto volume 1
Read where the ninja action began in the manga
Fiction based on your favorite characters' adventures
NARUTO
INNOCENT HEART, DEMONIC BLOOD
Original Concept by Masashi Kishimoto
Written by Masatoshi Kusakabe
SHONEN JUMP FICTION
JOURNEY INTO THE WORLD OF NARUTO BOOKS!
UZUMAKI
The Art of NARUTO
ART OF SHONEN JUMP
Hardcover art book with full-color images, a Masashi Kishimoto interview and a double-sided poster
NARUTO © 1999 by Masashi Kishimoto/SHUEISHA Inc.
NARUTO -SHIRO NO DOUJI, KEPPU NO KIJIN-© 2002 by Masashi Kishimoto, Masatoshi Kusakabe/SHUEISHA Inc.
UZUMAKI -NARUTO ILLUSTRATION BOOK- © 2004 by Masashi Kishimoto/SHUEISHA Inc.
RATED T FOR TEEN
ratings.viz.com
VIZ media
www.viz.com

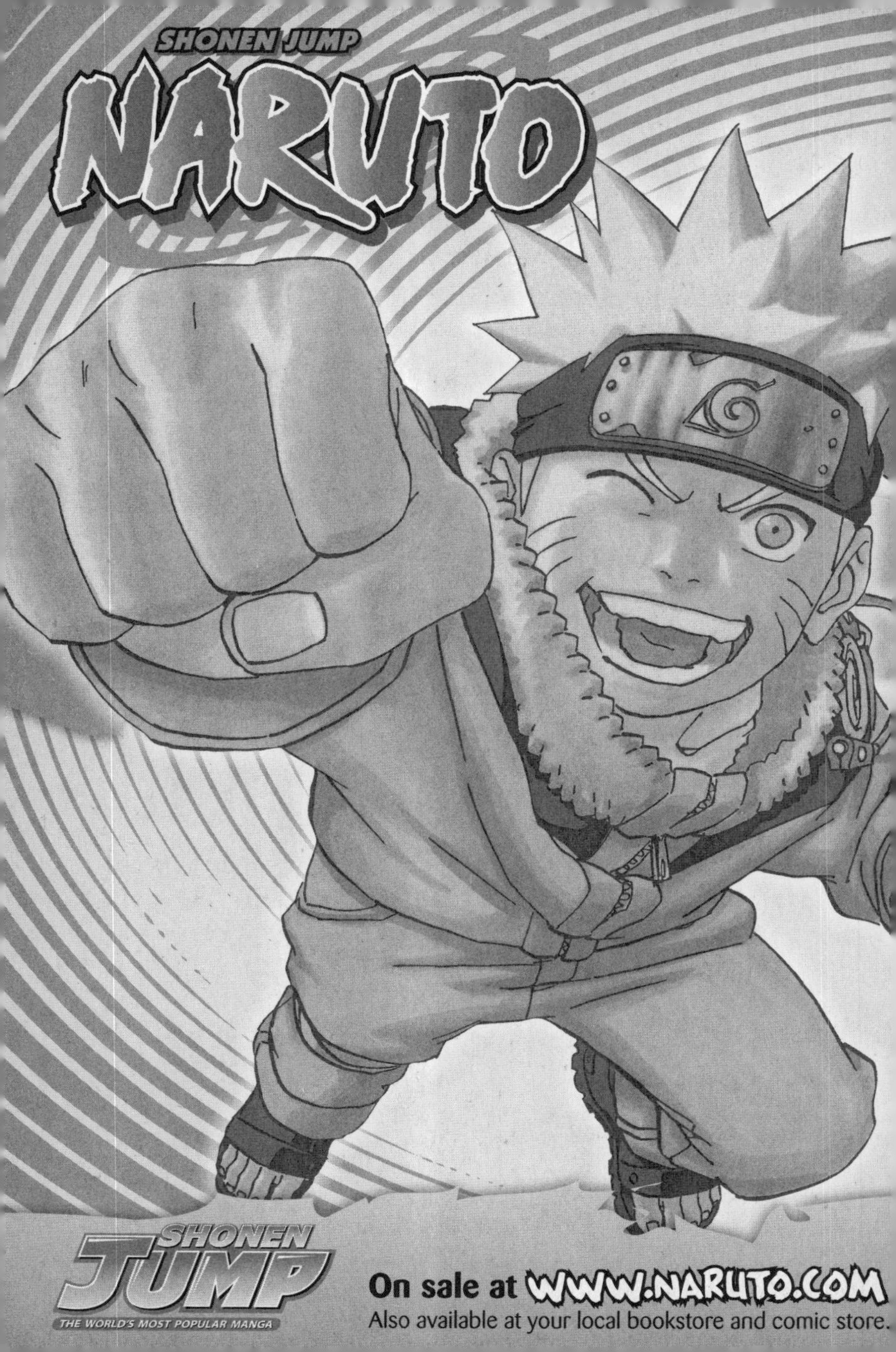
SHONEN JUMP
NARUTO
SHONEN JUMP
THE WORLD'S MOST POPULAR MANGA
On sale at WWW.NARUTO.COM
Also available at your local bookstore and comic store.

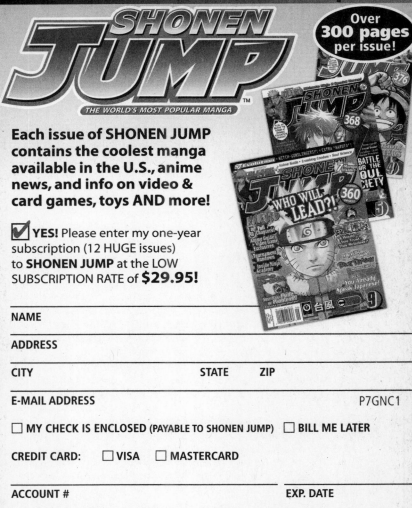